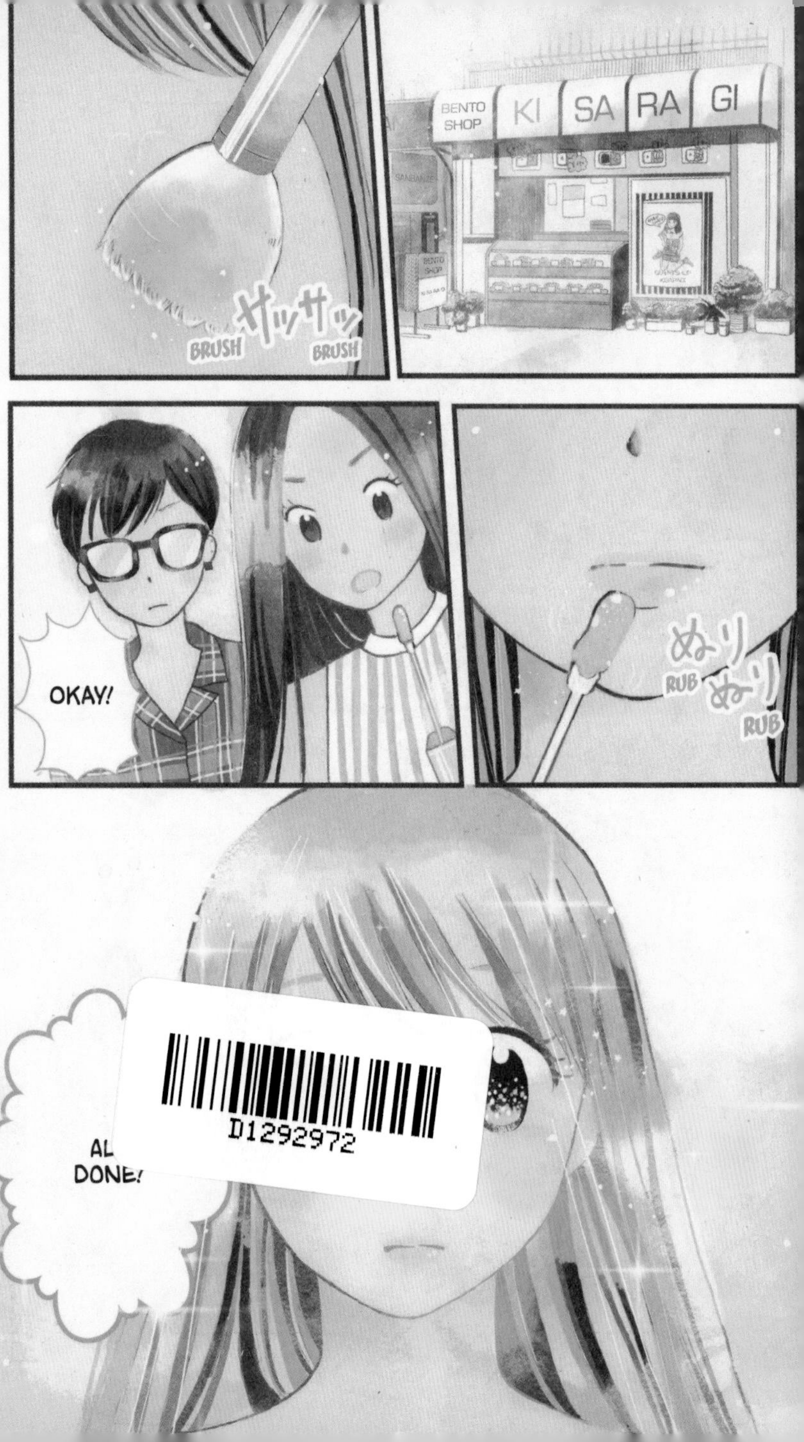
BENTO SHOP
KI SA RA GI
サッサッ
BRUSH
BRUSH
ぬり
RUB
ぬり
RUB
OKAY!
AL
DONE!

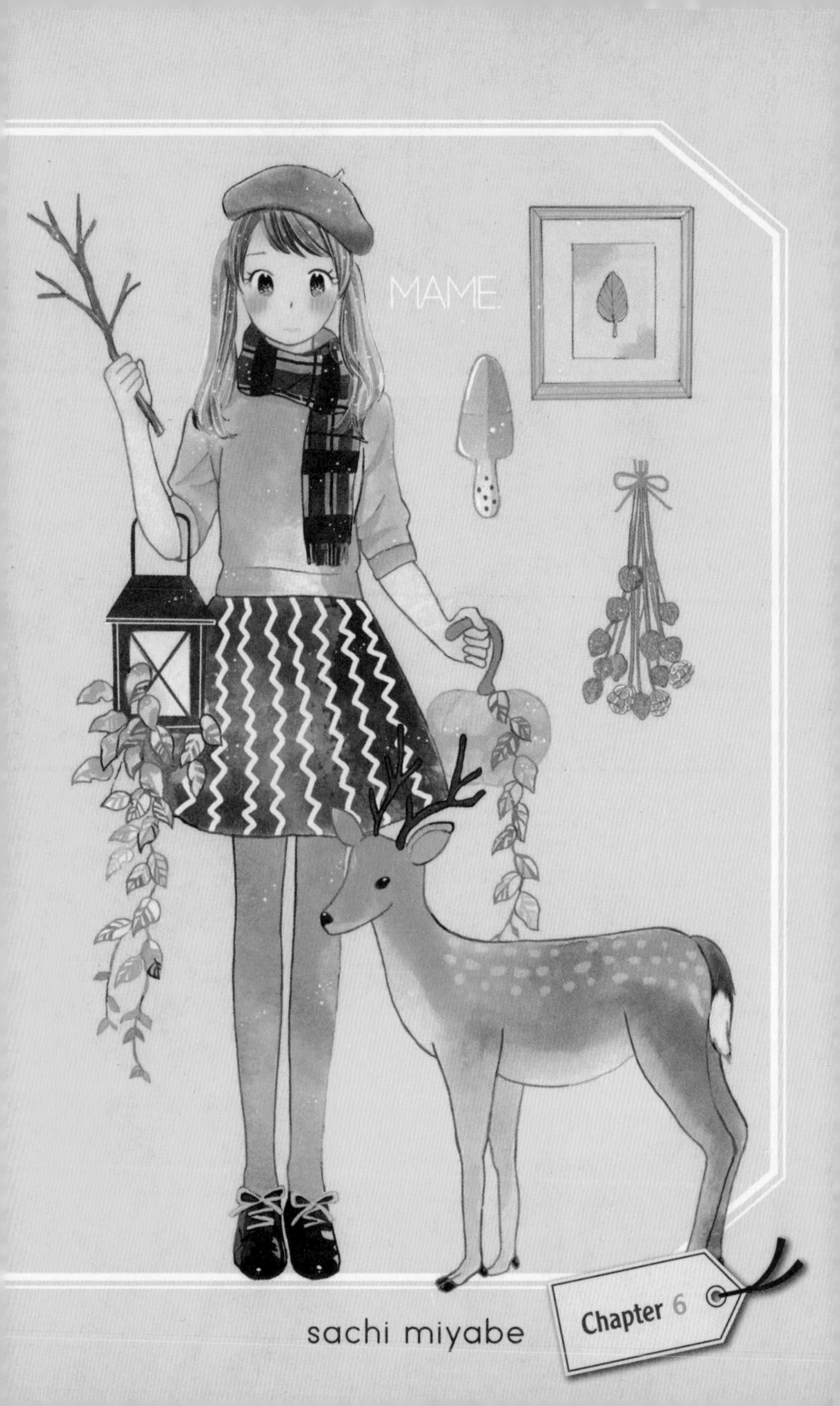
MAME.
Chapter 6
sachi miyabe

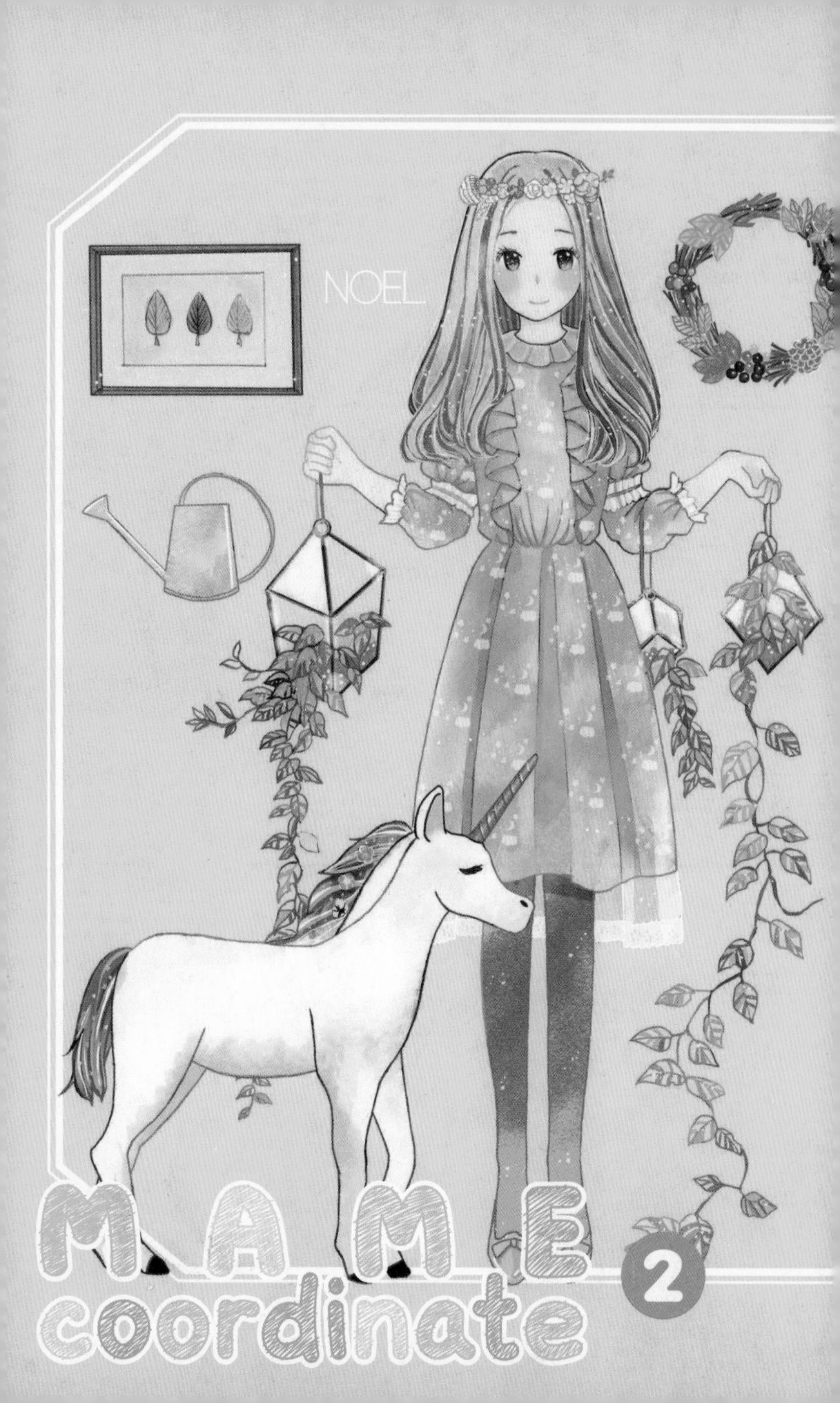
NOEL
MAME
coordinate
2

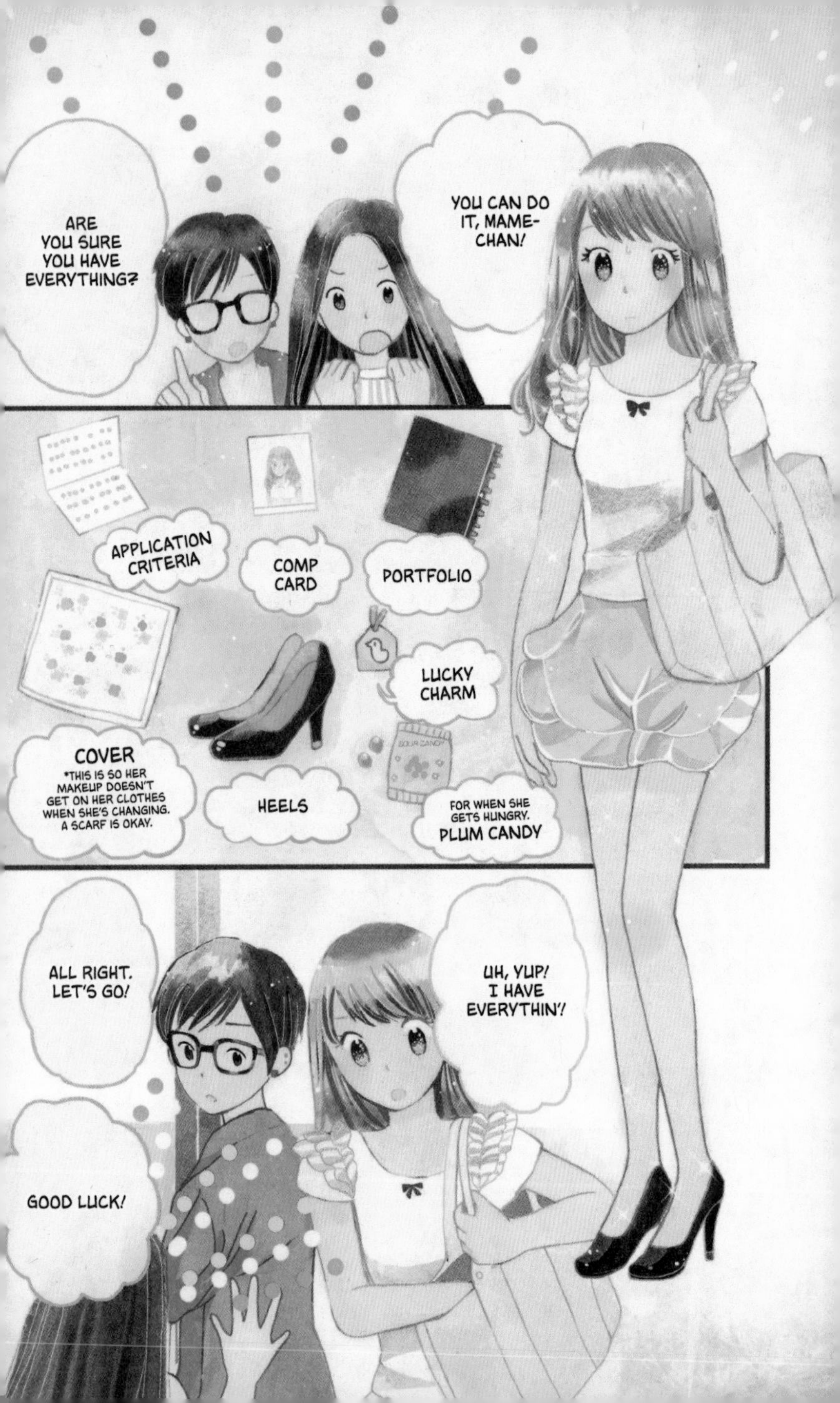
YOU CAN DO IT, MAME-CHAN!
ARE YOU SURE YOU HAVE EVERYTHING?
PORTFOLIO
COMP CARD
APPLICATION CRITERIA
LUCKY CHARM
FOR WHEN SHE GETS HUNGRY. PLUM CANDY
HEELS
COVER *THIS IS SO HER MAKEUP DOESN'T GET ON HER CLOTHES WHEN SHE'S CHANGING. A SCARF IS OKAY.
UH, YUP! I HAVE EVERYTHIN'!
ALL RIGHT. LET'S GO!
GOOD LUCK!

# Contents

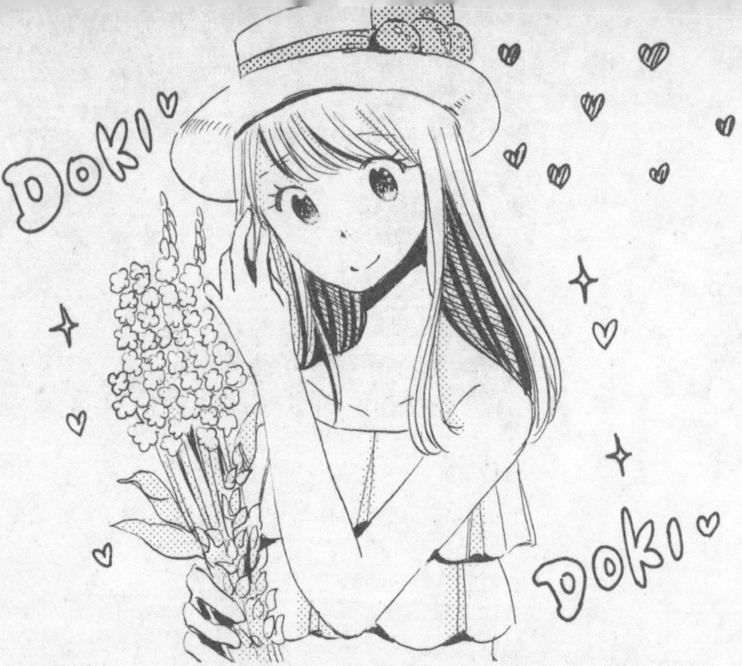
Doki
Doki

# MAME coordinate 2

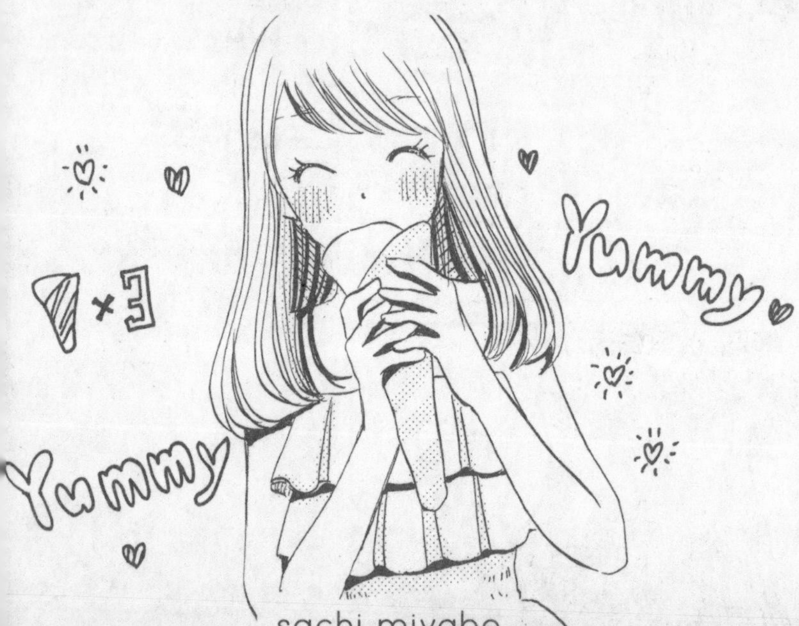
Yummy
Yummy

sachi miyabe

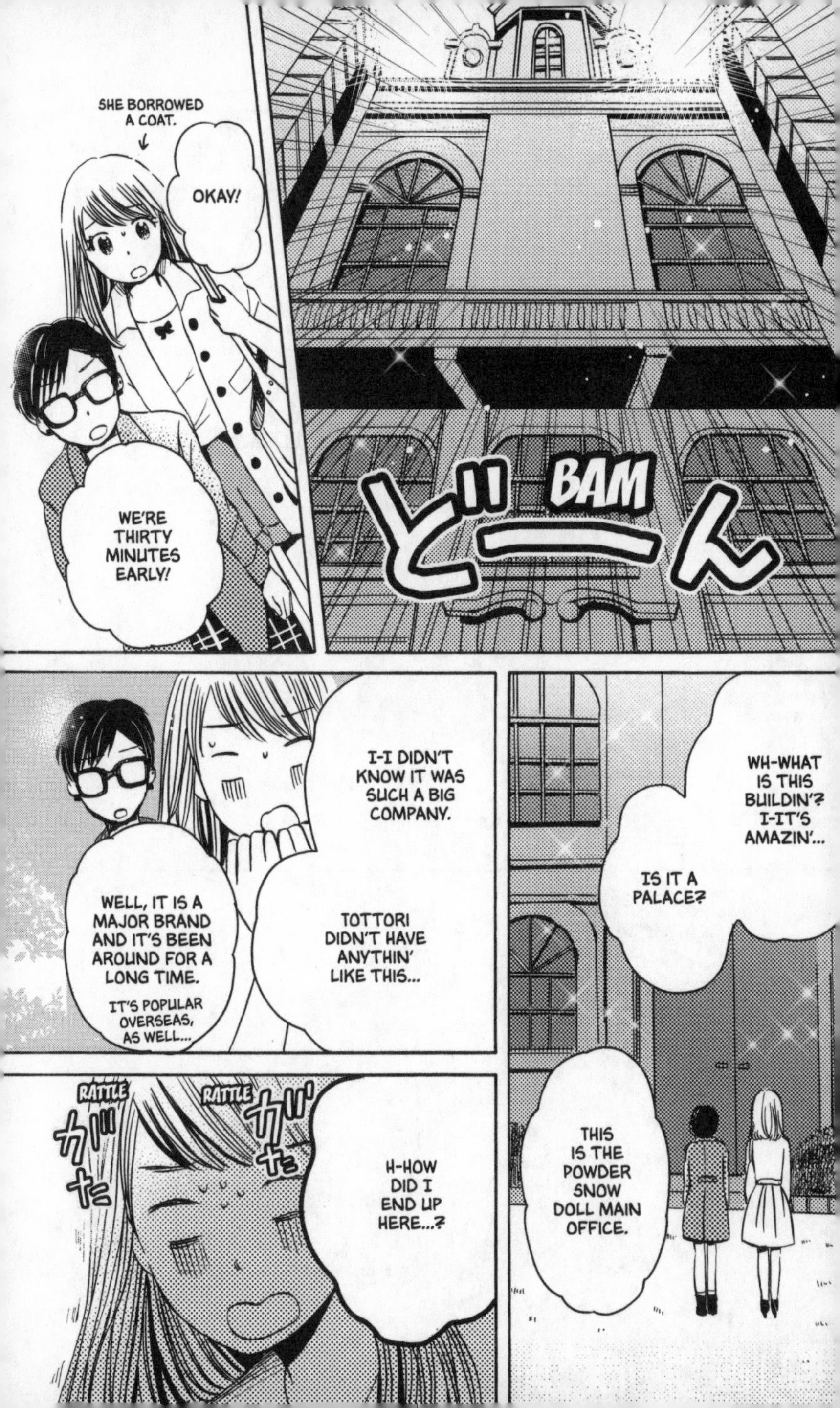
どーん
BAM
SHE BORROWED A COAT.
OKAY!
WE'RE THIRTY MINUTES EARLY!
WH-WHAT IS THIS BUILDIN'? I-IT'S AMAZIN'...
IS IT A PALACE?
THIS IS THE POWDER SNOW DOLL MAIN OFFICE.
I-I DIDN'T KNOW IT WAS SUCH A BIG COMPANY.
TOTTORI DIDN'T HAVE ANYTHIN' LIKE THIS...
WELL, IT IS A MAJOR BRAND AND IT'S BEEN AROUND FOR A LONG TIME.
IT'S POPULAR OVERSEAS, AS WELL...
H-HOW DID I END UP HERE...?
ガタ RATTLE
ガタ RATTLE

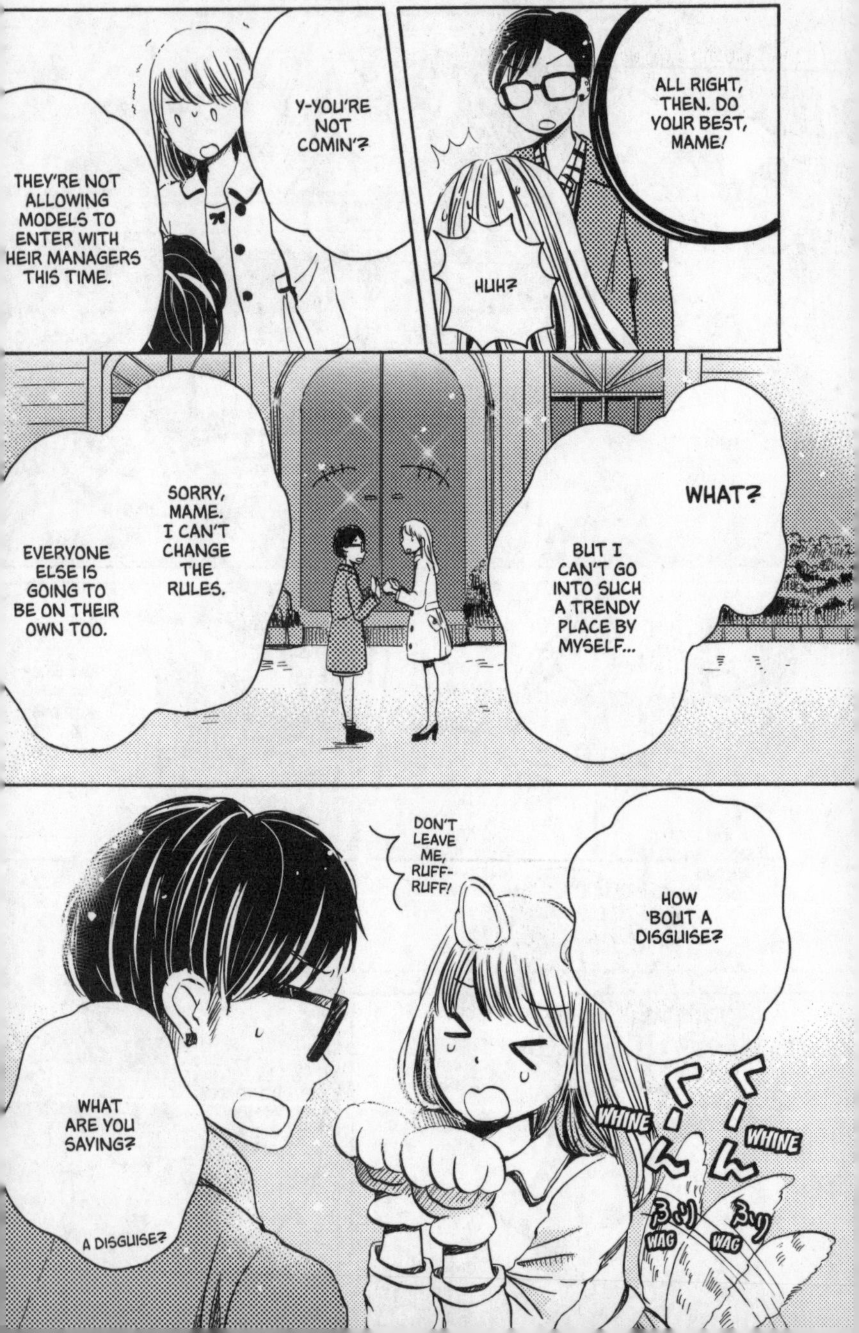
ALL RIGHT, THEN. DO YOUR BEST, MAME!
HUH?
Y-YOU'RE NOT COMIN'?
THEY'RE NOT ALLOWING MODELS TO ENTER WITH HEIR MANAGERS THIS TIME.
WHAT?
BUT I CAN'T GO INTO SUCH A TRENDY PLACE BY MYSELF...
SORRY, MAME. I CAN'T CHANGE THE RULES.
EVERYONE ELSE IS GOING TO BE ON THEIR OWN TOO.
HOW 'BOUT A DISGUISE?
DON'T LEAVE ME, RUFF-RUFF!
WHINE
WHINE
WAG
WAG
WHAT ARE YOU SAYING?
A DISGUISE?

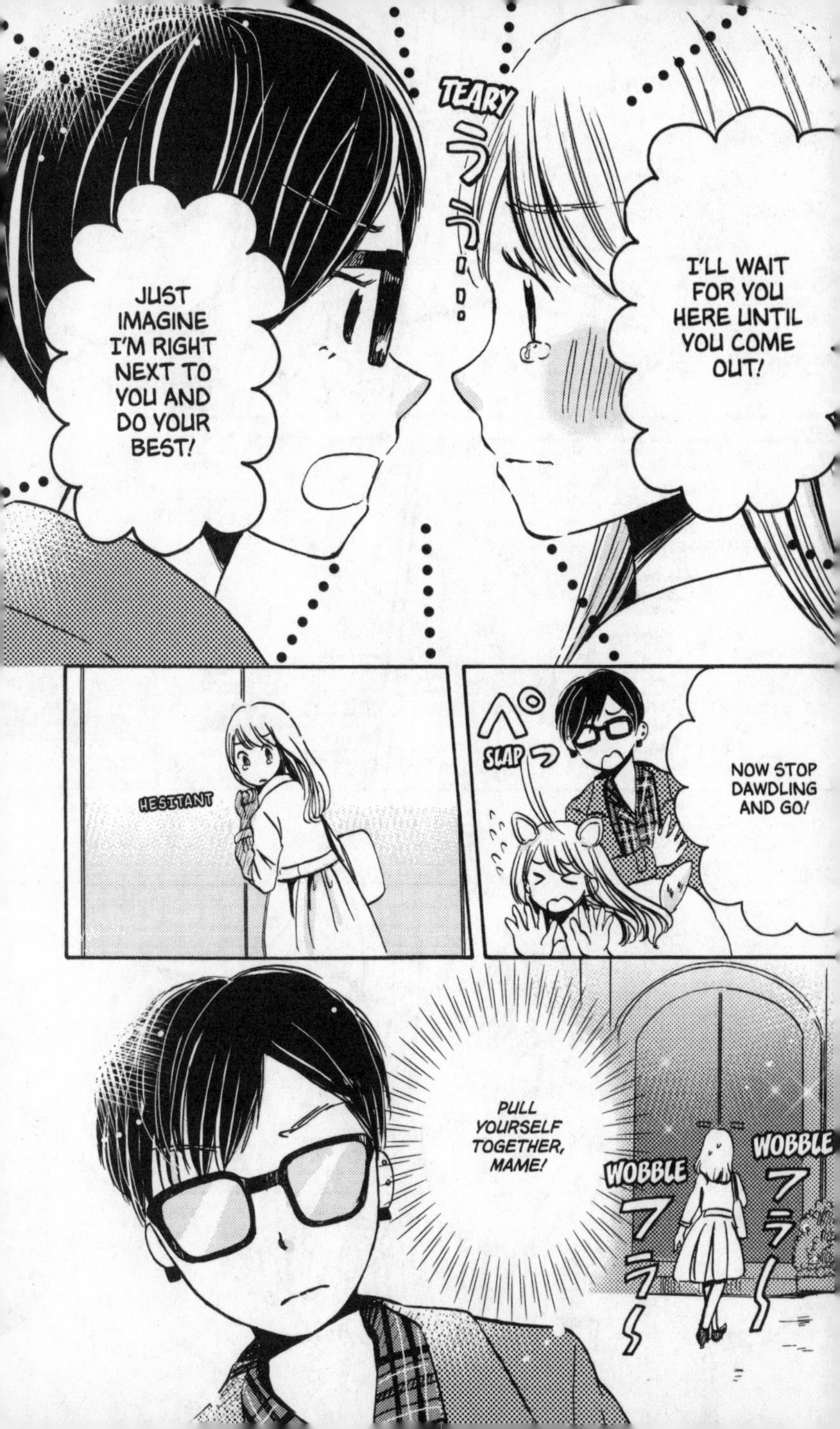
I'LL WAIT FOR YOU HERE UNTIL YOU COME OUT!
TEARY
JUST IMAGINE I'M RIGHT NEXT TO YOU AND DO YOUR BEST!
SLAP
NOW STOP DAWDLING AND GO!
HESITANT
WOBBLE
PULL YOURSELF TOGETHER, MAME!
WOBBLE

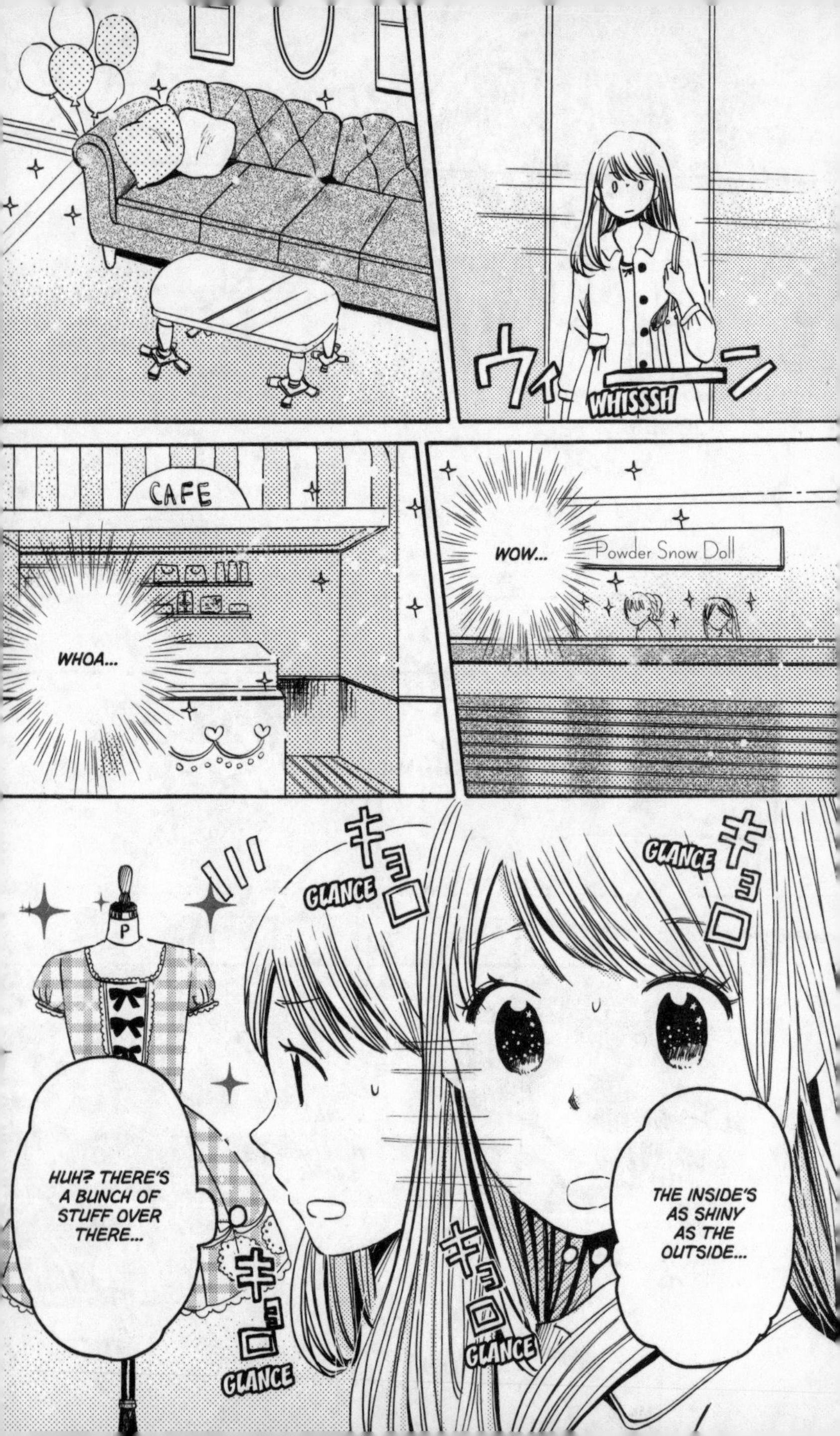
ウィーン
WHISSSH
WOW...
Powder Snow Doll
CAFE
WHOA...
キョロ
GLANCE
キョロ
GLANCE
THE INSIDE'S AS SHINY AS THE OUTSIDE...
キョロ
GLANCE
HUH? THERE'S A BUNCH OF STUFF OVER THERE...
キョロ
GLANCE

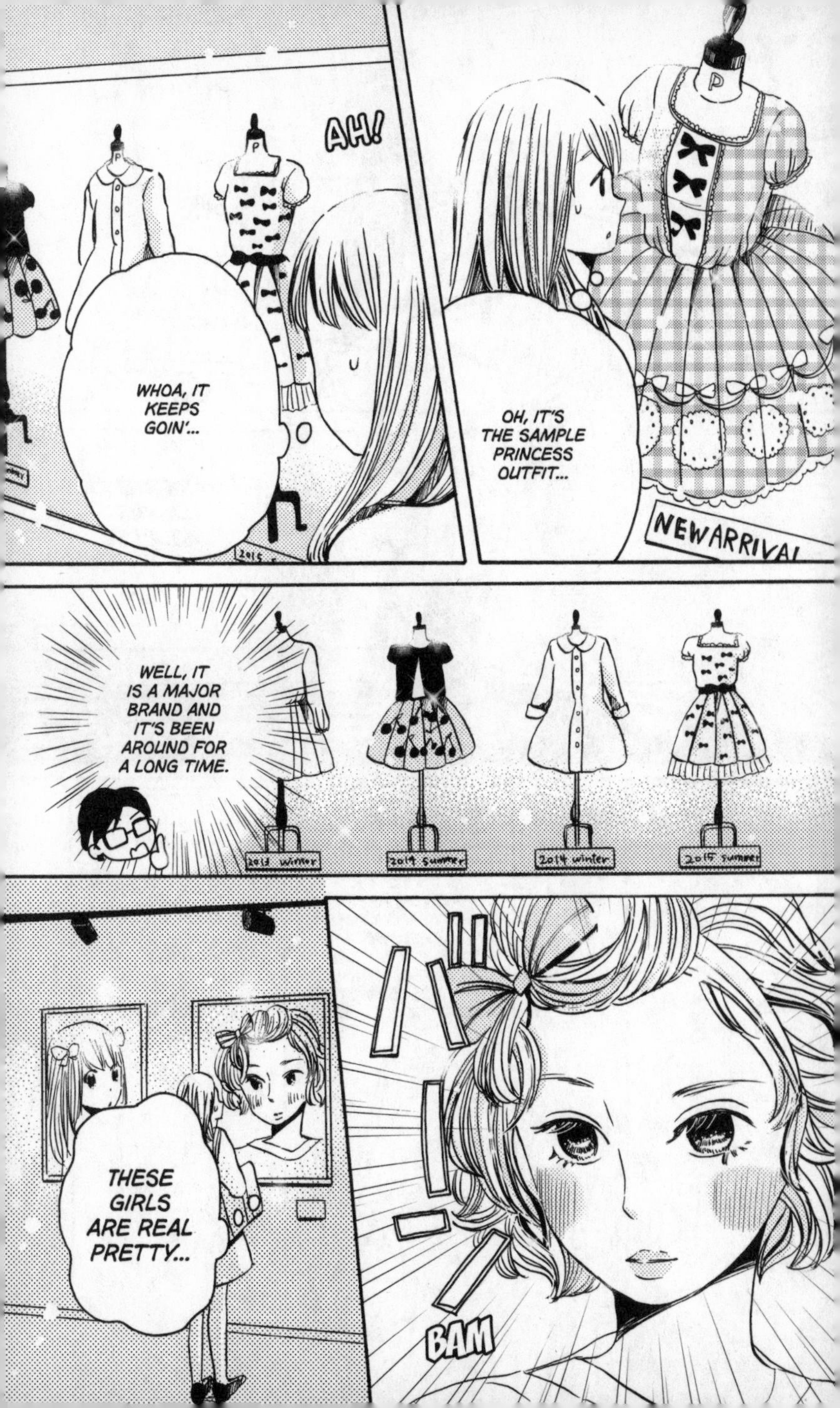
OH, IT'S THE SAMPLE PRINCESS OUTFIT...
NEWARRIVAL
AH!
WHOA, IT KEEPS GOIN'...
WELL, IT IS A MAJOR BRAND AND IT'S BEEN AROUND FOR A LONG TIME.
BAM
THESE GIRLS ARE REAL PRETTY...

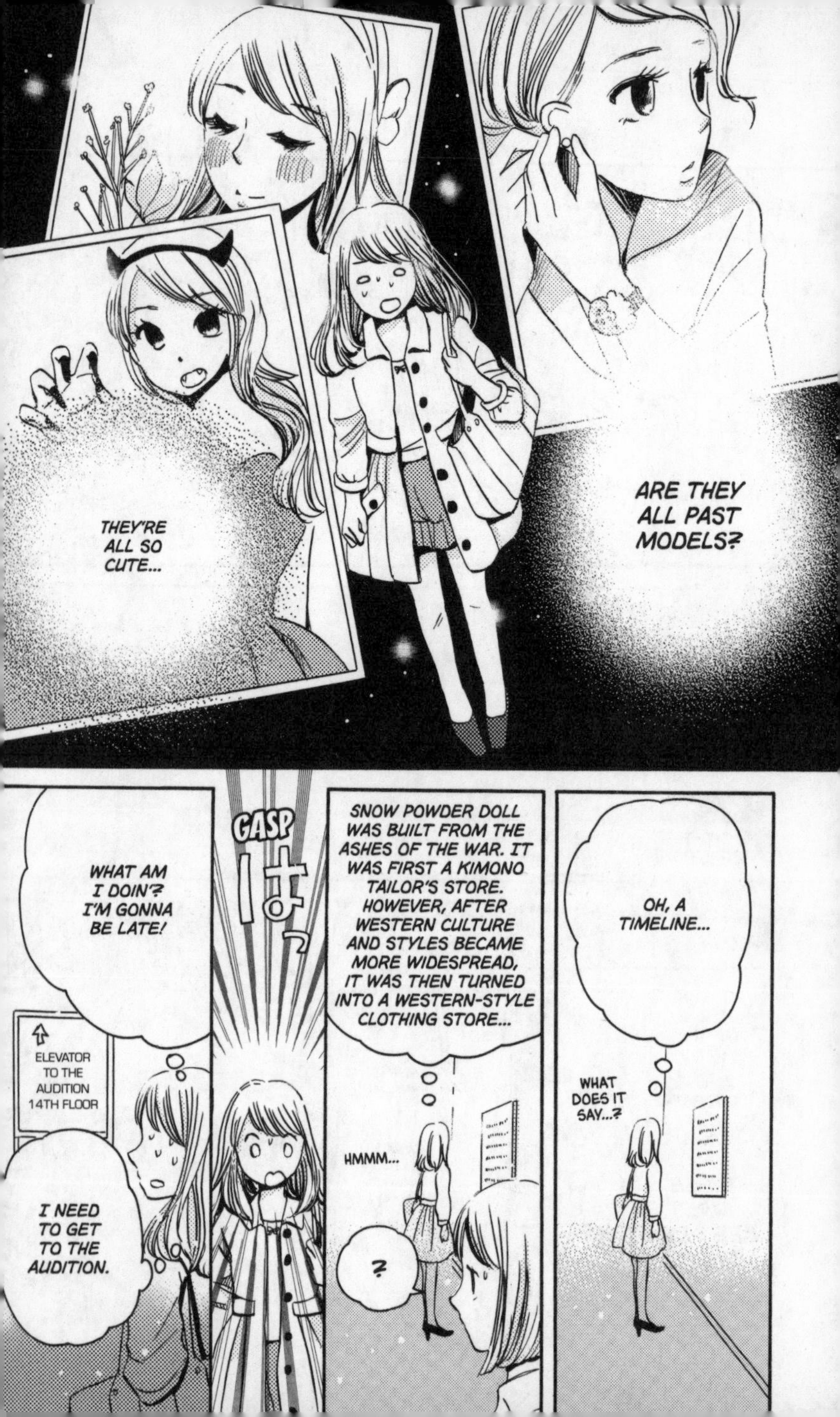
ARE THEY ALL PAST MODELS?
THEY'RE ALL SO CUTE...
OH, A TIMELINE...
WHAT DOES IT SAY...?
SNOW POWDER DOLL WAS BUILT FROM THE ASHES OF THE WAR. IT WAS FIRST A KIMONO TAILOR'S STORE. HOWEVER, AFTER WESTERN CULTURE AND STYLES BECAME MORE WIDESPREAD, IT WAS THEN TURNED INTO A WESTERN-STYLE CLOTHING STORE...
HMMM...
?
GASP
はっ
WHAT AM I DOIN'? I'M GONNA BE LATE!
ELEVATOR TO THE AUDITION 14TH FLOOR
I NEED TO GET TO THE AUDITION.

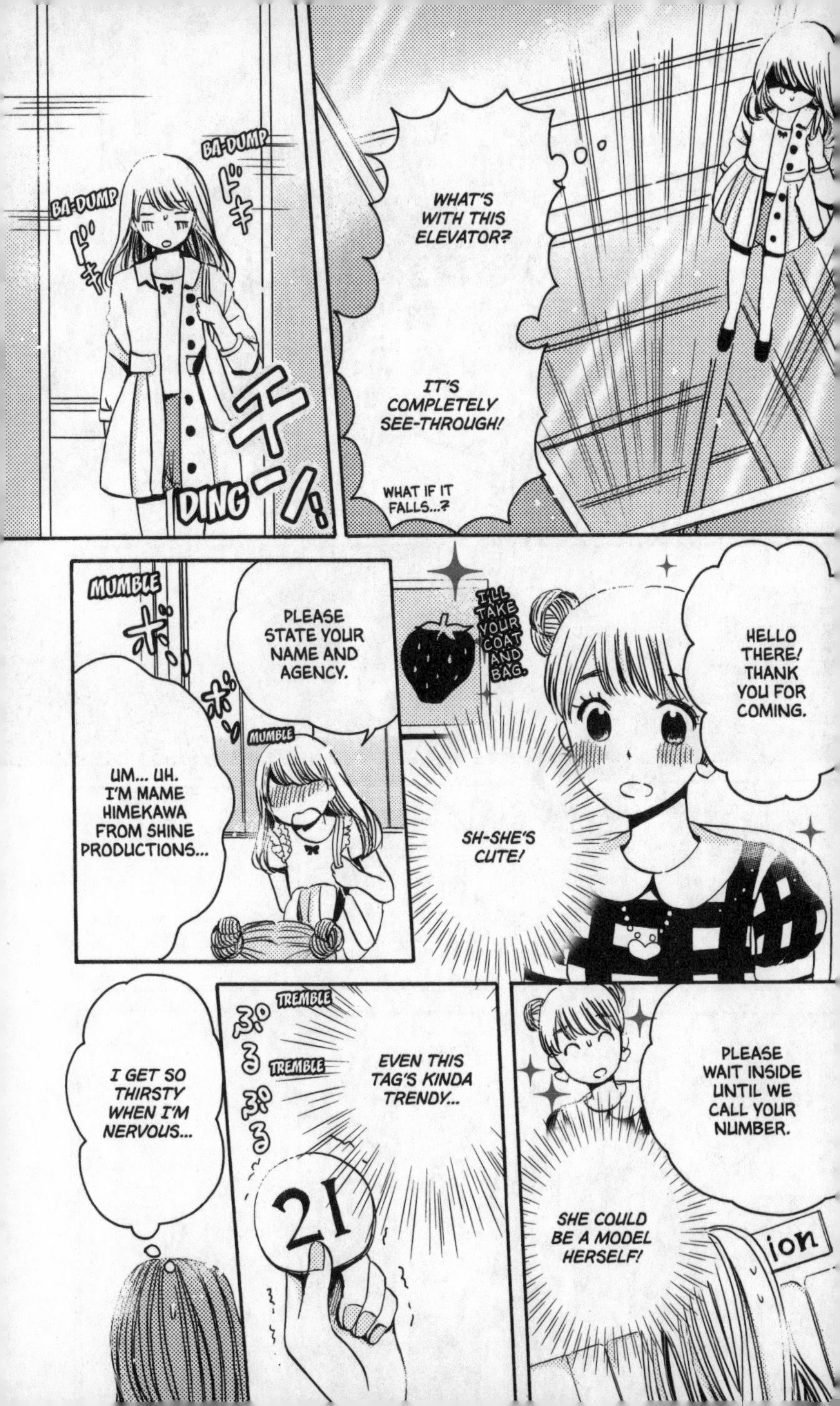
WHAT'S WITH THIS ELEVATOR?
IT'S COMPLETELY SEE-THROUGH!
WHAT IF IT FALLS...?
BA-DUMP
ドキ
BA-DUMP
ドキ
チーン
DING
HELLO THERE! THANK YOU FOR COMING.
I'LL TAKE YOUR COAT AND BAG.
SH-SHE'S CUTE!
PLEASE STATE YOUR NAME AND AGENCY.
MUMBLE
ボ
ボ
MUMBLE
UM... UH. I'M MAME HIMEKAWA FROM SHINE PRODUCTIONS...
PLEASE WAIT INSIDE UNTIL WE CALL YOUR NUMBER.
SHE COULD BE A MODEL HERSELF!
ion
TREMBLE
ぷる
TREMBLE
ぷる
EVEN THIS TAG'S KINDA TRENDY...
21
I GET SO THIRSTY WHEN I'M NERVOUS...

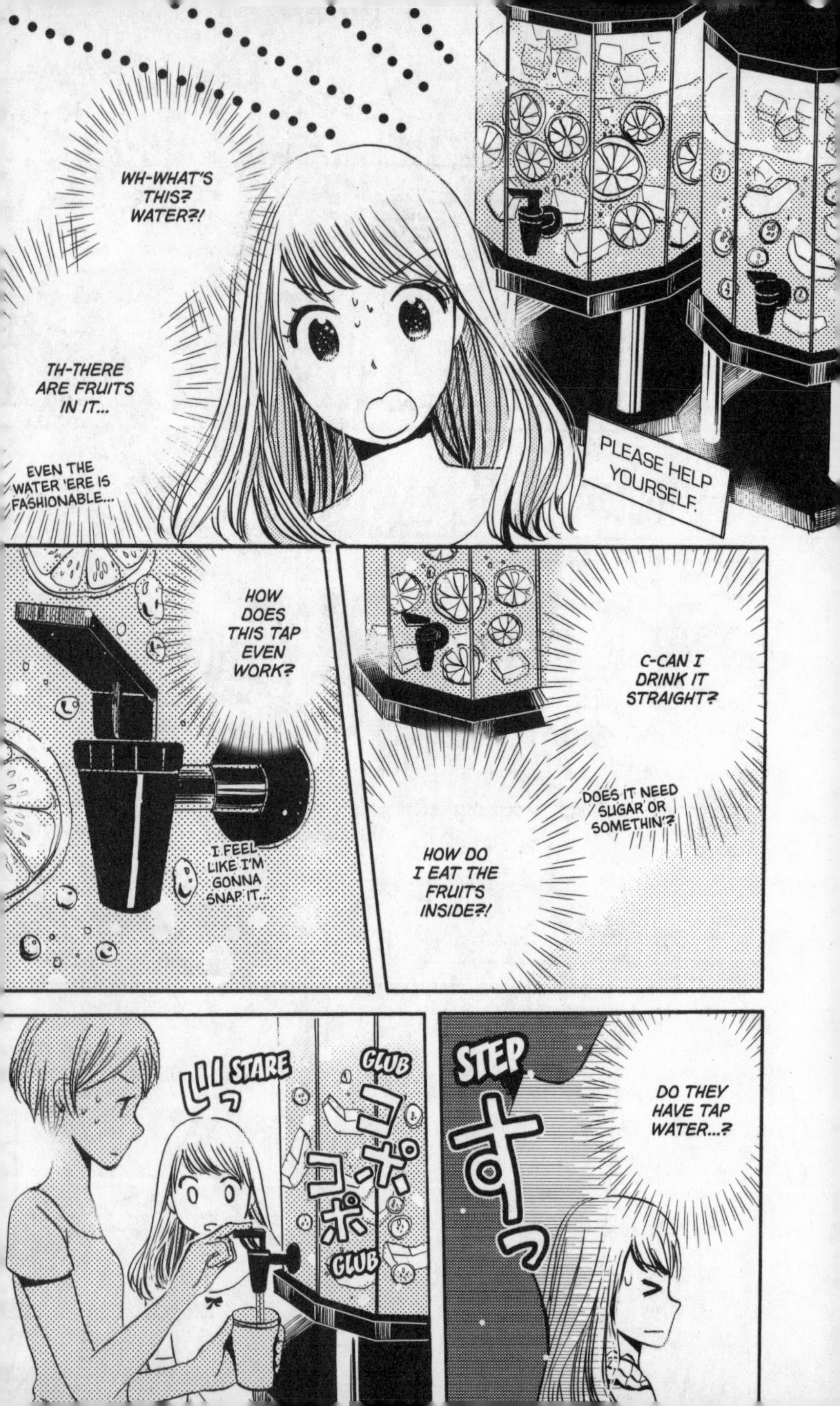
WH-WHAT'S THIS? WATER?!
TH-THERE ARE FRUITS IN IT...
PLEASE HELP YOURSELF.
EVEN THE WATER 'ERE IS FASHIONABLE...
C-CAN I DRINK IT STRAIGHT?
DOES IT NEED SUGAR OR SOMETHIN'?
HOW DO I EAT THE FRUITS INSIDE?!
HOW DOES THIS TAP EVEN WORK?
I FEEL LIKE I'M GONNA SNAP IT...
STEP
すっ
DO THEY HAVE TAP WATER...?
GLUB
コポ
STARE
じーっ
コポ
GLUB

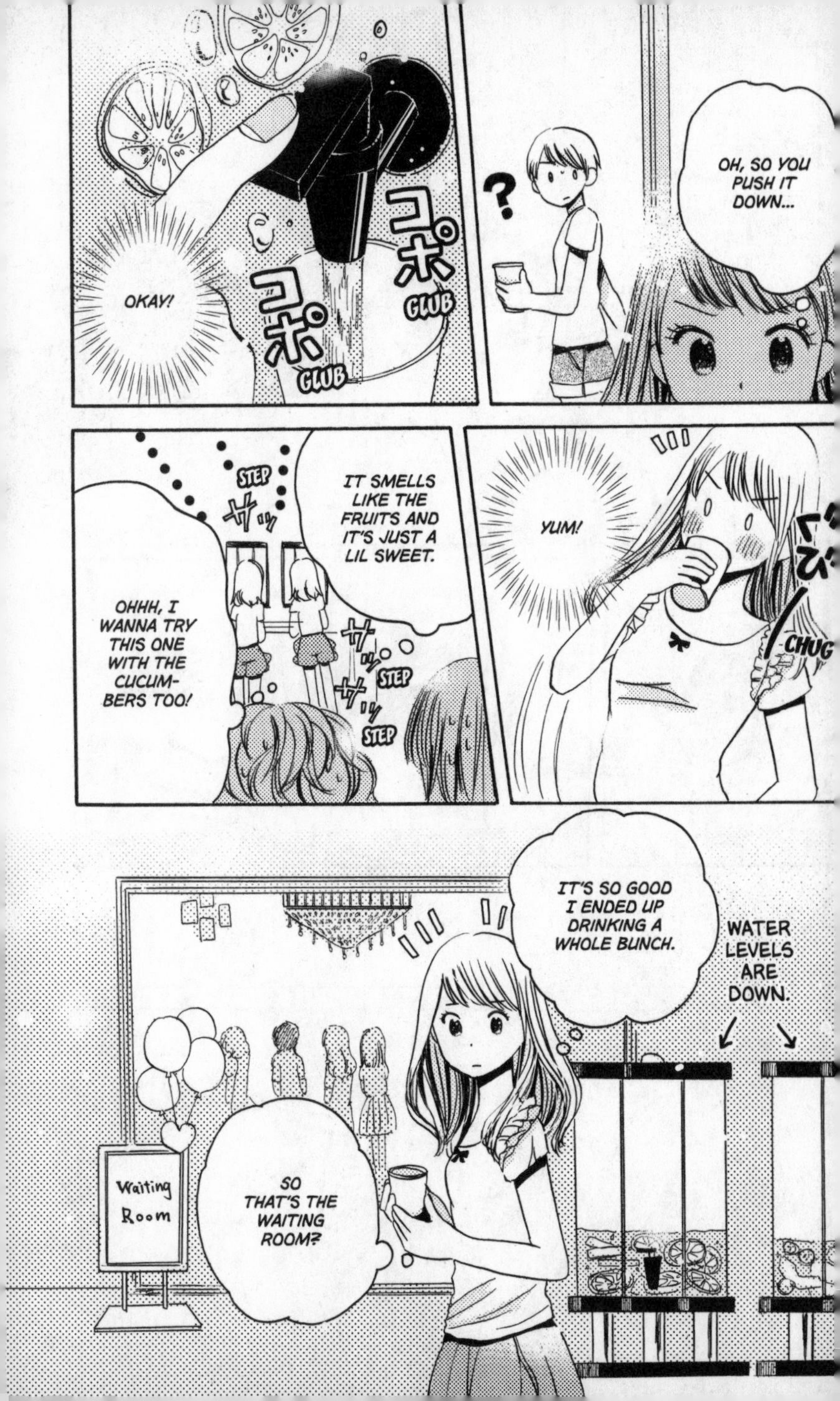
OH, SO YOU PUSH IT DOWN...
?
コポ
GLUB
OKAY!
コポ
GLUB
YUM!
CHUG
IT SMELLS LIKE THE FRUITS AND IT'S JUST A LIL SWEET.
STEP
サッ
サッ
STEP
サッ
STEP
OHHH, I WANNA TRY THIS ONE WITH THE CUCUMBERS TOO!
WATER LEVELS ARE DOWN.
IT'S SO GOOD I ENDED UP DRINKING A WHOLE BUNCH.
SO THAT'S THE WAITING ROOM?
Waiting Room

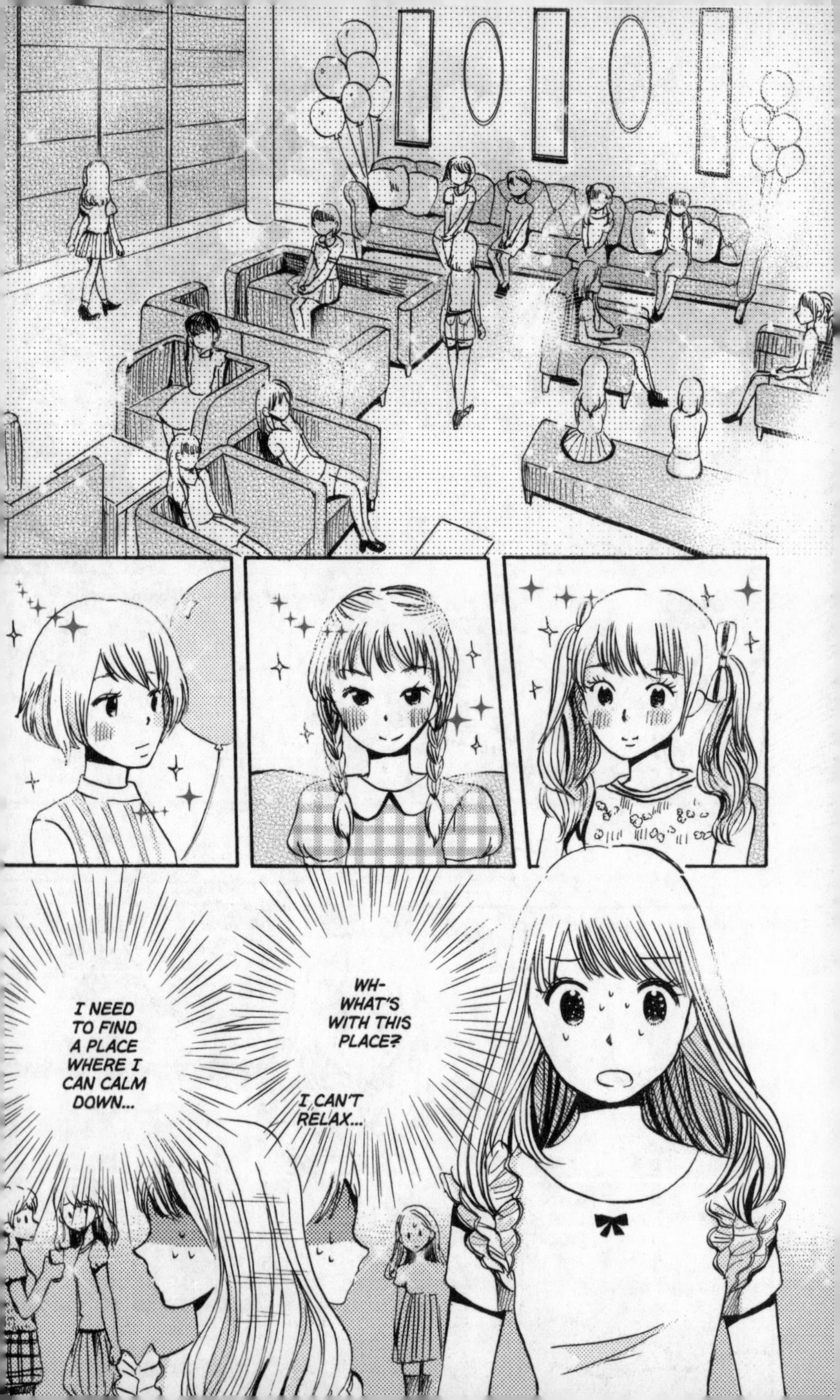
WH- WHAT'S WITH THIS PLACE?
I CAN'T RELAX...
I NEED TO FIND A PLACE WHERE I CAN CALM DOWN...

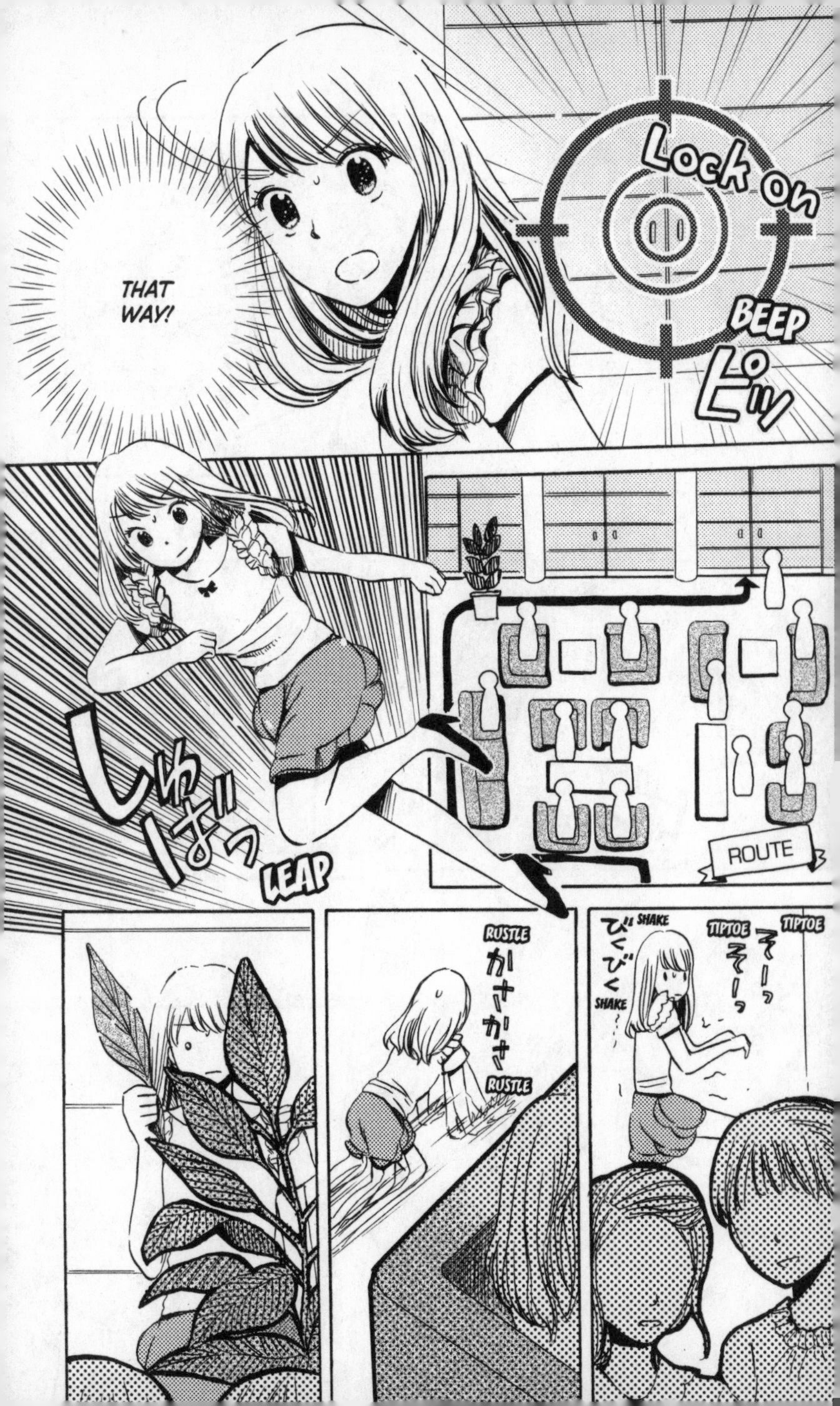
Lock on
BEEP
ピッ
THAT WAY!
ROUTE
しゅばっ
LEAP
TIPTOE
そーっ
TIPTOE
そーっ
SHAKE
びくびく
SHAKE
RUSTLE
かさかさ
RUSTLE

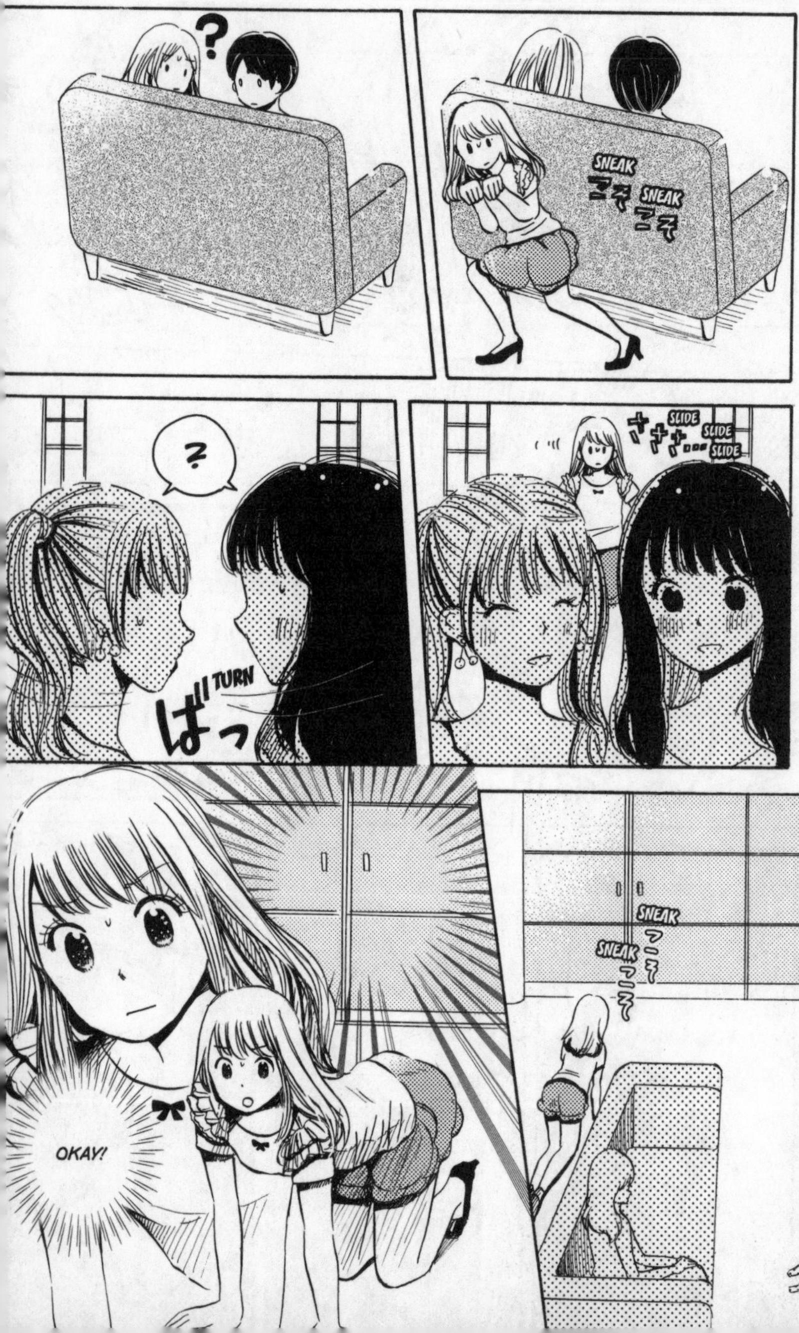

SNEAK
こそ
SNEAK
こそ
?
SLIDE
ささ...
SLIDE
SLIDE
?
TURN
ばっ
SNEAK
こそ
SNEAK
こそ
OKAY!

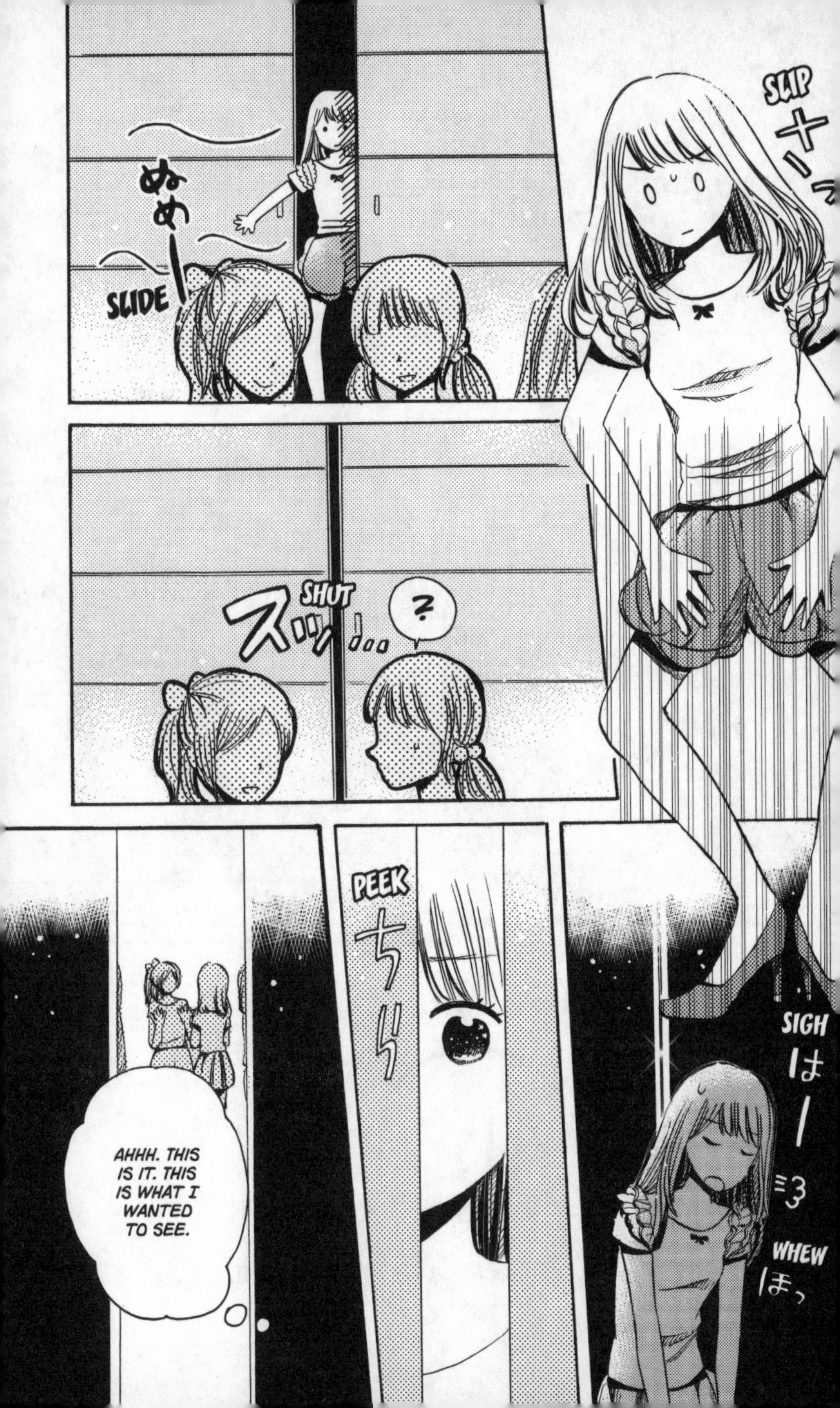
SLIP
さっ
SLIDE
ぬめー
SHUT
スッ
?
SIGH
はーっ
WHEW
ほっ
PEEK
ちら
AHHH. THIS IS IT. THIS IS WHAT I WANTED TO SEE.

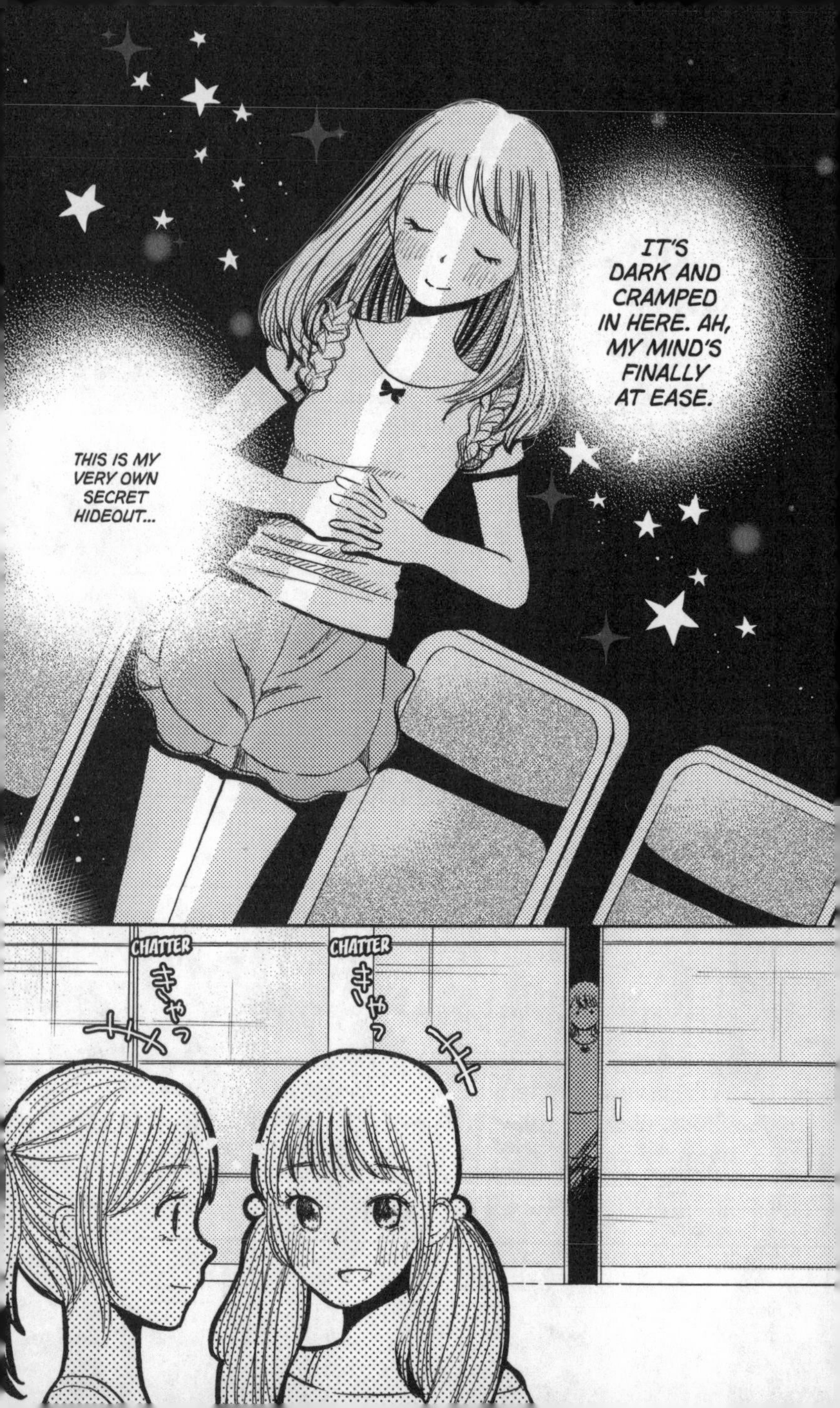
IT'S DARK AND CRAMPED IN HERE. AH, MY MIND'S FINALLY AT EASE.
THIS IS MY VERY OWN SECRET HIDEOUT...
CHATTER
CHATTER

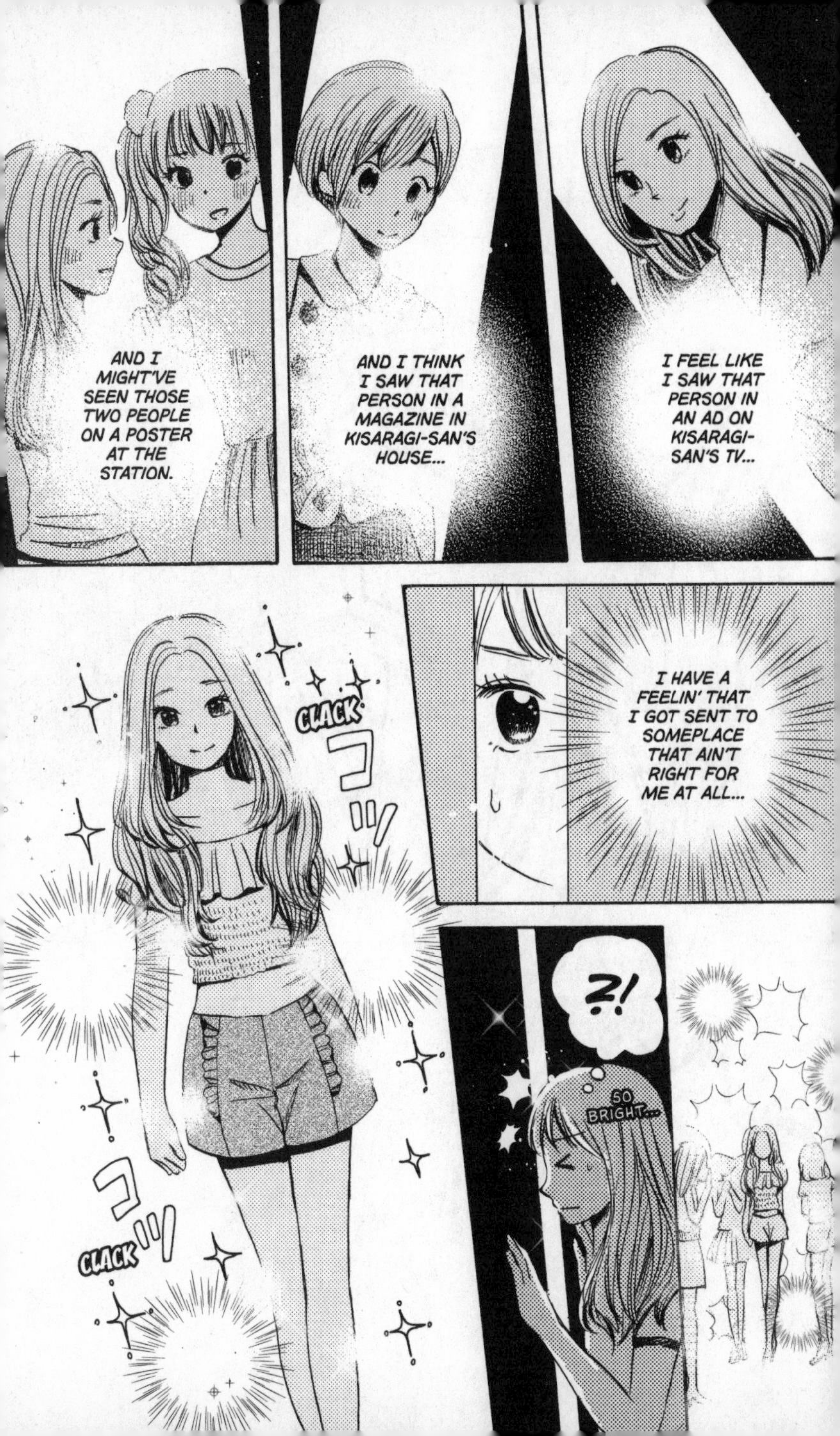
I FEEL LIKE I SAW THAT PERSON IN AN AD ON KISARAGI-SAN'S TV...
AND I THINK I SAW THAT PERSON IN A MAGAZINE IN KISARAGI-SAN'S HOUSE...
AND I MIGHT'VE SEEN THOSE TWO PEOPLE ON A POSTER AT THE STATION.
I HAVE A FEELIN' THAT I GOT SENT TO SOMEPLACE THAT AIN'T RIGHT FOR ME AT ALL...
?!
SO BRIGHT...
CLACK
CLACK

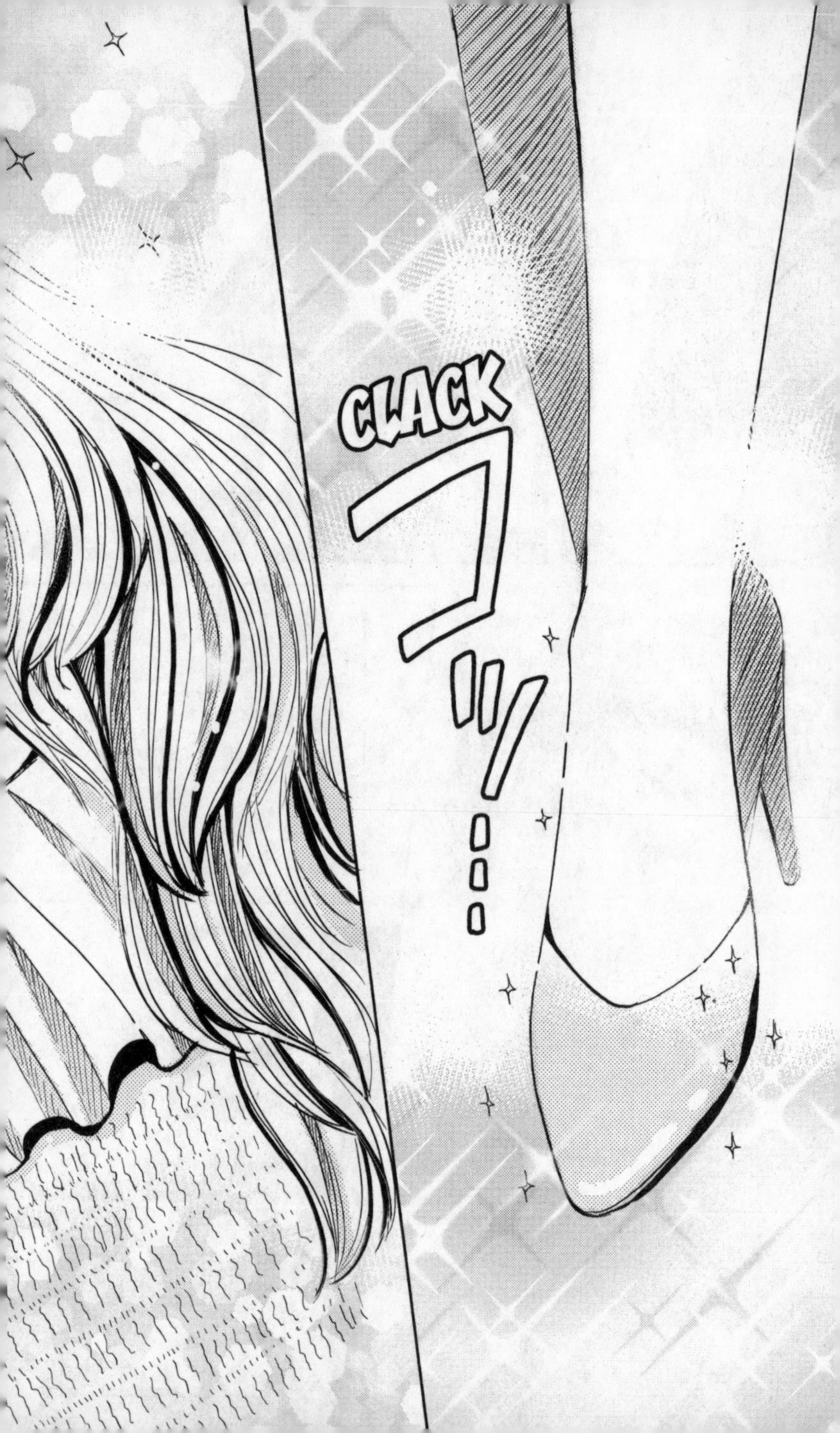
CLACK
コツ…

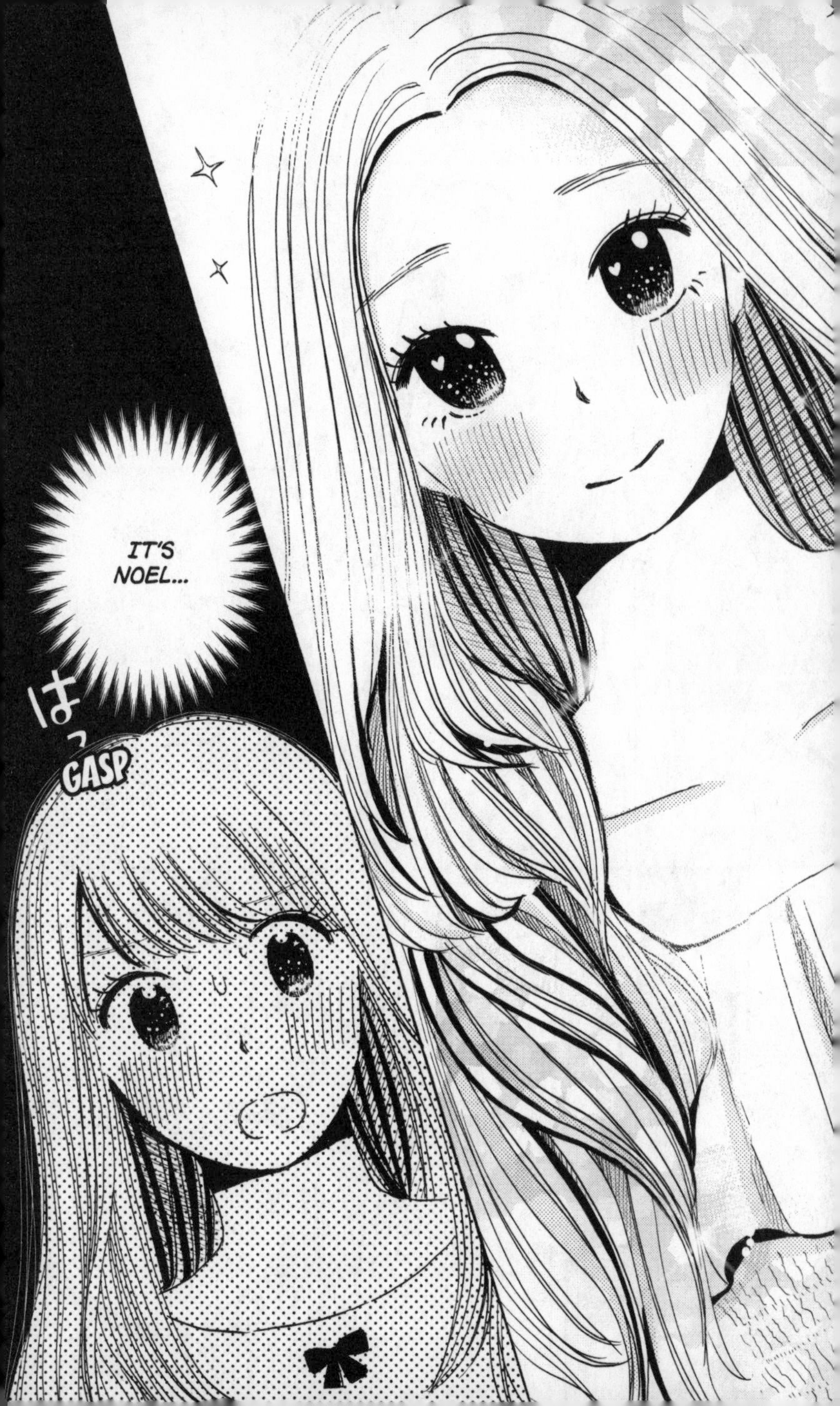
IT'S NOEL...
はっ
GASP

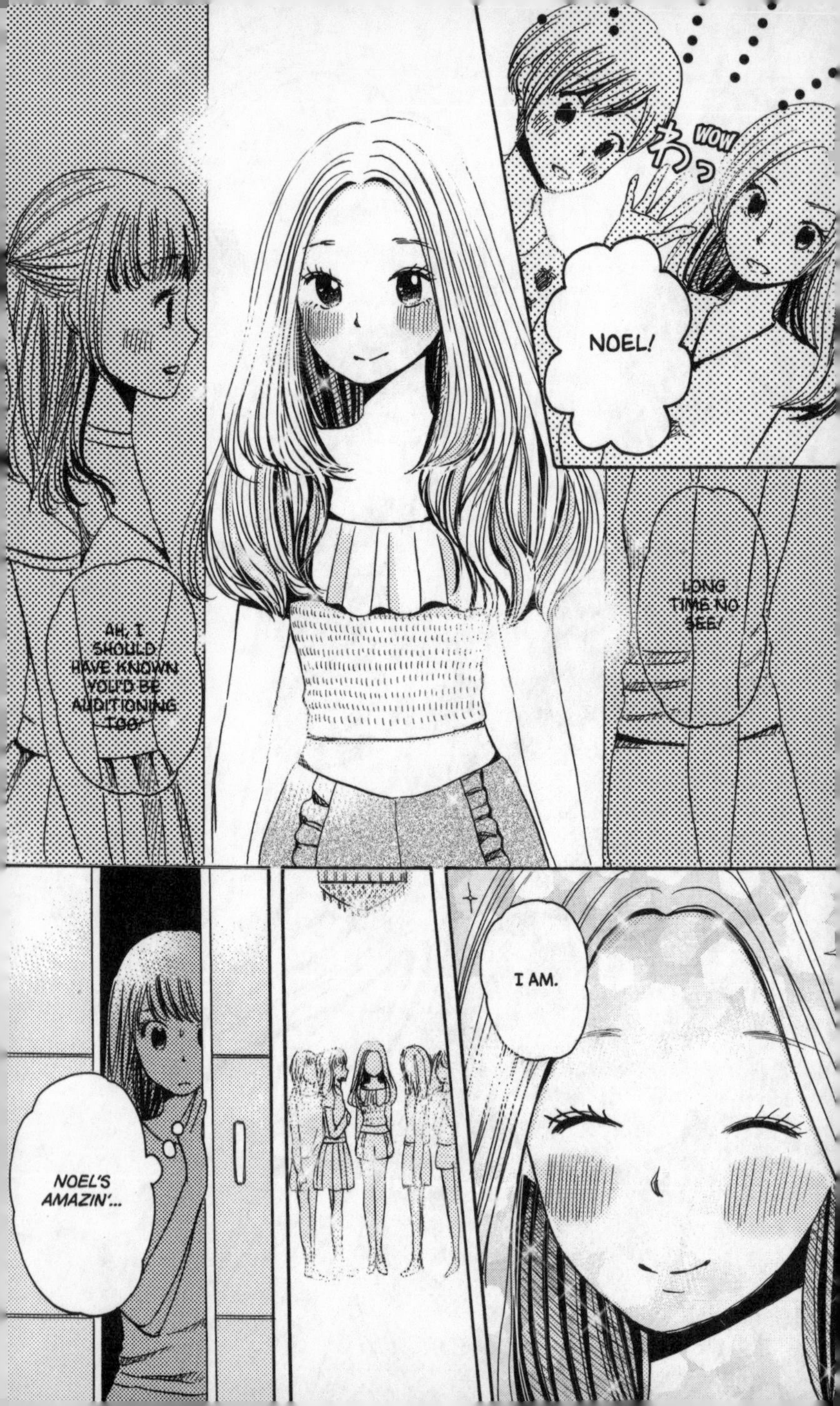
わっ
WOW
NOEL!
LONG TIME NO SEE!
AH, I SHOULD HAVE KNOWN YOU'D BE AUDITIONING TOO!
I AM.
NOEL'S AMAZIN'...

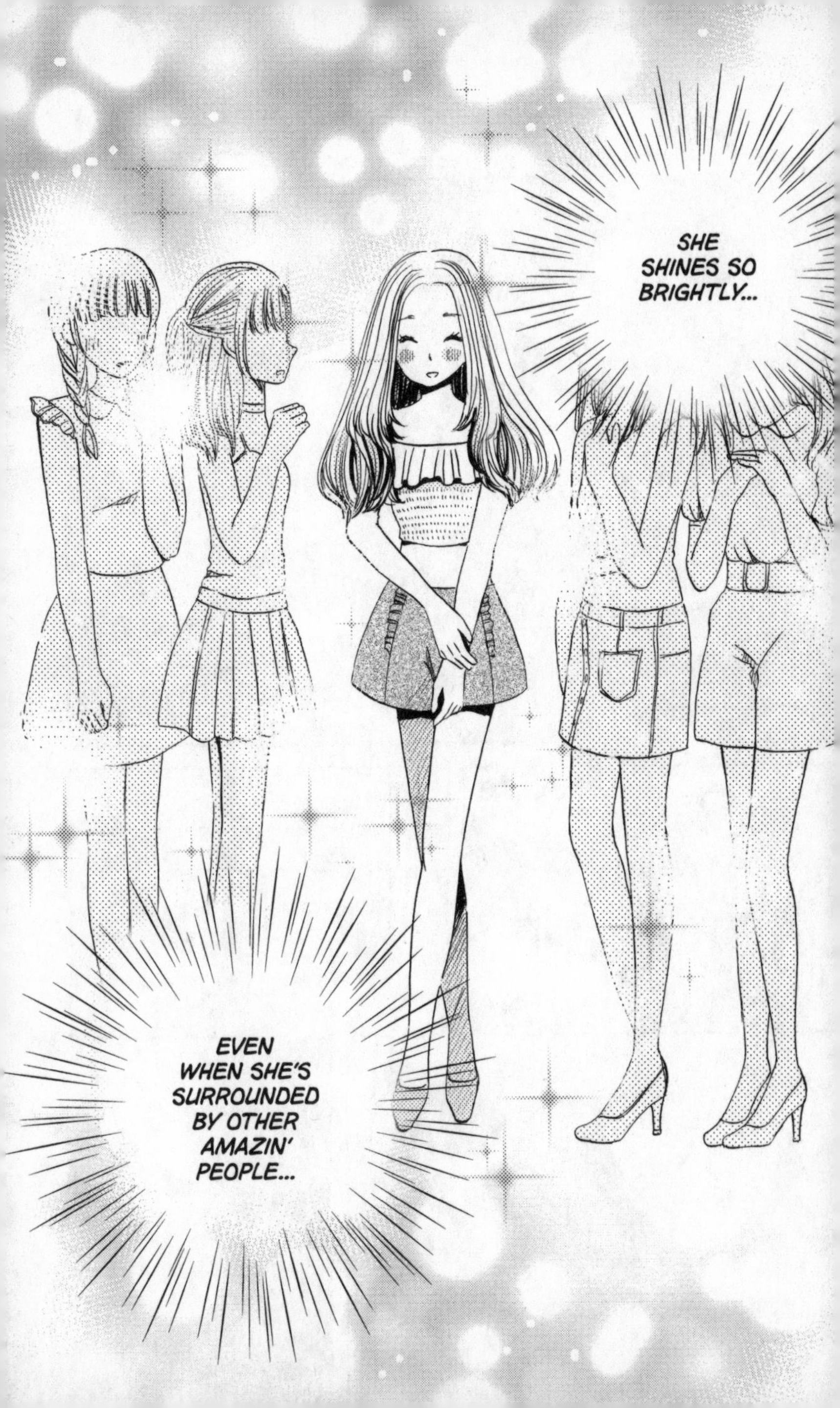
SHE SHINES SO BRIGHTLY...
EVEN WHEN SHE'S SURROUNDED BY OTHER AMAZIN' PEOPLE...

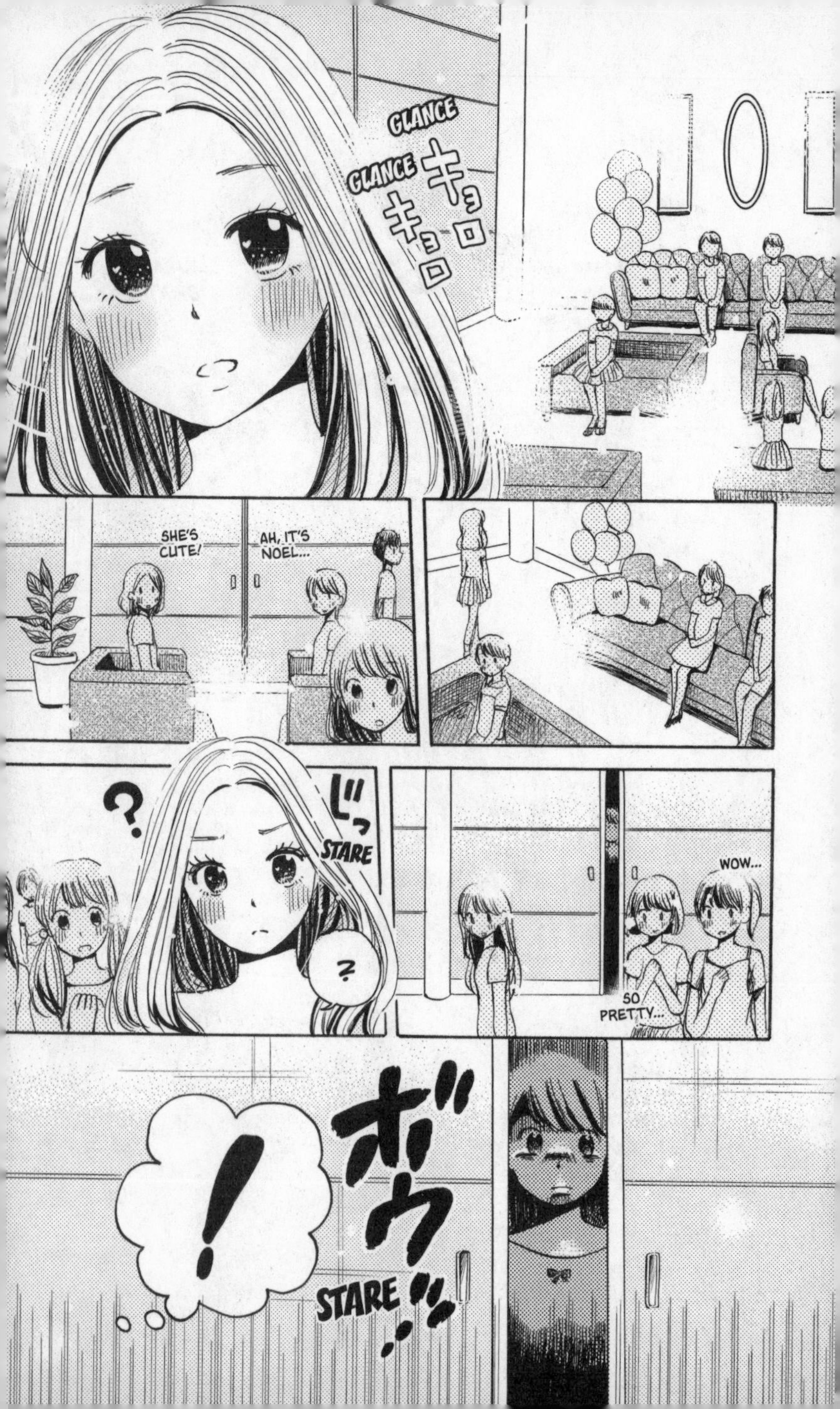

GLANCE
GLANCE
キョロキョロ
AH, IT'S NOEL...
SHE'S CUTE!
WOW...
SO PRETTY...
じっ
STARE
?
?
!
STARE

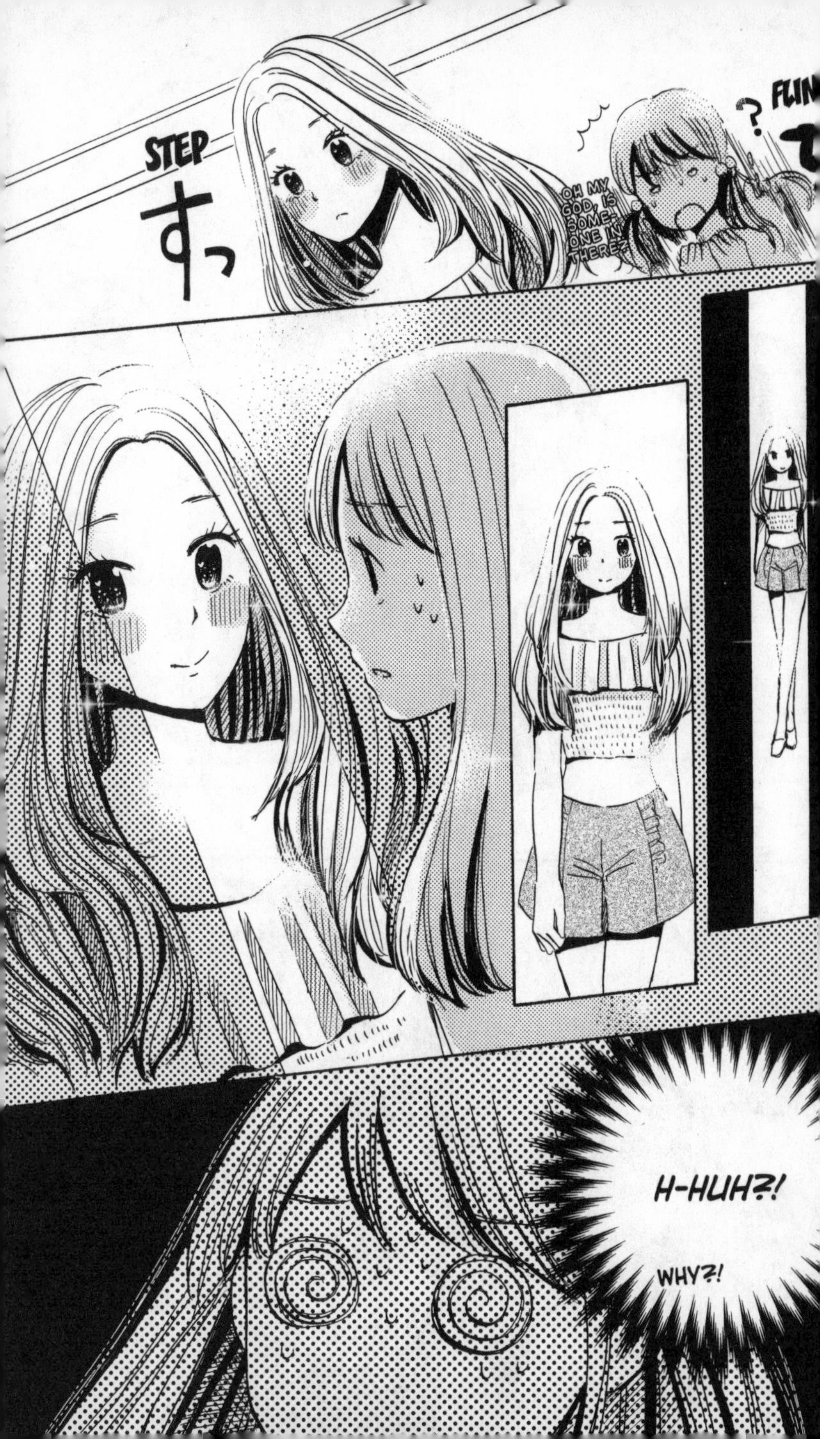
FLIN
?
OH MY GOD, IS SOME-ONE IN THERE?!
STEP
すっ
H-HUH?!
WHY?!

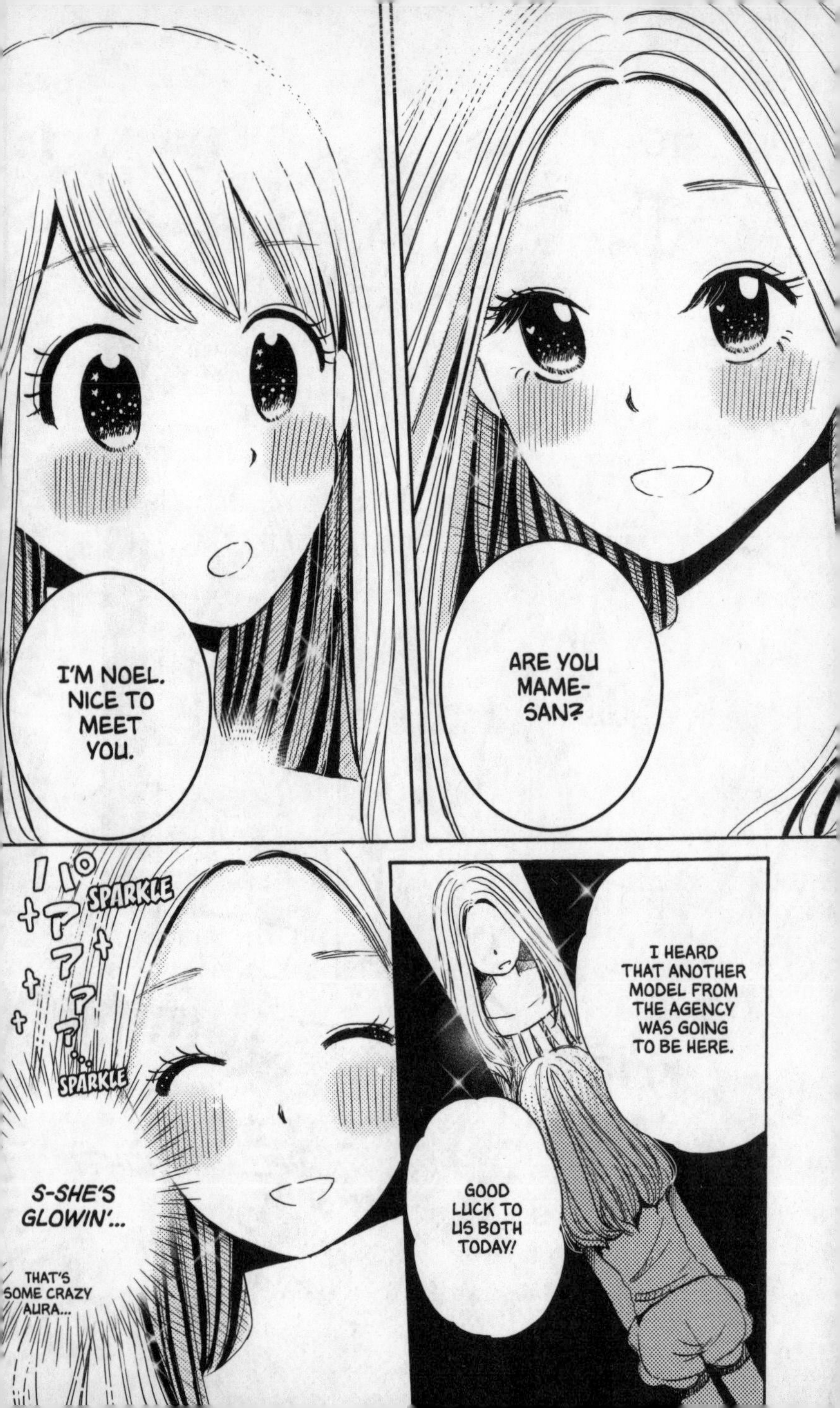
ARE YOU MAME-SAN?
I'M NOEL. NICE TO MEET YOU.
I HEARD THAT ANOTHER MODEL FROM THE AGENCY WAS GOING TO BE HERE.
GOOD LUCK TO US BOTH TODAY!
SPARKLE
SPARKLE
S-SHE'S GLOWIN'...
THAT'S SOME CRAZY AURA...

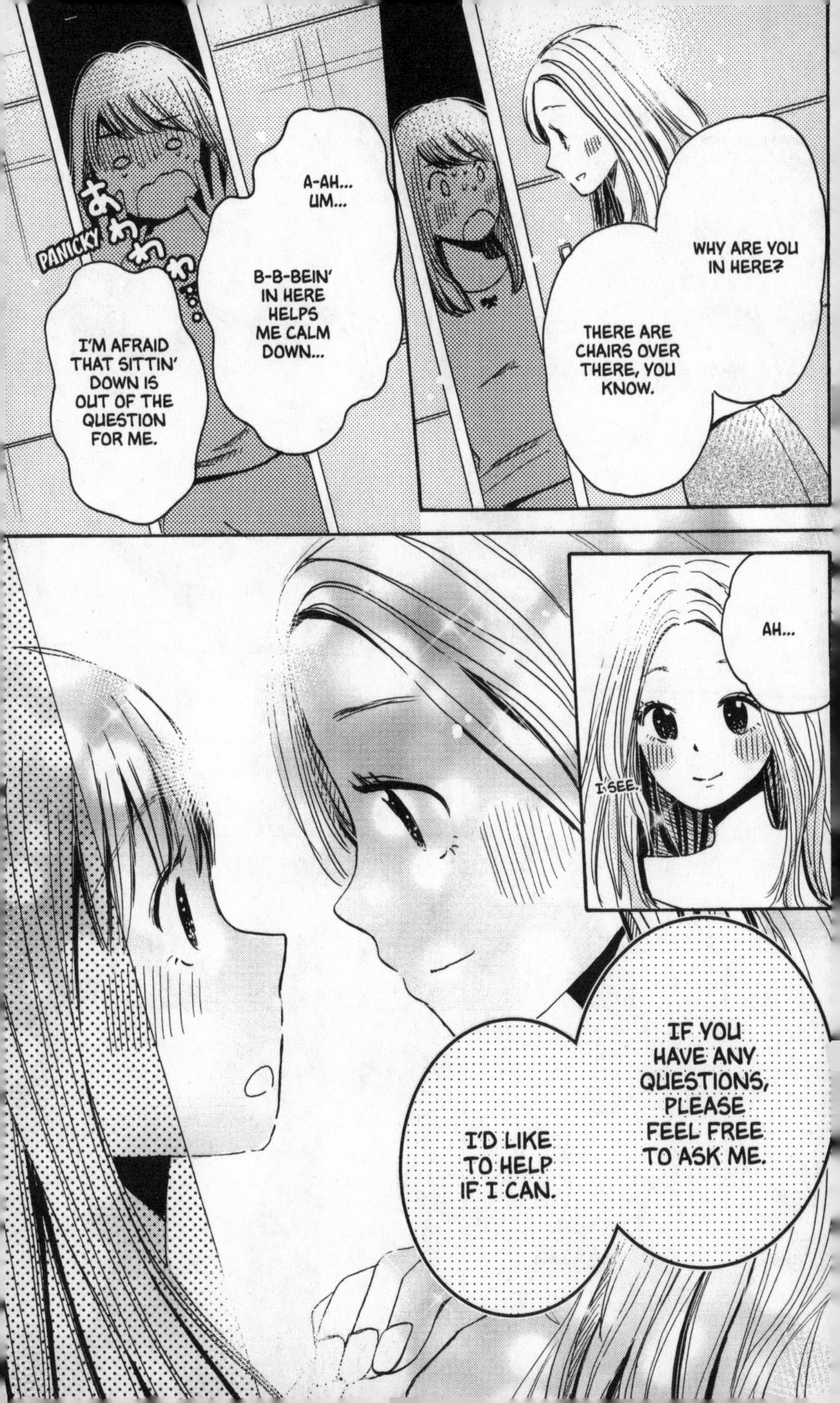
WHY ARE YOU IN HERE?
THERE ARE CHAIRS OVER THERE, YOU KNOW.
A-AH... UM...
B-B-BEIN' IN HERE HELPS ME CALM DOWN...
あわわわ…
PANICKY
I'M AFRAID THAT SITTIN' DOWN IS OUT OF THE QUESTION FOR ME.
AH...
I SEE.
IF YOU HAVE ANY QUESTIONS, PLEASE FEEL FREE TO ASK ME.
I'D LIKE TO HELP IF I CAN.

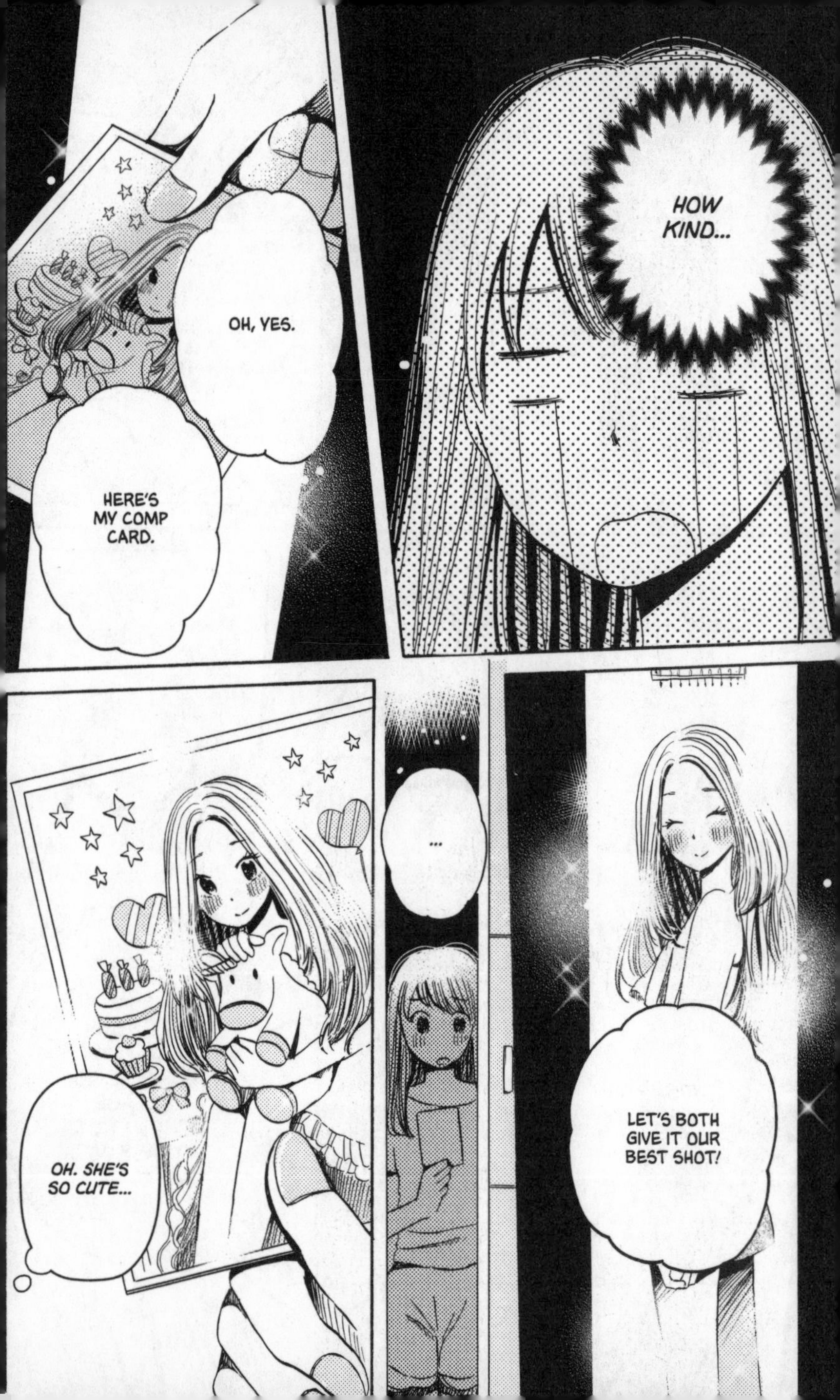
HOW KIND...
OH, YES.
HERE'S MY COMP CARD.
LET'S BOTH GIVE IT OUR BEST SHOT!
...
OH. SHE'S SO CUTE...

NOEL...
SHE'S PRETTY, ELEGANT, AND KIND...
SHE'S THE PERFECT HUMAN...
WE'RE GOING TO WIN. WE'LL BEAT HER.
BUT I DON'T REMEMBER HOW...
KISARAGI-SAAAN!

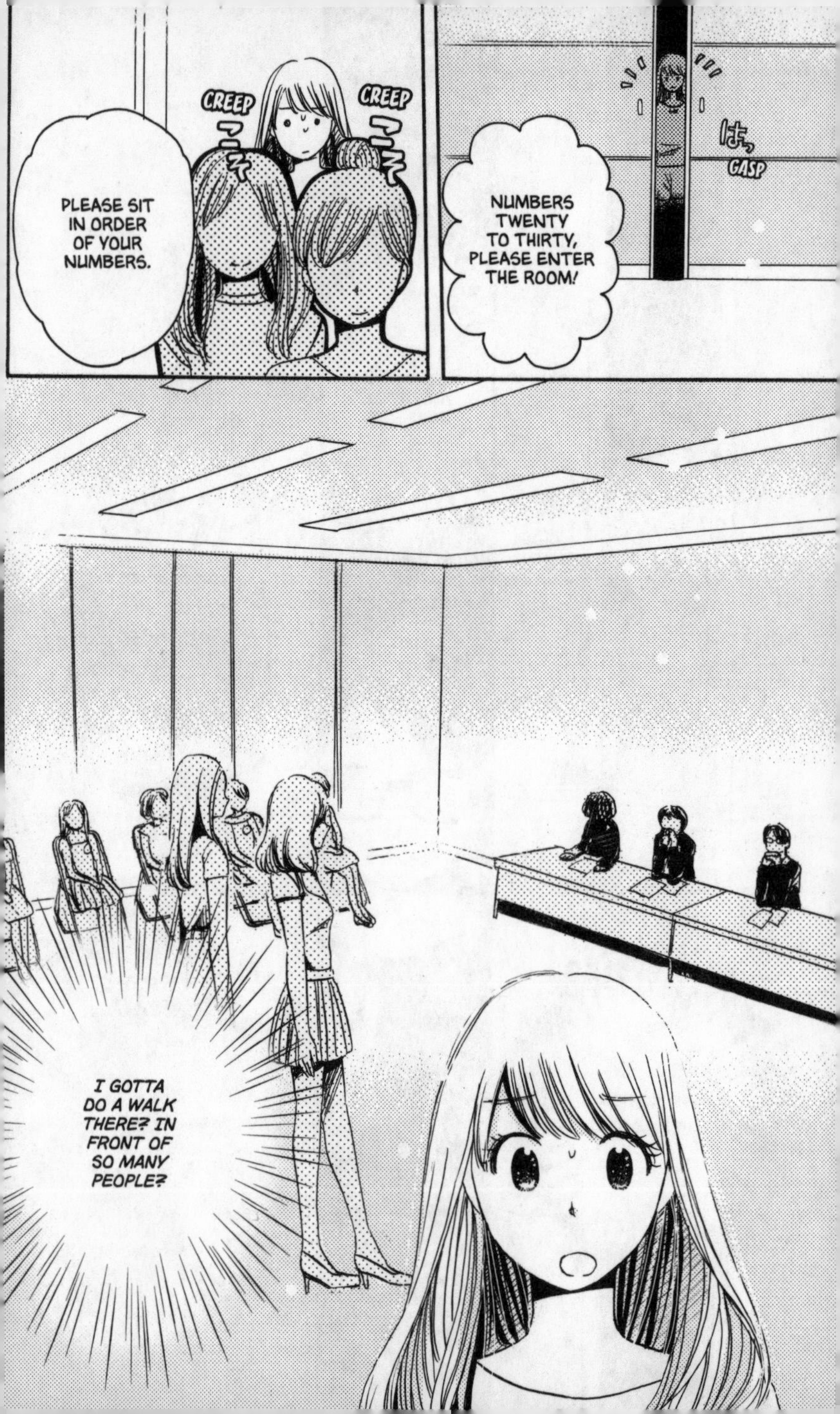
はっ
GASP
NUMBERS TWENTY TO THIRTY, PLEASE ENTER THE ROOM!
CREEP
CREEP
PLEASE SIT IN ORDER OF YOUR NUMBERS.
I GOTTA DO A WALK THERE? IN FRONT OF SO MANY PEOPLE?

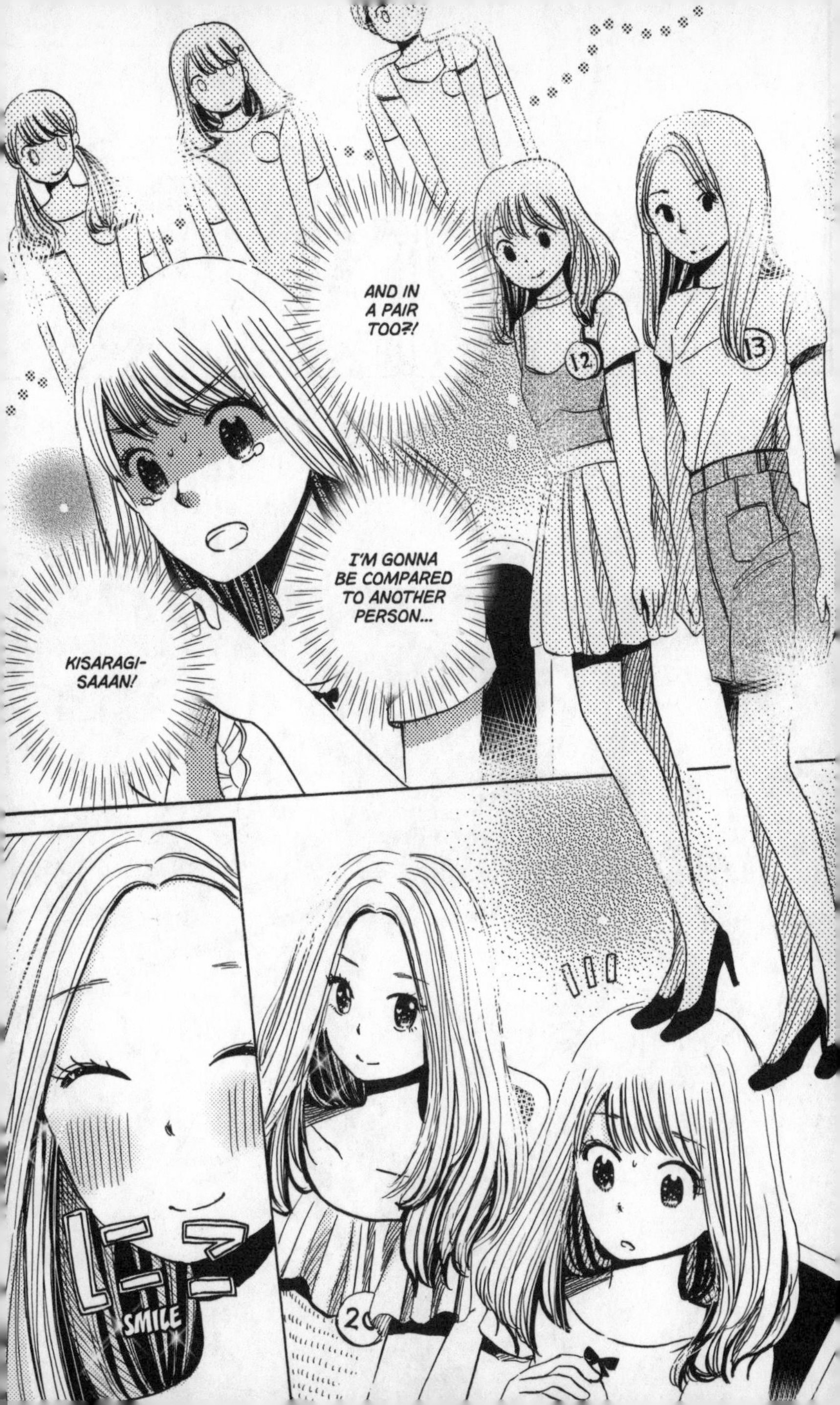
AND IN A PAIR TOO?!
I'M GONNA BE COMPARED TO ANOTHER PERSON...
KISARAGI-SAAAN!
SMILE

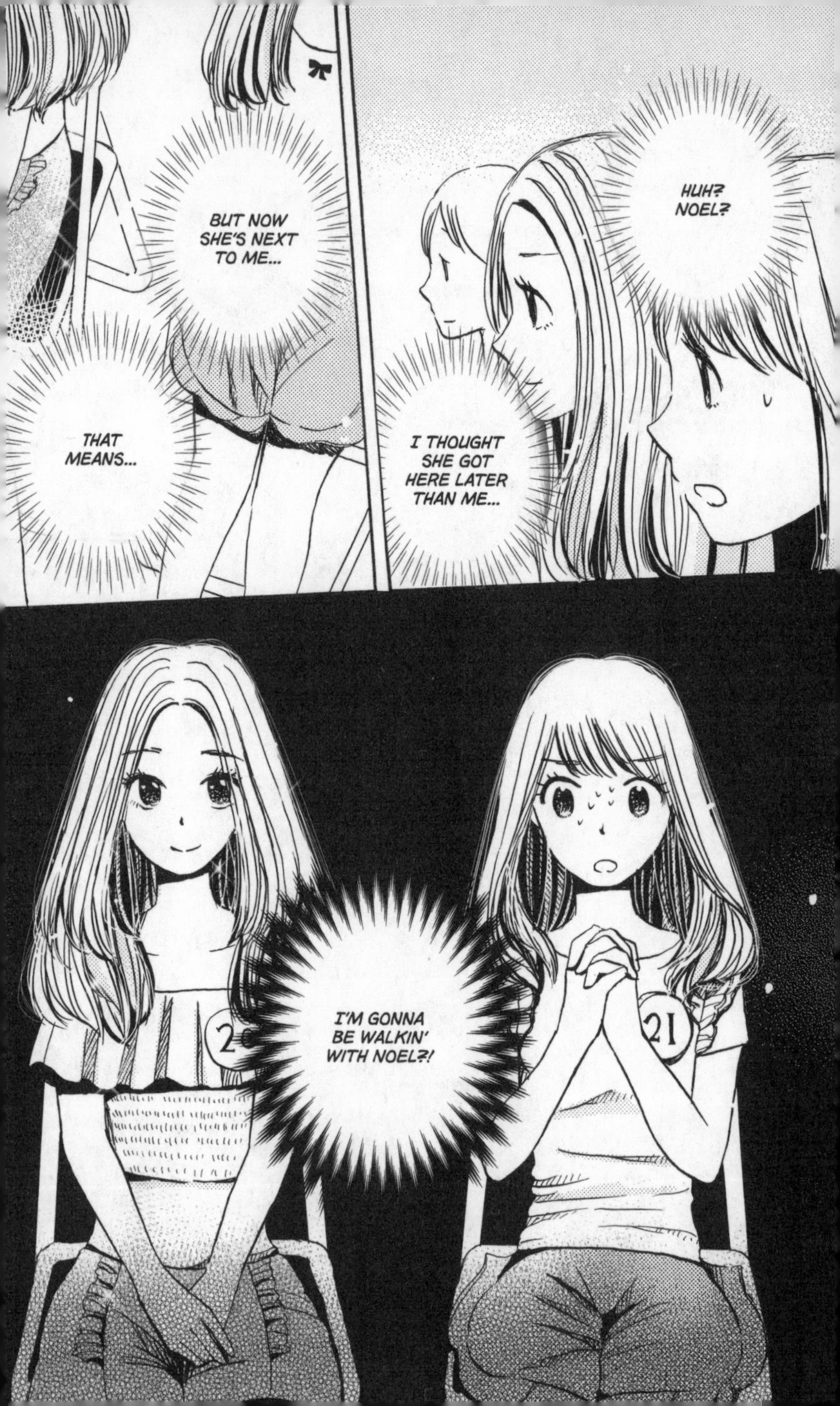
HUH? NOEL?
I THOUGHT SHE GOT HERE LATER THAN ME...
BUT NOW SHE'S NEXT TO ME...
THAT MEANS...
21
I'M GONNA BE WALKIN' WITH NOEL?!

M A M E
coordinate

## THE ORIGIN OF A NAME

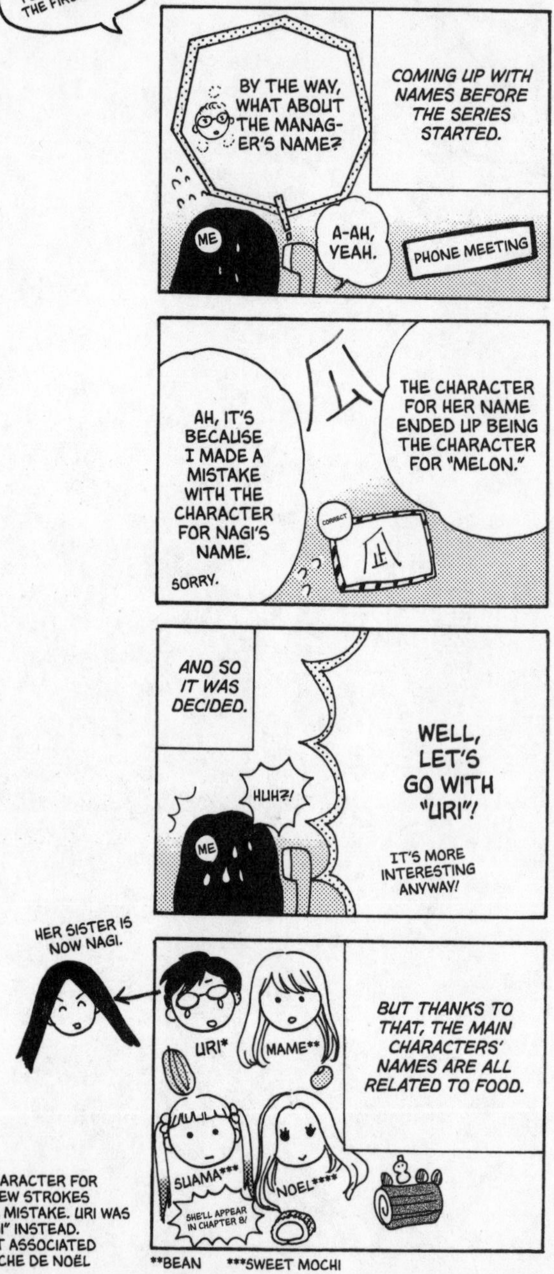
SOMETHING I FORGOT TO PUT IN THE FIRST VOLUME.
COMING UP WITH NAMES BEFORE THE SERIES STARTED.
BY THE WAY, WHAT ABOUT THE MANAGER'S NAME?
PHONE MEETING
A-AH, YEAH.
ME
THE CHARACTER FOR HER NAME ENDED UP BEING THE CHARACTER FOR "MELON."
CORRECT
AH, IT'S BECAUSE I MADE A MISTAKE WITH THE CHARACTER FOR NAGI'S NAME.
SORRY.
WELL, LET'S GO WITH "URI"!
IT'S MORE INTERESTING ANYWAY!
AND SO IT WAS DECIDED.
HUH?!
ME
BUT THANKS TO THAT, THE MAIN CHARACTERS' NAMES ARE ALL RELATED TO FOOD.
MAME**
URI*
HER SISTER IS NOW NAGI.
NOEL****
SUAMA***
SHE'LL APPEAR IN CHAPTER 8!

*"URI" MEANS "MELON." THE CHARACTER FOR "URI" AND "NAGI" ARE JUST A FEW STROKES APART, SO THE ARTIST MADE A MISTAKE. URI WAS SUPPOSED TO BE CALLED "NAGI" INSTEAD.
****IN JAPANESE, NOEL IS BEST ASSOCIATED WITH THE CHRISTMAS CAKE BÛCHE DE NOËL

**BEAN ***SWEET MOCHI

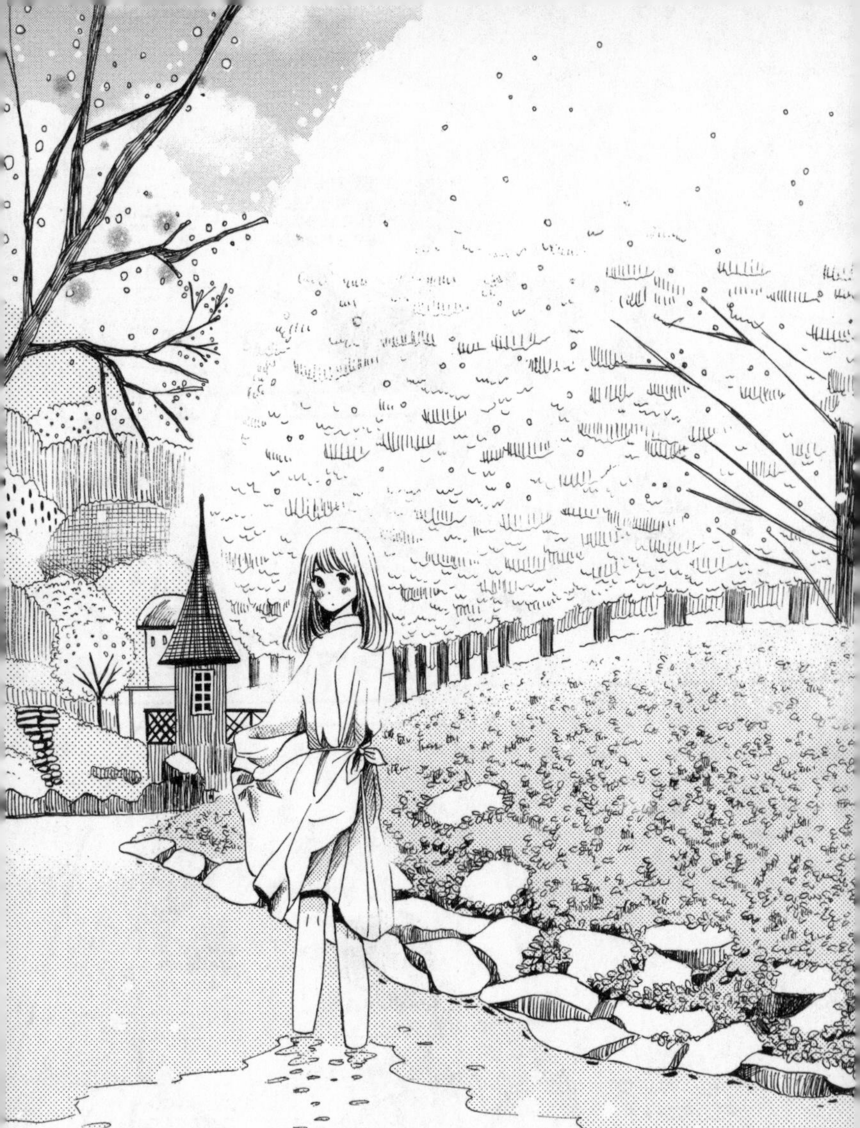

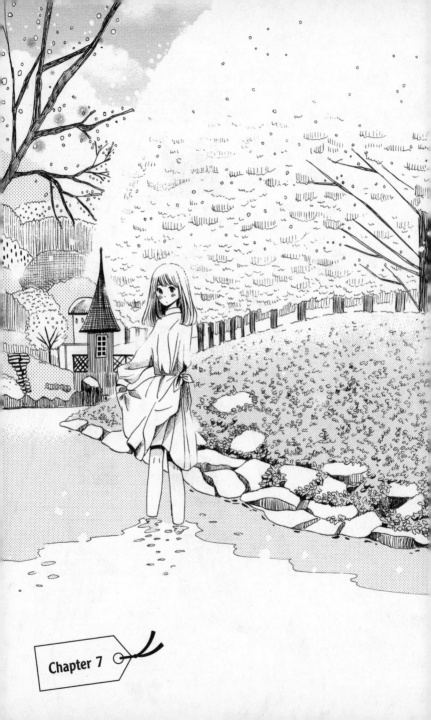

# Chapter 7

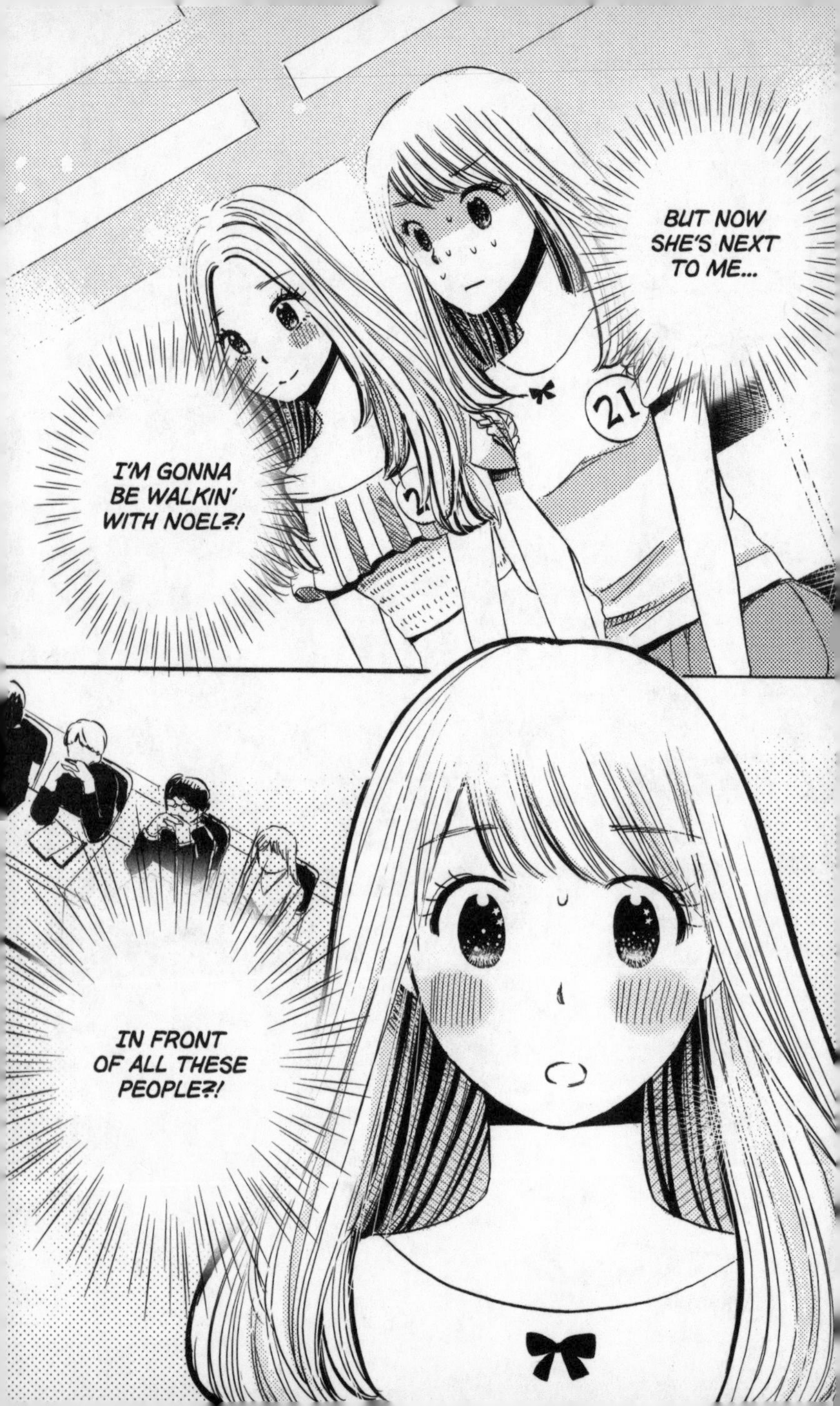
BUT NOW SHE'S NEXT TO ME...
I'M GONNA BE WALKIN' WITH NOEL?!
IN FRONT OF ALL THESE PEOPLE?!

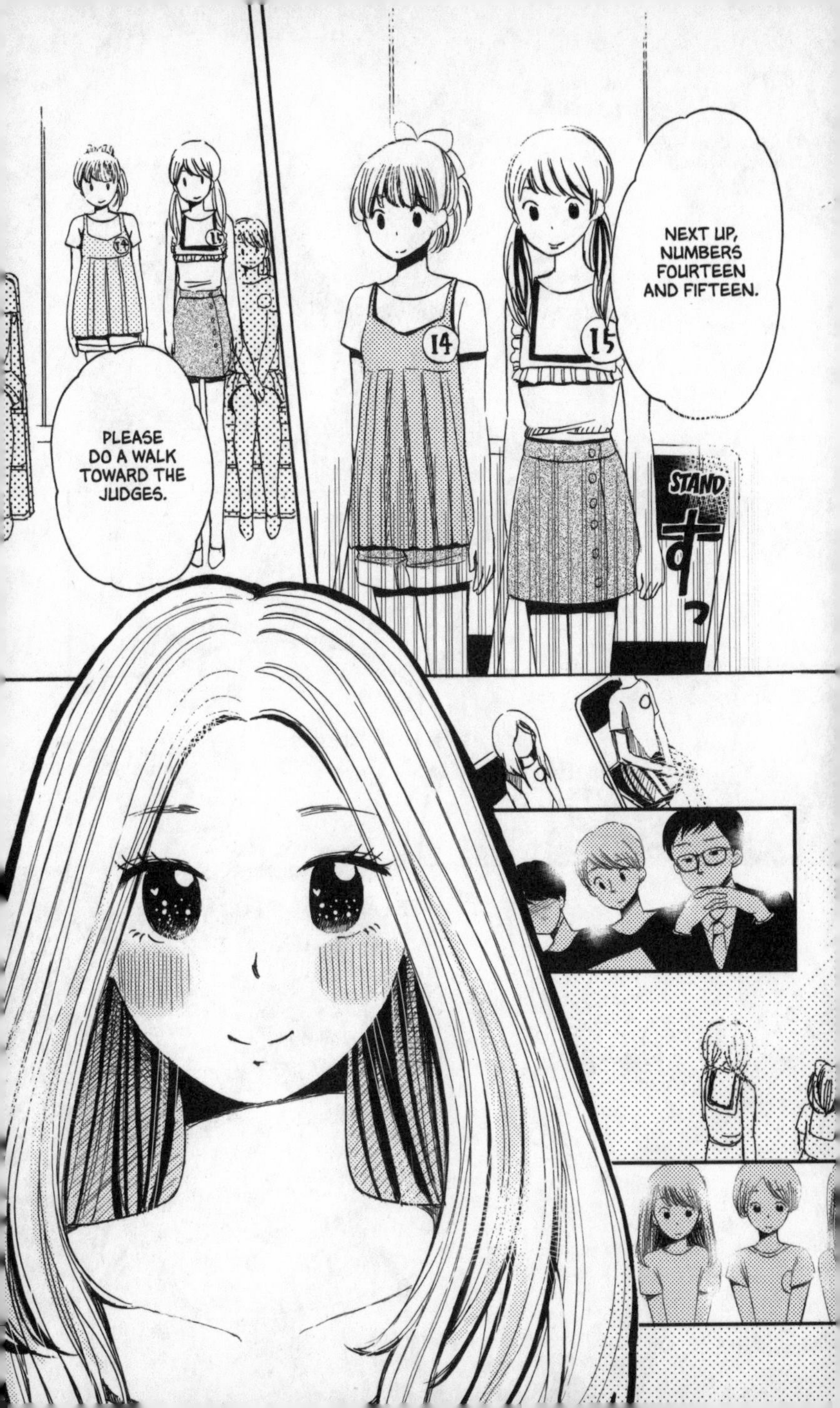
NEXT UP, NUMBERS FOURTEEN AND FIFTEEN.
STAND
すっ
PLEASE DO A WALK TOWARD THE JUDGES.

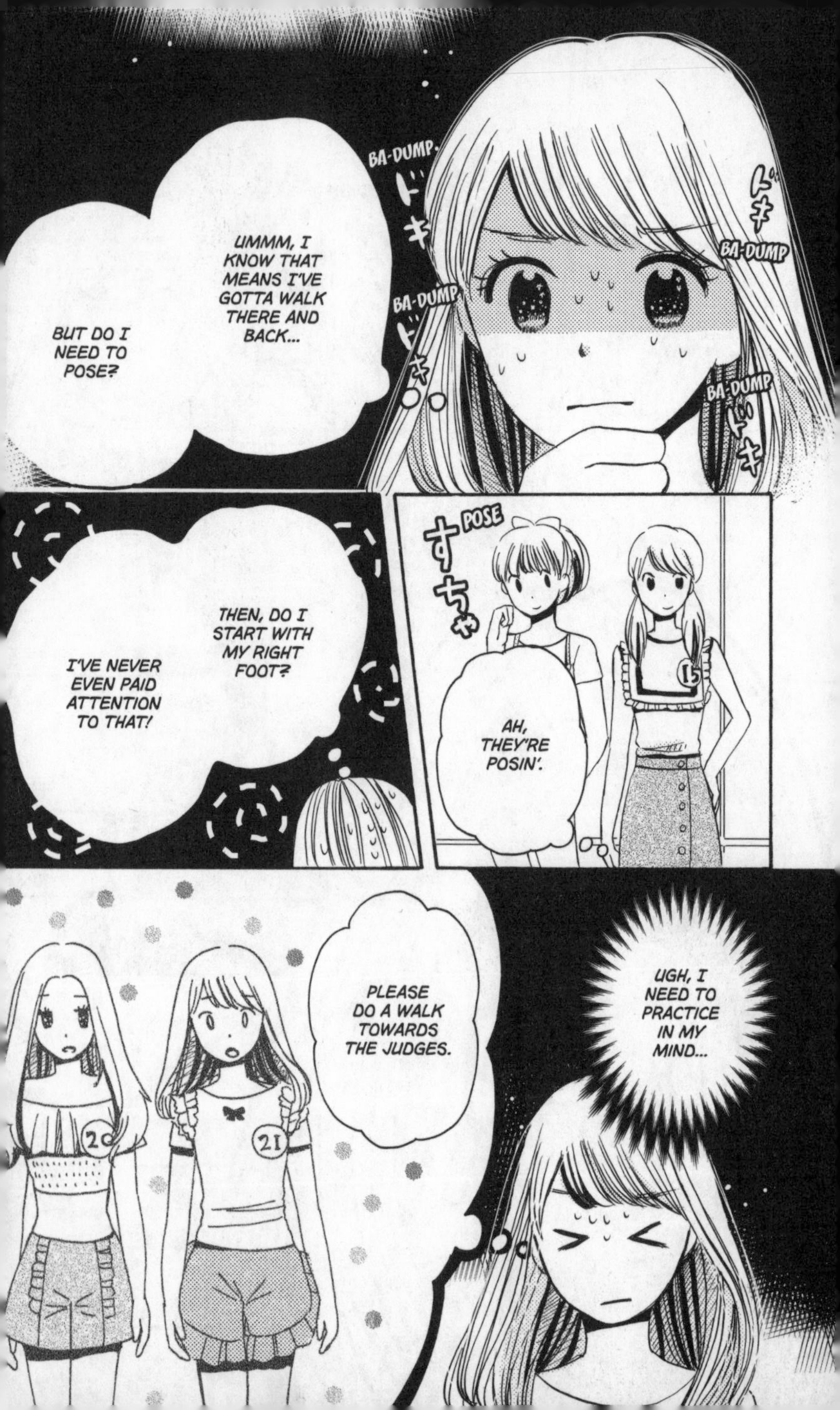
ドキ
BA-DUMP
BA-DUMP.
ドキ
UMMM, I KNOW THAT MEANS I'VE GOTTA WALK THERE AND BACK...
BA-DUMP
ドキ
BA-DUMP
ドキ
BUT DO I NEED TO POSE?
POSE
すちゃ
AH, THEY'RE POSIN'.
THEN, DO I START WITH MY RIGHT FOOT?
I'VE NEVER EVEN PAID ATTENTION TO THAT!
UGH, I NEED TO PRACTICE IN MY MIND...
PLEASE DO A WALK TOWARDS THE JUDGES.

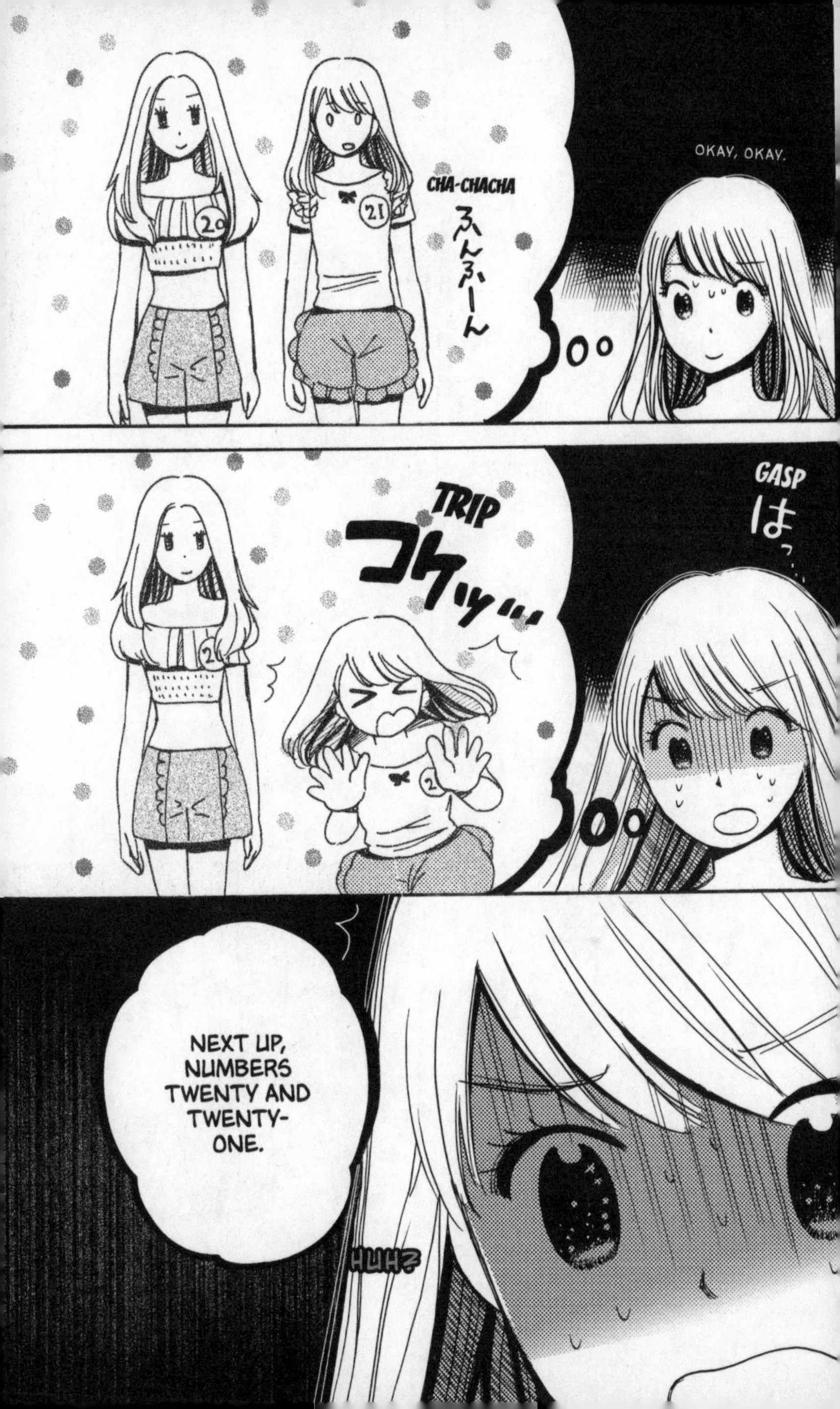
OKAY, OKAY.
CHA-CHACHA
ふんふーん
GASP
はっ
TRIP
コケッ
NEXT UP, NUMBERS TWENTY AND TWENTY-ONE.
HUH?

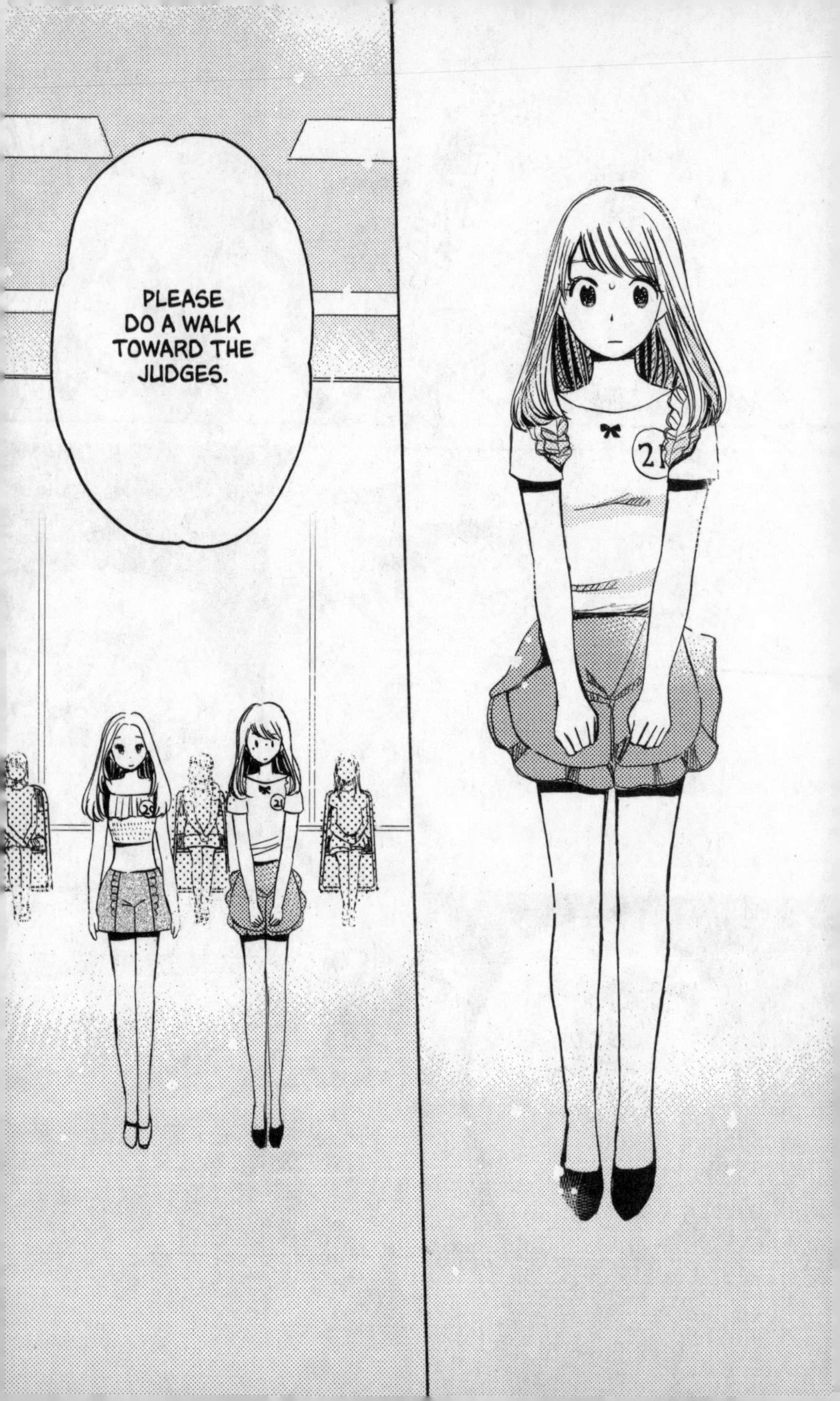
PLEASE DO A WALK TOWARD THE JUDGES.

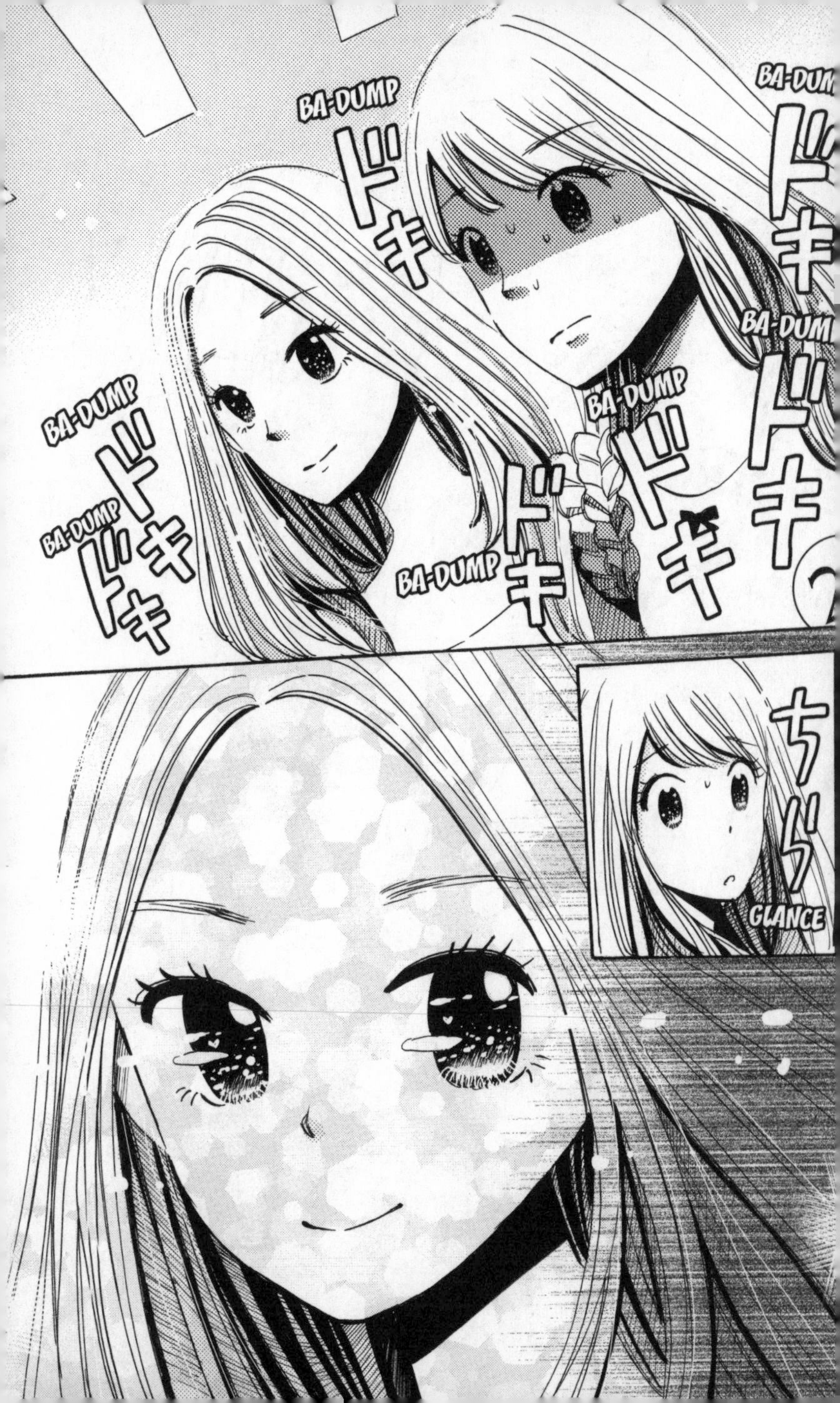

BA-DUM
ドキ
BA-DUM
ドキ
BA-DUMP
ドキ
BA-DUMP
ドキ
BA-DUMP
ドキ
BA-DUMP
ドキ
BA-DUMP
ドキ
ちら
GLANCE

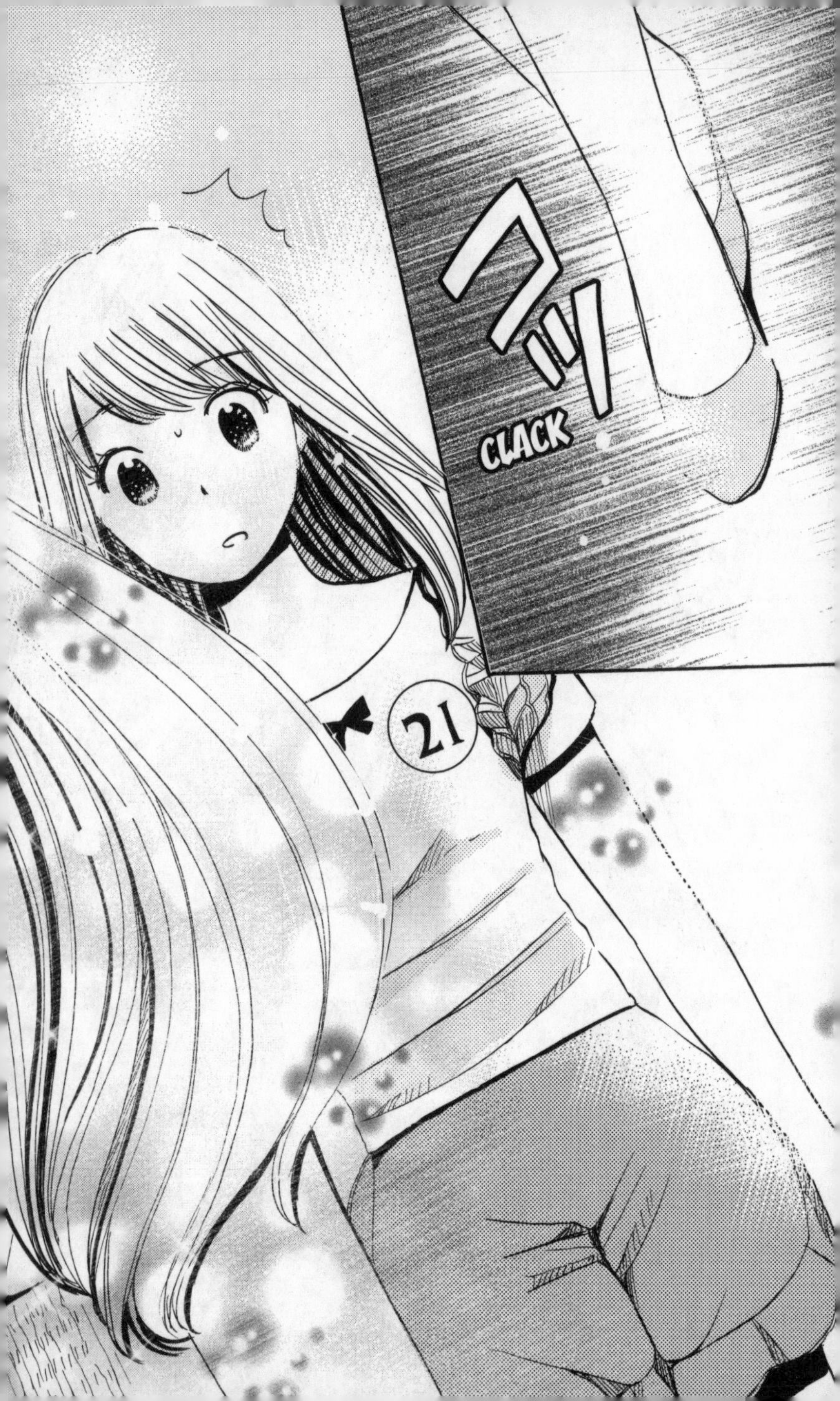

カッ
CLACK
21

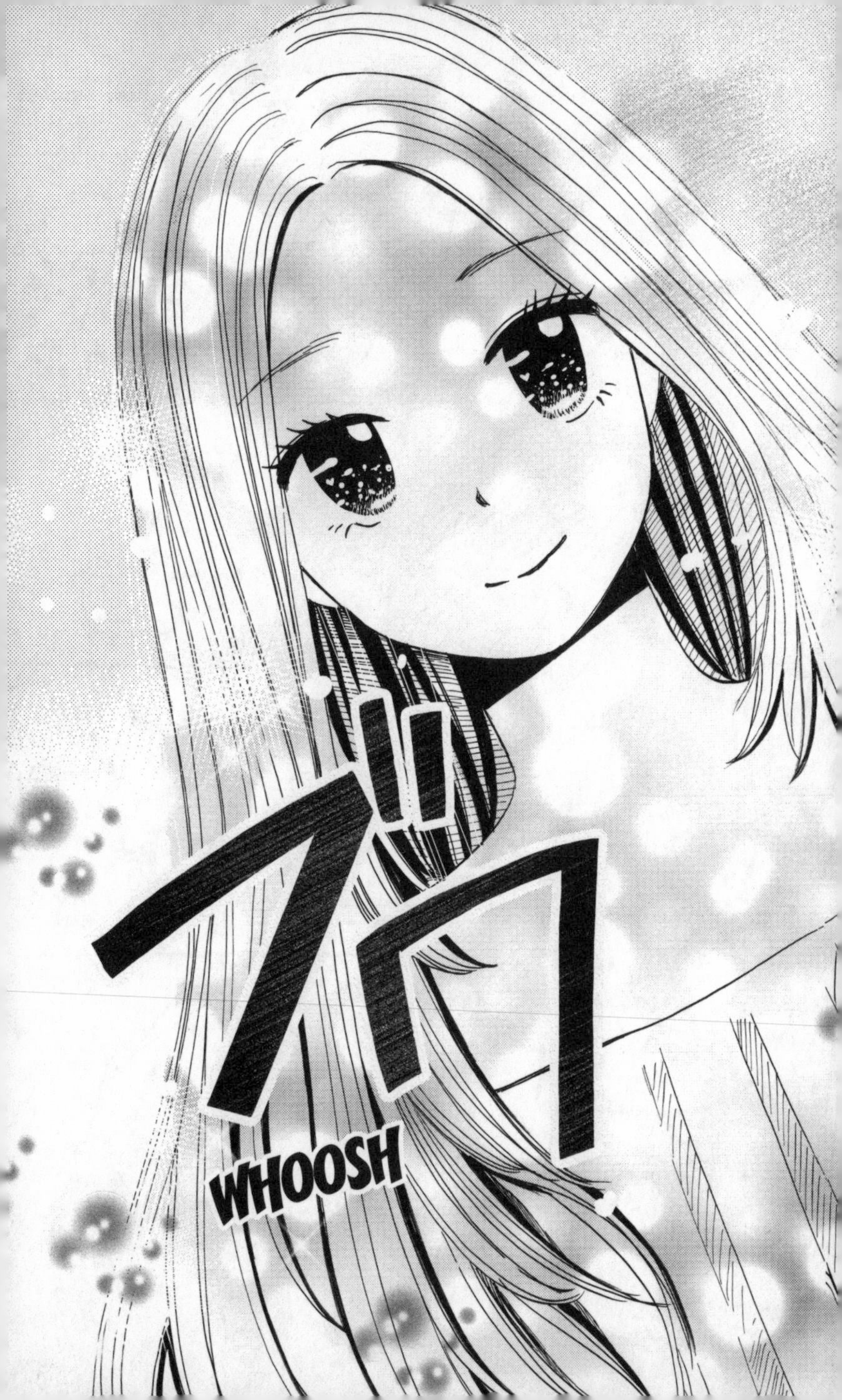
WHOOSH

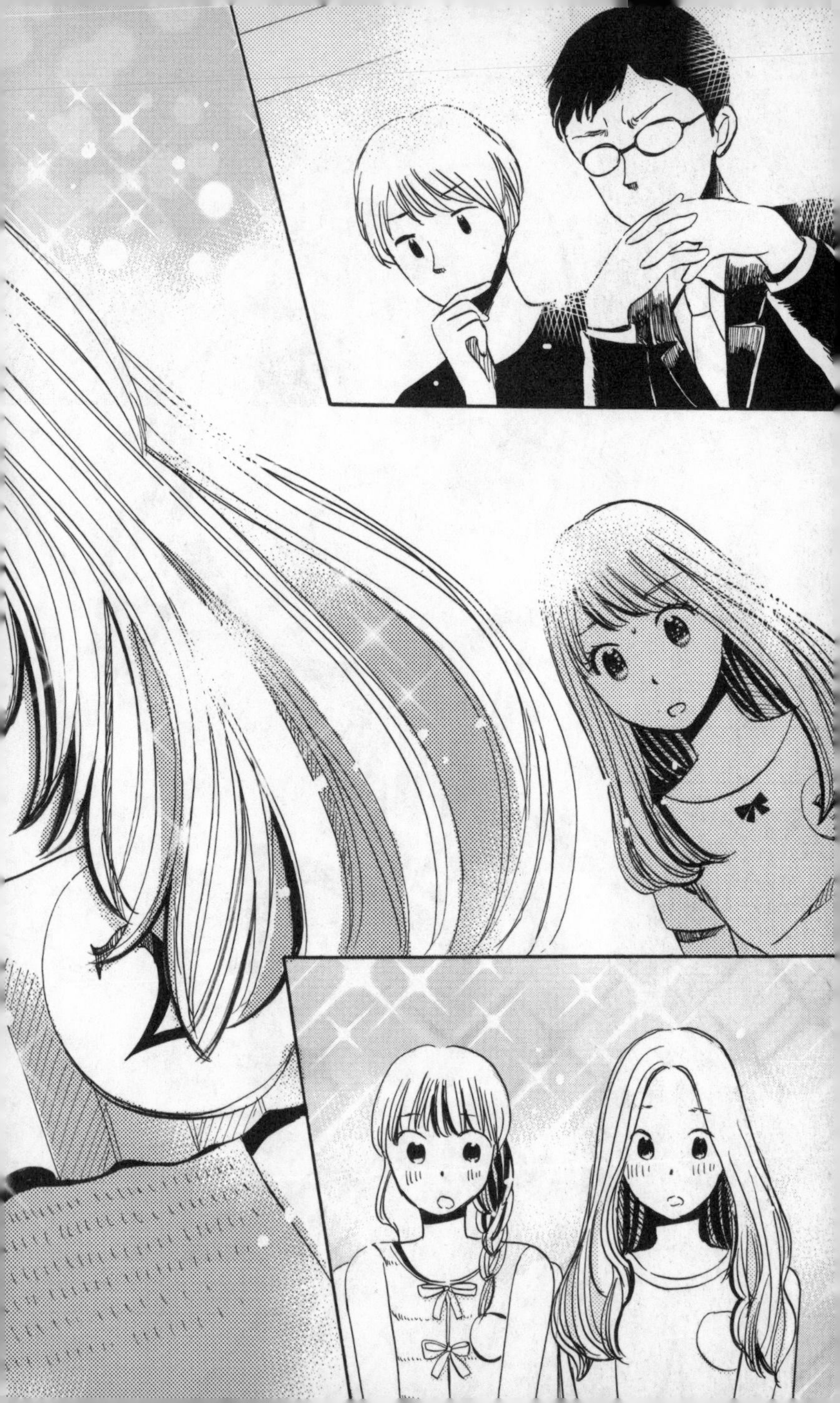

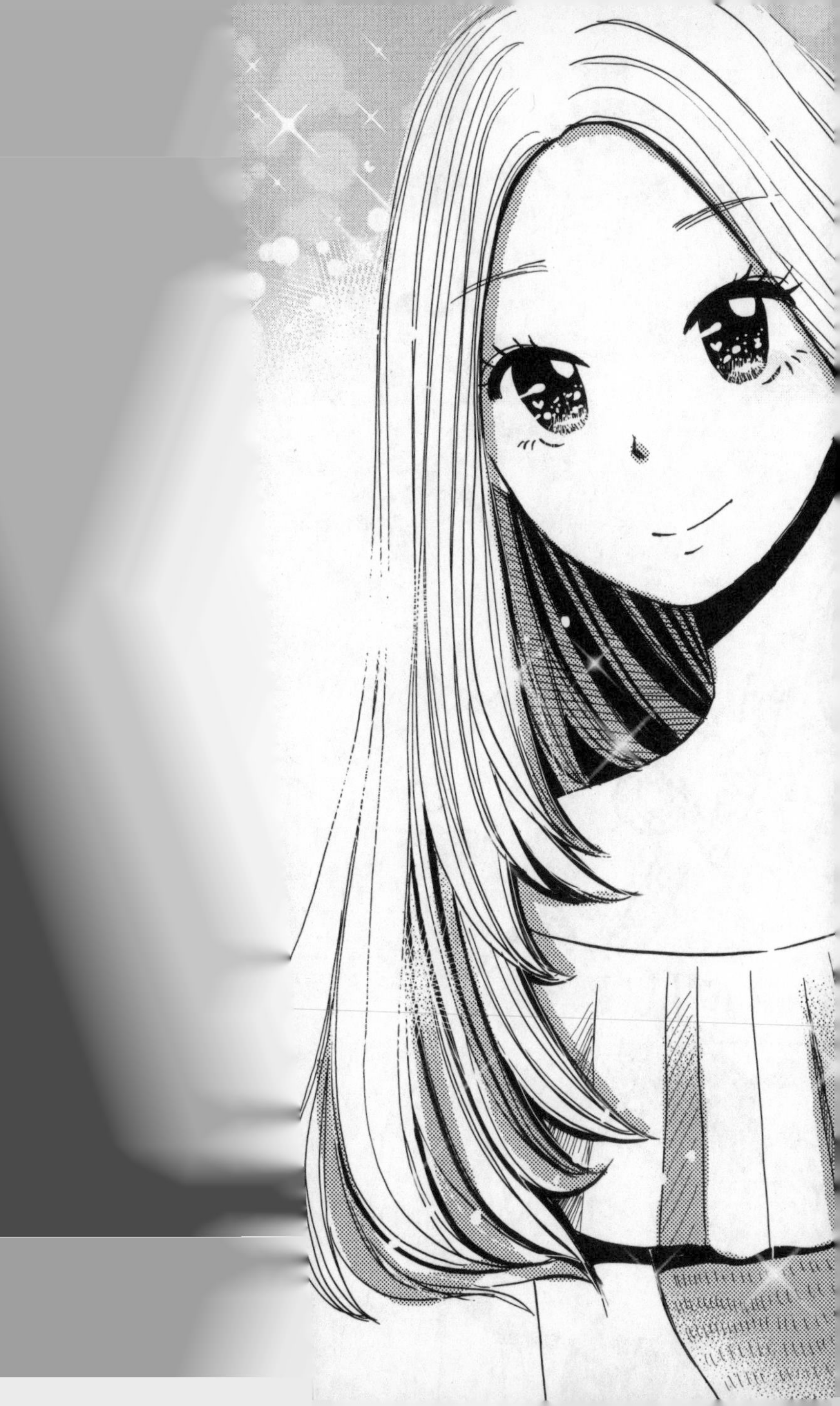

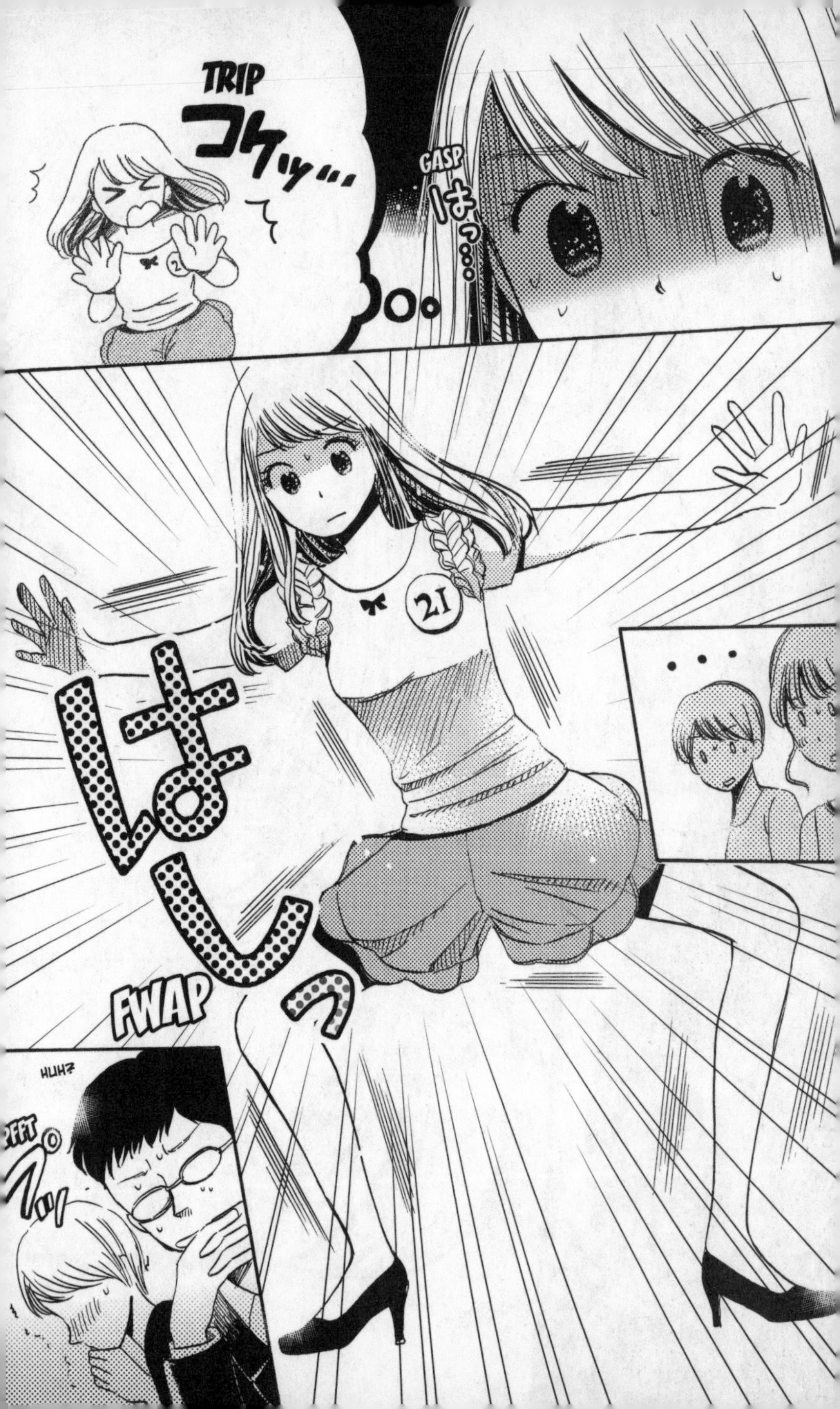
GASP
はっ…
Oo
TRIP
コケッ…
FWAP
はしっ
• • •
HUH?
PFFT
プッ

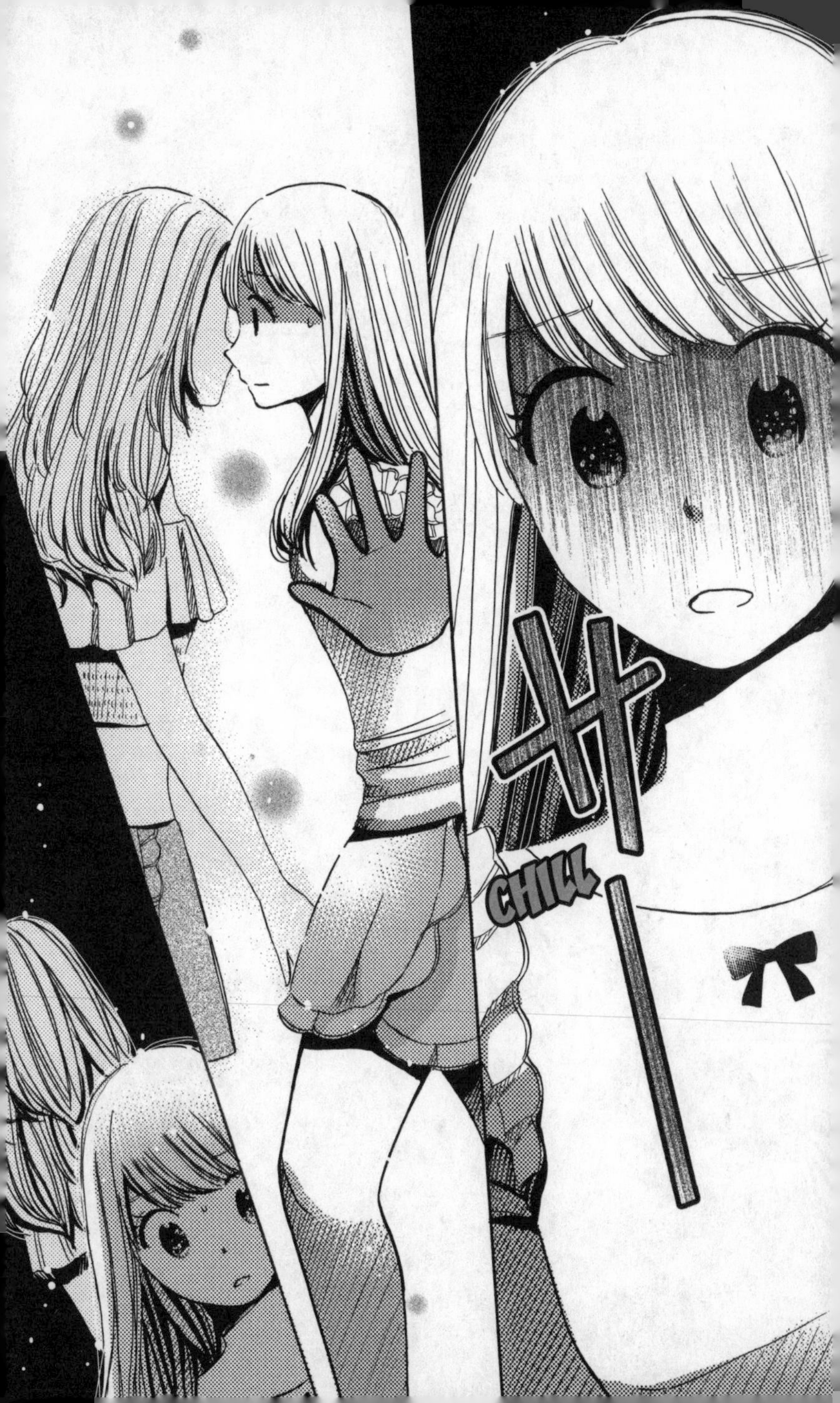
CHILL

# IT'S OVER...

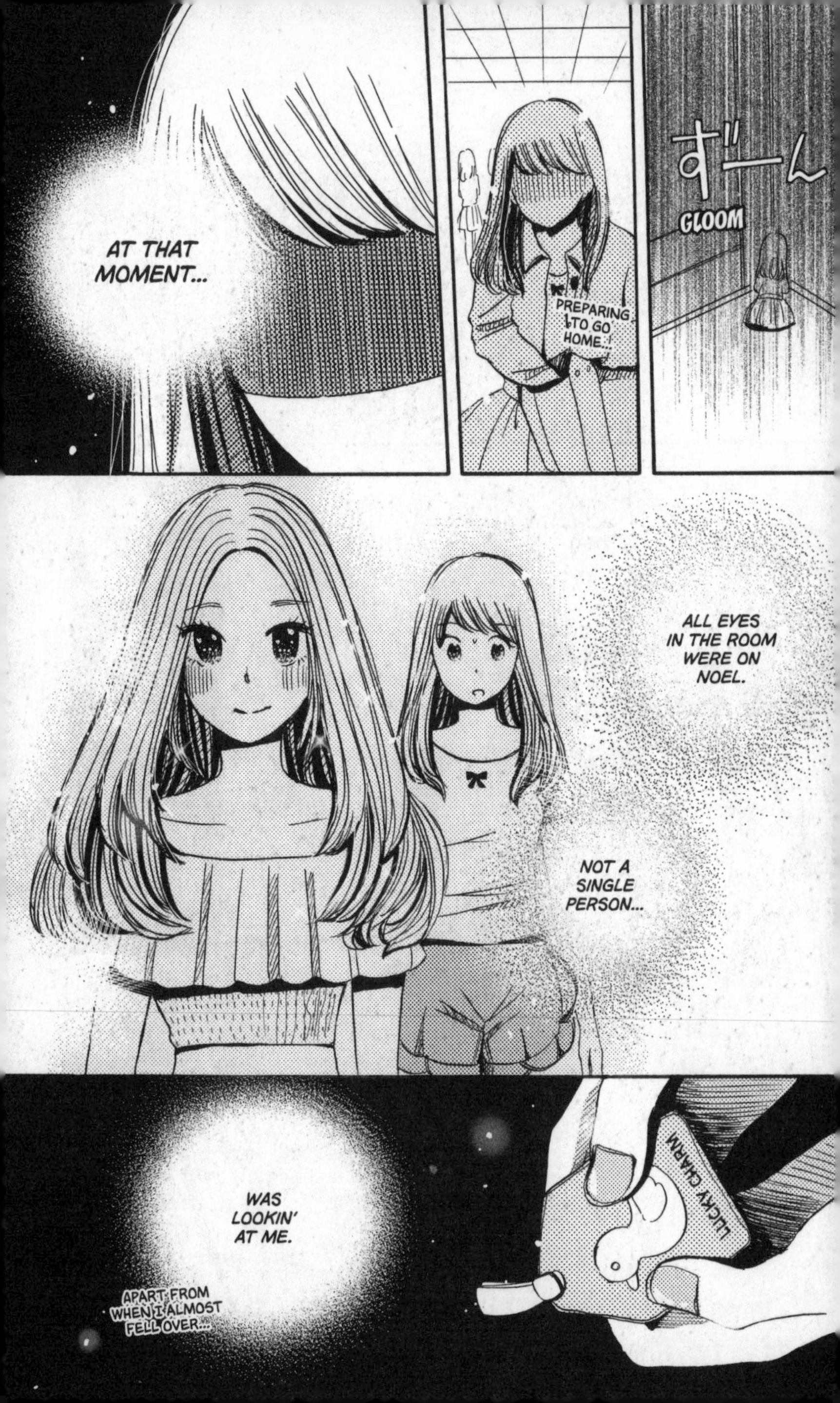
ずーん
GLOOM
PREPARING TO GO HOME...
AT THAT MOMENT...
ALL EYES IN THE ROOM WERE ON NOEL.
NOT A SINGLE PERSON...
LUCKY CHARM
WAS LOOKIN' AT ME.
APART FROM WHEN I ALMOST FELL OVER...

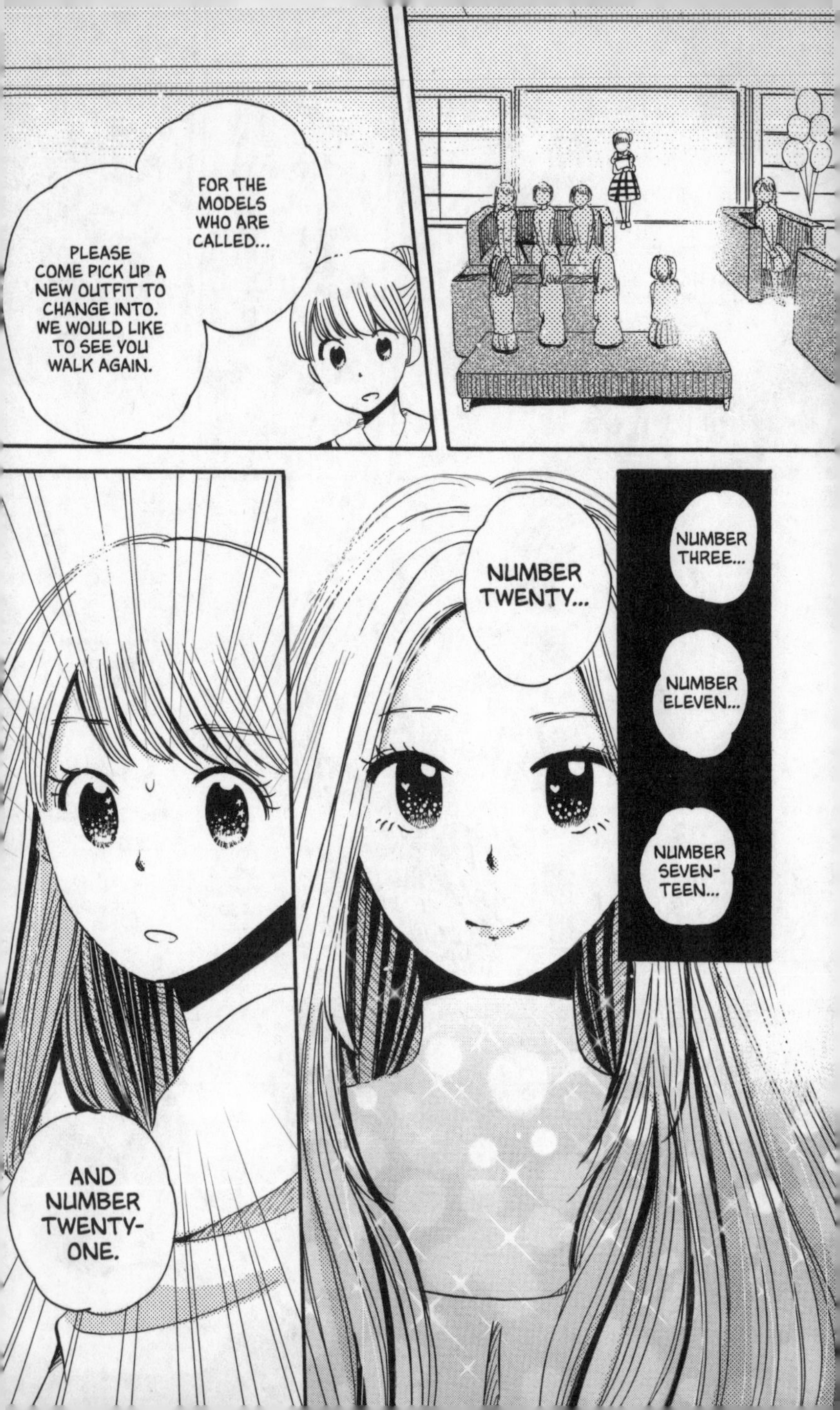
FOR THE MODELS WHO ARE CALLED...
PLEASE COME PICK UP A NEW OUTFIT TO CHANGE INTO. WE WOULD LIKE TO SEE YOU WALK AGAIN.
NUMBER THREE...
NUMBER ELEVEN...
NUMBER SEVEN-TEEN...
NUMBER TWENTY...
AND NUMBER TWENTY-ONE.

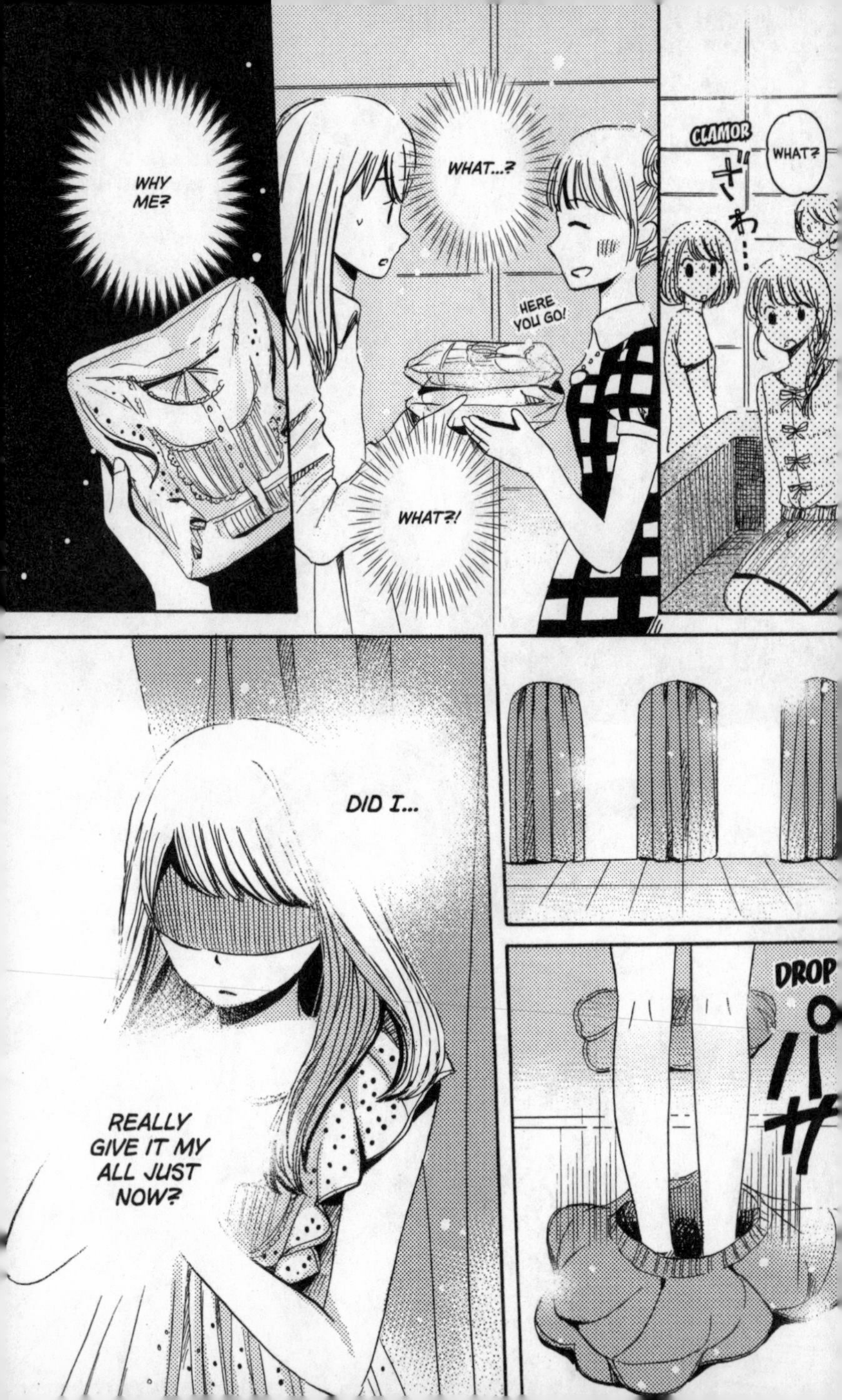
WHAT?
CLAMOR
ざわ…
WHAT...?
HERE YOU GO!
WHAT?!
WHY ME?
DROP
パサ
DID I...
REALLY GIVE IT MY ALL JUST NOW?

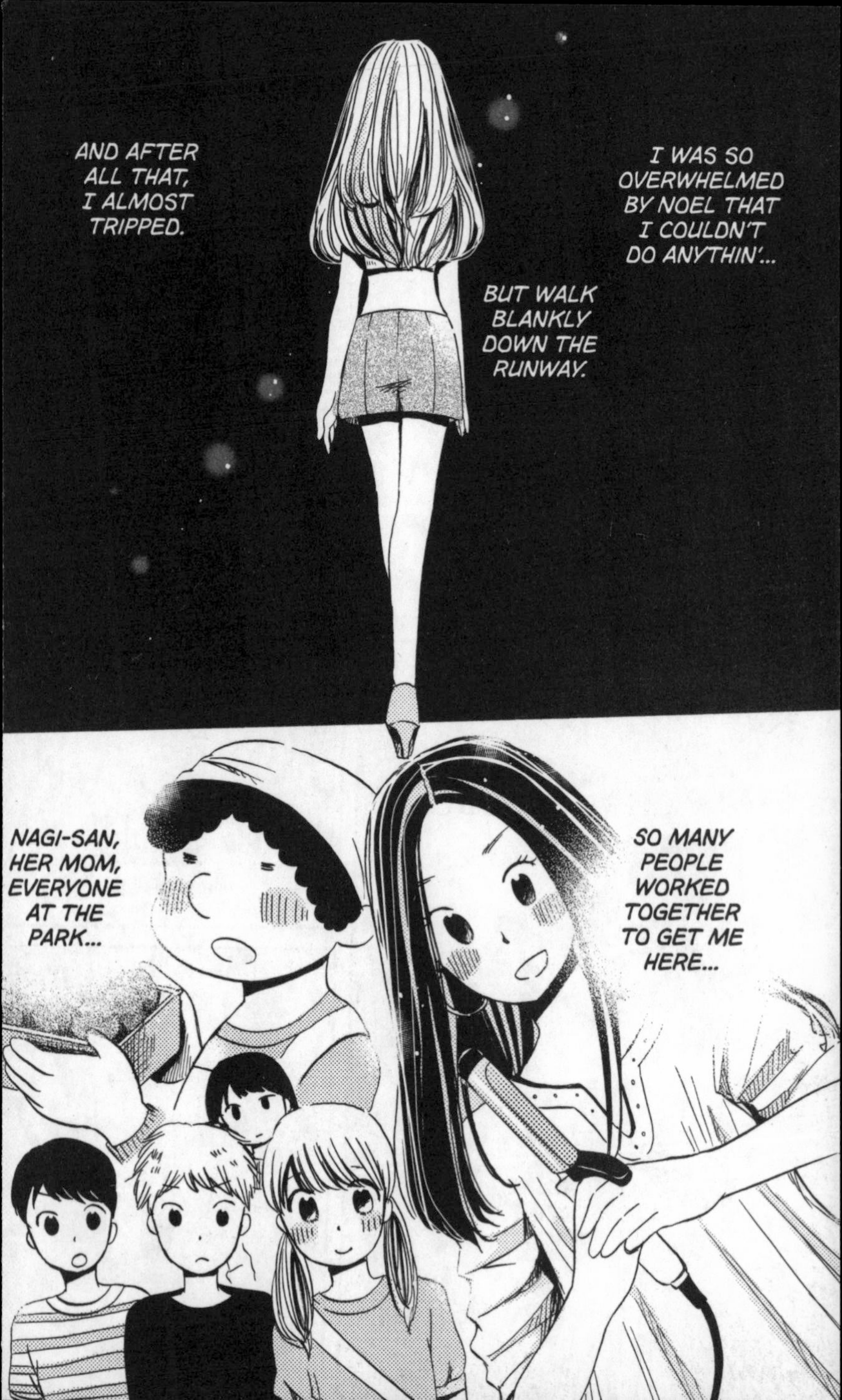
I WAS SO OVERWHELMED BY NOEL THAT I COULDN'T DO ANYTHIN'...
BUT WALK BLANKLY DOWN THE RUNWAY.
AND AFTER ALL THAT, I ALMOST TRIPPED.
SO MANY PEOPLE WORKED TOGETHER TO GET ME HERE...
NAGI-SAN, HER MOM, EVERYONE AT THE PARK...

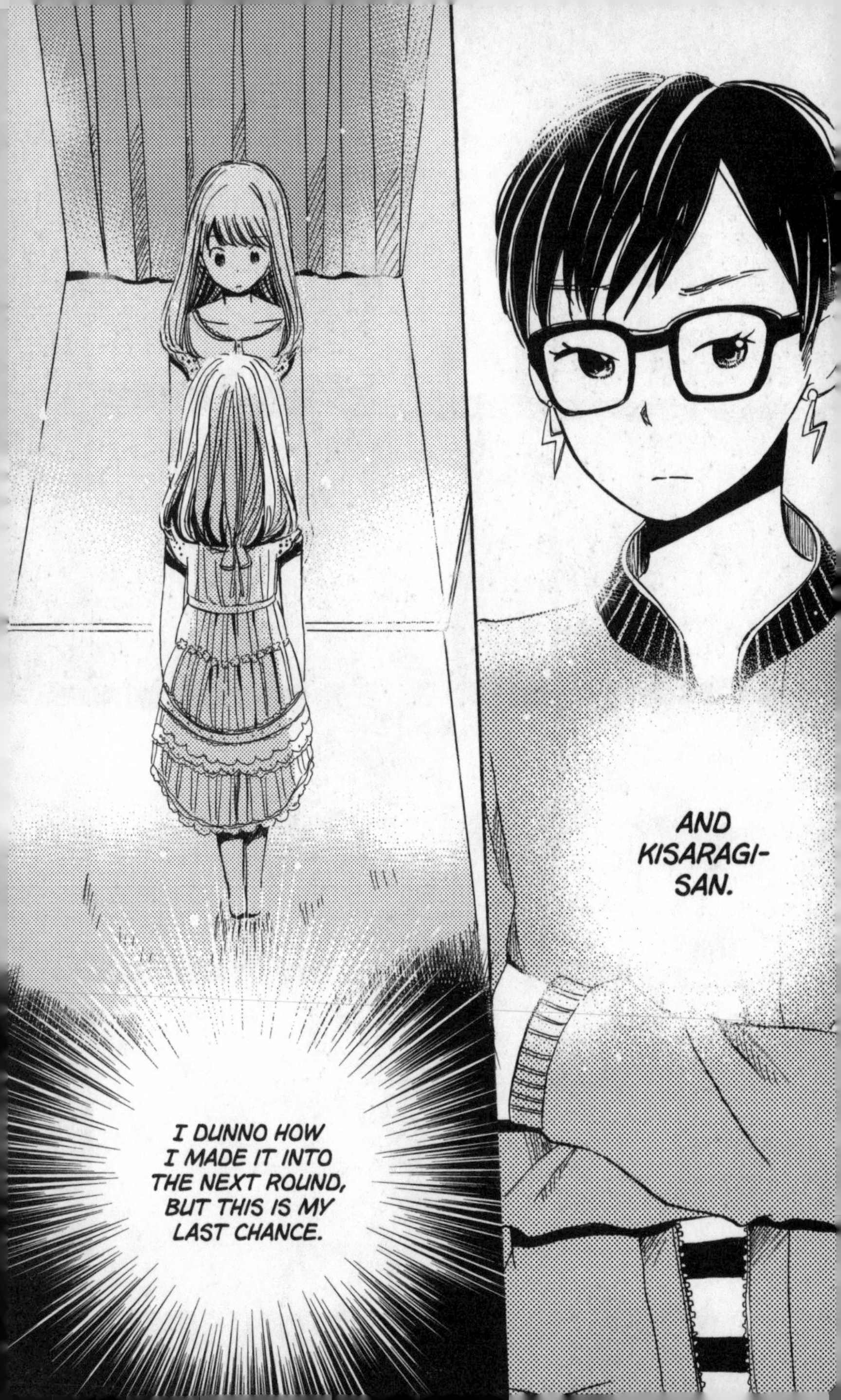
AND KISARAGI-SAN.
I DUNNO HOW I MADE IT INTO THE NEXT ROUND, BUT THIS IS MY LAST CHANCE.

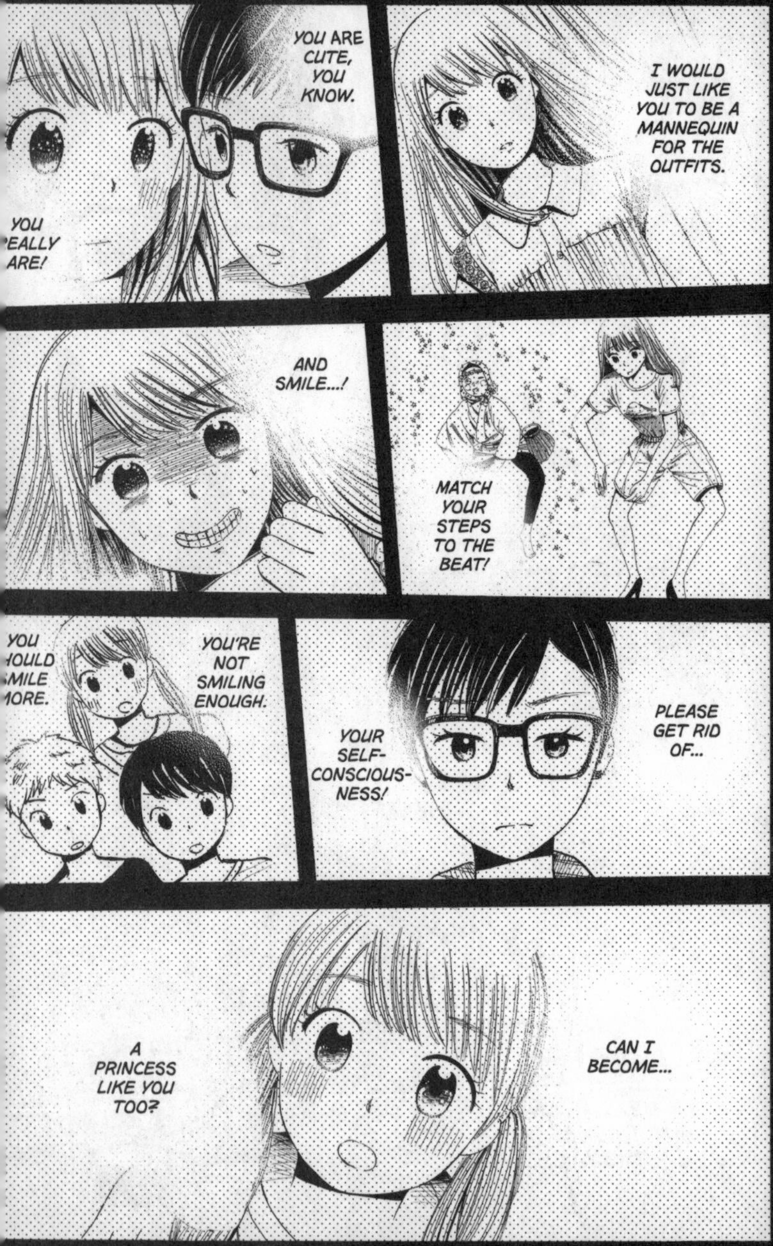

I WOULD JUST LIKE YOU TO BE A MANNEQUIN FOR THE OUTFITS.
YOU ARE CUTE, YOU KNOW.
YOU EALLY ARE!
MATCH YOUR STEPS TO THE BEAT!
AND SMILE...!
PLEASE GET RID OF...
YOUR SELF-CONSCIOUS-NESS!
YOU'RE NOT SMILING ENOUGH.
YOU HOULD MILE ORE.
CAN I BECOME...
A PRINCESS LIKE YOU TOO?

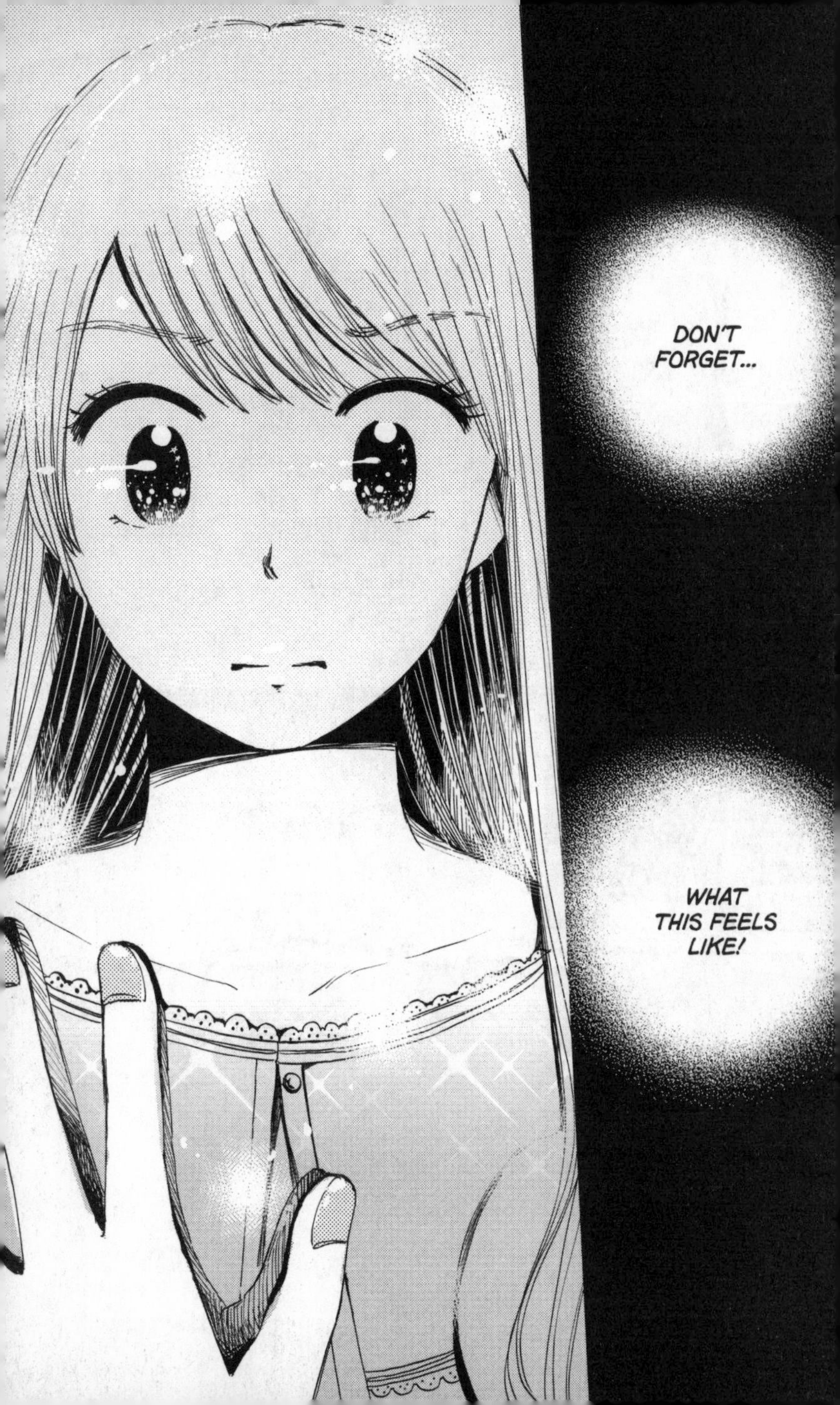
DON'T FORGET...
WHAT THIS FEELS LIKE!

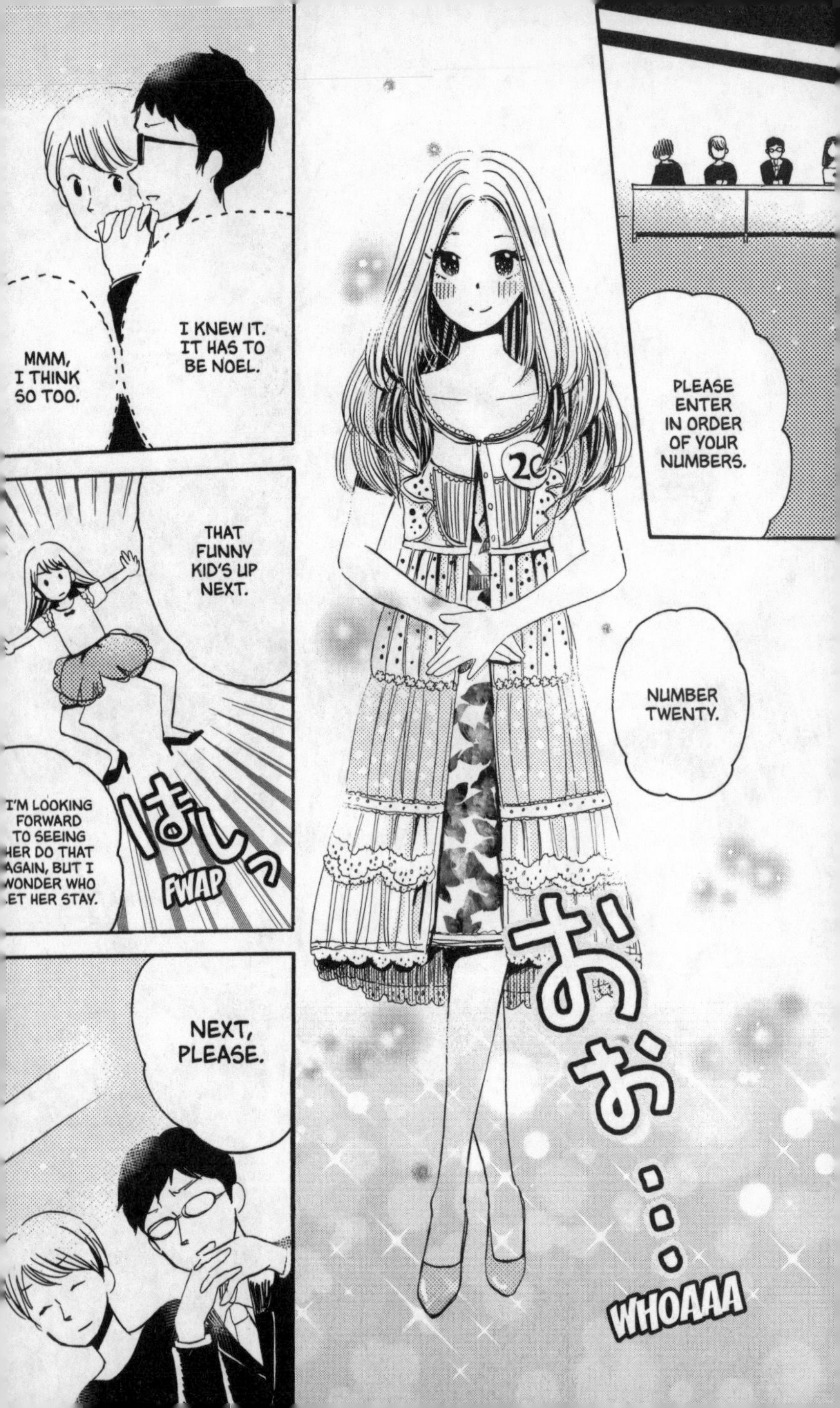
PLEASE ENTER IN ORDER OF YOUR NUMBERS.
NUMBER TWENTY.
おお…
WHOAAA
I KNEW IT. IT HAS TO BE NOEL.
MMM, I THINK SO TOO.
THAT FUNNY KID'S UP NEXT.
はしっ
FWAP
I'M LOOKING FORWARD TO SEEING HER DO THAT AGAIN, BUT I WONDER WHO LET HER STAY.
NEXT, PLEASE.

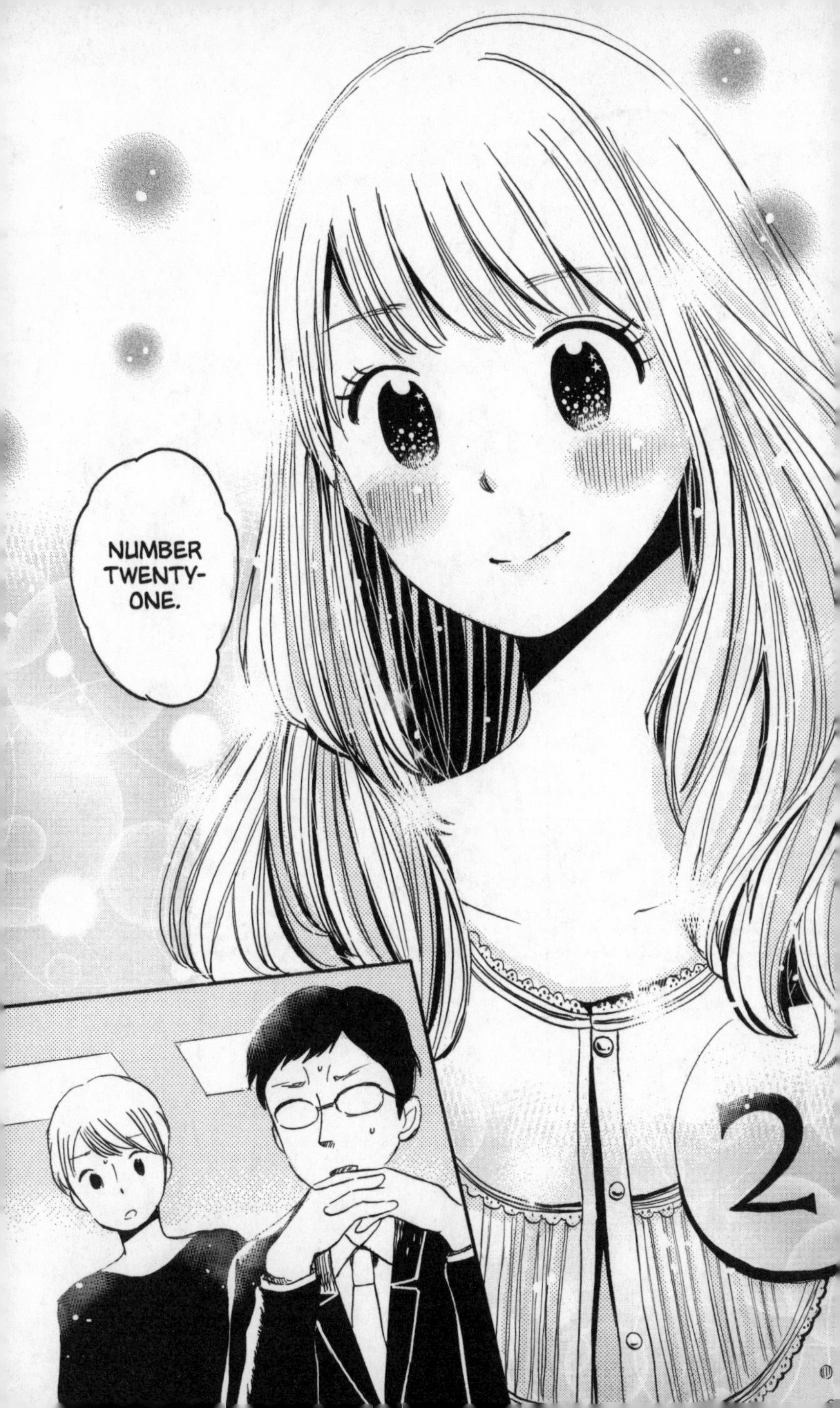
NUMBER TWENTY-ONE.

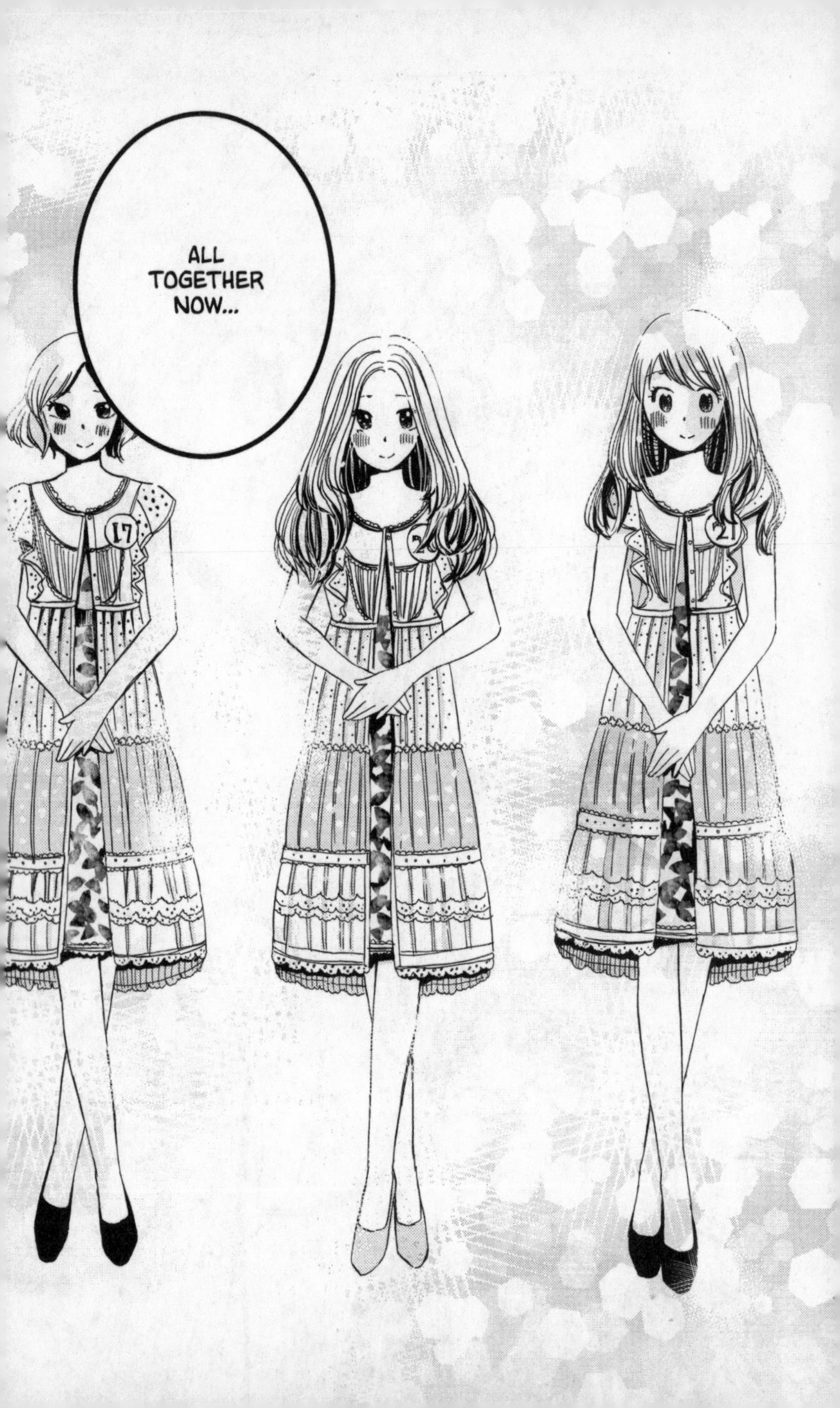
ALL TOGETHER NOW...

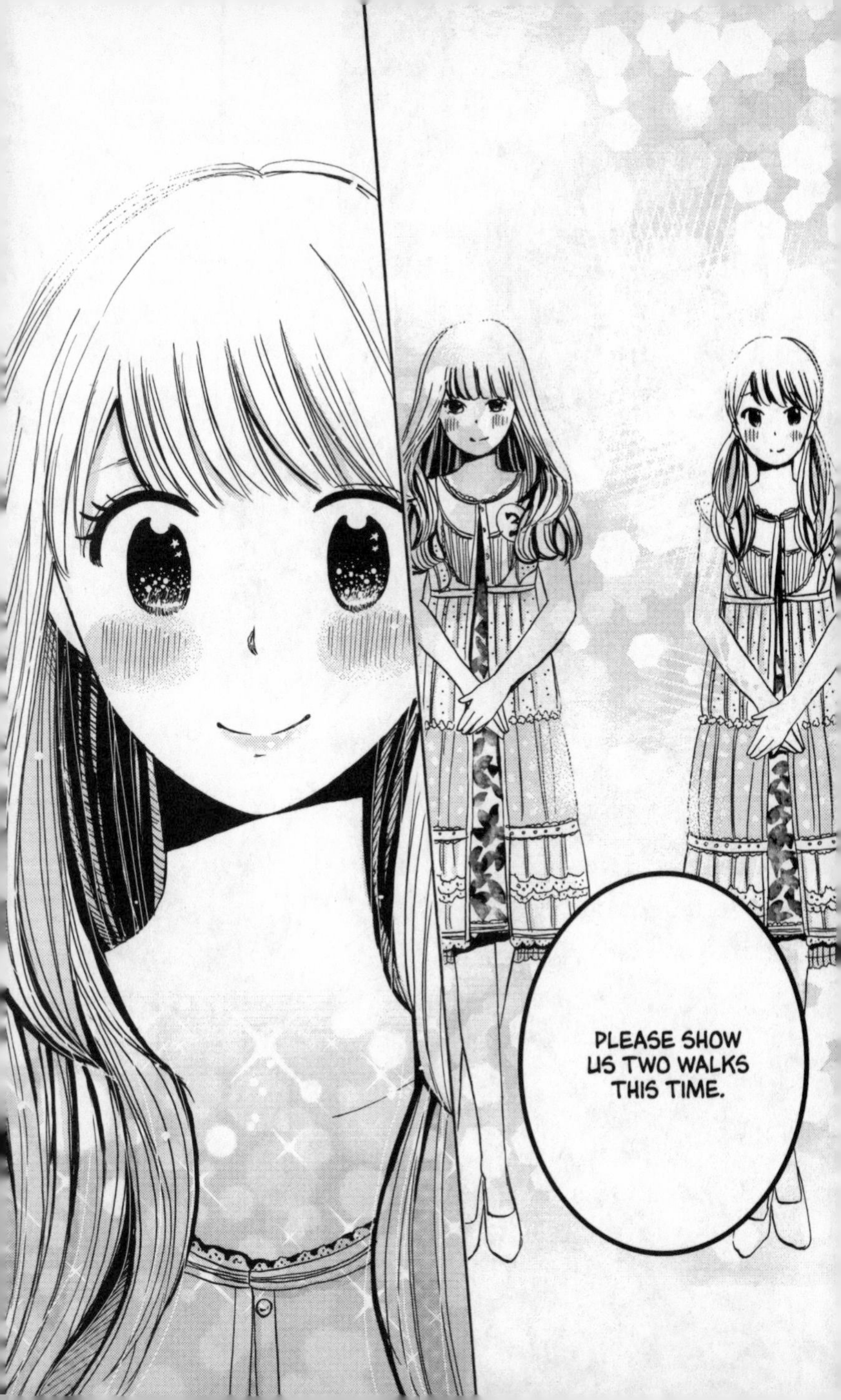
PLEASE SHOW US TWO WALKS THIS TIME.

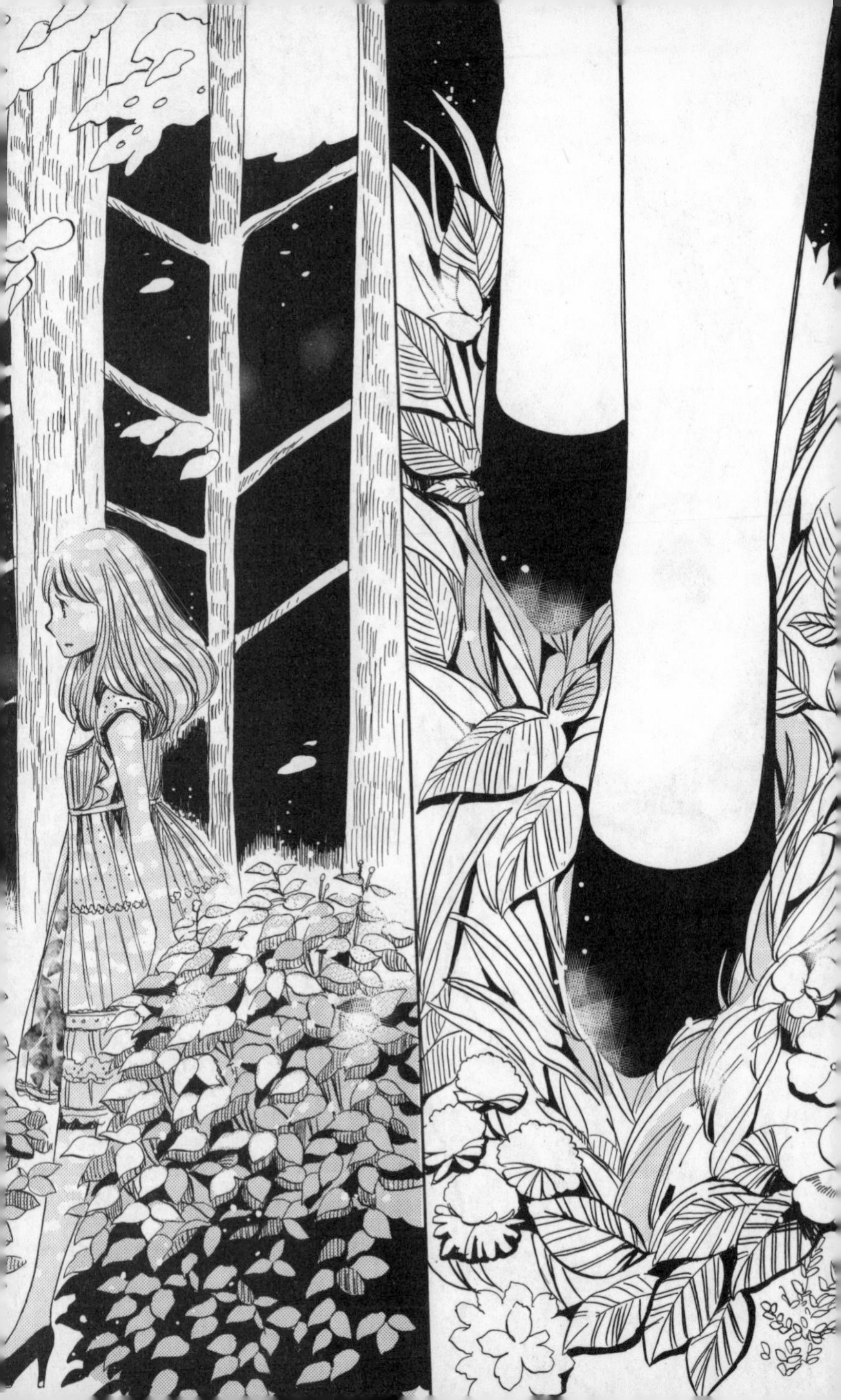

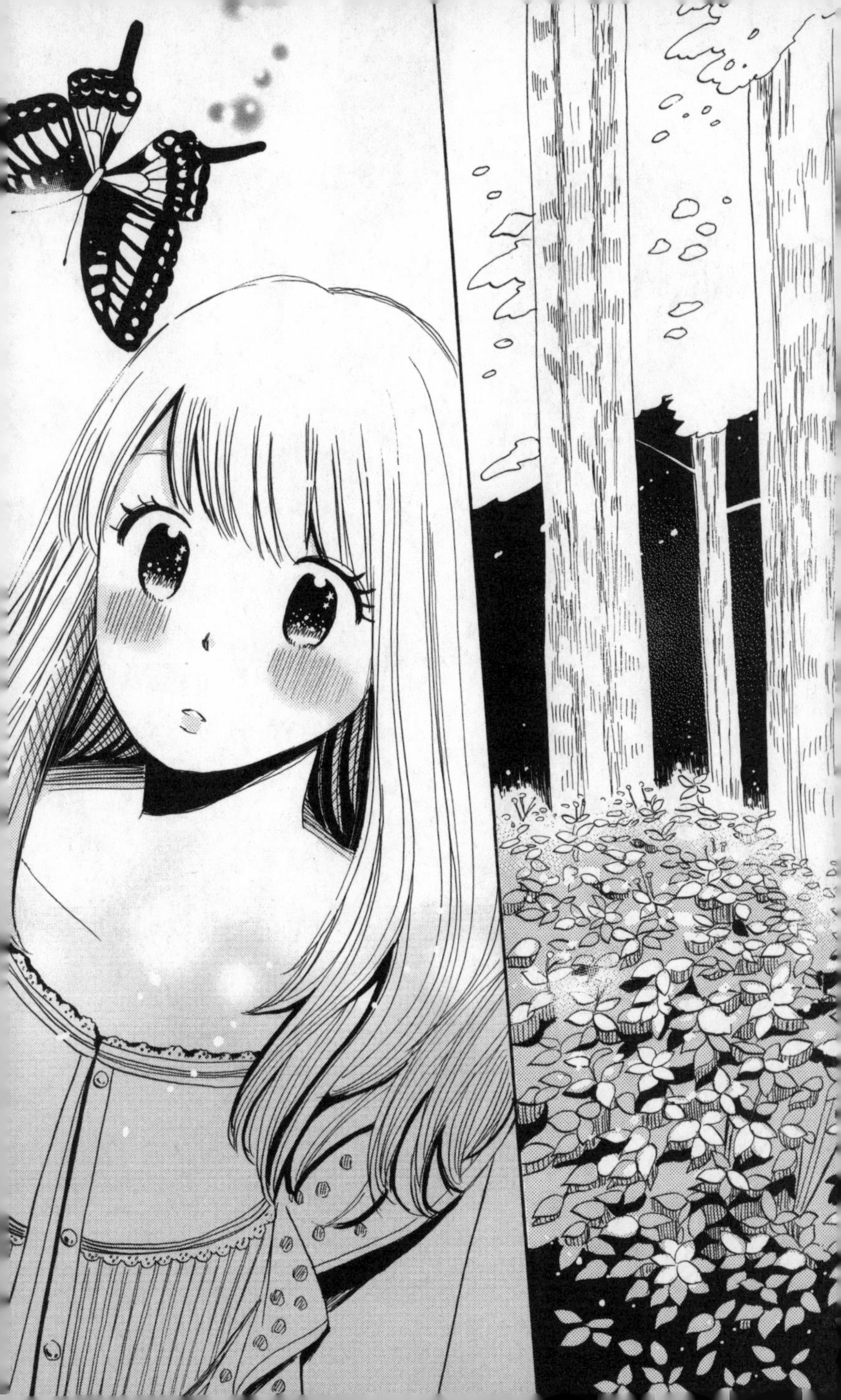

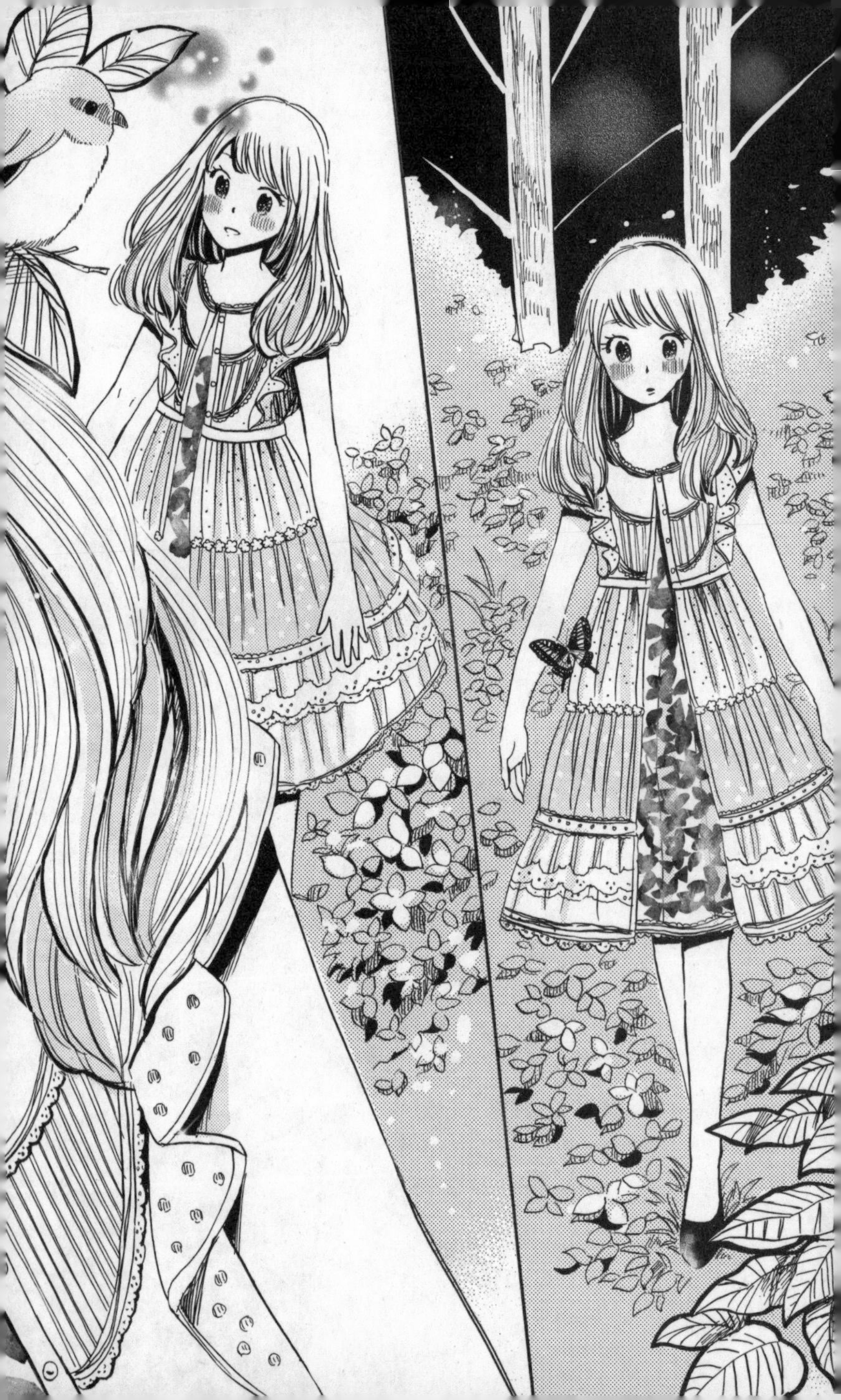

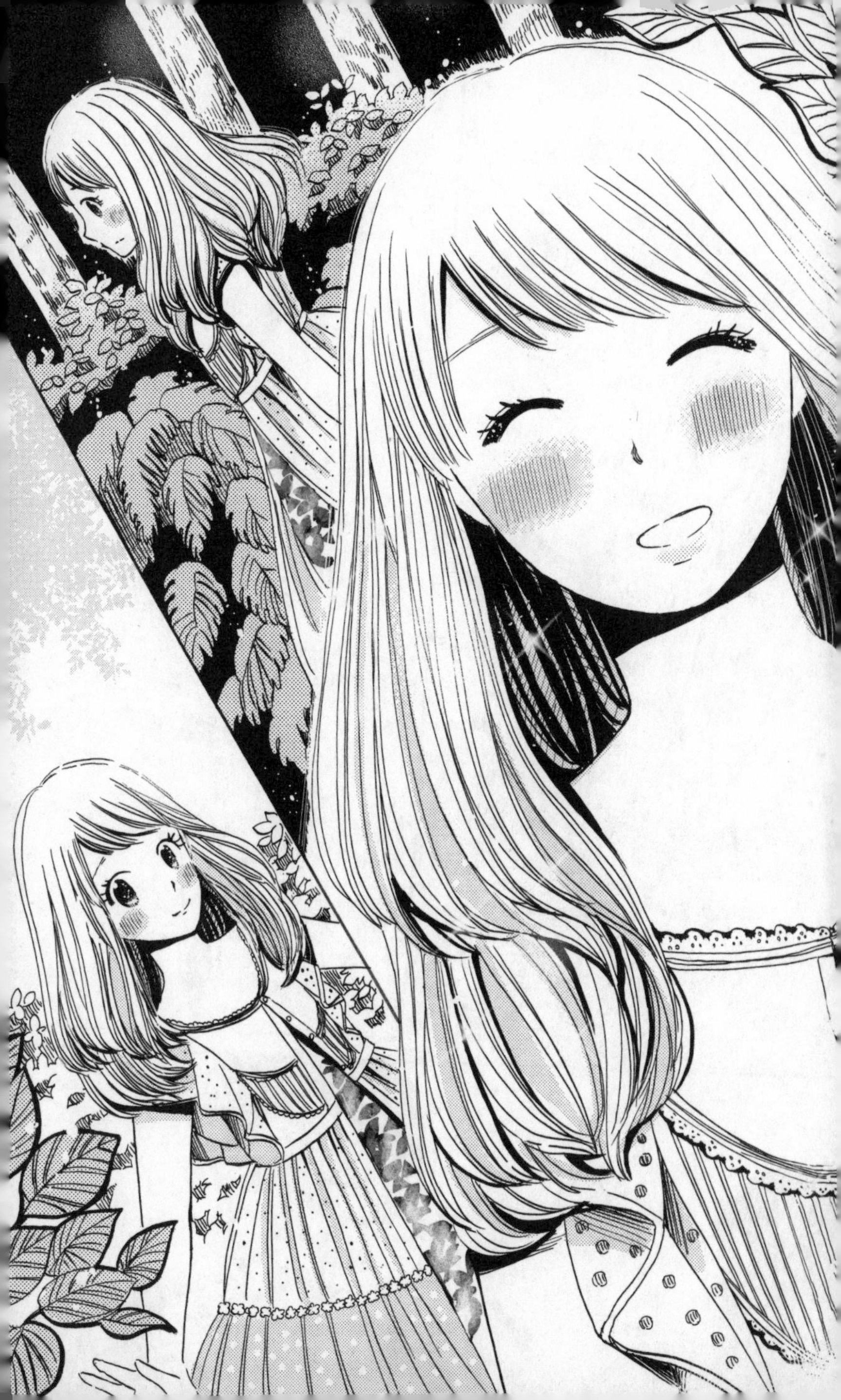

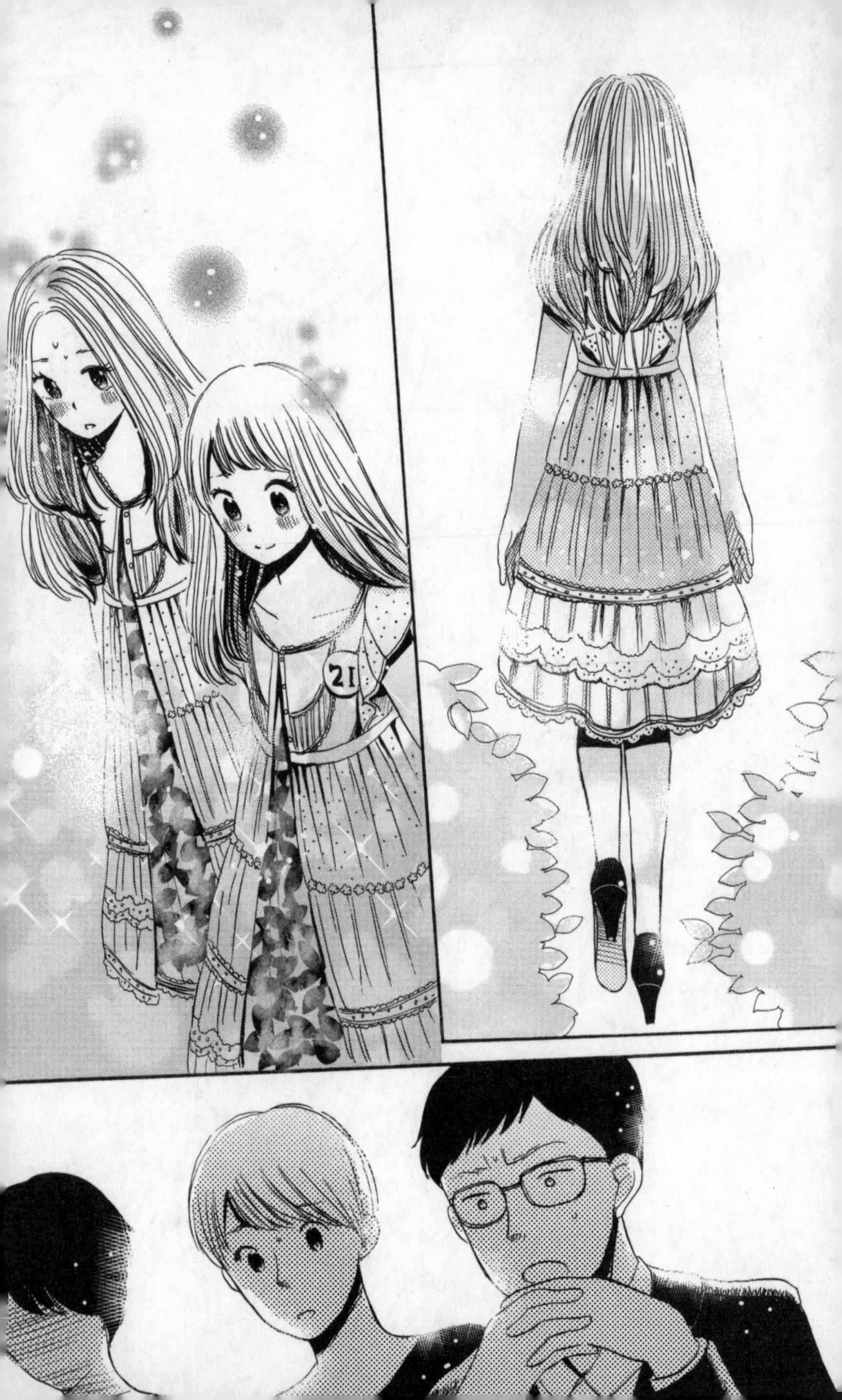
21

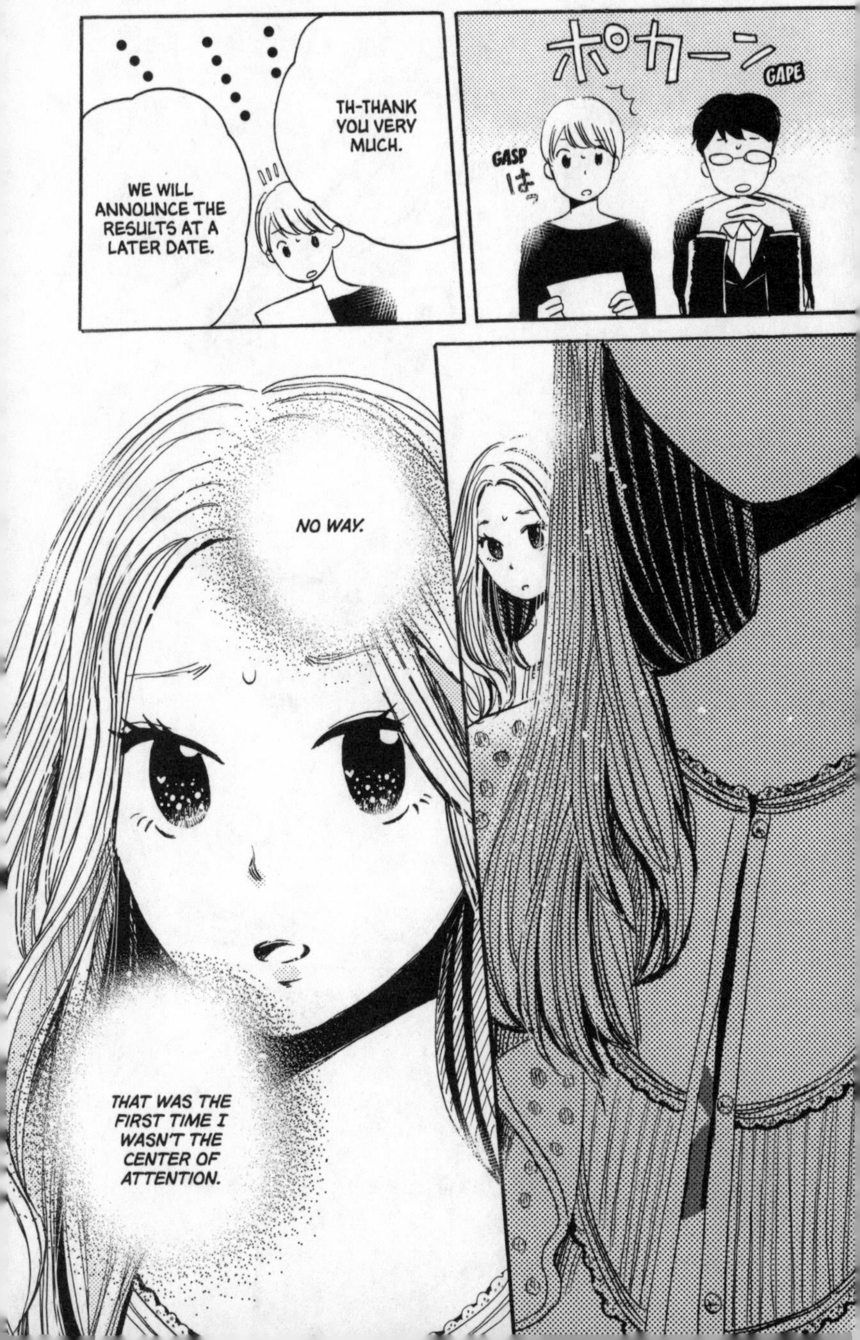
ポカーン
GAPE
GASP
はっ
TH-THANK YOU VERY MUCH.
WE WILL ANNOUNCE THE RESULTS AT A LATER DATE.
NO WAY.
THAT WAS THE FIRST TIME I WASN'T THE CENTER OF ATTENTION.

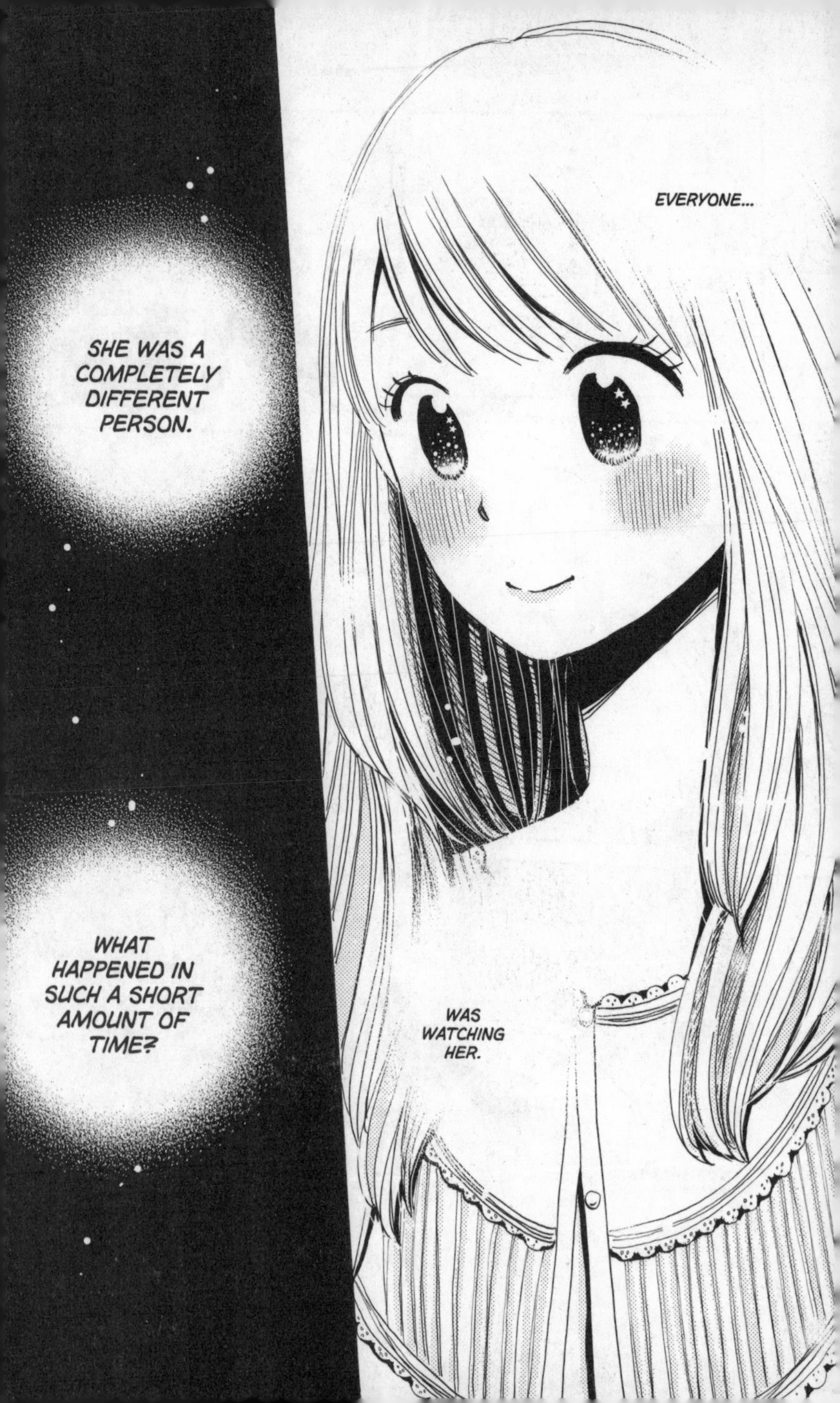
EVERYONE...
WAS WATCHING HER.
SHE WAS A COMPLETELY DIFFERENT PERSON.
WHAT HAPPENED IN SUCH A SHORT AMOUNT OF TIME?

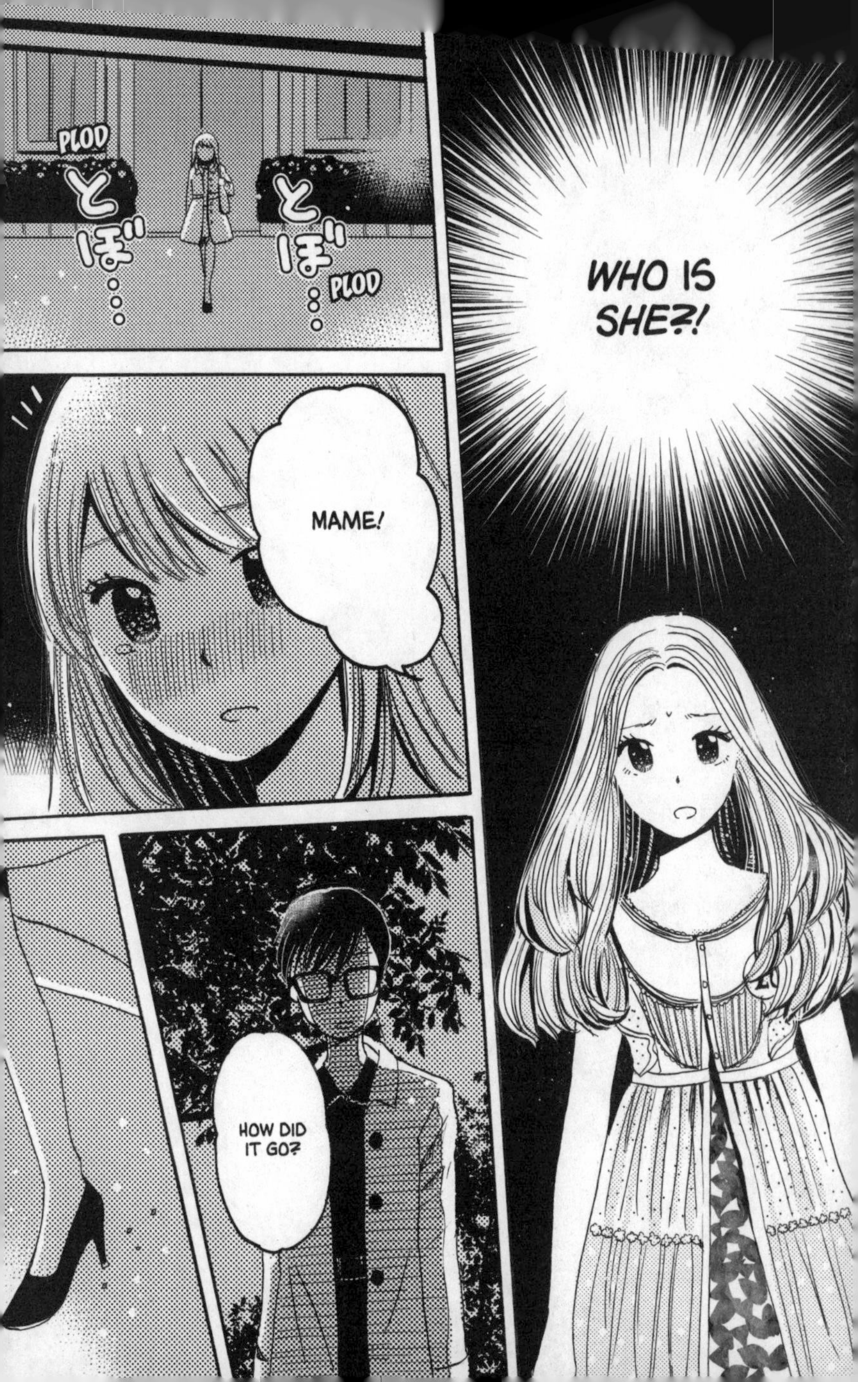
WHO IS SHE?!
とぼ…
PLOD
PLOD
とぼ…
MAME!
HOW DID IT GO?

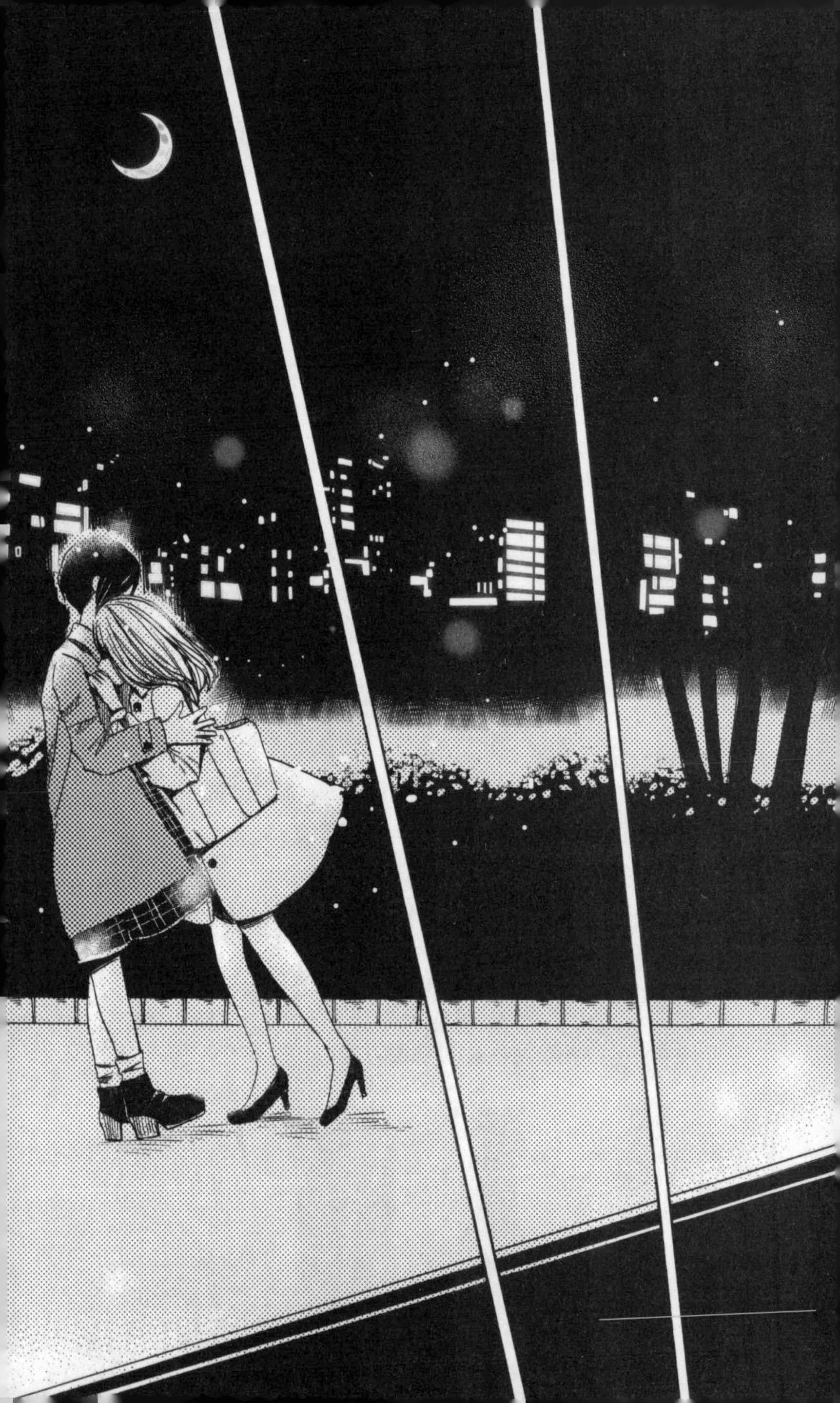

M A M E
coordinate

# OOTD CORNER

AUDITION OUTFITS
FRILLY RIBBON JERSEY BLOUSE (POWDER SNOW DOLL)
FRILLY OFF-THE-SHOULDER BLOUSE
DENIM SHORTS WITH FRILLS
ORGANDIE SHORTS
ALWAYS SHOW OFF LEGS
4-INCH HEELS
3-INCH HEELS

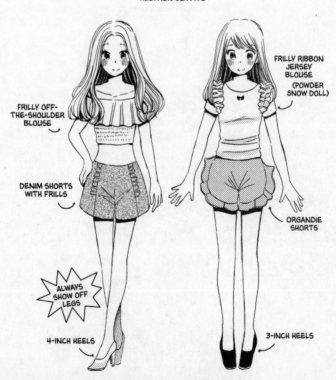

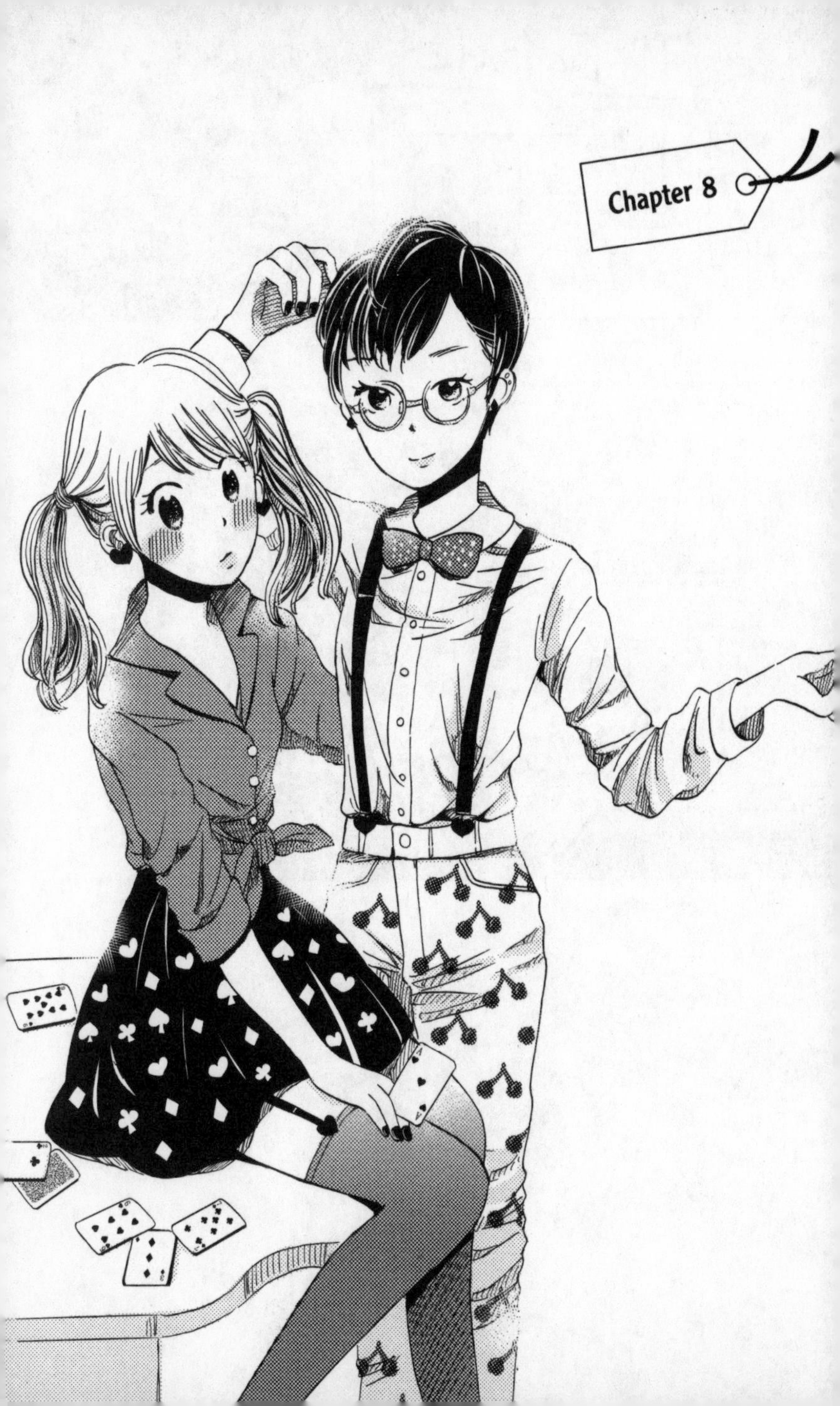
Chapter 8

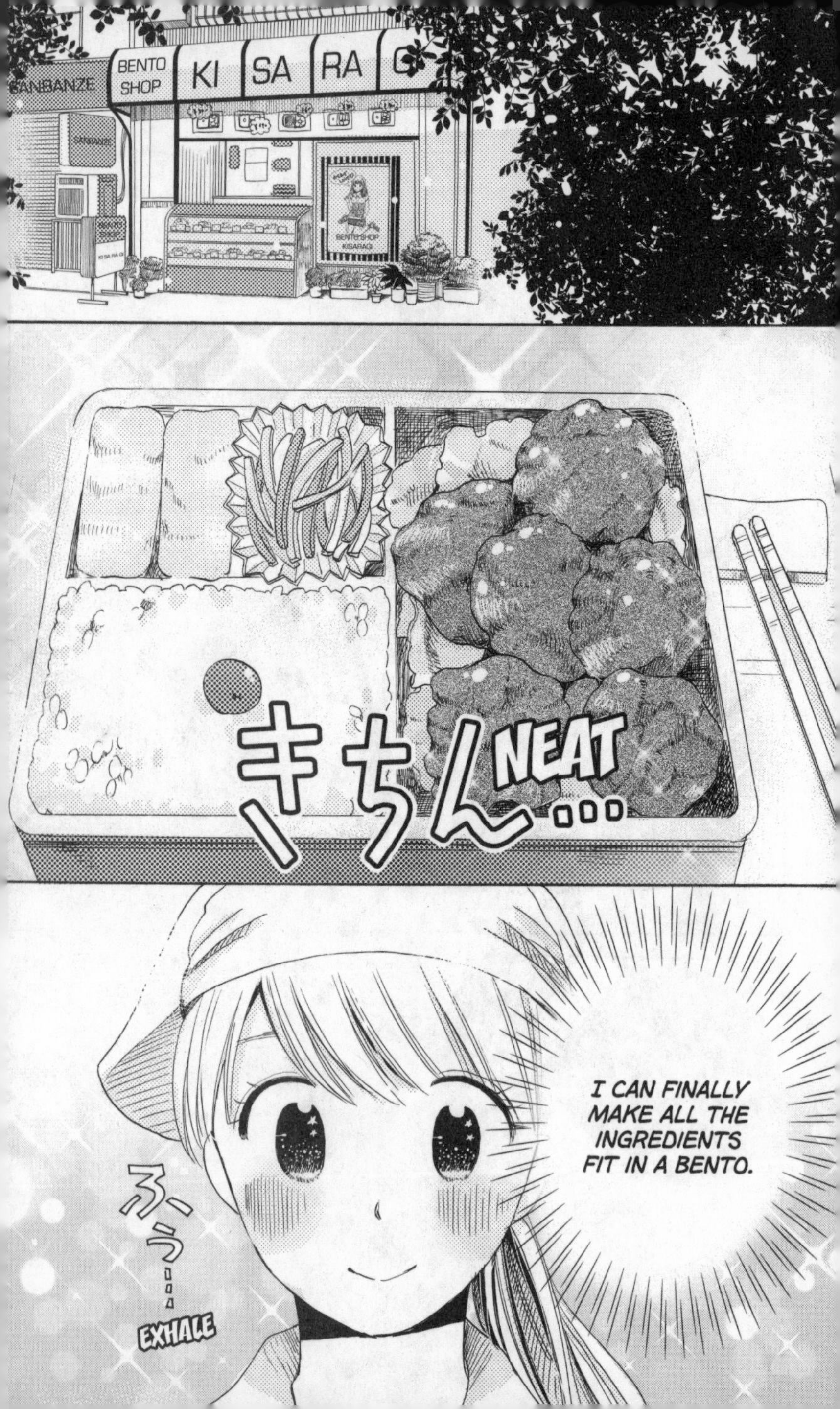

SANBANZE
BENTO SHOP
KI SA RA
BENTO-SHOP KISARAGI
きちん…
NEAT
I CAN FINALLY MAKE ALL THE INGREDIENTS FIT IN A BENTO.
ふぅ…
EXHALE

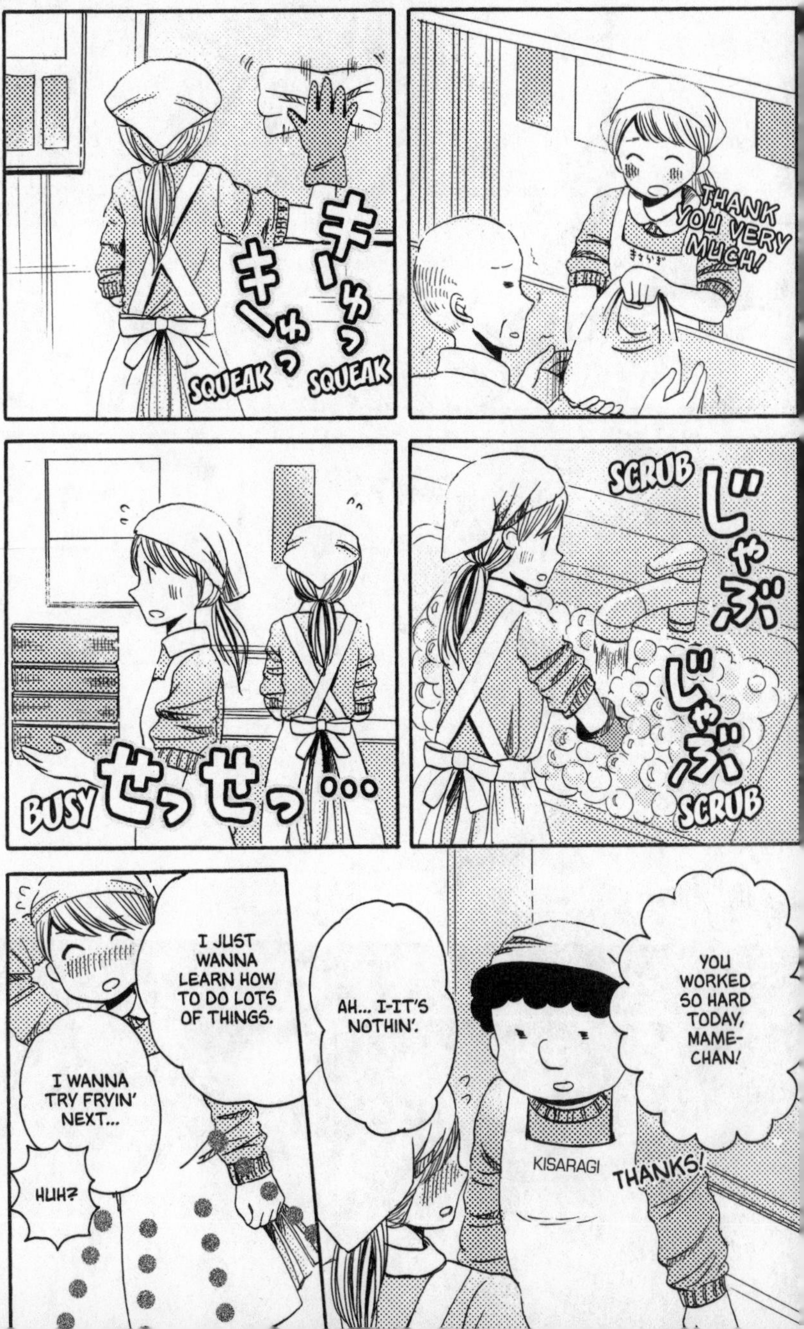
THANK YOU VERY MUCH!
キュッ
SQUEAK
キュッ
SQUEAK
SCRUB
じゃぶ
じゃぶ
SCRUB
BUSY
せっせっ…
YOU WORKED SO HARD TODAY, MAME-CHAN!
THANKS!
KISARAGI
AH... I-IT'S NOTHIN'.
I JUST WANNA LEARN HOW TO DO LOTS OF THINGS.
I WANNA TRY FRYIN' NEXT...
HUH?

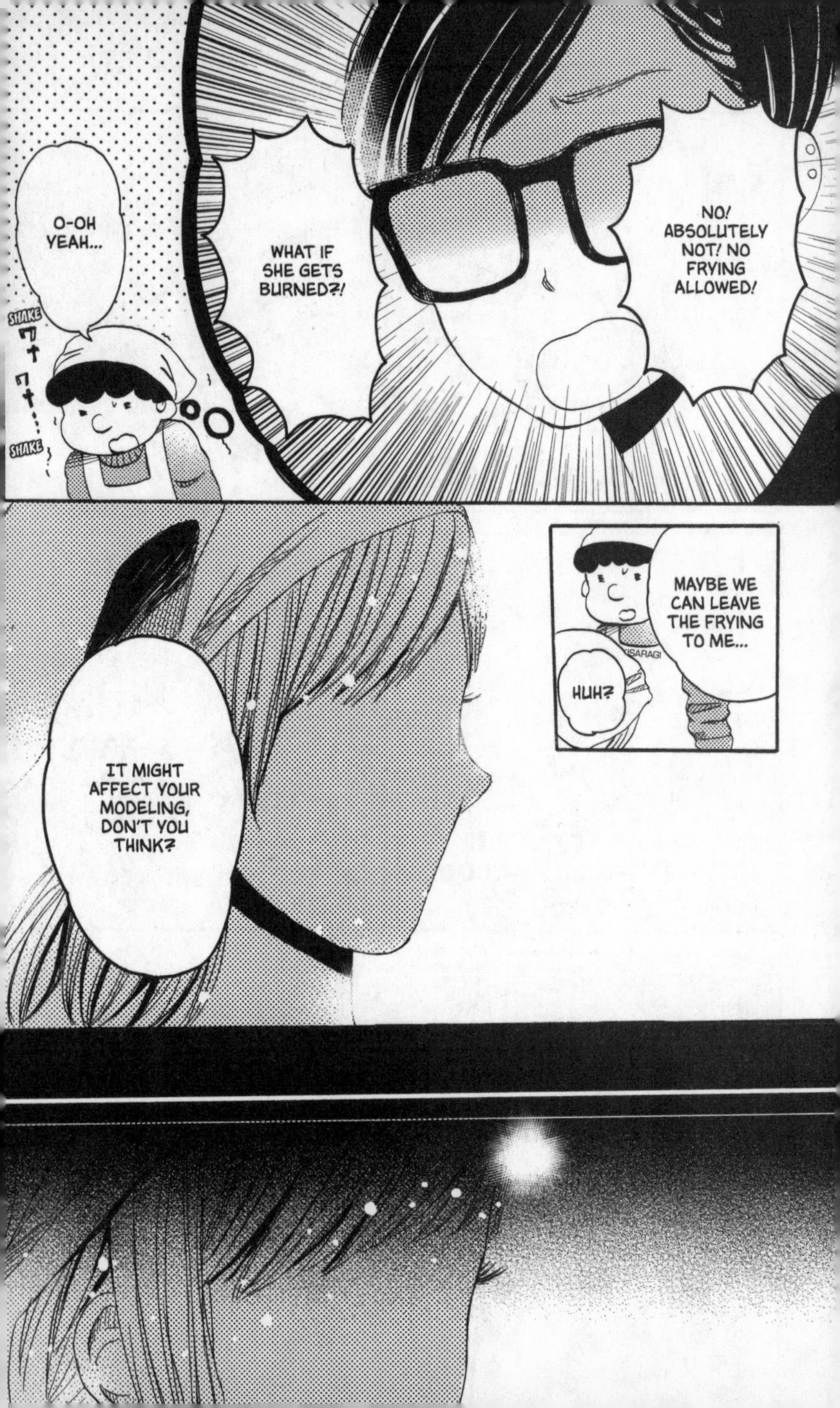
NO! ABSOLUTELY NOT! NO FRYING ALLOWED!
WHAT IF SHE GETS BURNED?!
O-OH YEAH...
SHAKE
SHAKE
MAYBE WE CAN LEAVE THE FRYING TO ME...
HUH?
IT MIGHT AFFECT YOUR MODELING, DON'T YOU THINK?

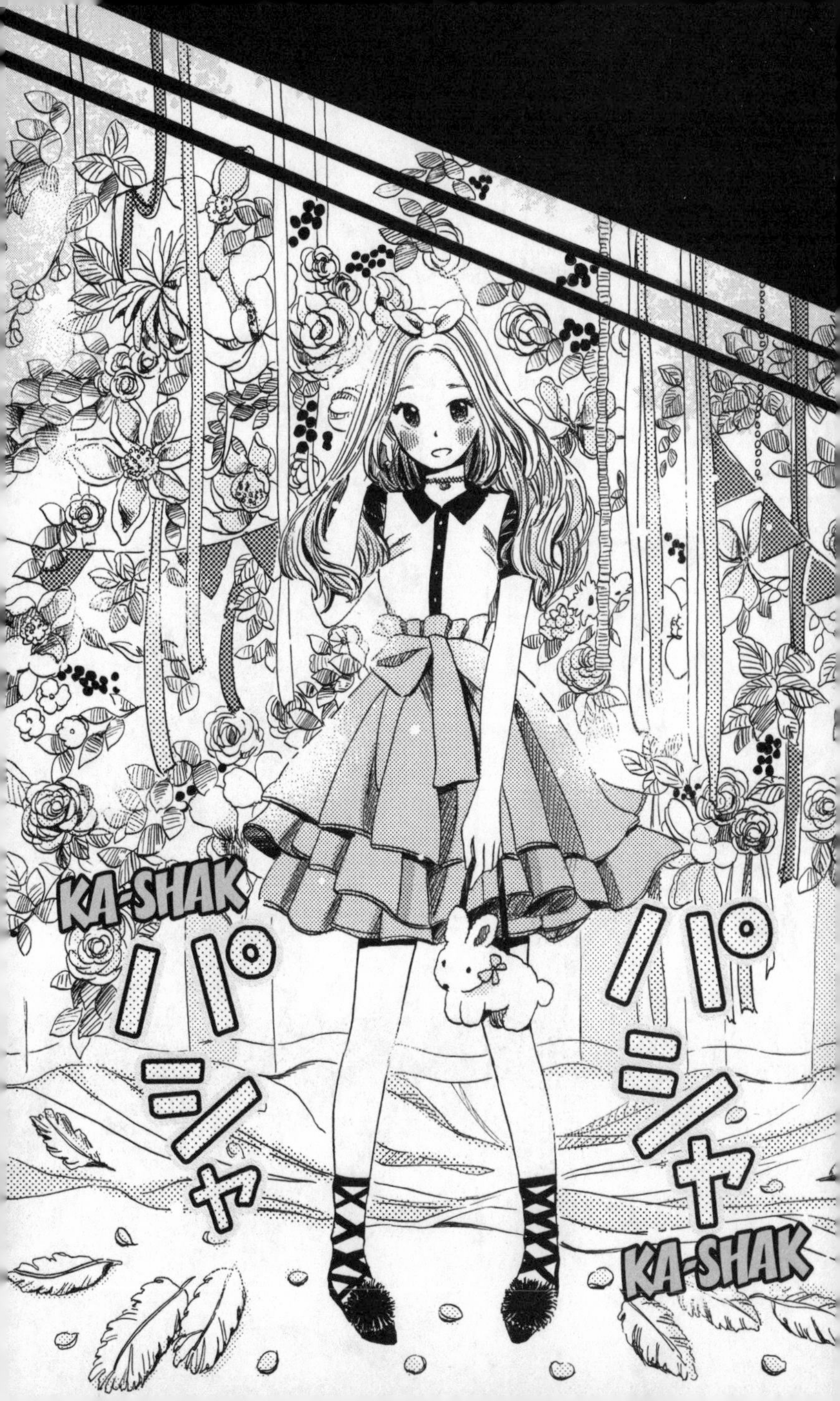
パシャ
KA-SHAK
パシャ
KA-SHAK

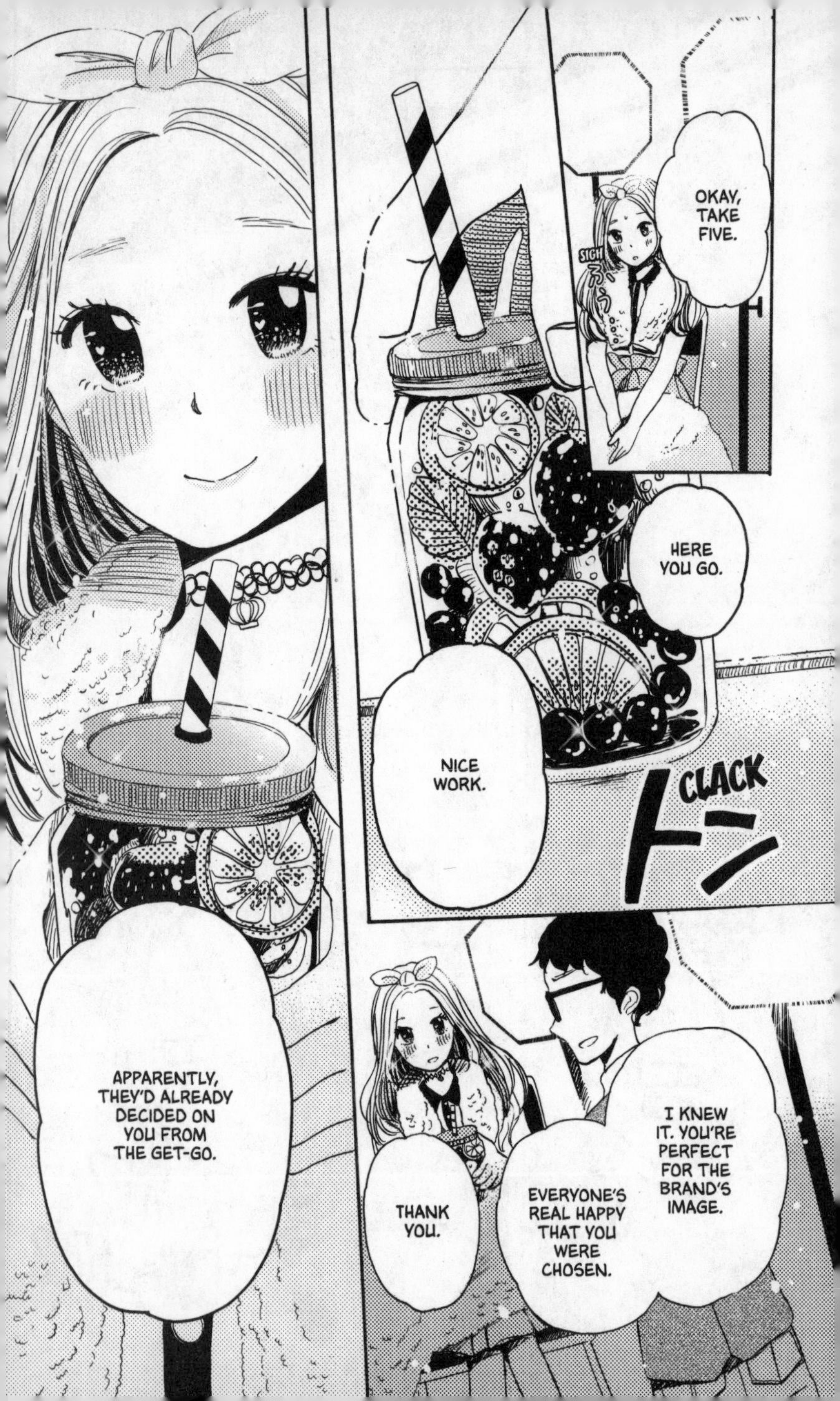
OKAY, TAKE FIVE.
SIGH
ふう
HERE YOU GO.
NICE WORK.
CLACK
トン
I KNEW IT. YOU'RE PERFECT FOR THE BRAND'S IMAGE.
EVERYONE'S REAL HAPPY THAT YOU WERE CHOSEN.
THANK YOU.
APPARENTLY, THEY'D ALREADY DECIDED ON YOU FROM THE GET-GO.

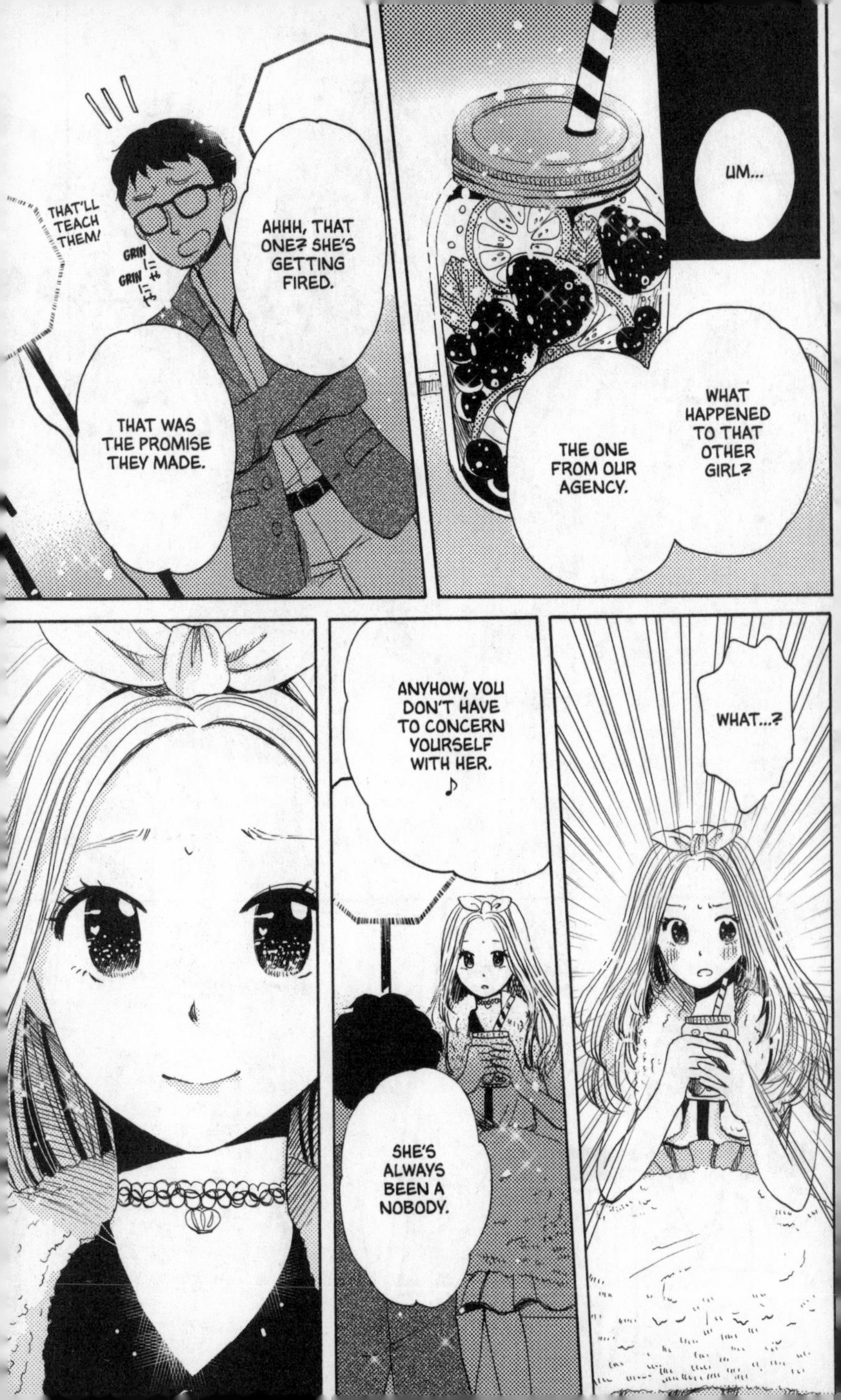
UM...
WHAT HAPPENED TO THAT OTHER GIRL?
THE ONE FROM OUR AGENCY.
AHHH, THAT ONE? SHE'S GETTING FIRED.
THAT'LL TEACH THEM!
GRIN にや
GRIN にや
THAT WAS THE PROMISE THEY MADE.
WHAT...?
ANYHOW, YOU DON'T HAVE TO CONCERN YOURSELF WITH HER. ♪
SHE'S ALWAYS BEEN A NOBODY.

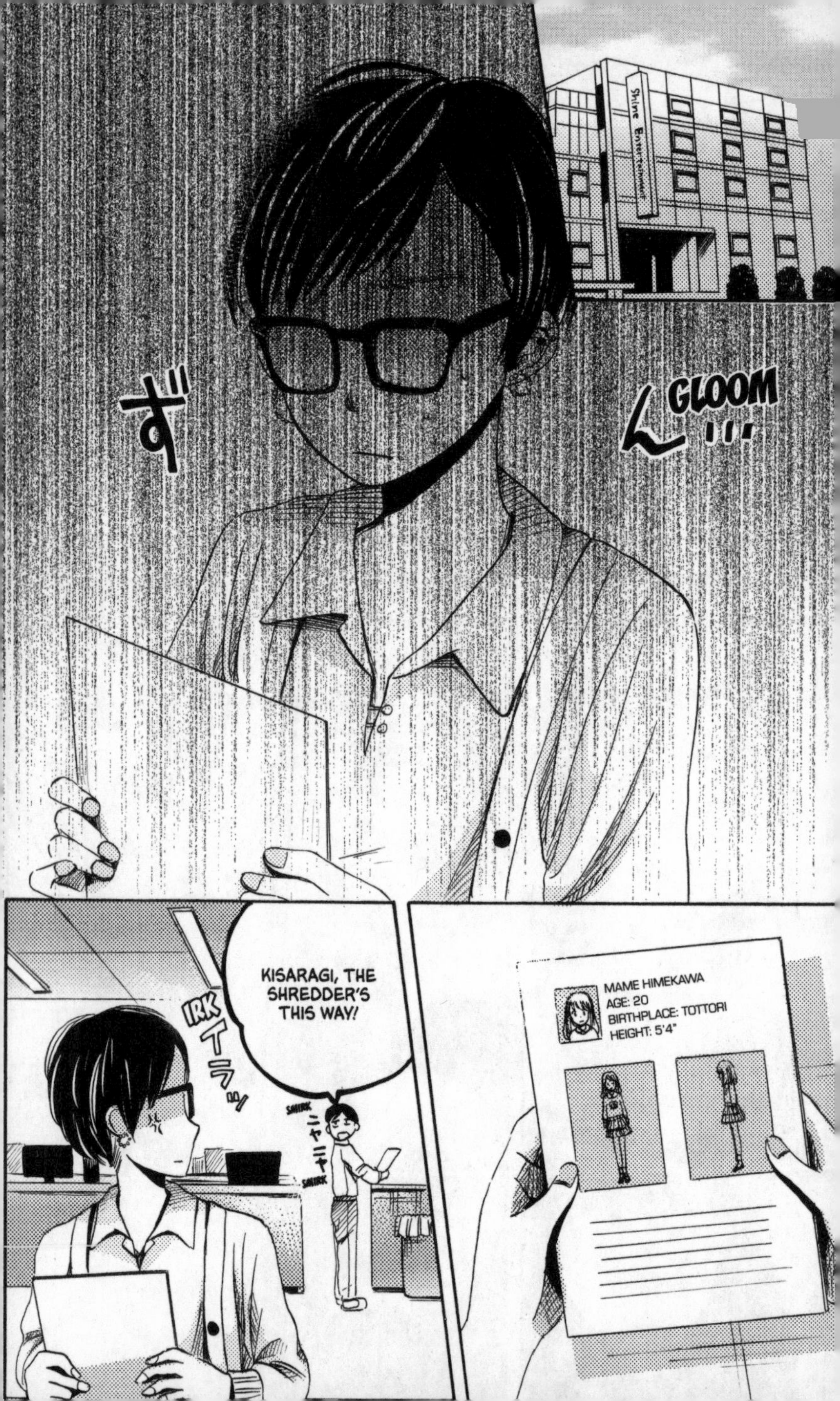
Shine Entertainment
ずん
GLOOM
MAME HIMEKAWA
AGE: 20
BIRTHPLACE: TOTTORI
HEIGHT: 5'4"
KISARAGI, THE SHREDDER'S THIS WAY!
IRK
イラッ
SMIRK
ニヤニヤ
SMIRK

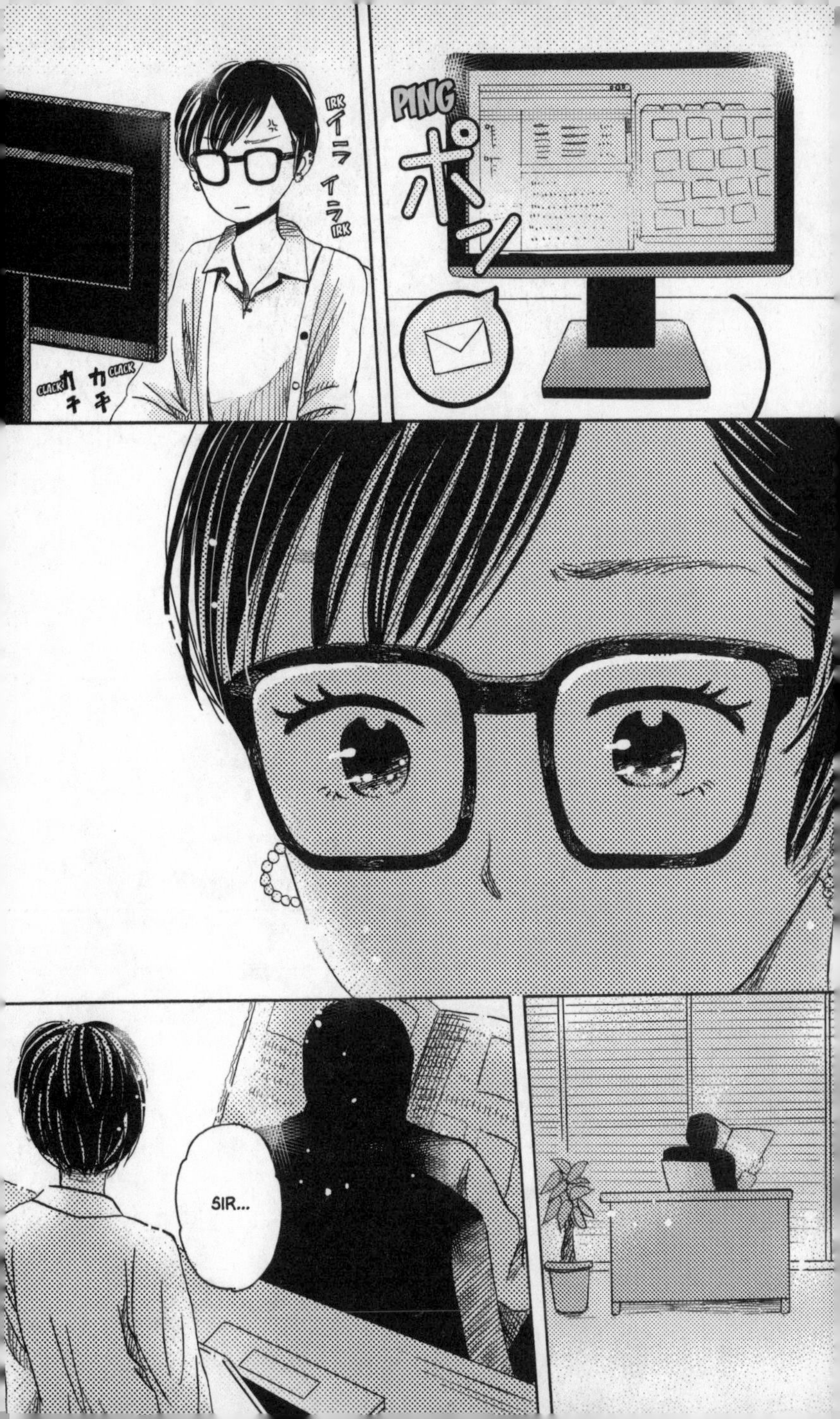
PING
ポン
IRK
イラ
イラ
IRK
CLACK
カチ
カチ
CLACK
SIR...

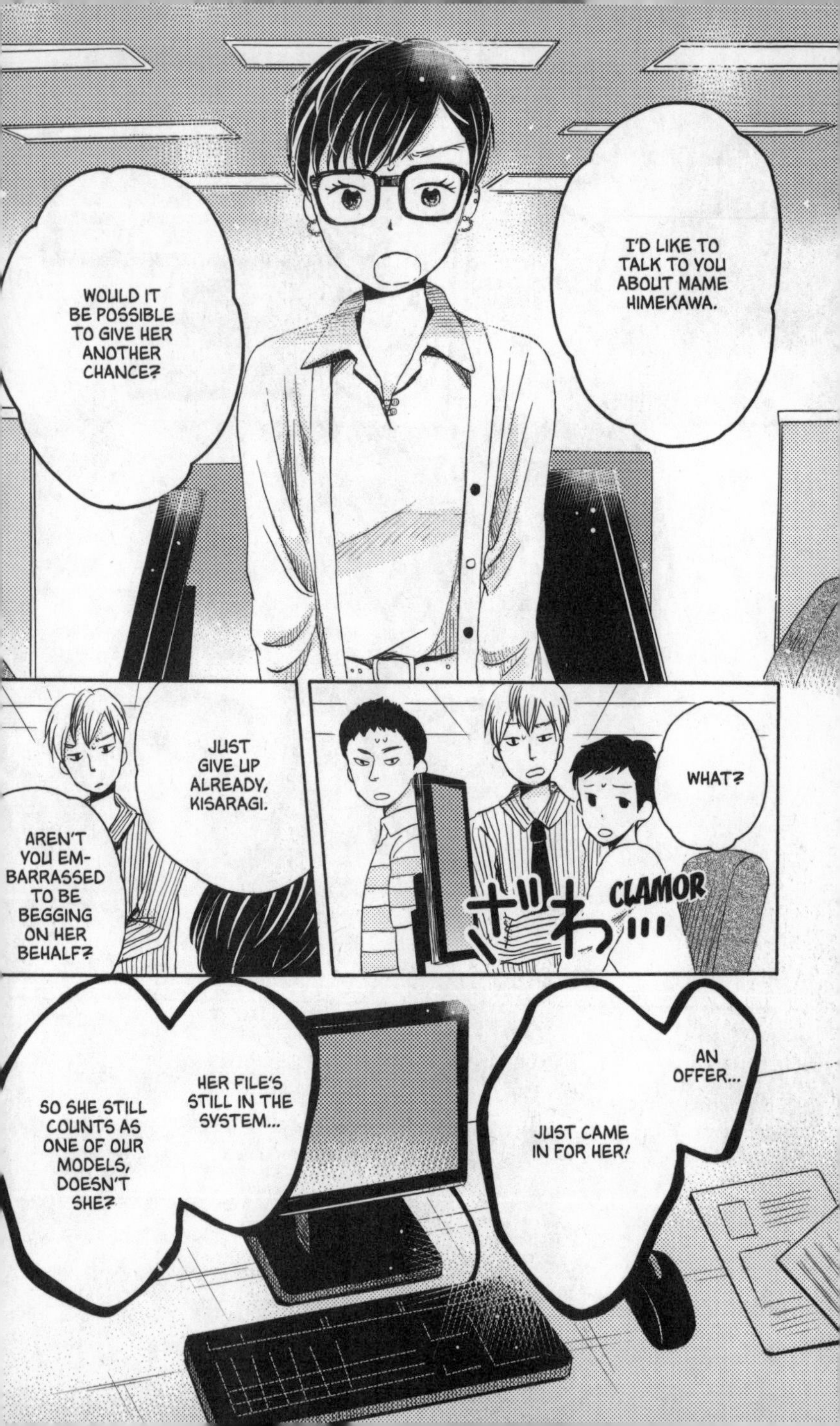
I'D LIKE TO TALK TO YOU ABOUT MAME HIMEKAWA.
WOULD IT BE POSSIBLE TO GIVE HER ANOTHER CHANCE?
WHAT?
ざわ…
CLAMOR
JUST GIVE UP ALREADY, KISARAGI.
AREN'T YOU EM-BARRASSED TO BE BEGGING ON HER BEHALF?
AN OFFER...
JUST CAME IN FOR HER!
HER FILE'S STILL IN THE SYSTEM...
SO SHE STILL COUNTS AS ONE OF OUR MODELS, DOESN'T SHE?

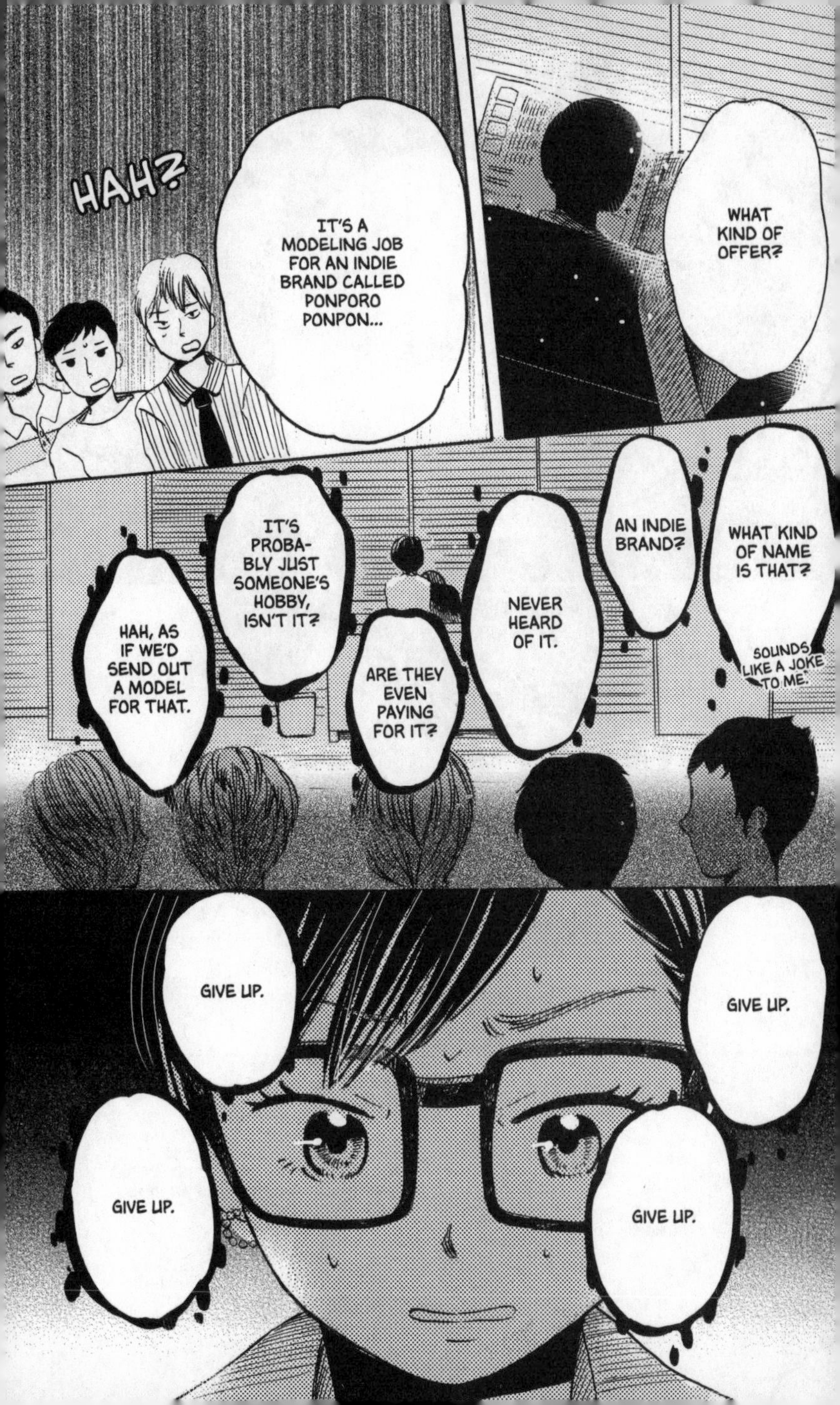
WHAT KIND OF OFFER?
IT'S A MODELING JOB FOR AN INDIE BRAND CALLED PONPORO PONPON...
HAH?
WHAT KIND OF NAME IS THAT?
SOUNDS LIKE A JOKE TO ME.
AN INDIE BRAND?
NEVER HEARD OF IT.
ARE THEY EVEN PAYING FOR IT?
IT'S PROBA-BLY JUST SOMEONE'S HOBBY, ISN'T IT?
HAH, AS IF WE'D SEND OUT A MODEL FOR THAT.
GIVE UP.
GIVE UP.
GIVE UP.
GIVE UP.

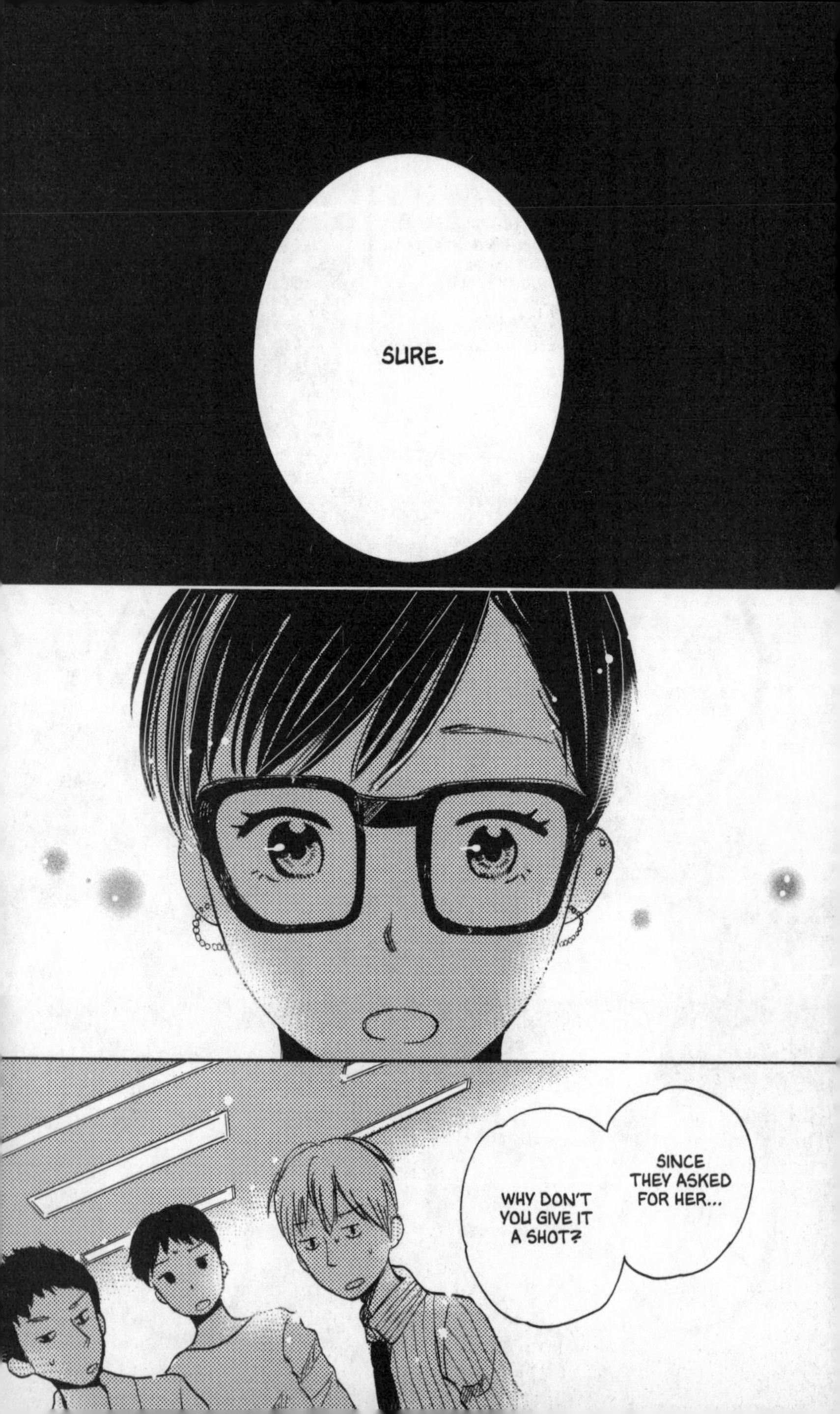
SURE.
SINCE THEY ASKED FOR HER...
WHY DON'T YOU GIVE IT A SHOT?

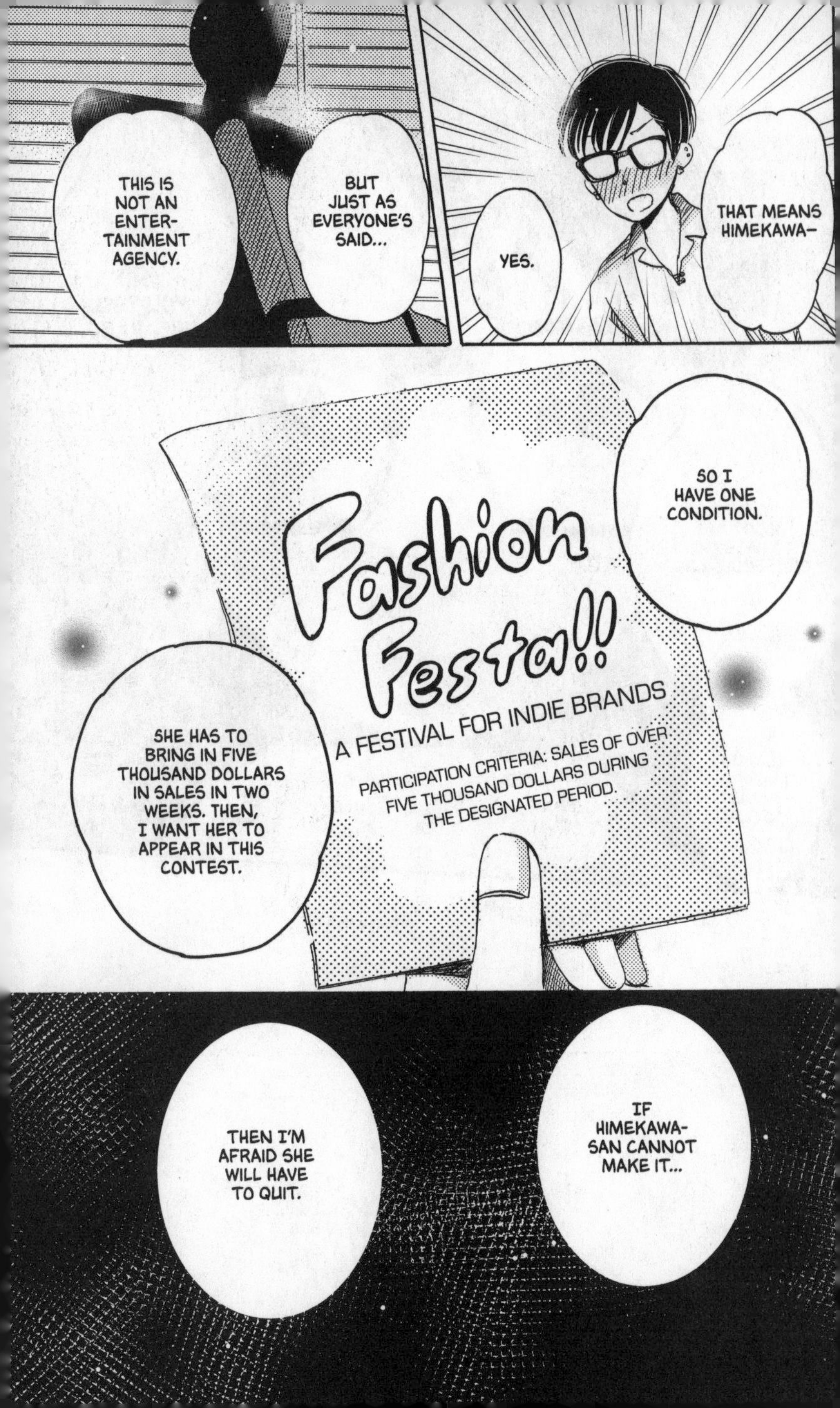
THAT MEANS HIMEKAWA—
YES.
BUT JUST AS EVERYONE'S SAID...
THIS IS NOT AN ENTERTAINMENT AGENCY.
SO I HAVE ONE CONDITION.
Fashion Festa!!
A FESTIVAL FOR INDIE BRANDS
PARTICIPATION CRITERIA: SALES OF OVER FIVE THOUSAND DOLLARS DURING THE DESIGNATED PERIOD.
SHE HAS TO BRING IN FIVE THOUSAND DOLLARS IN SALES IN TWO WEEKS. THEN, I WANT HER TO APPEAR IN THIS CONTEST.
IF HIMEKAWA-SAN CANNOT MAKE IT...
THEN I'M AFRAID SHE WILL HAVE TO QUIT.

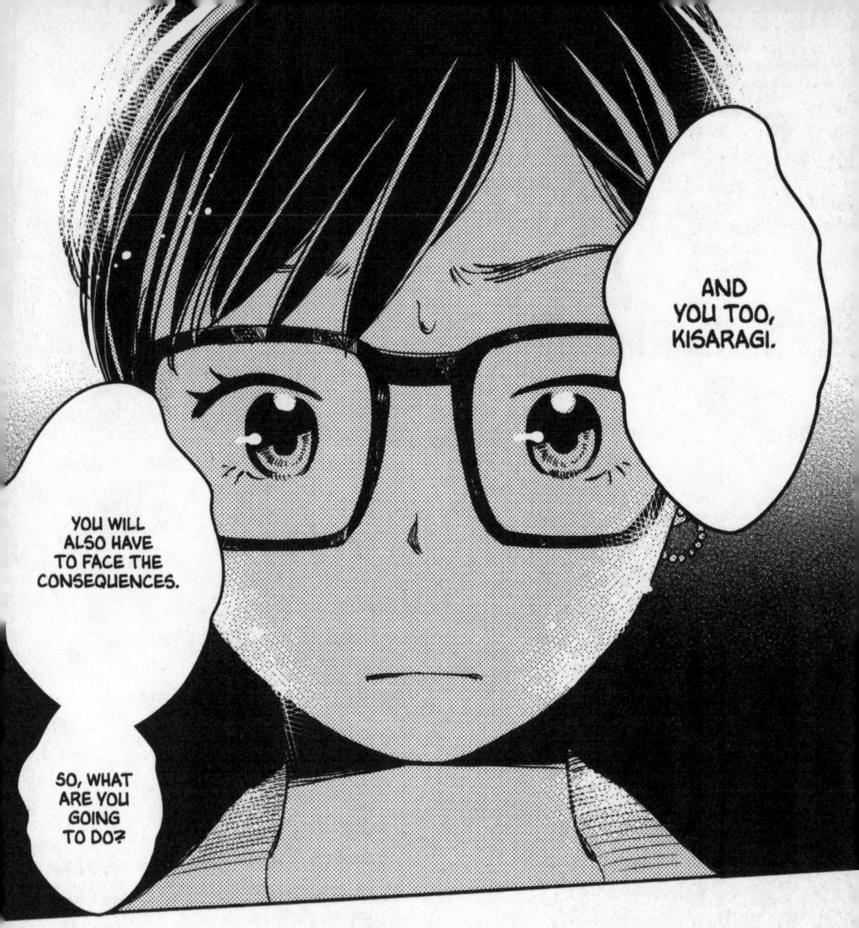
AND YOU TOO, KISARAGI.
YOU WILL ALSO HAVE TO FACE THE CONSEQUENCES.
SO, WHAT ARE YOU GOING TO DO?
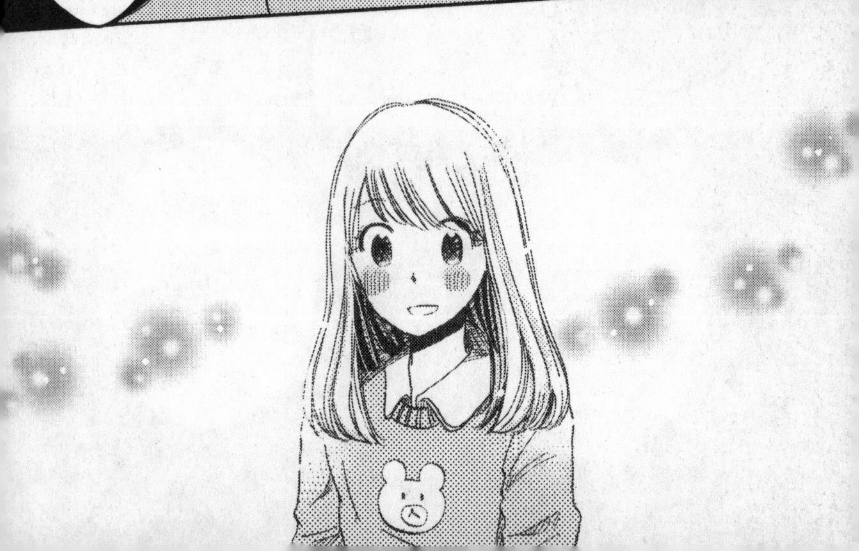

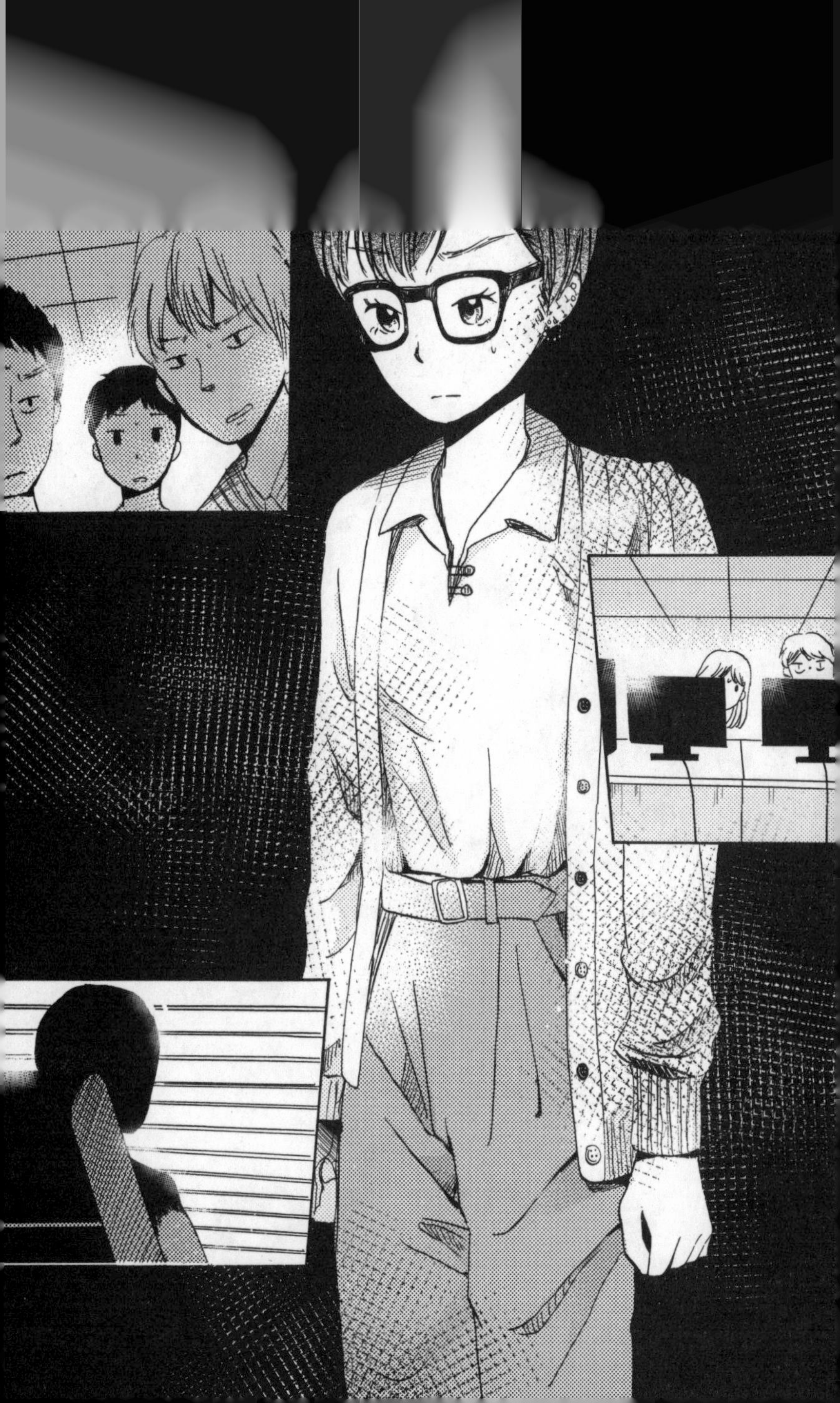

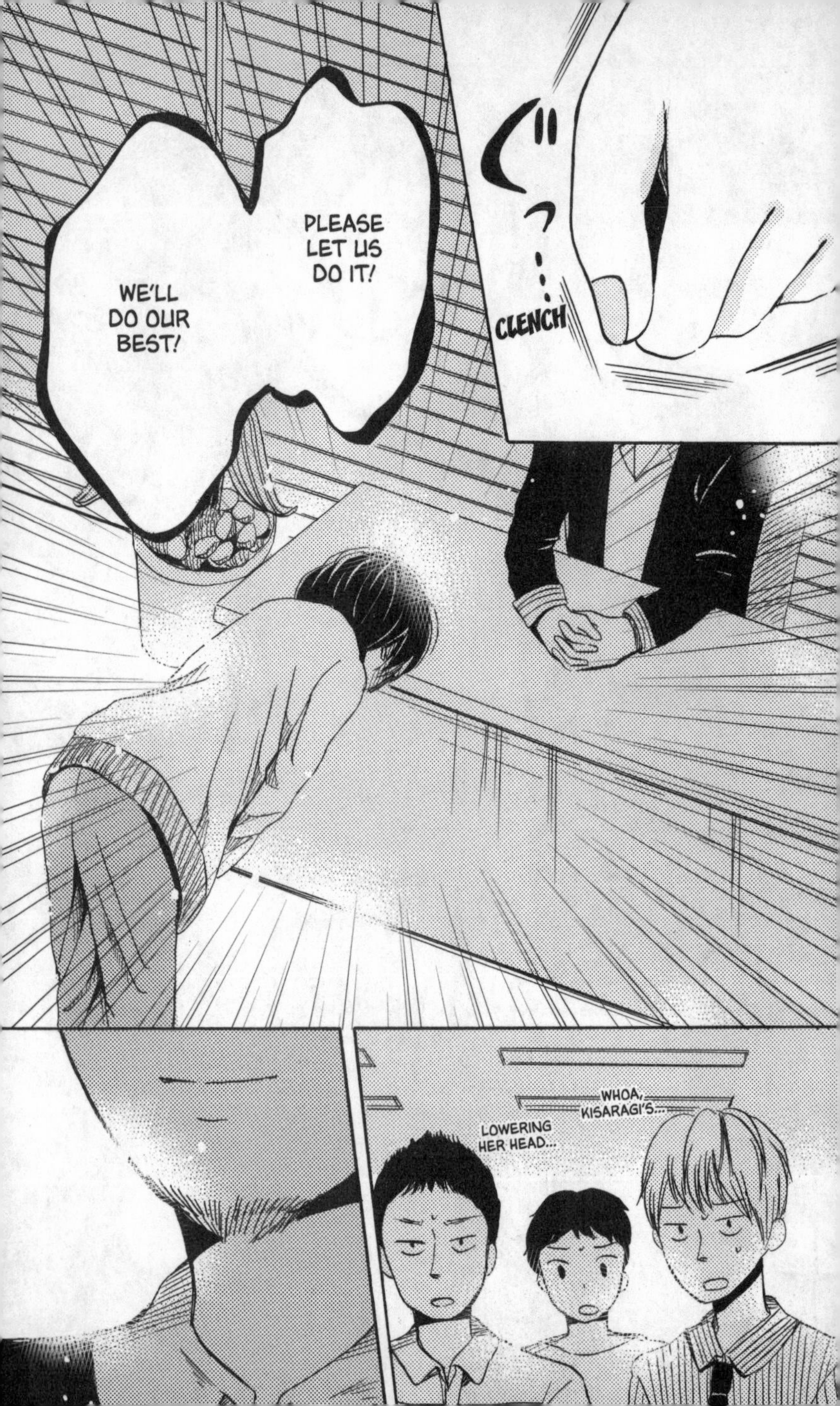
CLENCH
PLEASE LET US DO IT!
WE'LL DO OUR BEST!
WHOA, KISARAGI'S...
LOWERING HER HEAD...

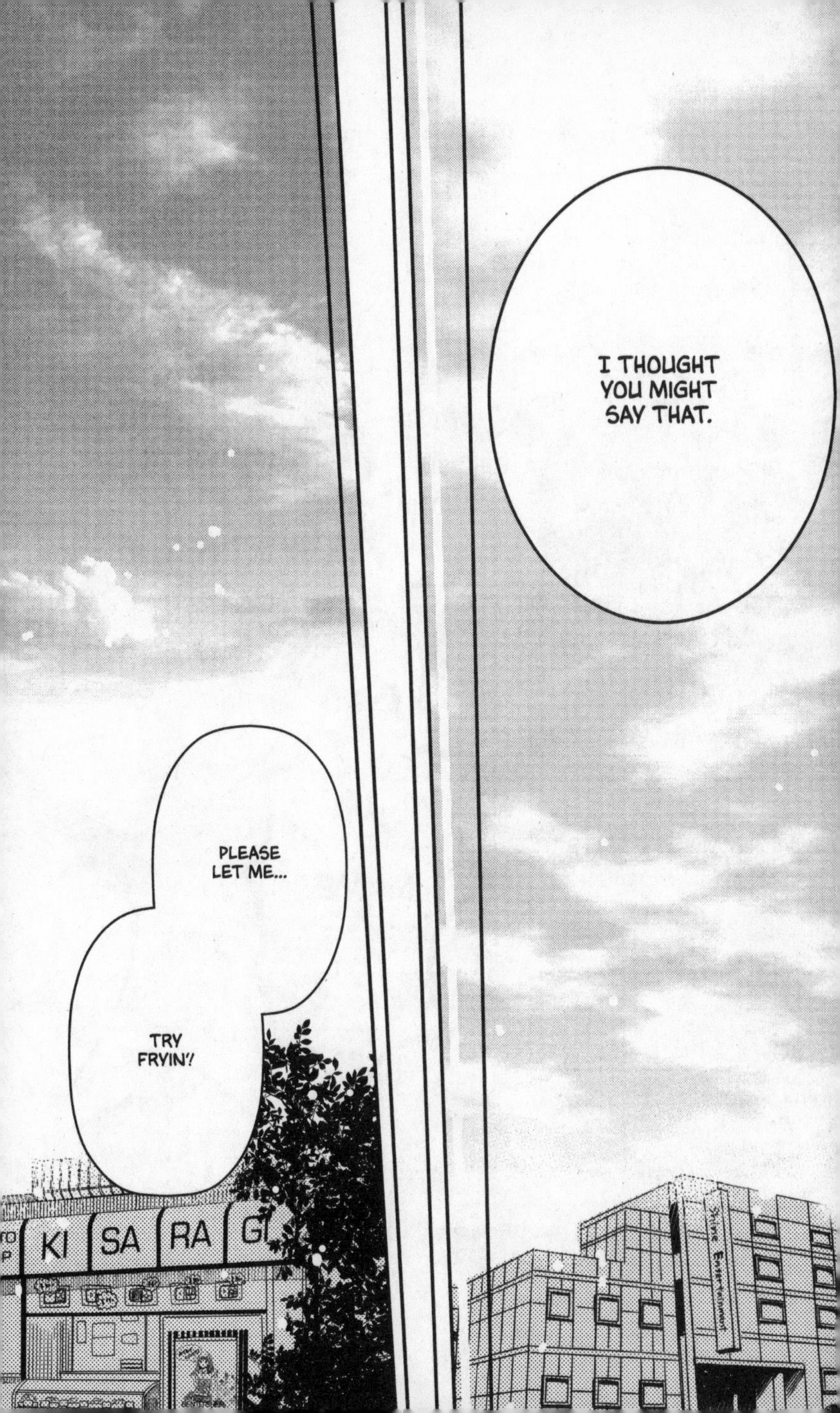
I THOUGHT YOU MIGHT SAY THAT.
PLEASE LET ME...
TRY FRYIN'!
KI SA RA GI

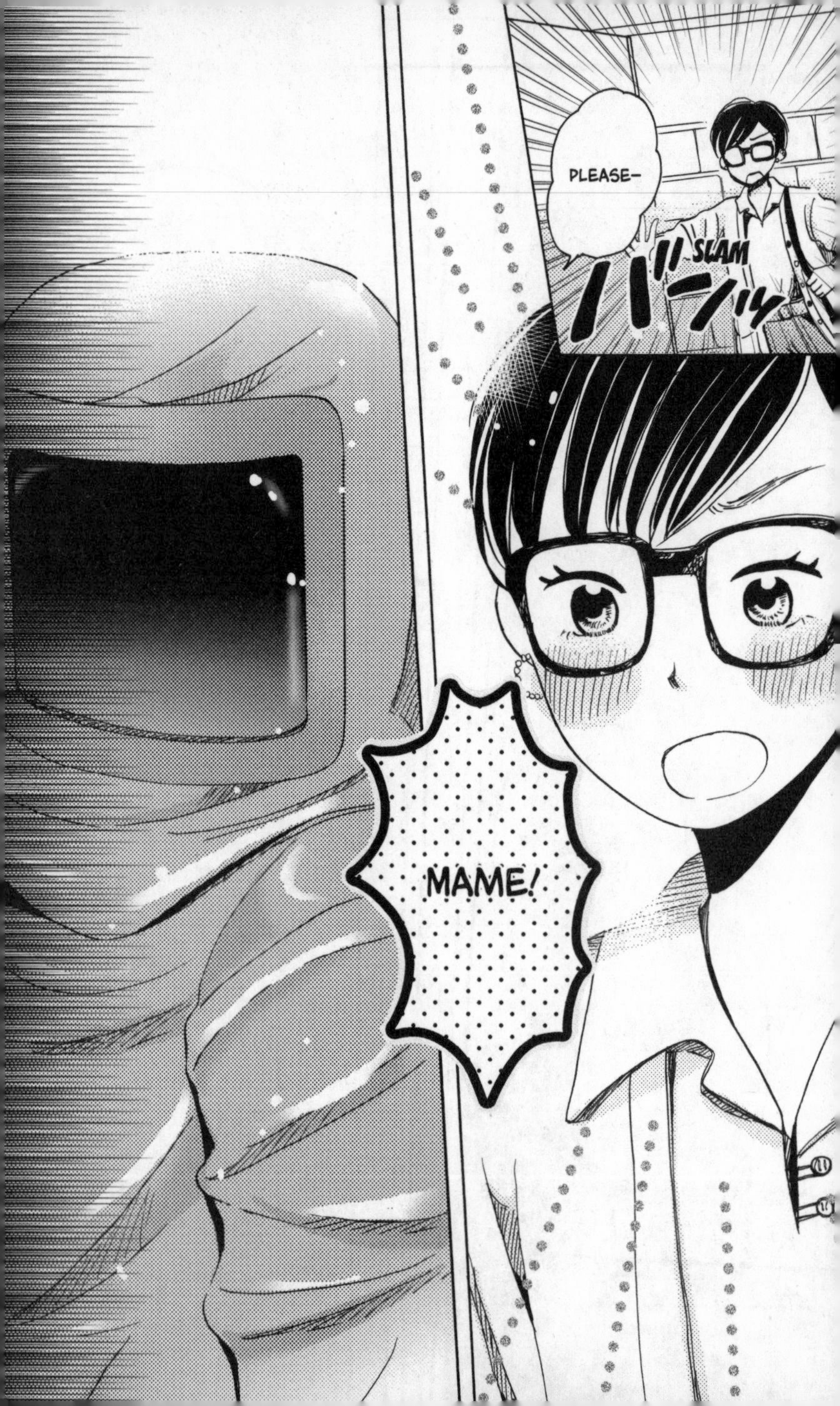
PLEASE-
SLAM
MAME!

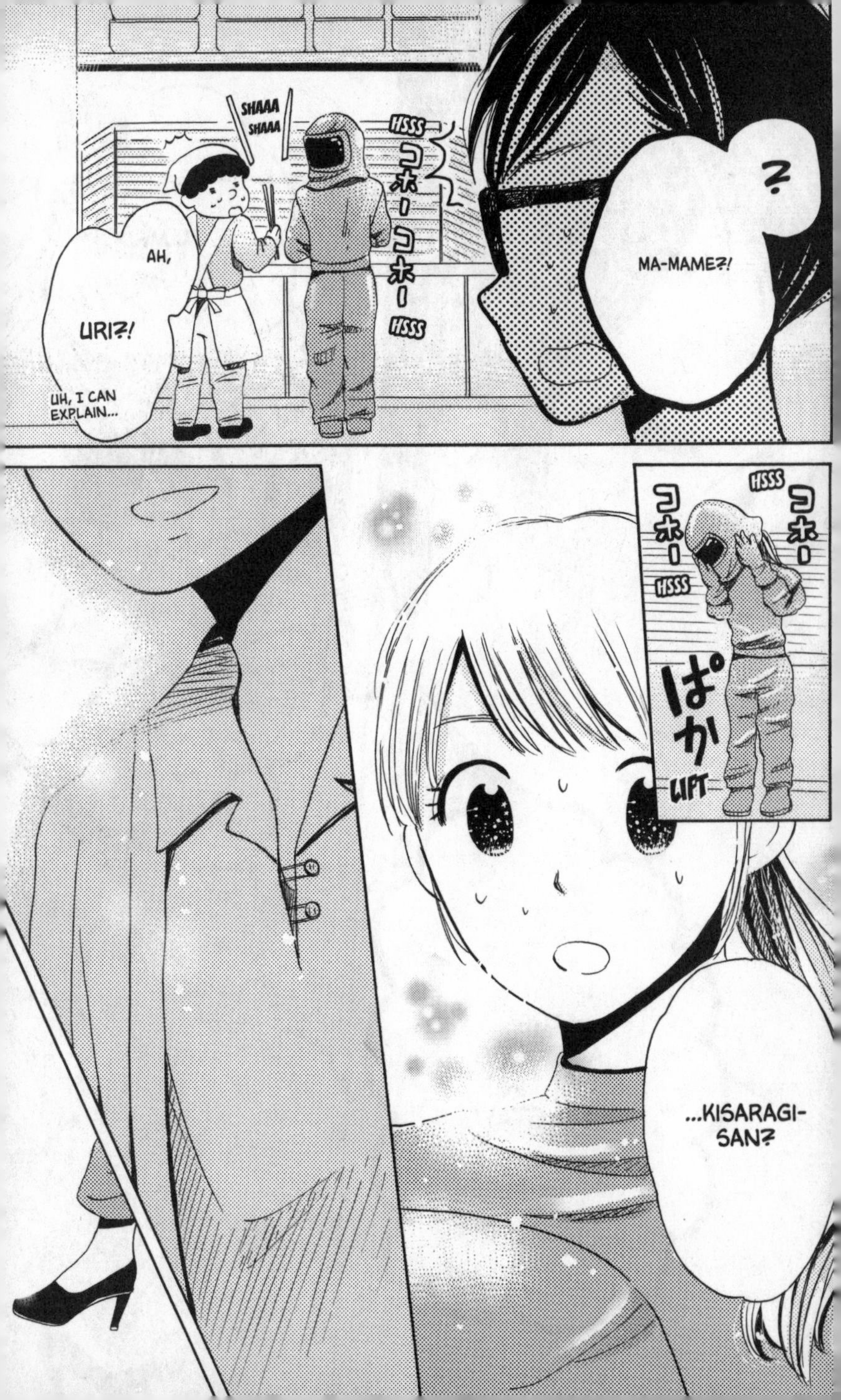
?
MA-MAME?!
SHAAA
SHAAA
HSSS
コホーコホー
HSSS
AH,
URI?!
UH, I CAN EXPLAIN...
HSSS
コホー
HSSS
ぱか
LIFT
...KISARAGI-SAN?

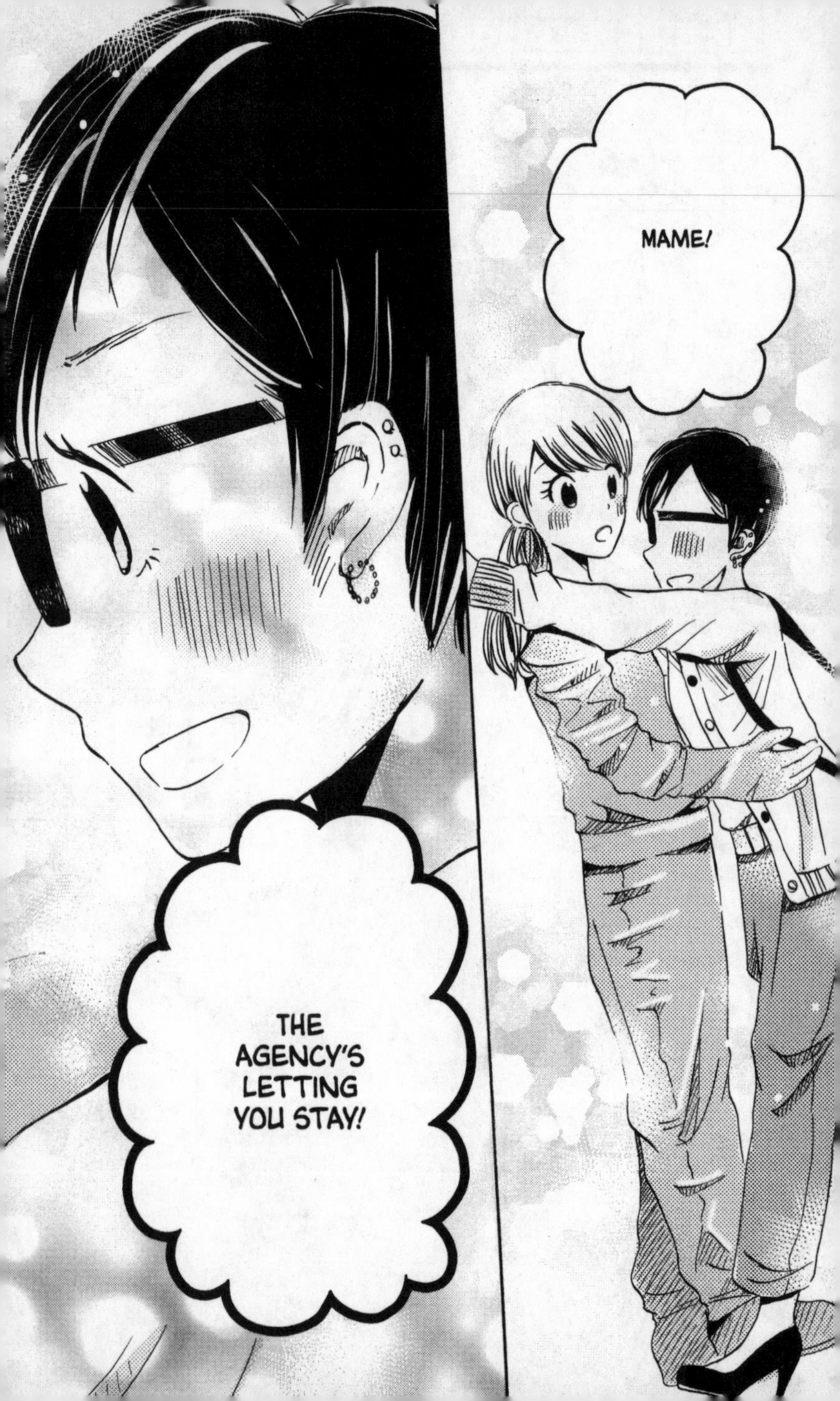
MAME!
THE AGENCY'S LETTING YOU STAY!

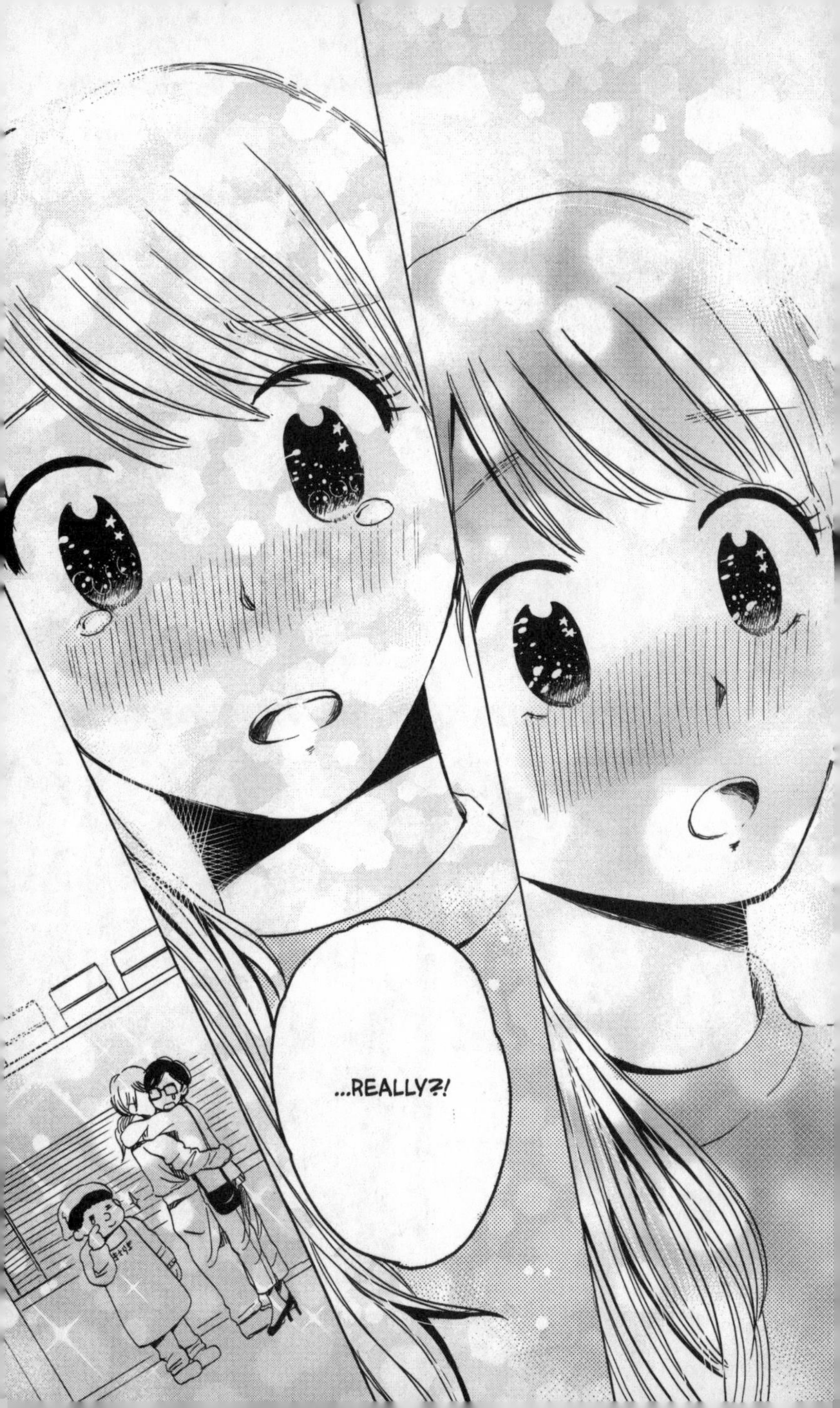
...REALLY?!

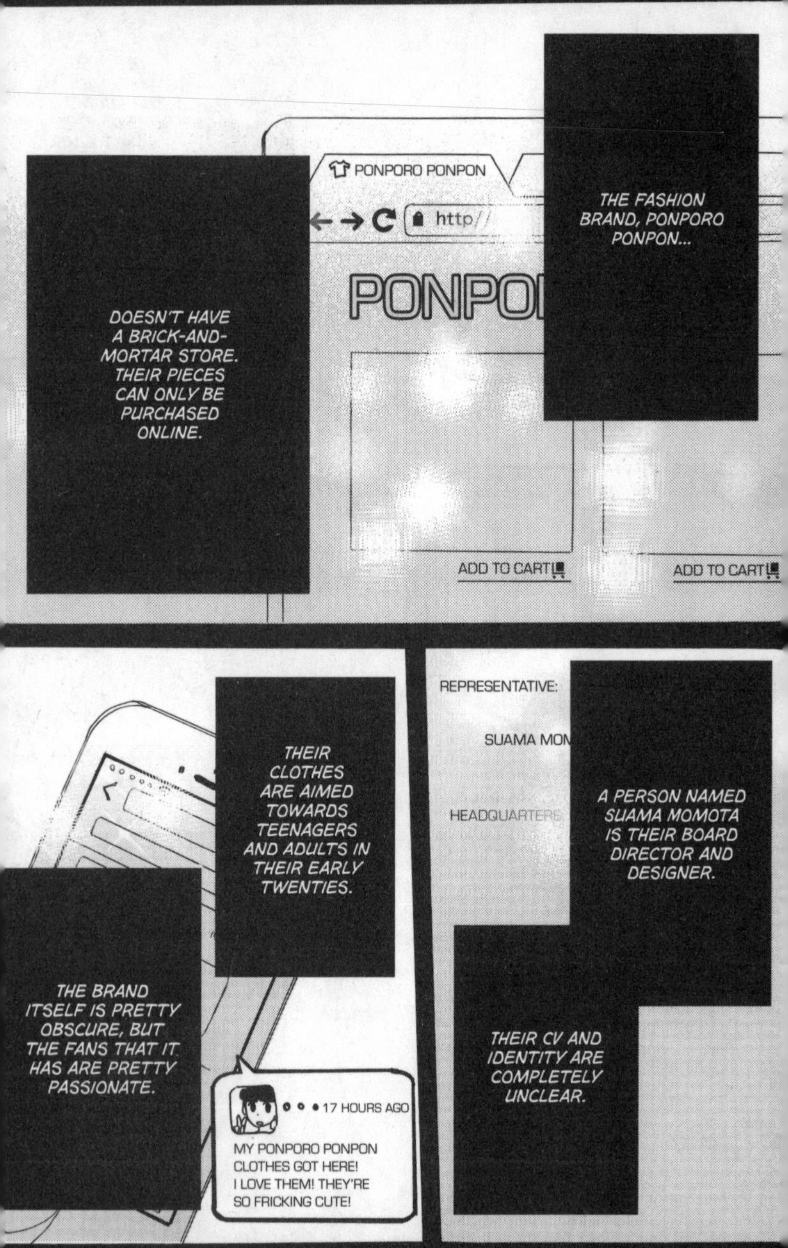
THE FASHION BRAND, PONPORO PONPON...
PONPORO PONPON
http//
DOESN'T HAVE A BRICK-AND-MORTAR STORE. THEIR PIECES CAN ONLY BE PURCHASED ONLINE.
ADD TO CART
ADD TO CART
REPRESENTATIVE:
A PERSON NAMED SUAMA MOMOTA IS THEIR BOARD DIRECTOR AND DESIGNER.
THEIR CV AND IDENTITY ARE COMPLETELY UNCLEAR.
THEIR CLOTHES ARE AIMED TOWARDS TEENAGERS AND ADULTS IN THEIR EARLY TWENTIES.
THE BRAND ITSELF IS PRETTY OBSCURE, BUT THE FANS THAT IT HAS ARE PRETTY PASSIONATE.
17 HOURS AGO
MY PONPORO PONPON CLOTHES GOT HERE! I LOVE THEM! THEY'RE SO FRICKING CUTE!

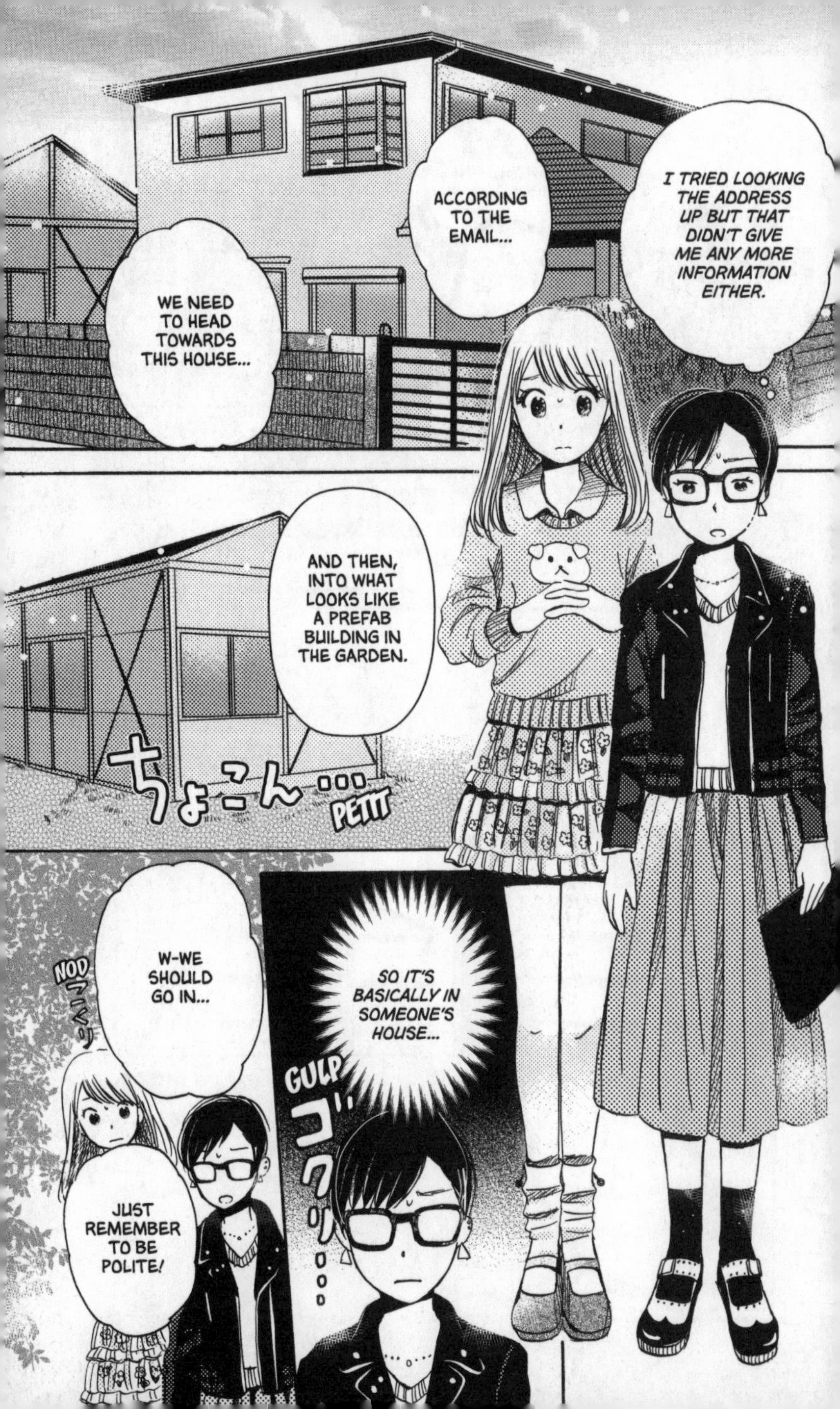
I TRIED LOOKING THE ADDRESS UP BUT THAT DIDN'T GIVE ME ANY MORE INFORMATION EITHER.
ACCORDING TO THE EMAIL...
WE NEED TO HEAD TOWARDS THIS HOUSE...
AND THEN, INTO WHAT LOOKS LIKE A PREFAB BUILDING IN THE GARDEN.
ちょこん...
PETIT
SO IT'S BASICALLY IN SOMEONE'S HOUSE...
GULP
W-WE SHOULD GO IN...
NOD
JUST REMEMBER TO BE POLITE!

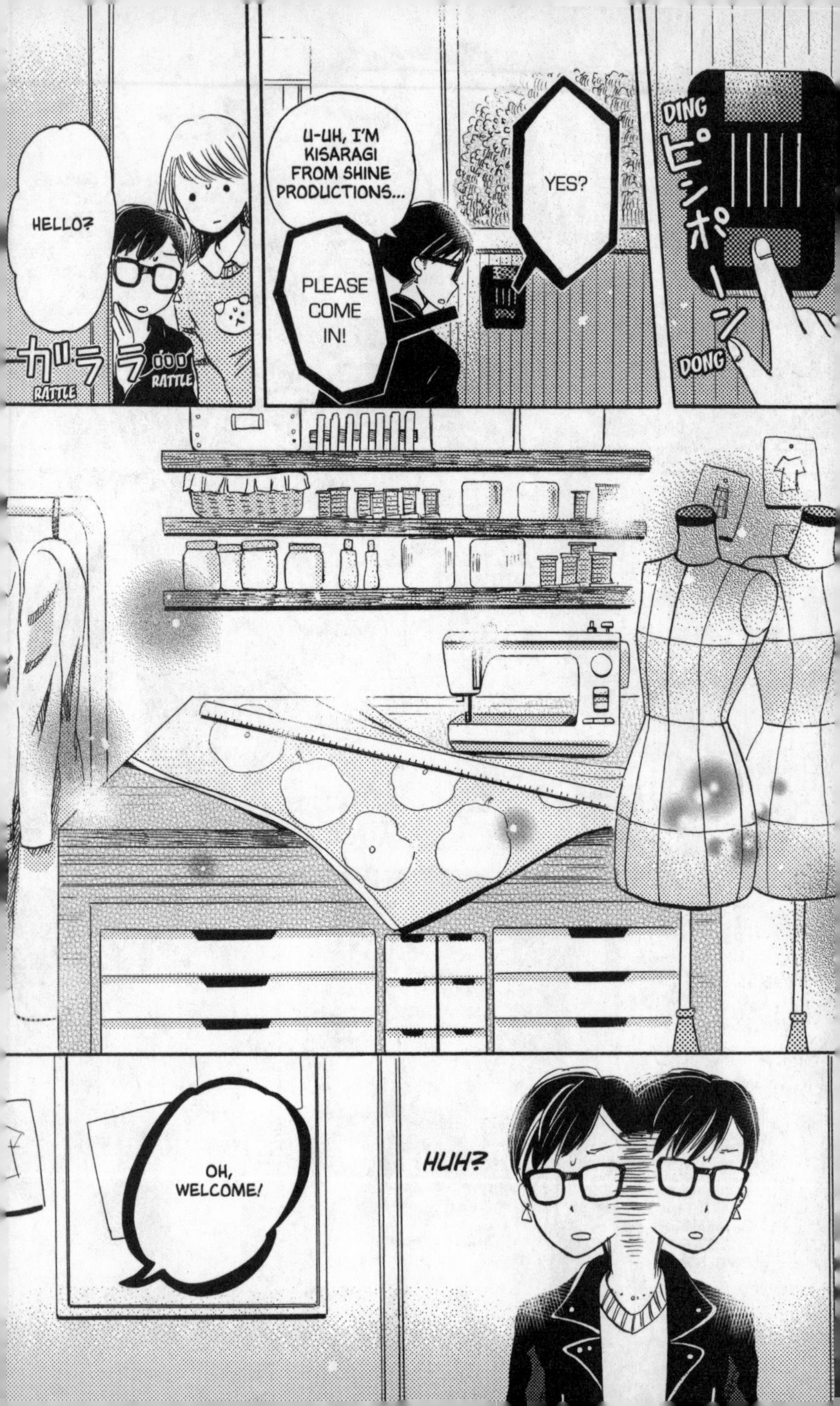
DING
ピンポーン
DONG
YES?
U-UH, I'M KISARAGI FROM SHINE PRODUCTIONS...
PLEASE COME IN!
HELLO?
ガラララ
RATTLE
RATTLE
HUH?
OH, WELCOME!

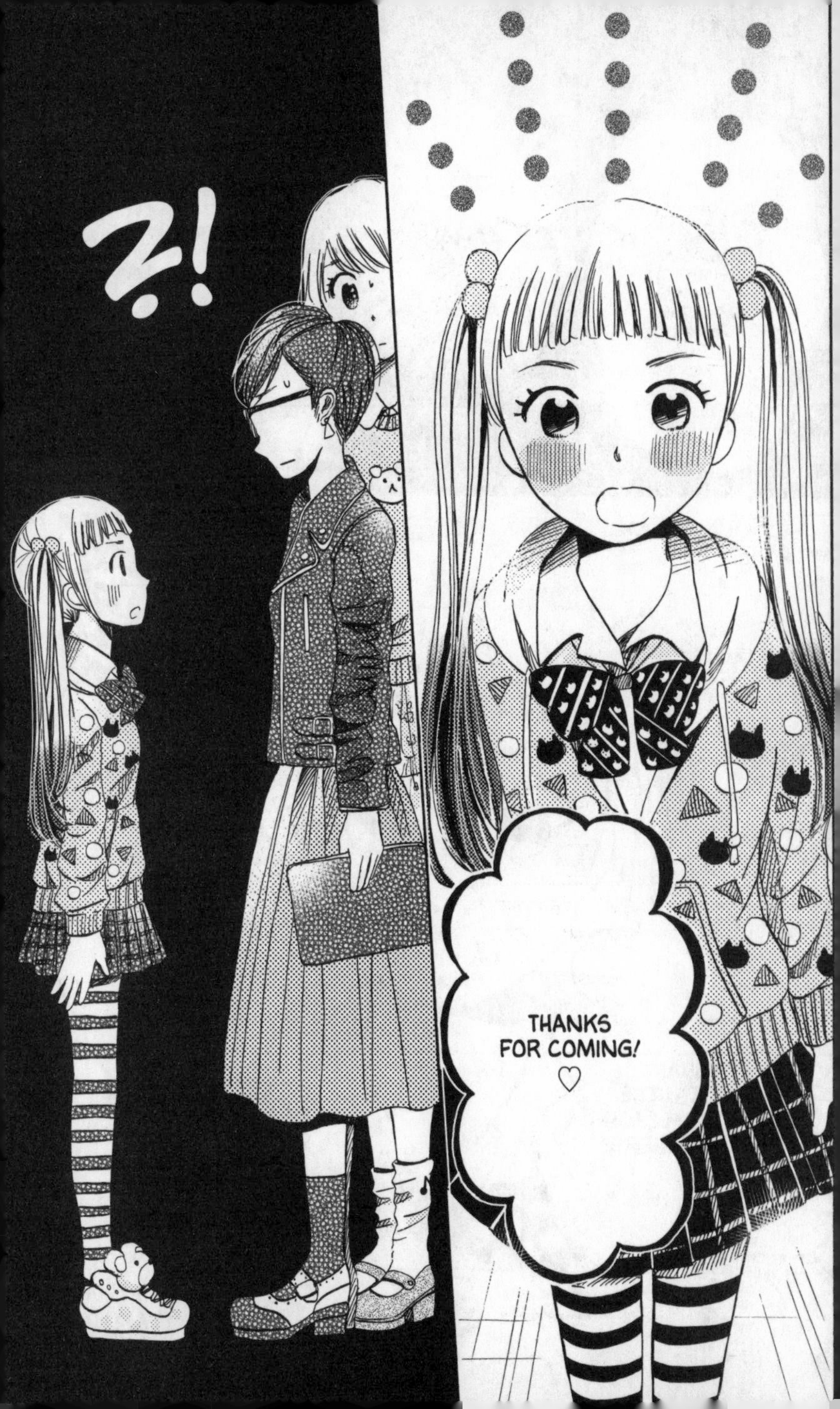
THANKS FOR COMING! ♡
?!

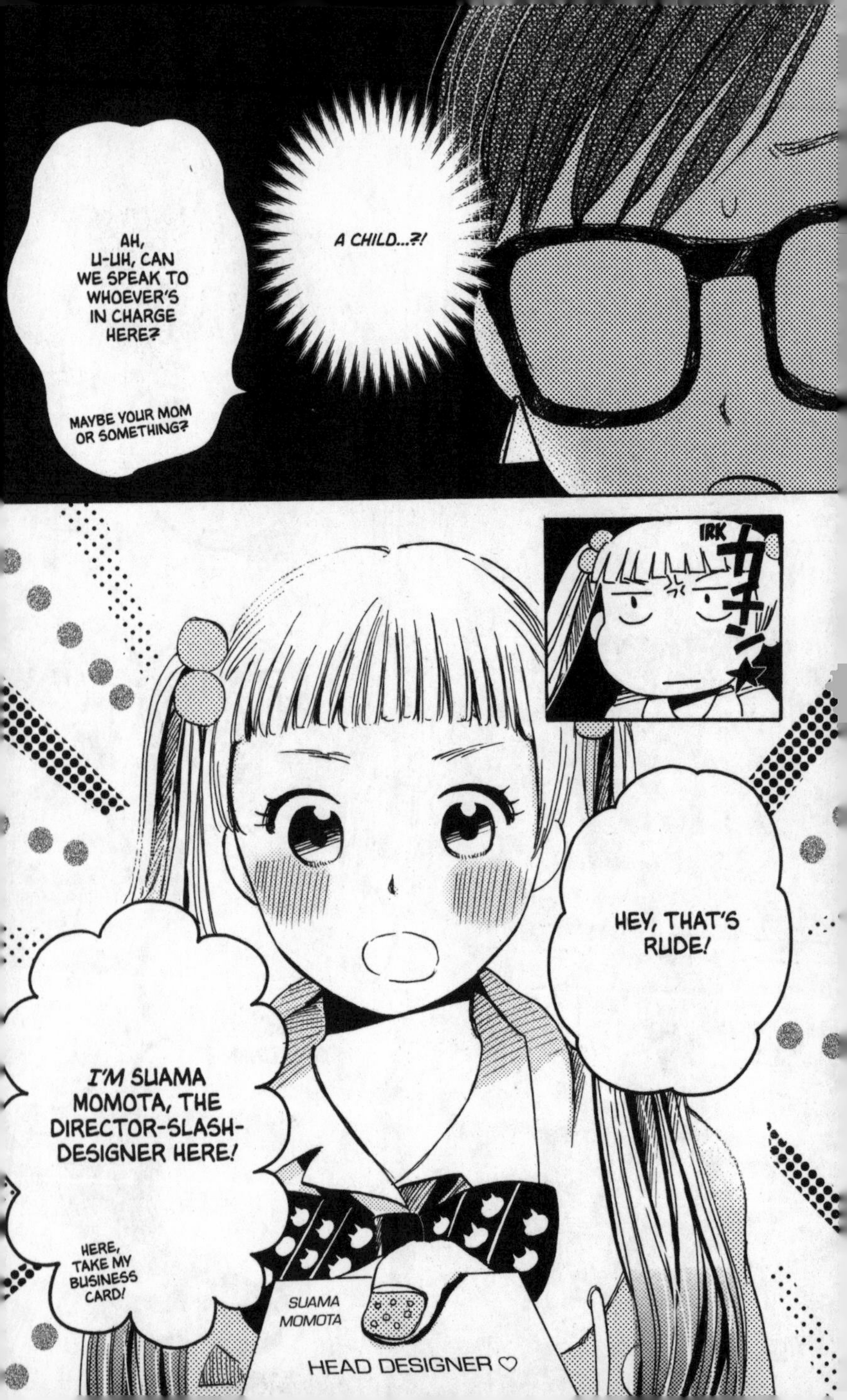
A CHILD...?!
AH, U-UH, CAN WE SPEAK TO WHOEVER'S IN CHARGE HERE?
MAYBE YOUR MOM OR SOMETHING?
IRK
HEY, THAT'S RUDE!
I'M SUAMA MOMOTA, THE DIRECTOR-SLASH-DESIGNER HERE!
HERE, TAKE MY BUSINESS CARD!
SUAMA MOMOTA
HEAD DESIGNER ♡

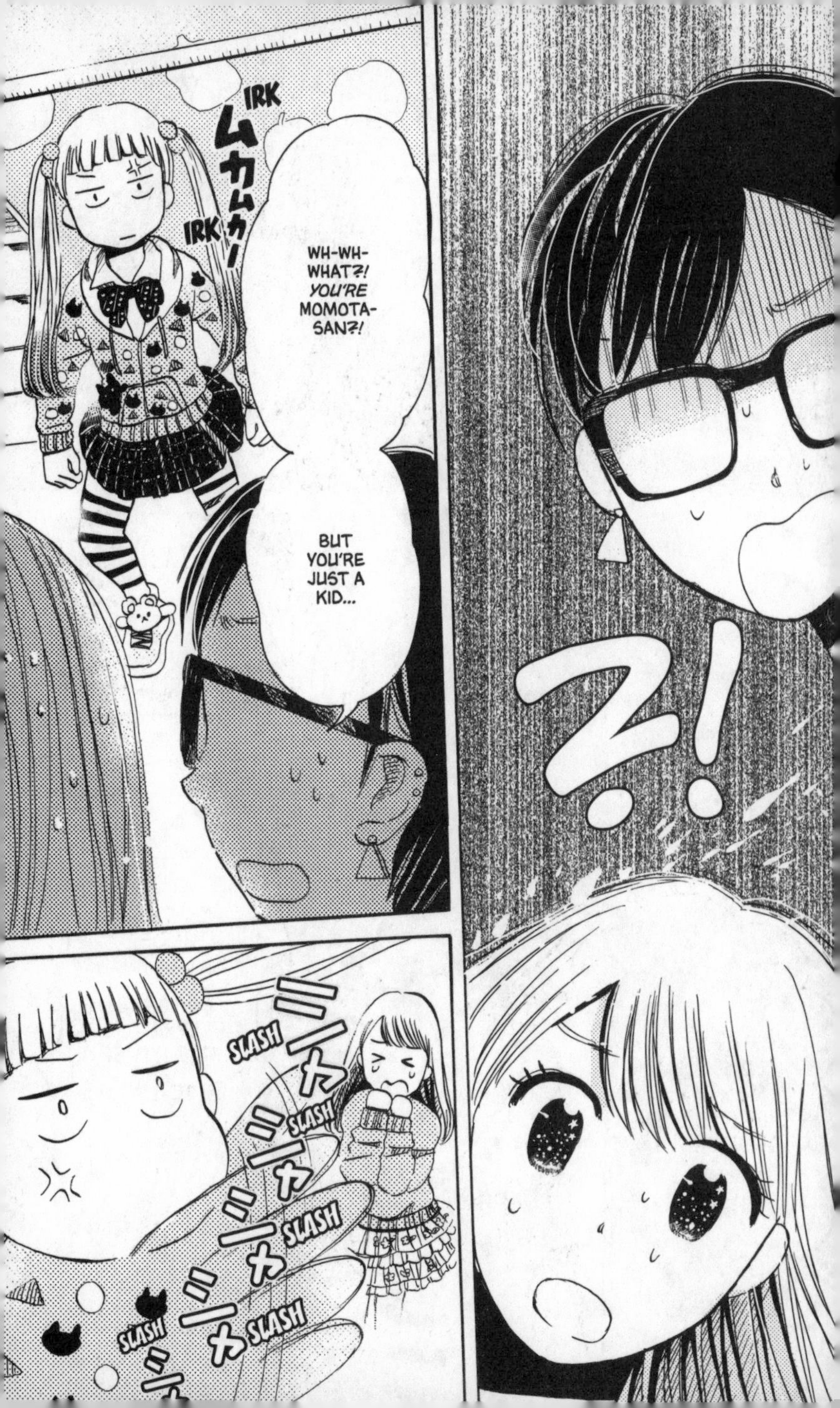
?!
IRK
IRK
WH-WH-WHAT?! YOU'RE MOMOTA-SAN?!
BUT YOU'RE JUST A KID...
SLASH
SLASH
SLASH
SLASH
SLASH

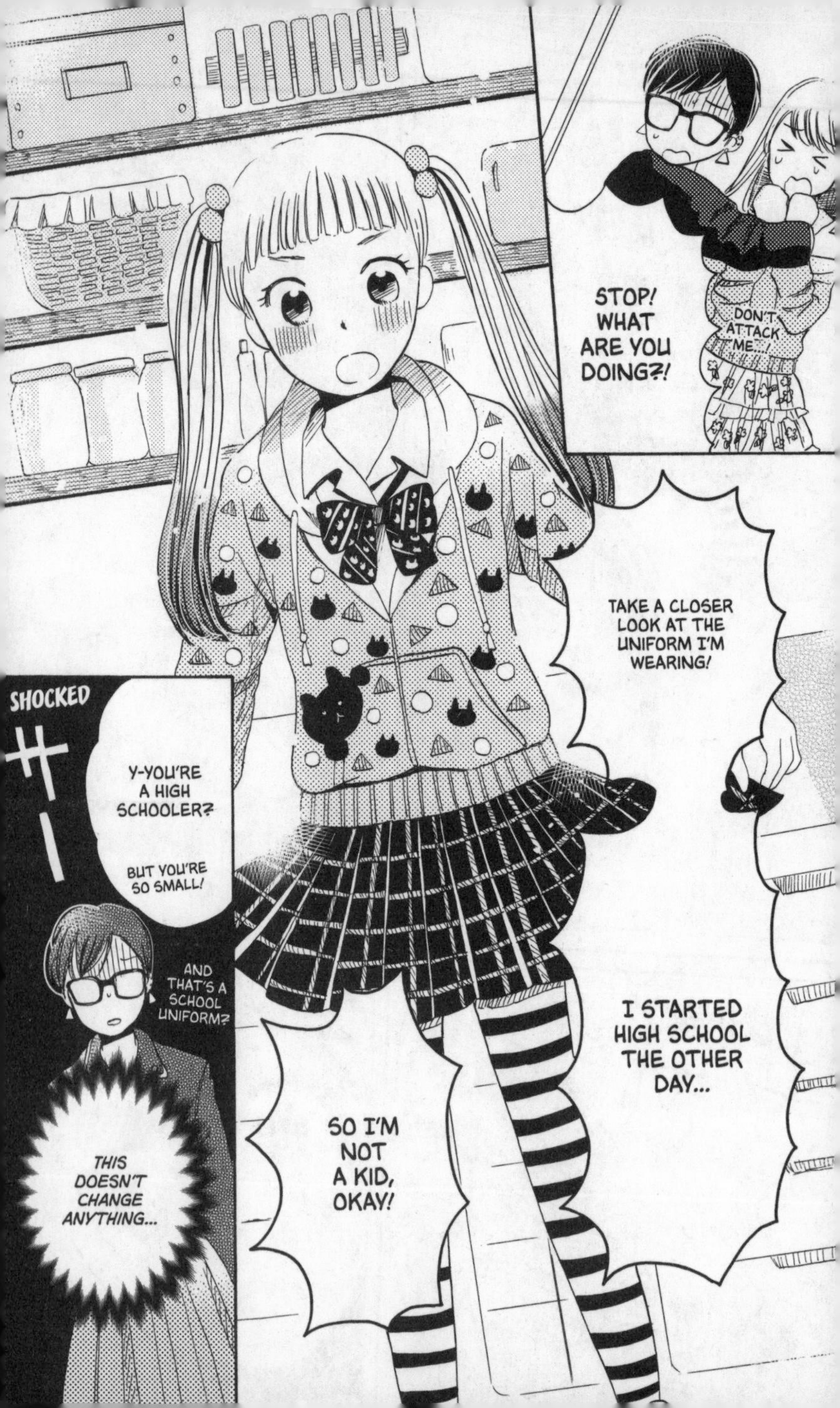

DON'T ATTACK ME...!
STOP! WHAT ARE YOU DOING?!
TAKE A CLOSER LOOK AT THE UNIFORM I'M WEARING!
I STARTED HIGH SCHOOL THE OTHER DAY...
SO I'M NOT A KID, OKAY!
SHOCKED
Y-YOU'RE A HIGH SCHOOLER?
BUT YOU'RE SO SMALL!
AND THAT'S A SCHOOL UNIFORM?
THIS DOESN'T CHANGE ANYTHING...

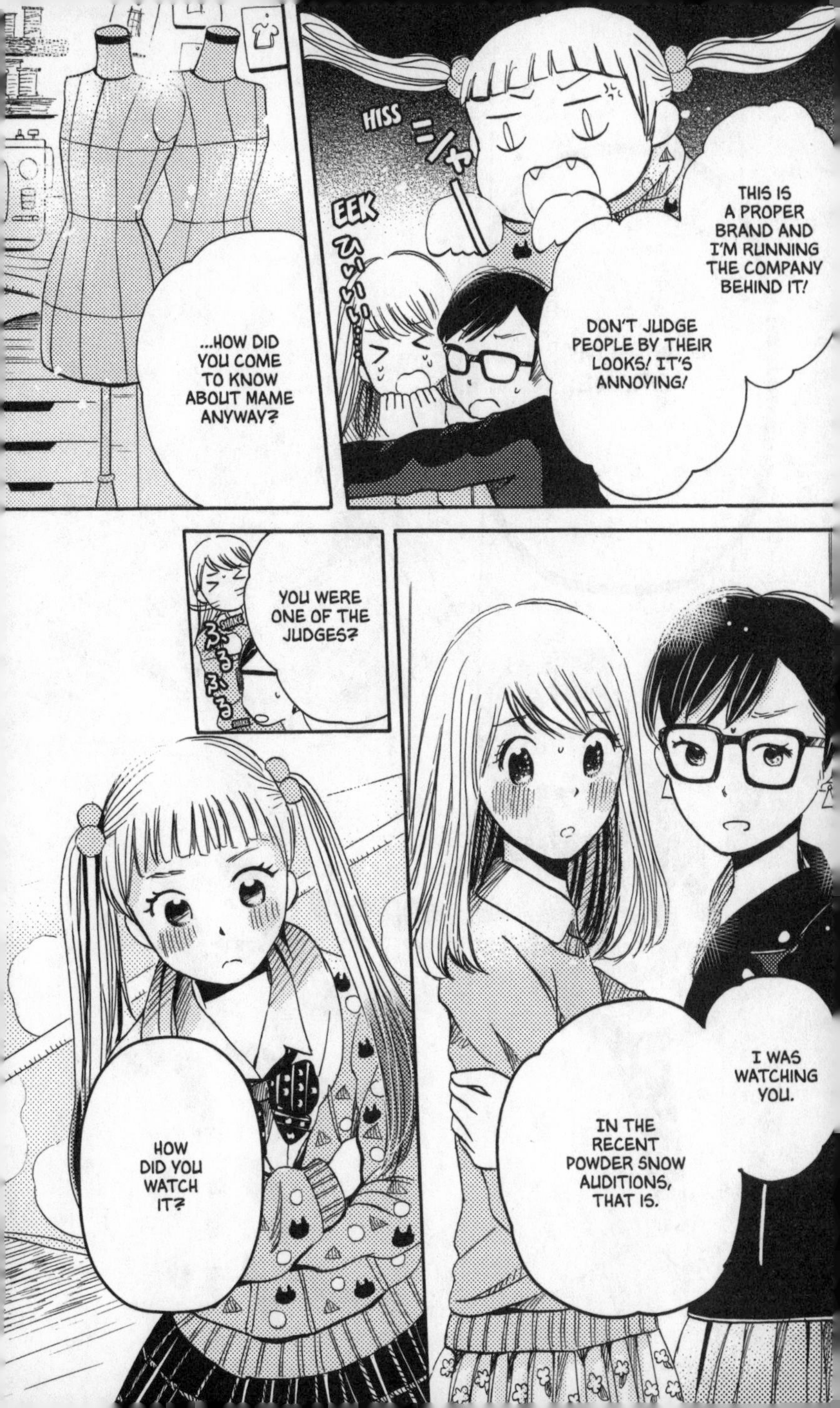
HISS
シャー
THIS IS A PROPER BRAND AND I'M RUNNING THE COMPANY BEHIND IT!
DON'T JUDGE PEOPLE BY THEIR LOOKS! IT'S ANNOYING!
EEK
...HOW DID YOU COME TO KNOW ABOUT MAME ANYWAY?
I WAS WATCHING YOU.
IN THE RECENT POWDER SNOW AUDITIONS, THAT IS.
YOU WERE ONE OF THE JUDGES?
SHAKE
ふるふる
SHAKE
HOW DID YOU WATCH IT?

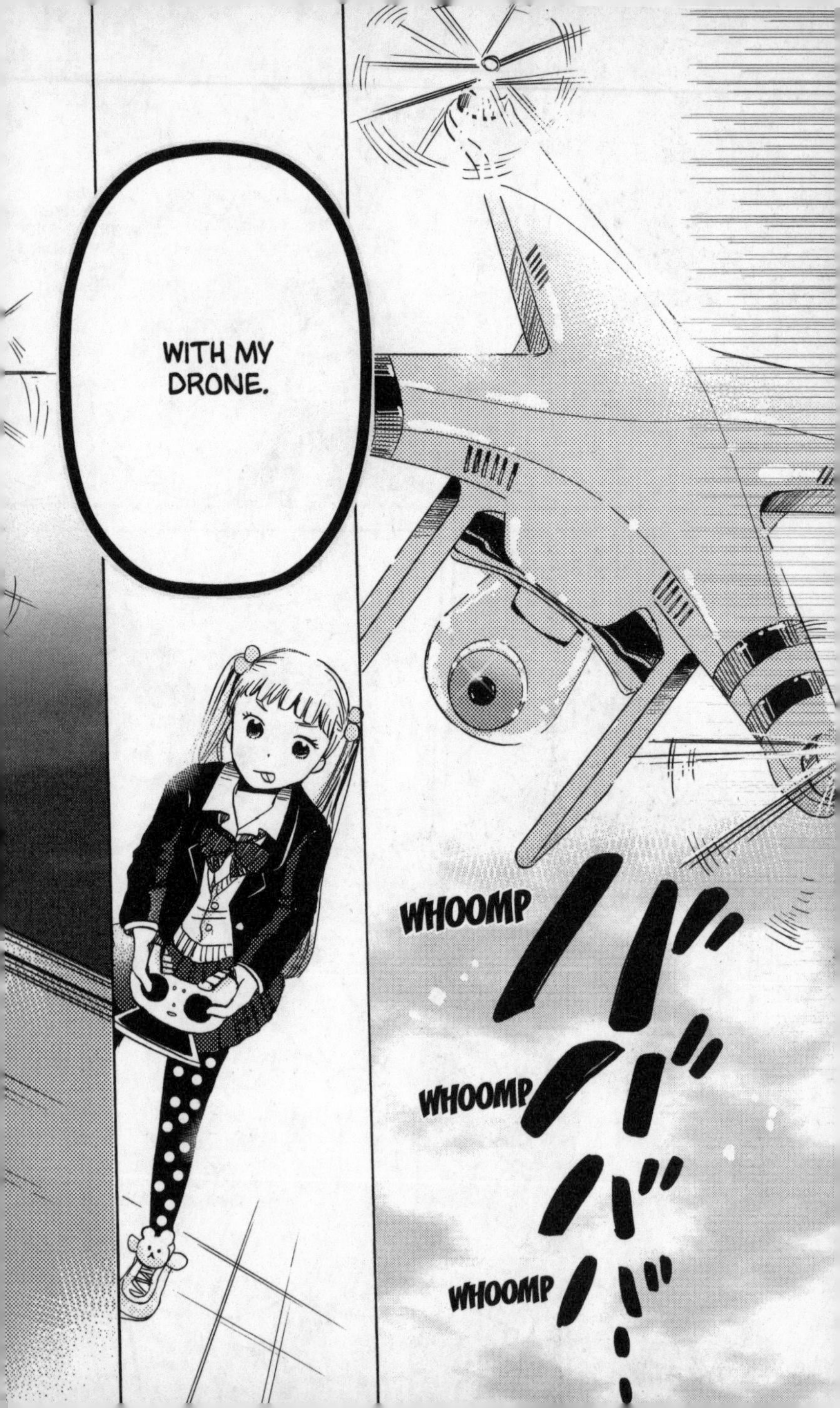
WITH MY DRONE.
WHOOMP
WHOOMP
WHOOMP

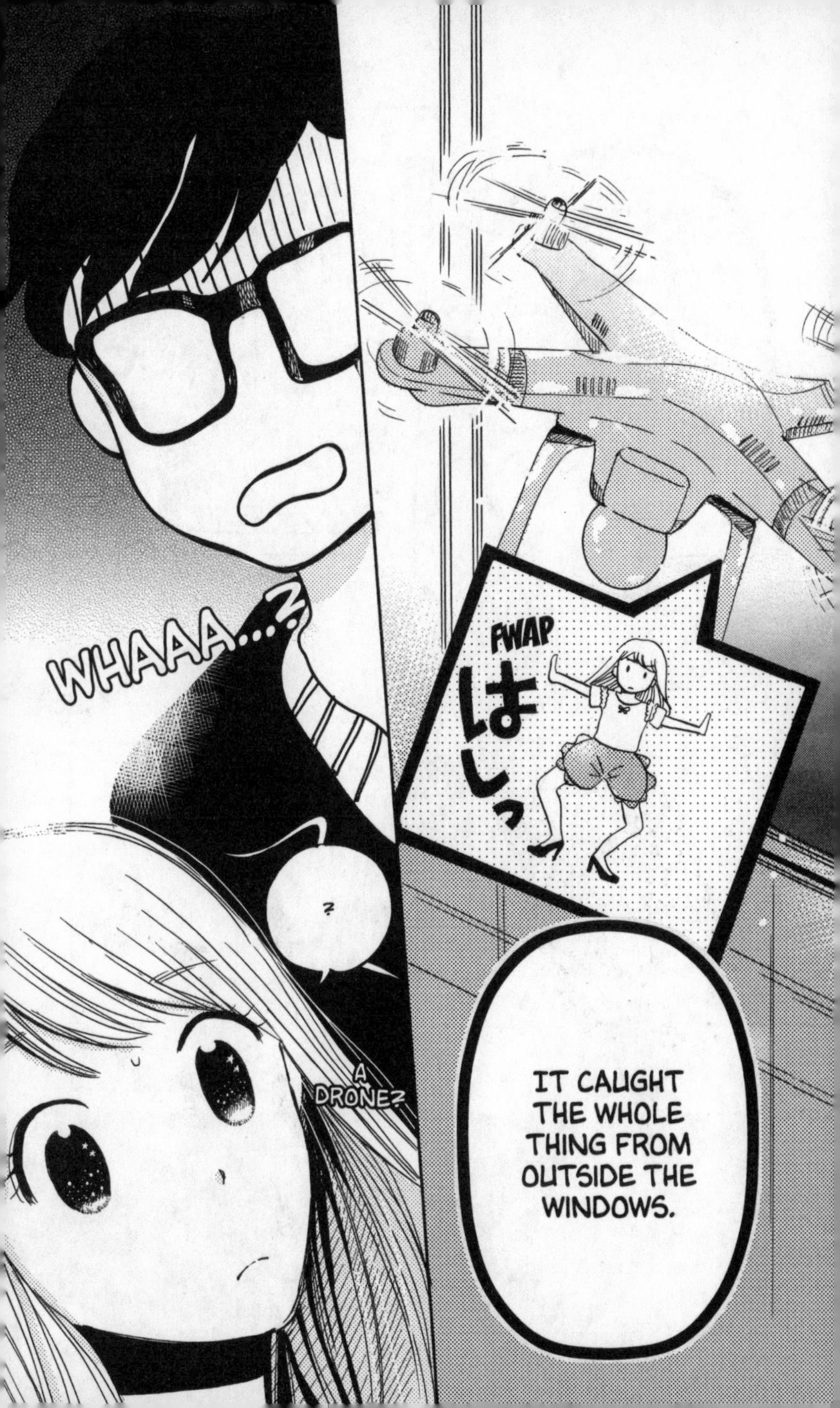

FWAP
はしっ
IT CAUGHT THE WHOLE THING FROM OUTSIDE THE WINDOWS.
WHAAA...?
?
A DRONE?

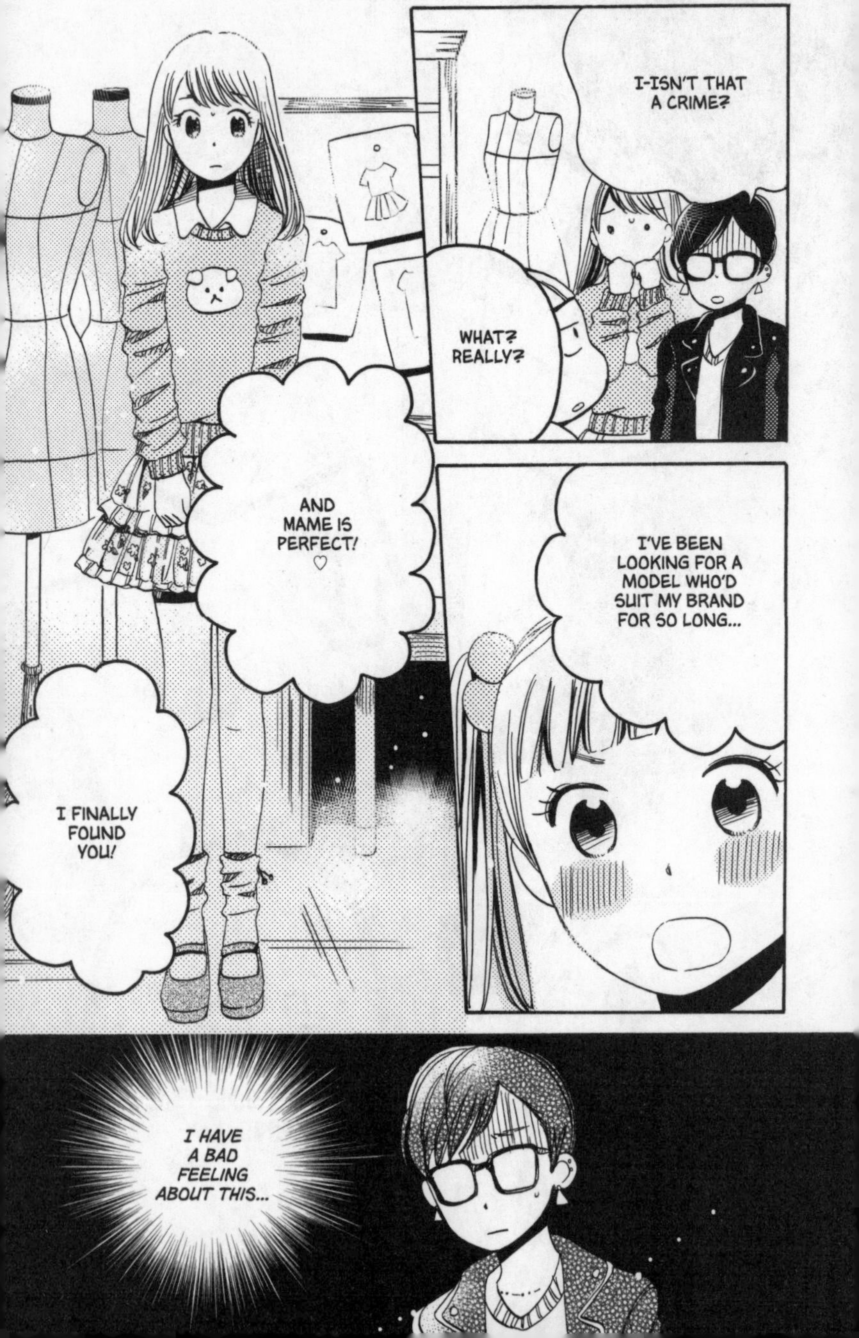

I-ISN'T THAT A CRIME?
WHAT? REALLY?
I'VE BEEN LOOKING FOR A MODEL WHO'D SUIT MY BRAND FOR SO LONG...
AND MAME IS PERFECT! ♡
I FINALLY FOUND YOU!
I HAVE A BAD FEELING ABOUT THIS...

# M A M E
## coordinate

OOTD
CORNER

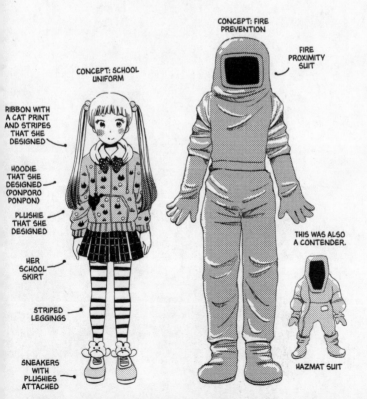

CONCEPT: FIRE PREVENTION
FIRE PROXIMITY SUIT
THIS WAS ALSO A CONTENDER.
HAZMAT SUIT
CONCEPT: SCHOOL UNIFORM
RIBBON WITH A CAT PRINT AND STRIPES THAT SHE DESIGNED
HOODIE THAT SHE DESIGNED (PONPORO PONPON)
PLUSHIE THAT SHE DESIGNED
HER SCHOOL SKIRT
STRIPED LEGGINGS
SNEAKERS WITH PLUSHIES ATTACHED

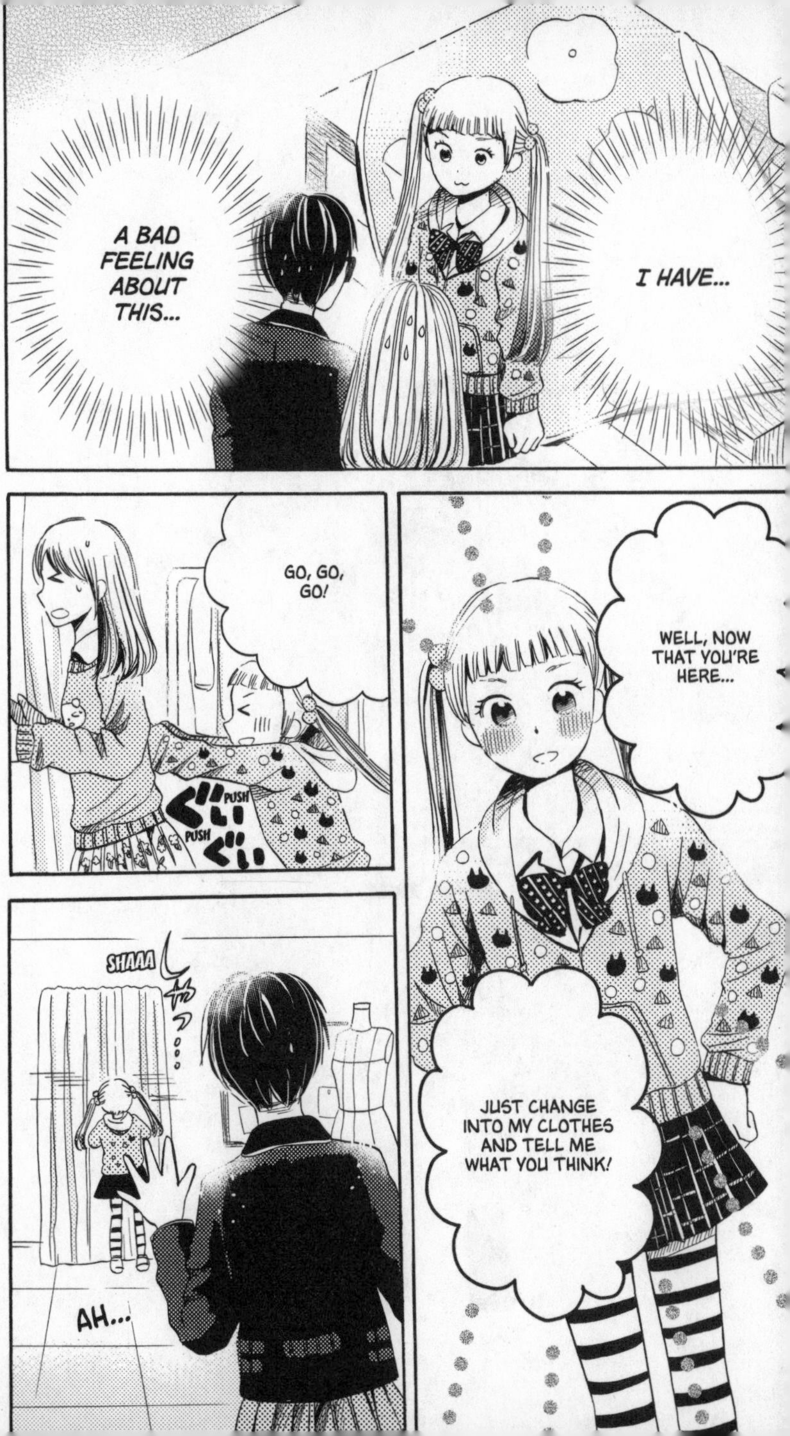
I HAVE...
A BAD FEELING ABOUT THIS...
WELL, NOW THAT YOU'RE HERE...
JUST CHANGE INTO MY CLOTHES AND TELL ME WHAT YOU THINK!
GO, GO, GO!
PUSH
PUSH
SHAAA
AH...

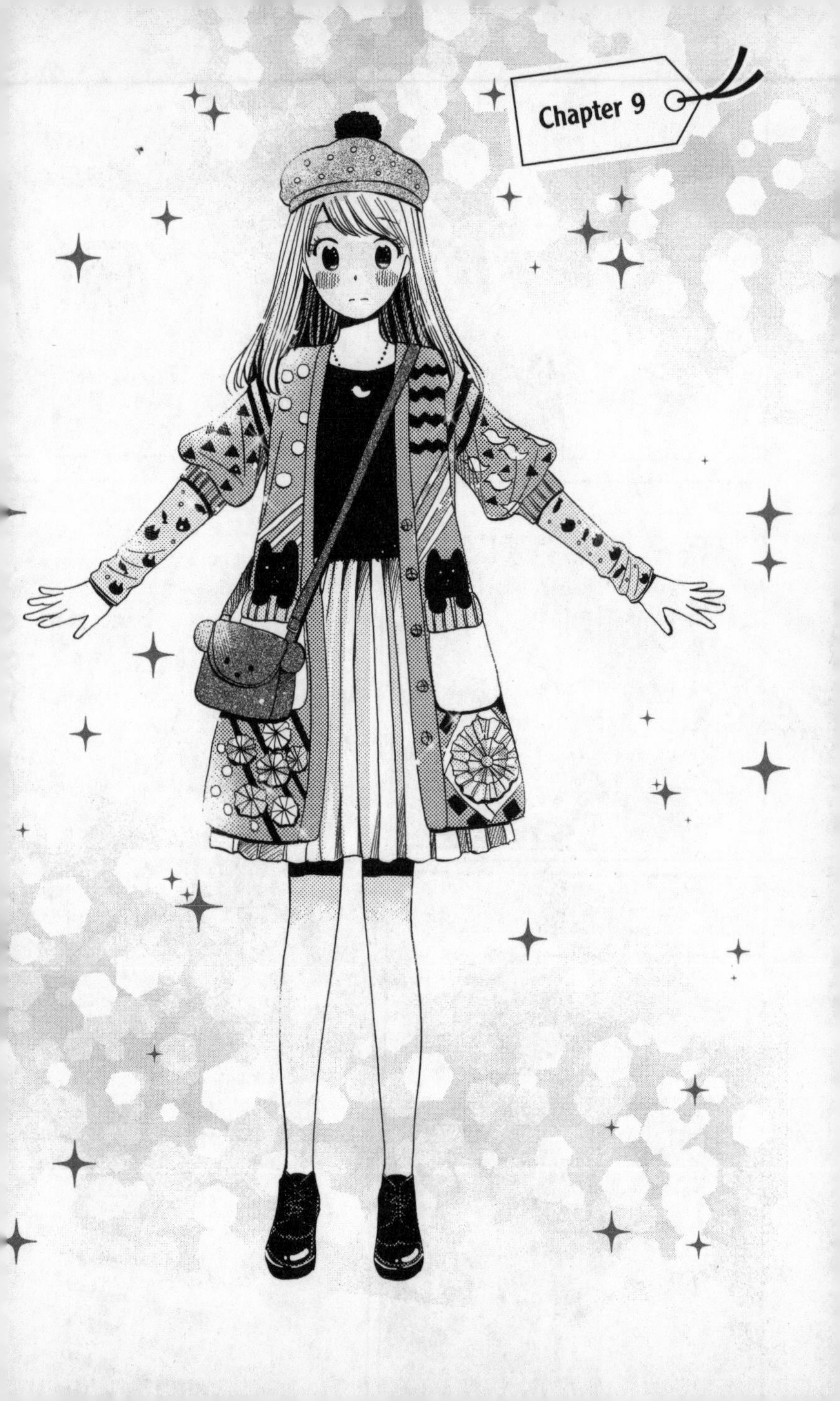
Chapter 9

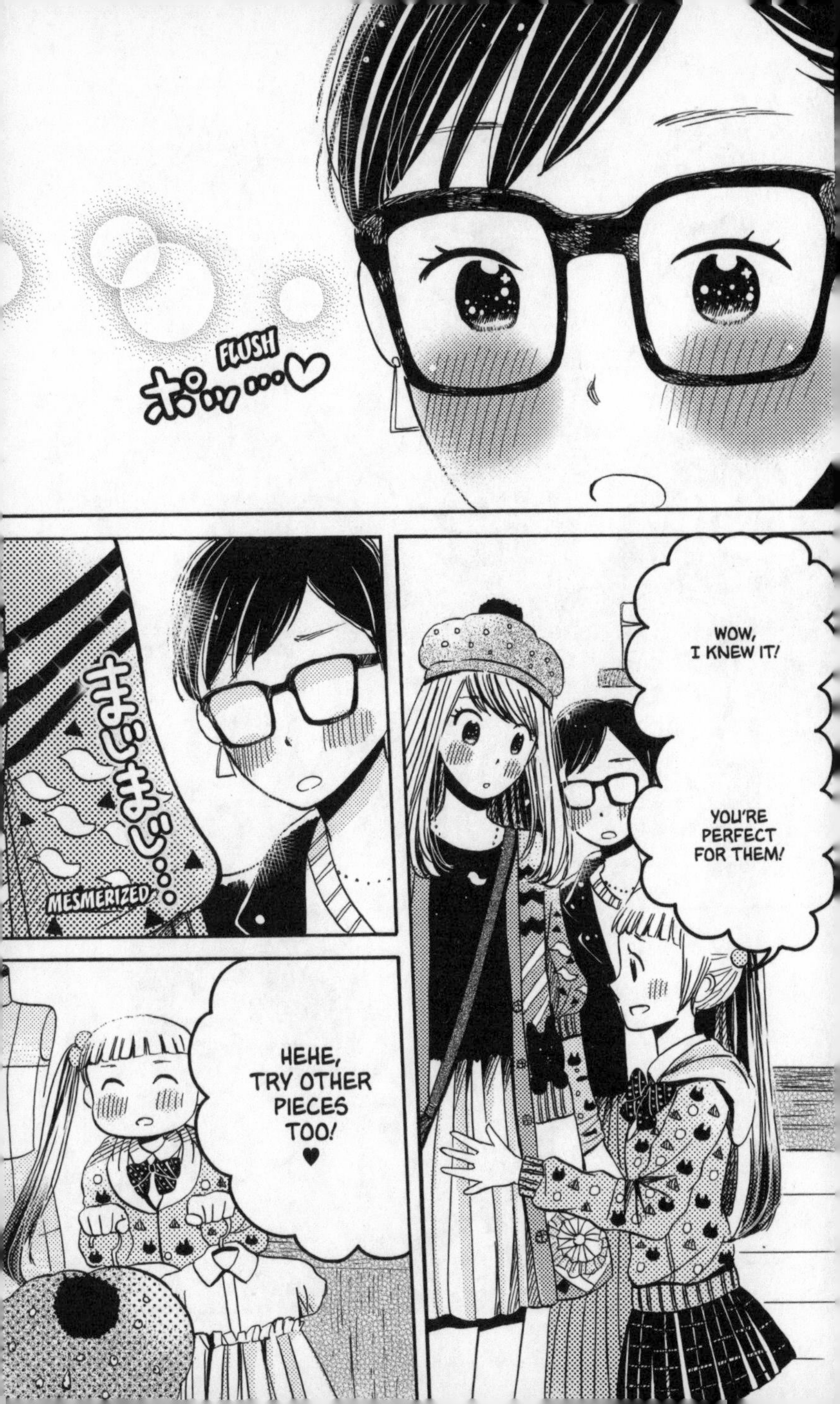

FLUSH
ポッ…♡
WOW, I KNEW IT!
YOU'RE PERFECT FOR THEM!
まじまじ…
MESMERIZED
HEHE, TRY OTHER PIECES TOO! ♥

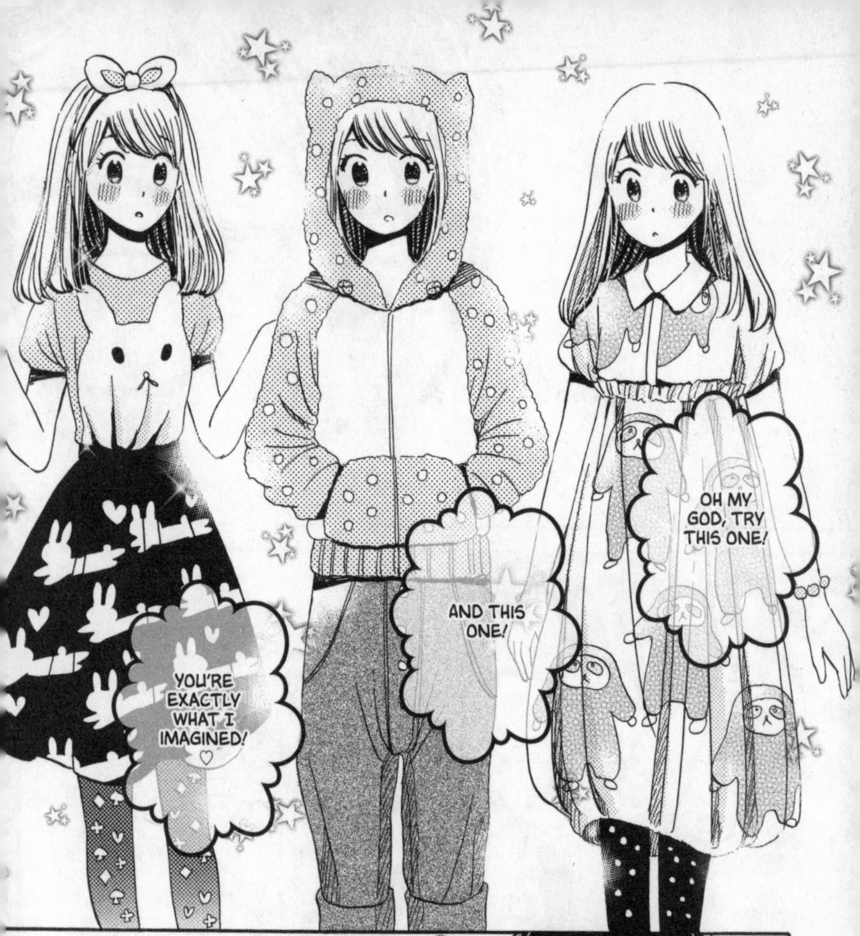
OH MY GOD, TRY THIS ONE!
AND THIS ONE!
YOU'RE EXACTLY WHAT I IMAGINED! ♡

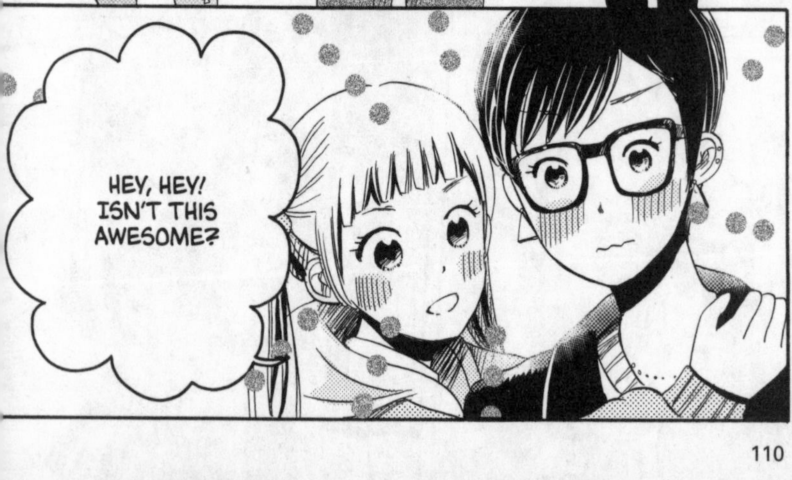
HEY, HEY! ISN'T THIS AWESOME?

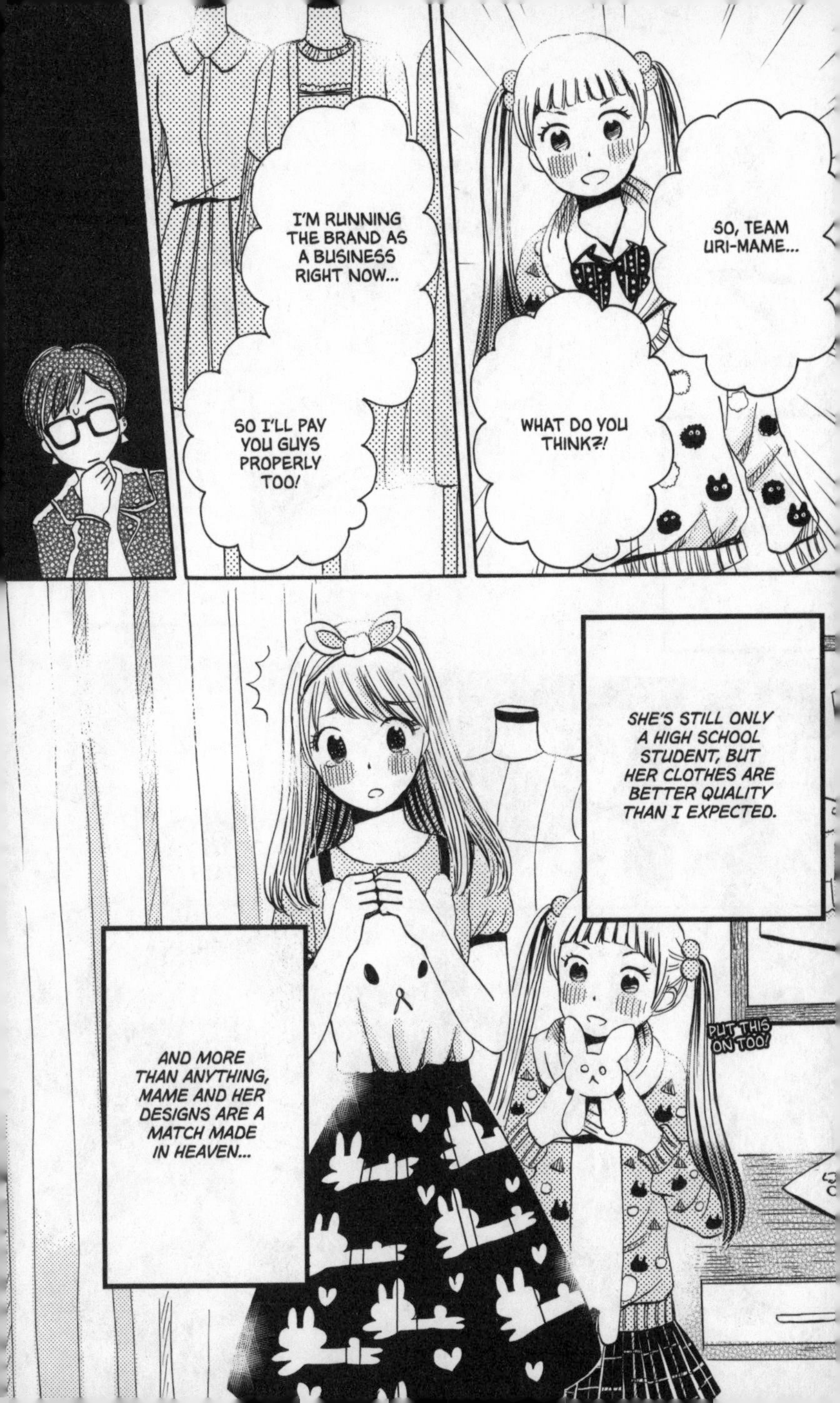
SO, TEAM URI-MAME...
WHAT DO YOU THINK?!
I'M RUNNING THE BRAND AS A BUSINESS RIGHT NOW...
SO I'LL PAY YOU GUYS PROPERLY TOO!
SHE'S STILL ONLY A HIGH SCHOOL STUDENT, BUT HER CLOTHES ARE BETTER QUALITY THAN I EXPECTED.
PUT THIS ON TOO!
AND MORE THAN ANYTHING, MAME AND HER DESIGNS ARE A MATCH MADE IN HEAVEN...

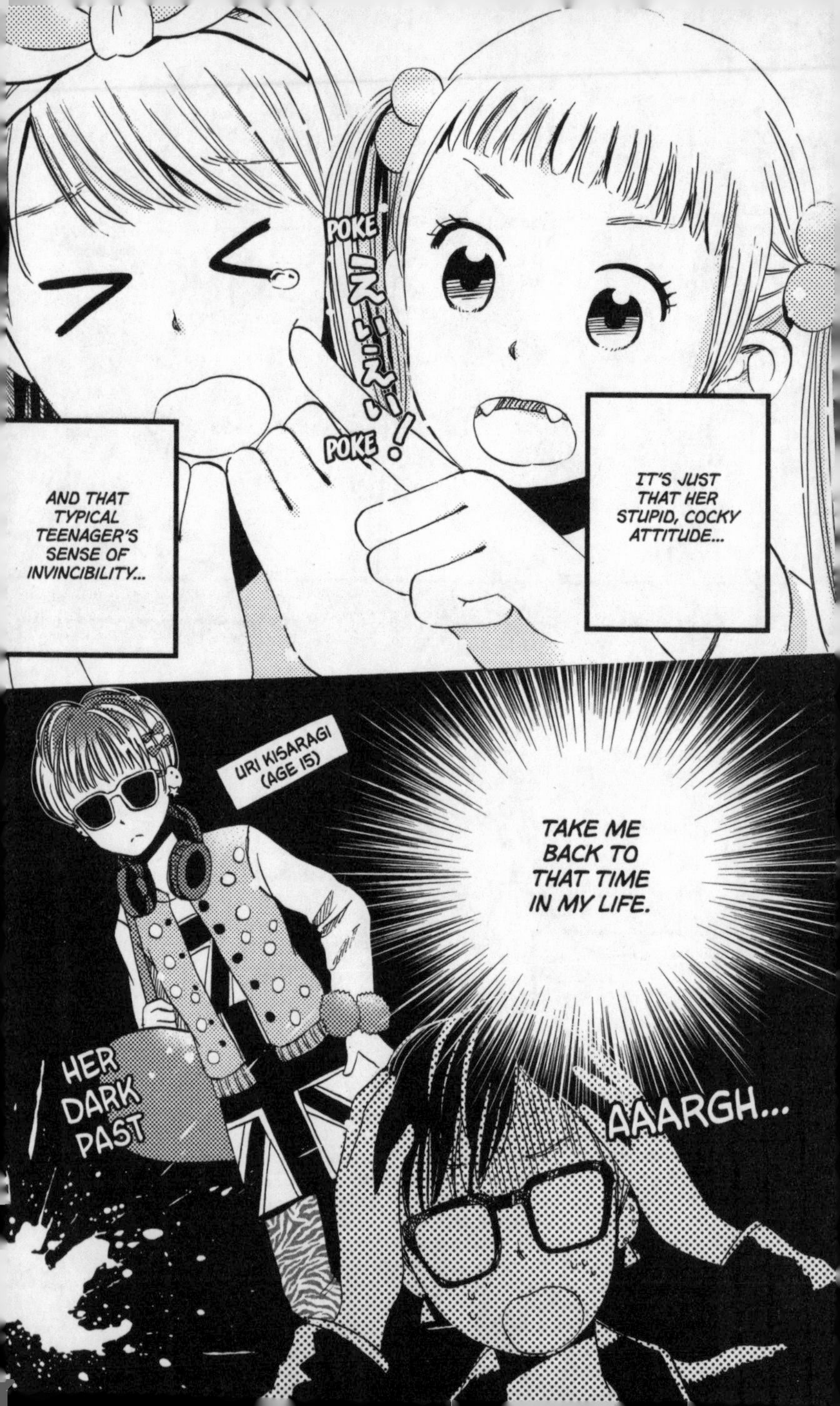
POKE
えいえい!
POKE
IT'S JUST THAT HER STUPID, COCKY ATTITUDE...
AND THAT TYPICAL TEENAGER'S SENSE OF INVINCIBILITY...
TAKE ME BACK TO THAT TIME IN MY LIFE.
URI KISARAGI (AGE 15)
AAARGH...
HER DARK PAST

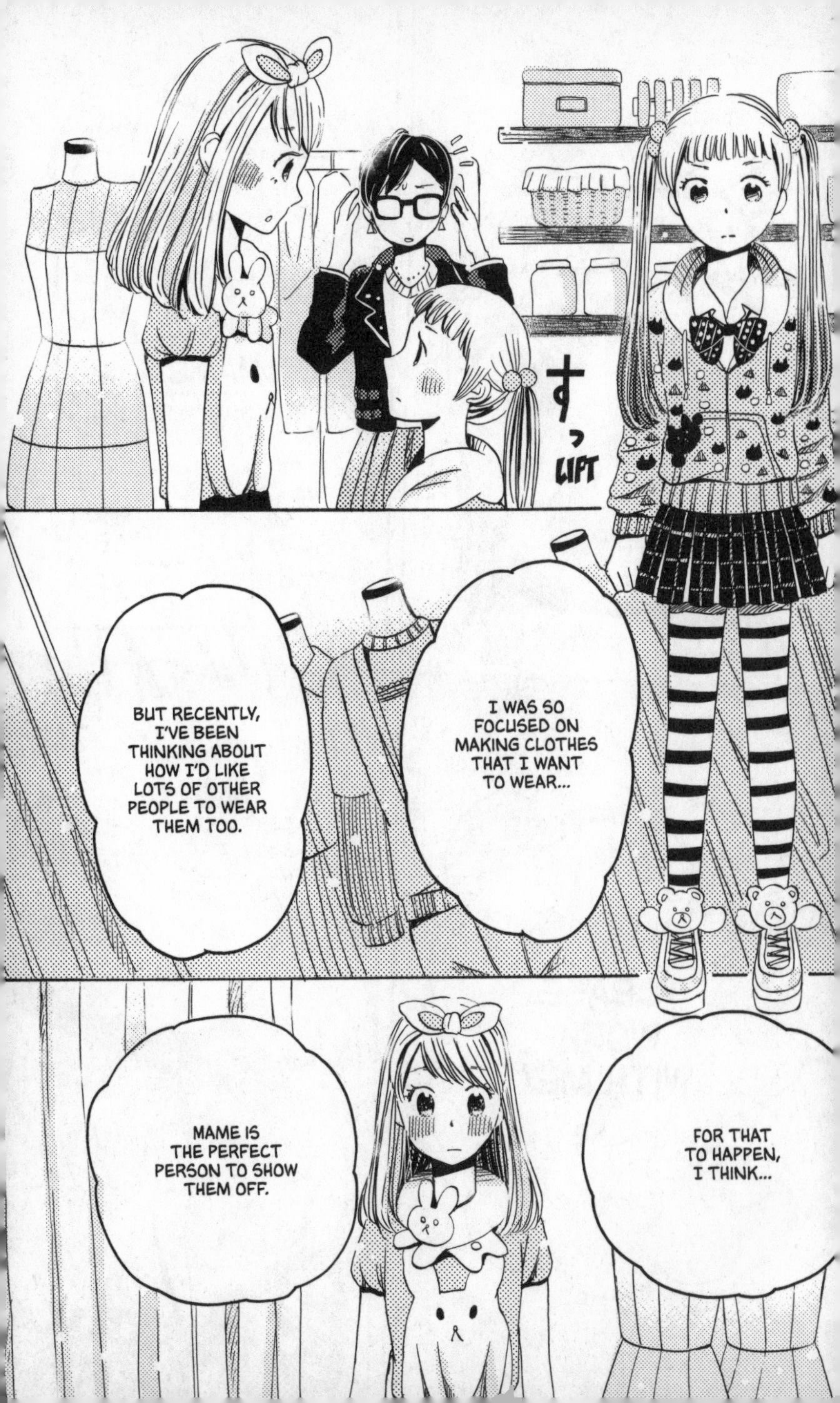

すっ
LIFT
I WAS SO FOCUSED ON MAKING CLOTHES THAT I WANT TO WEAR...
BUT RECENTLY, I'VE BEEN THINKING ABOUT HOW I'D LIKE LOTS OF OTHER PEOPLE TO WEAR THEM TOO.
FOR THAT TO HAPPEN, I THINK...
MAME IS THE PERFECT PERSON TO SHOW THEM OFF.

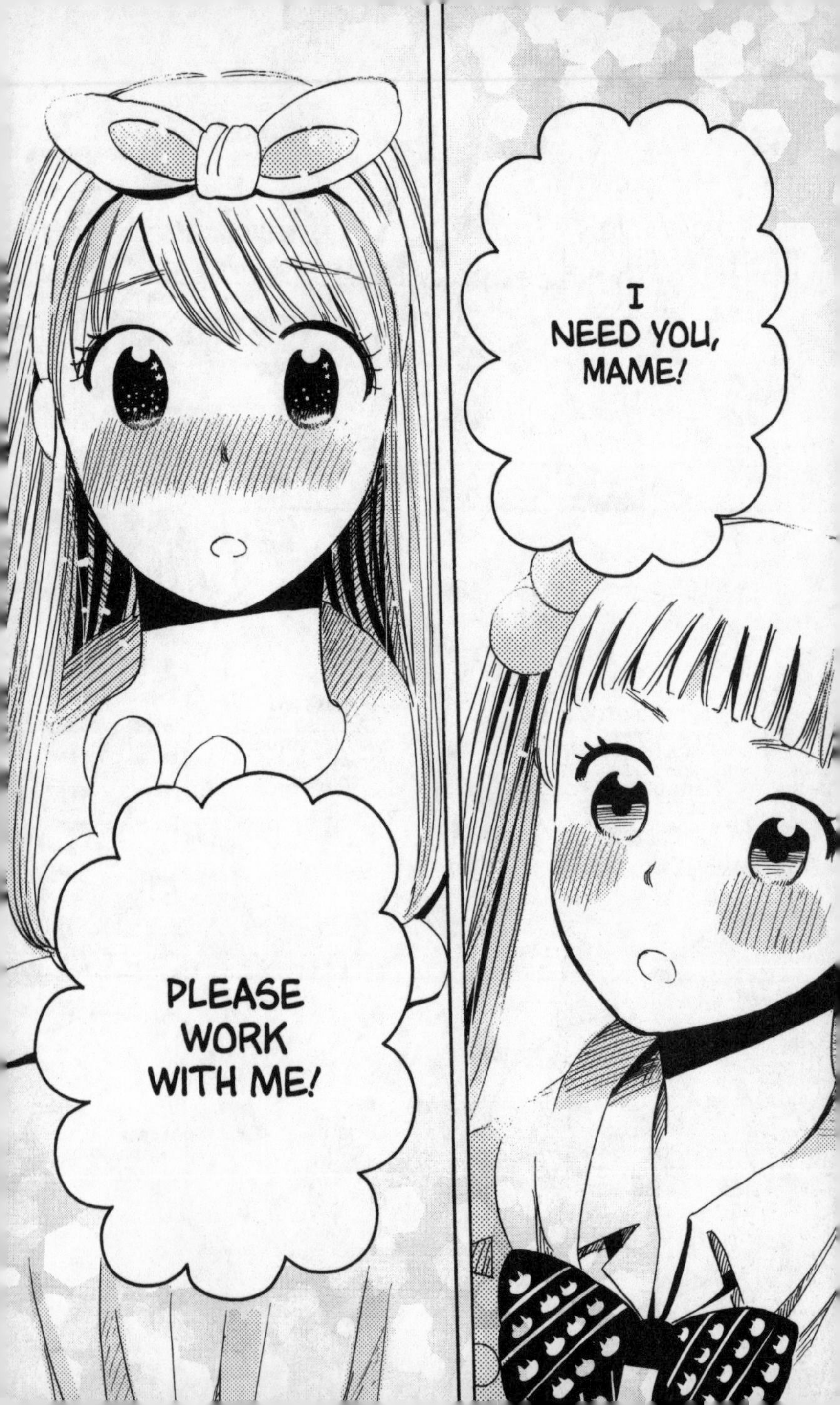
I NEED YOU, MAME!
PLEASE WORK WITH ME!

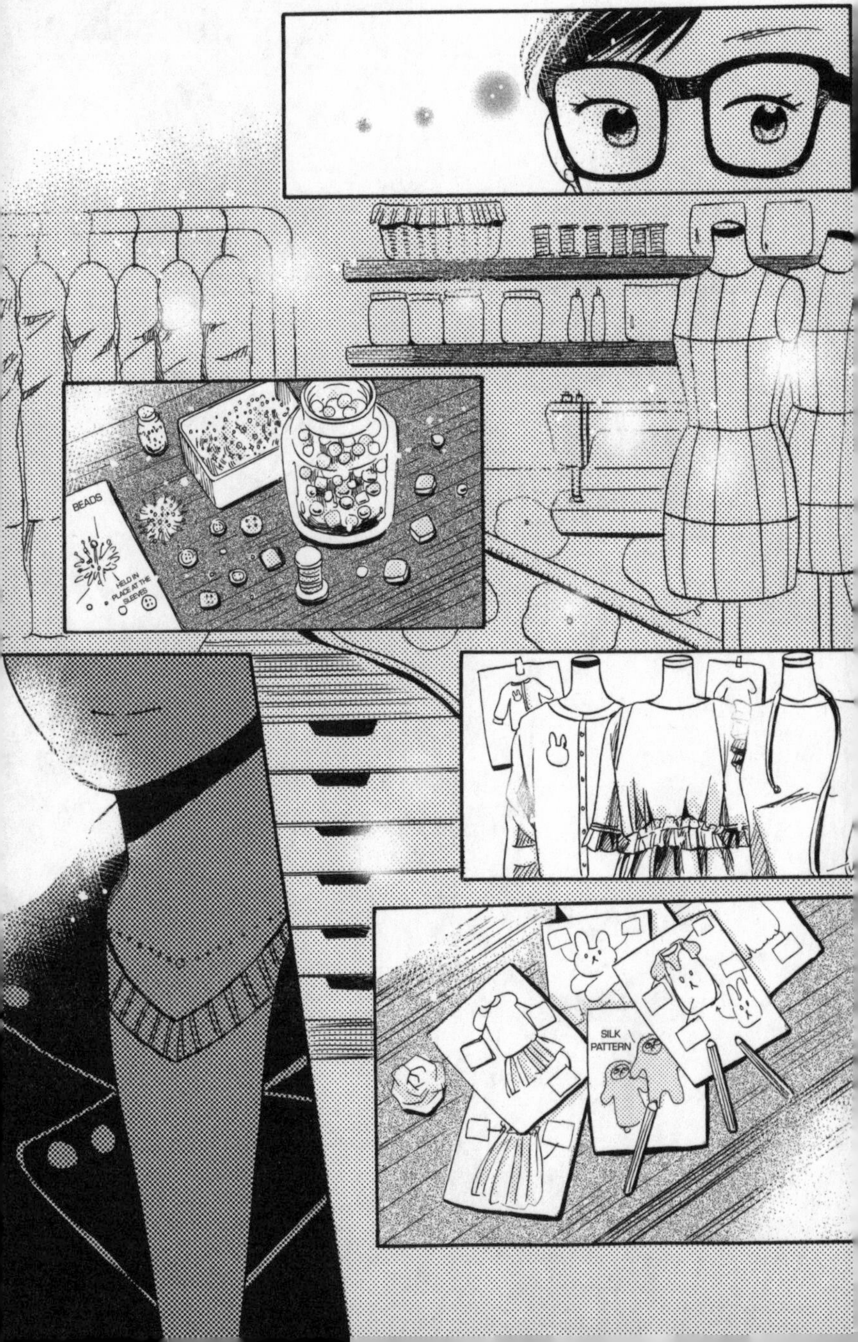
BEADS
HELD IN PLACE AT THE SLEEVES
SILK PATTERN

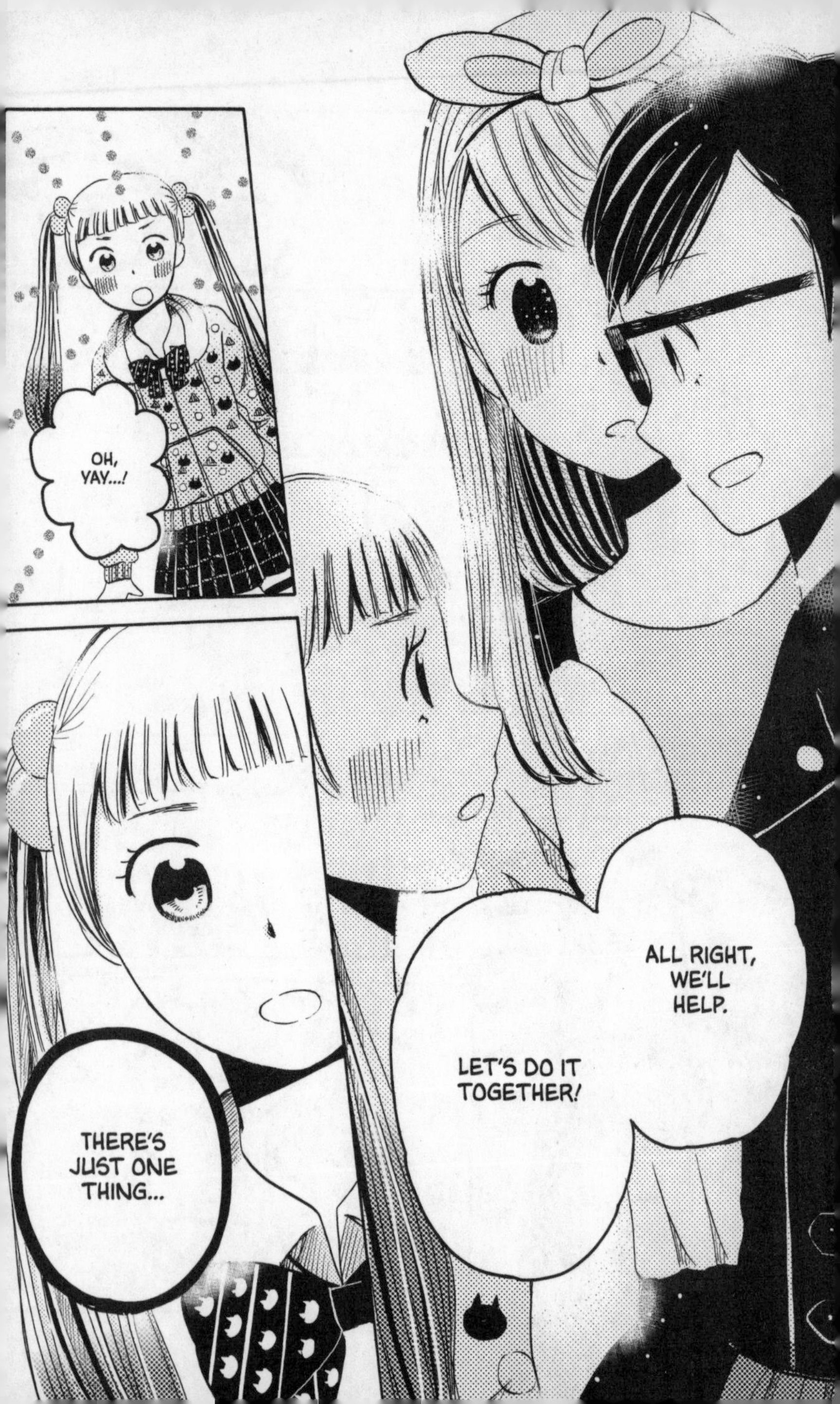
ALL RIGHT, WE'LL HELP.
LET'S DO IT TOGETHER!
OH, YAY...!
THERE'S JUST ONE THING...

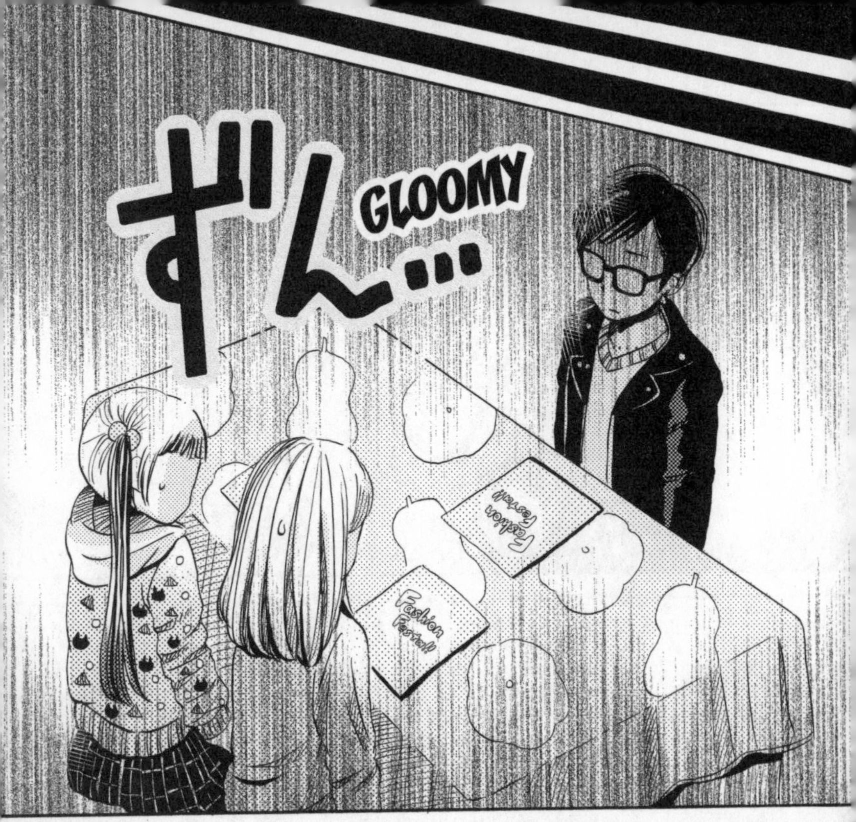
ずん...
GLOOMY
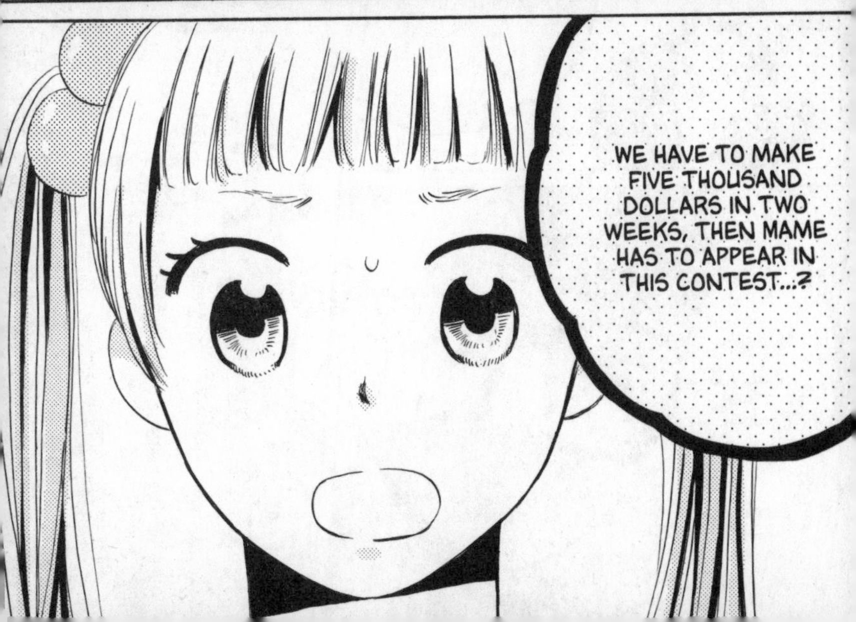
WE HAVE TO MAKE FIVE THOUSAND DOLLARS IN TWO WEEKS, THEN MAME HAS TO APPEAR IN THIS CONTEST...?

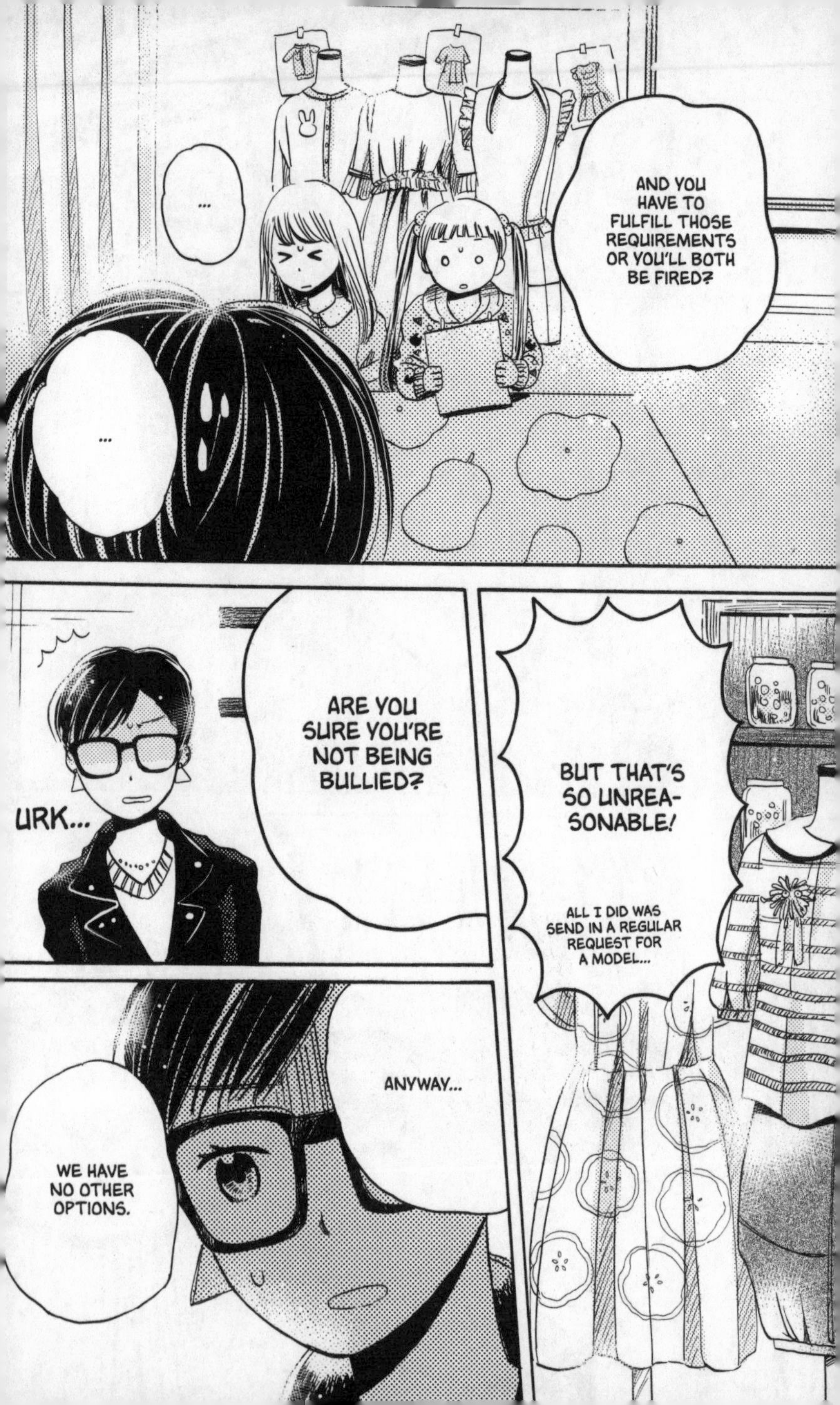
AND YOU HAVE TO FULFILL THOSE REQUIREMENTS OR YOU'LL BOTH BE FIRED?
...
...
BUT THAT'S SO UNREA-SONABLE!
ALL I DID WAS SEND IN A REGULAR REQUEST FOR A MODEL...
ARE YOU SURE YOU'RE NOT BEING BULLIED?
URK...
ANYWAY...
WE HAVE NO OTHER OPTIONS.

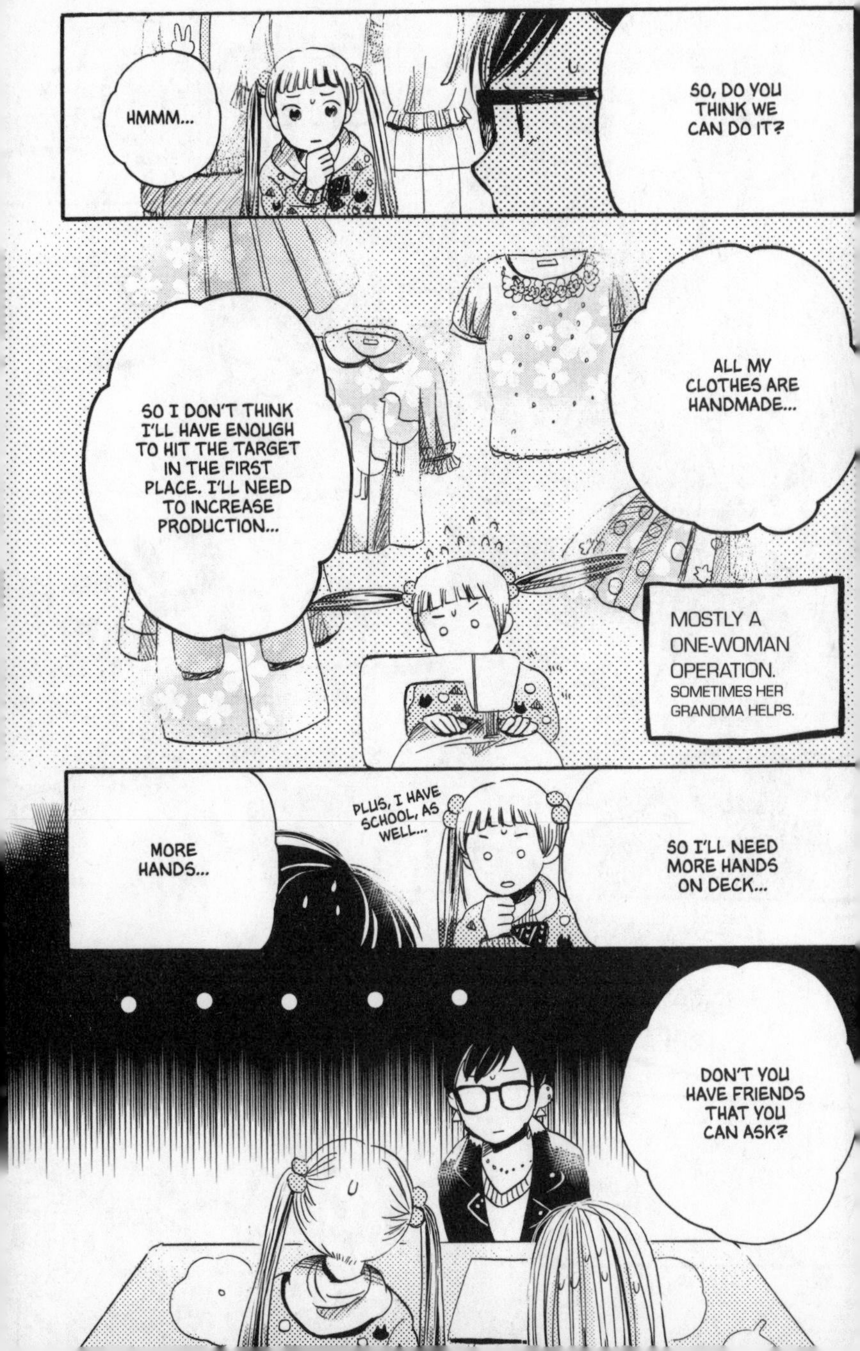

SO, DO YOU THINK WE CAN DO IT?
HMMM...
ALL MY CLOTHES ARE HANDMADE...
SO I DON'T THINK I'LL HAVE ENOUGH TO HIT THE TARGET IN THE FIRST PLACE. I'LL NEED TO INCREASE PRODUCTION...
MOSTLY A ONE-WOMAN OPERATION. SOMETIMES HER GRANDMA HELPS.
SO I'LL NEED MORE HANDS ON DECK...
PLUS, I HAVE SCHOOL, AS WELL...
MORE HANDS...
DON'T YOU HAVE FRIENDS THAT YOU CAN ASK?

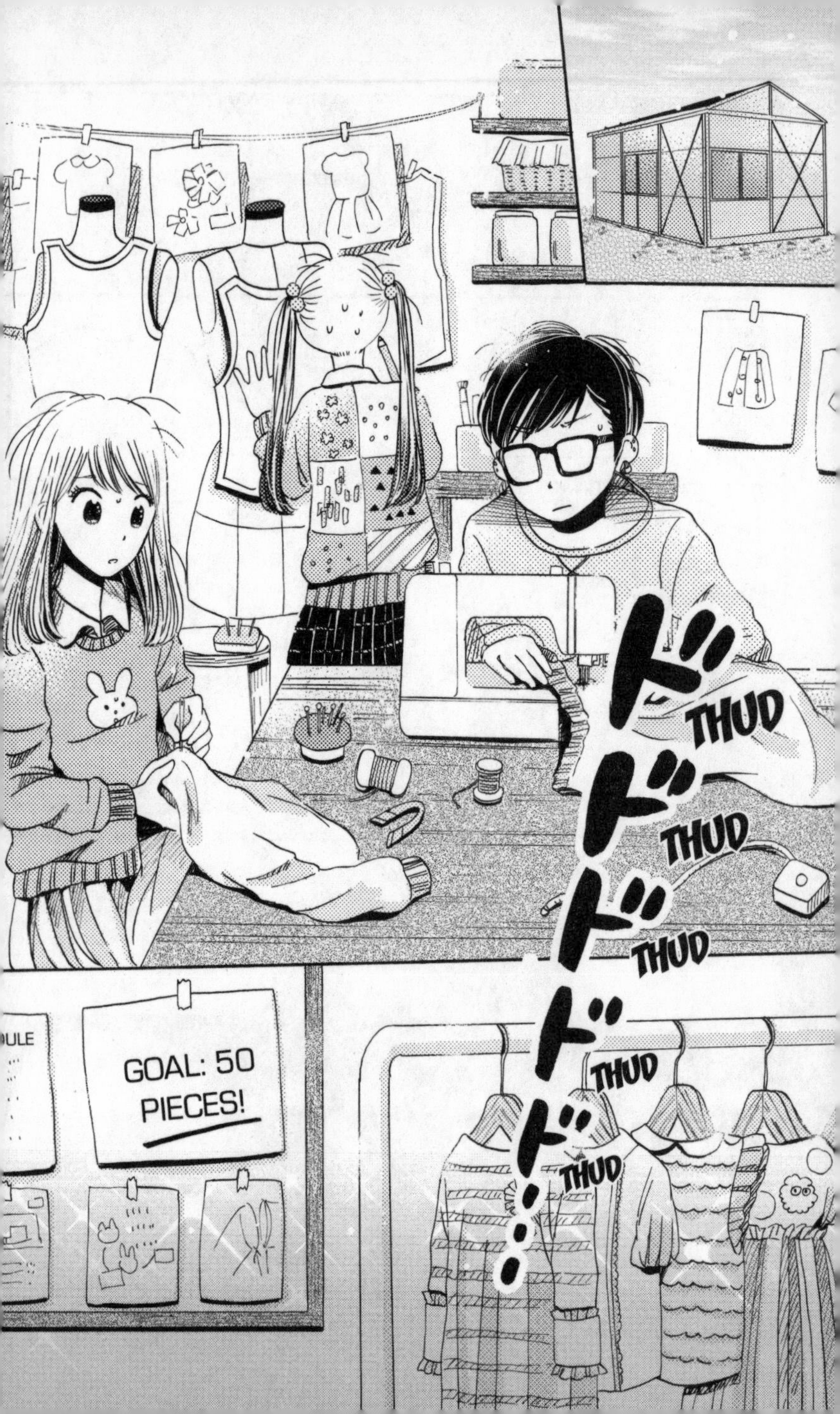ドドドドド…
THUD
THUD
THUD
THUD
THUD
GOAL: 50
PIECES!
DULE

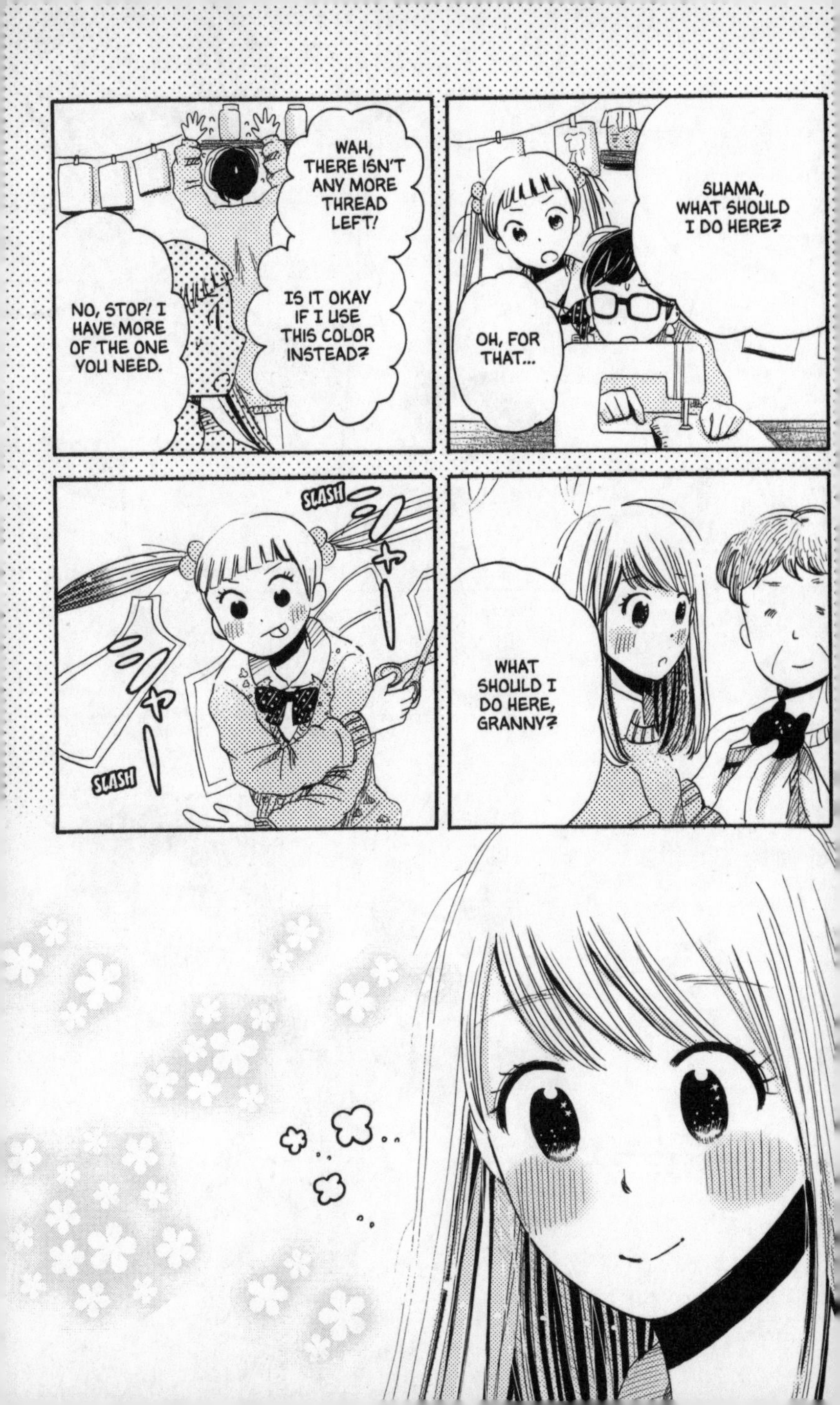
SUAMA, WHAT SHOULD I DO HERE?
OH, FOR THAT...
WAH, THERE ISN'T ANY MORE THREAD LEFT!
IS IT OKAY IF I USE THIS COLOR INSTEAD?
NO, STOP! I HAVE MORE OF THE ONE YOU NEED.
WHAT SHOULD I DO HERE, GRANNY?
SLASH
SLASH

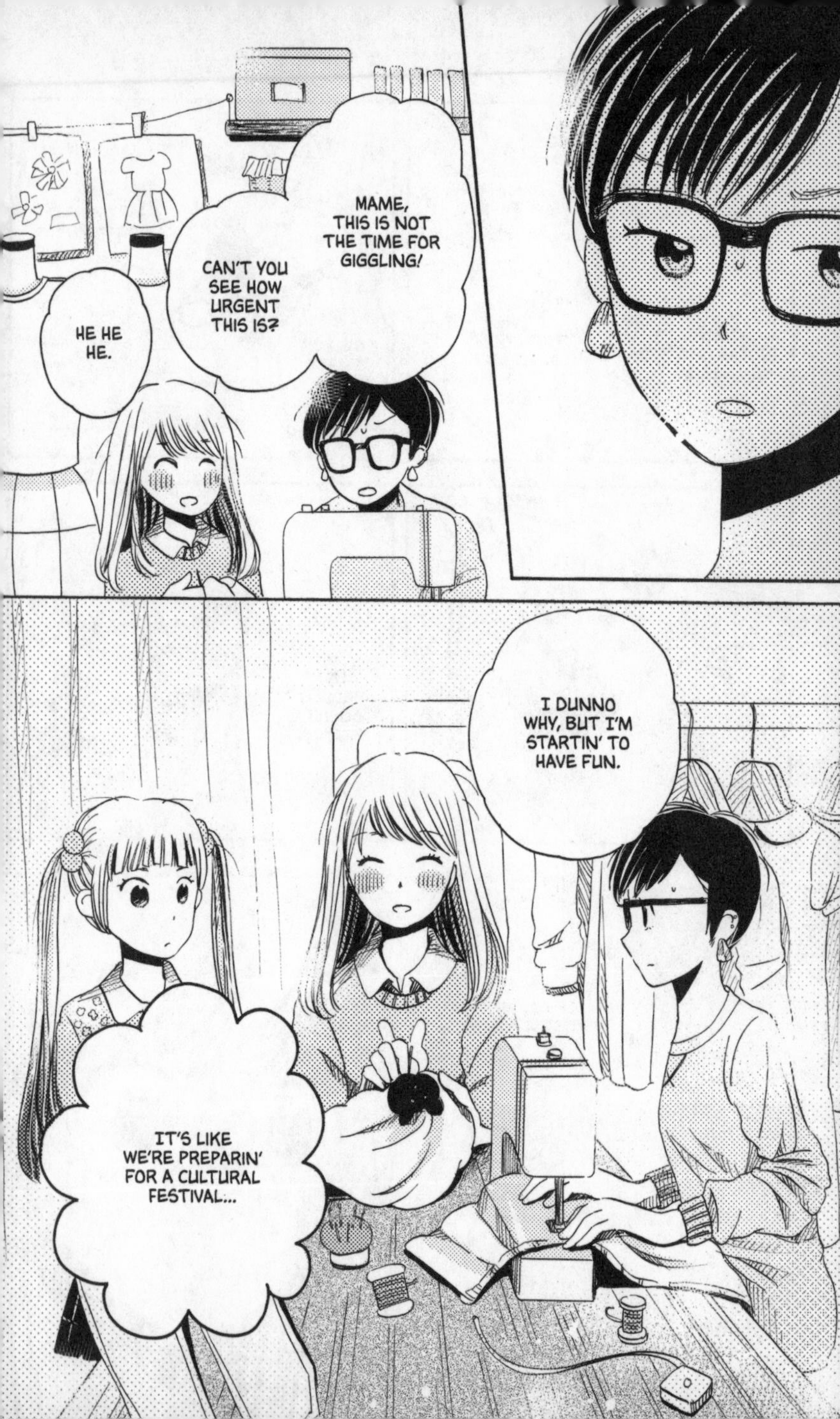
MAME, THIS IS NOT THE TIME FOR GIGGLING!
CAN'T YOU SEE HOW URGENT THIS IS?
HE HE HE.
I DUNNO WHY, BUT I'M STARTIN' TO HAVE FUN.
IT'S LIKE WE'RE PREPARIN' FOR A CULTURAL FESTIVAL...

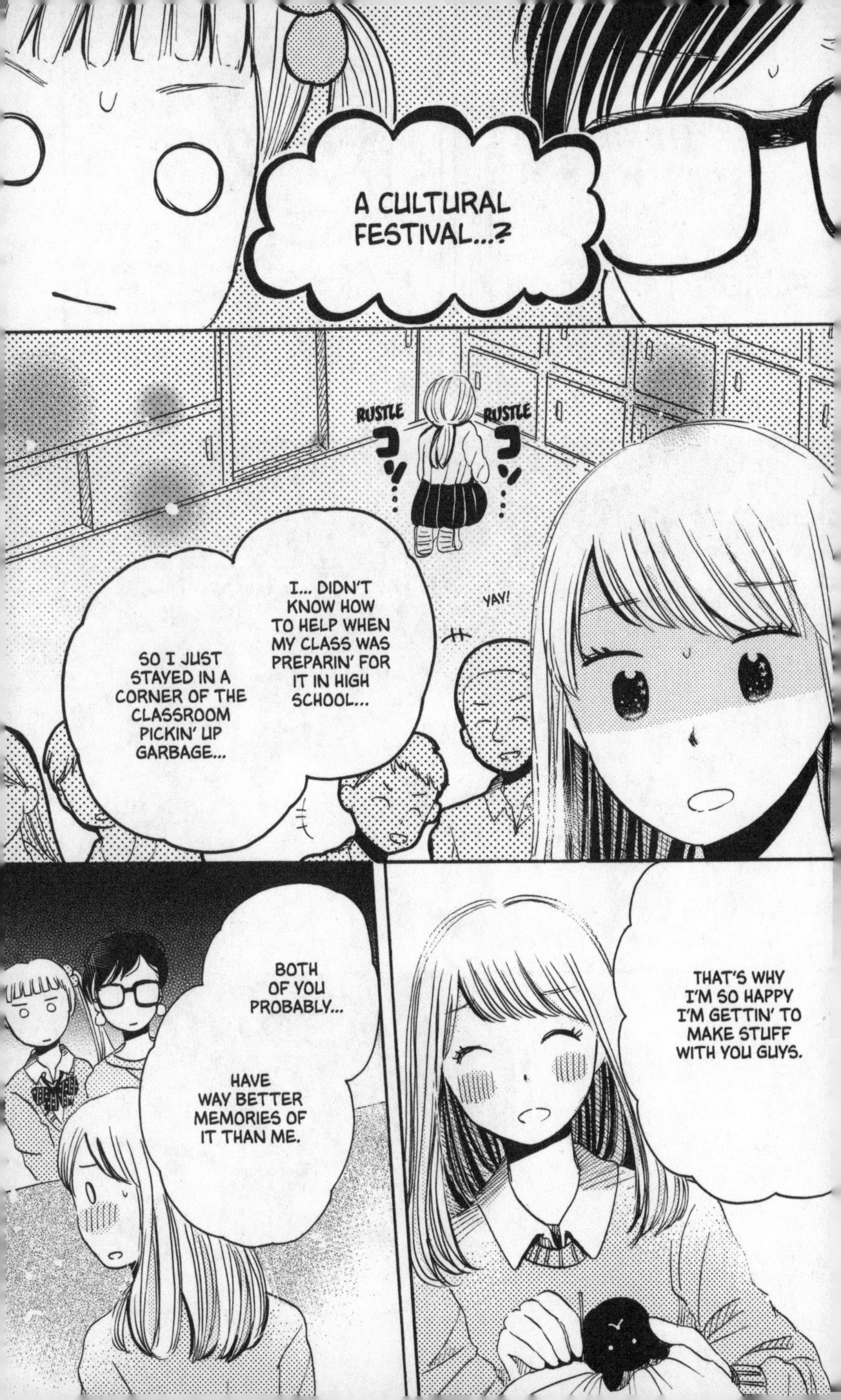
A CULTURAL FESTIVAL...?
RUSTLE
RUSTLE
YAY!
I... DIDN'T KNOW HOW TO HELP WHEN MY CLASS WAS PREPARIN' FOR IT IN HIGH SCHOOL...
SO I JUST STAYED IN A CORNER OF THE CLASSROOM PICKIN' UP GARBAGE...
THAT'S WHY I'M SO HAPPY I'M GETTIN' TO MAKE STUFF WITH YOU GUYS.
BOTH OF YOU PROBABLY...
HAVE WAY BETTER MEMORIES OF IT THAN ME.

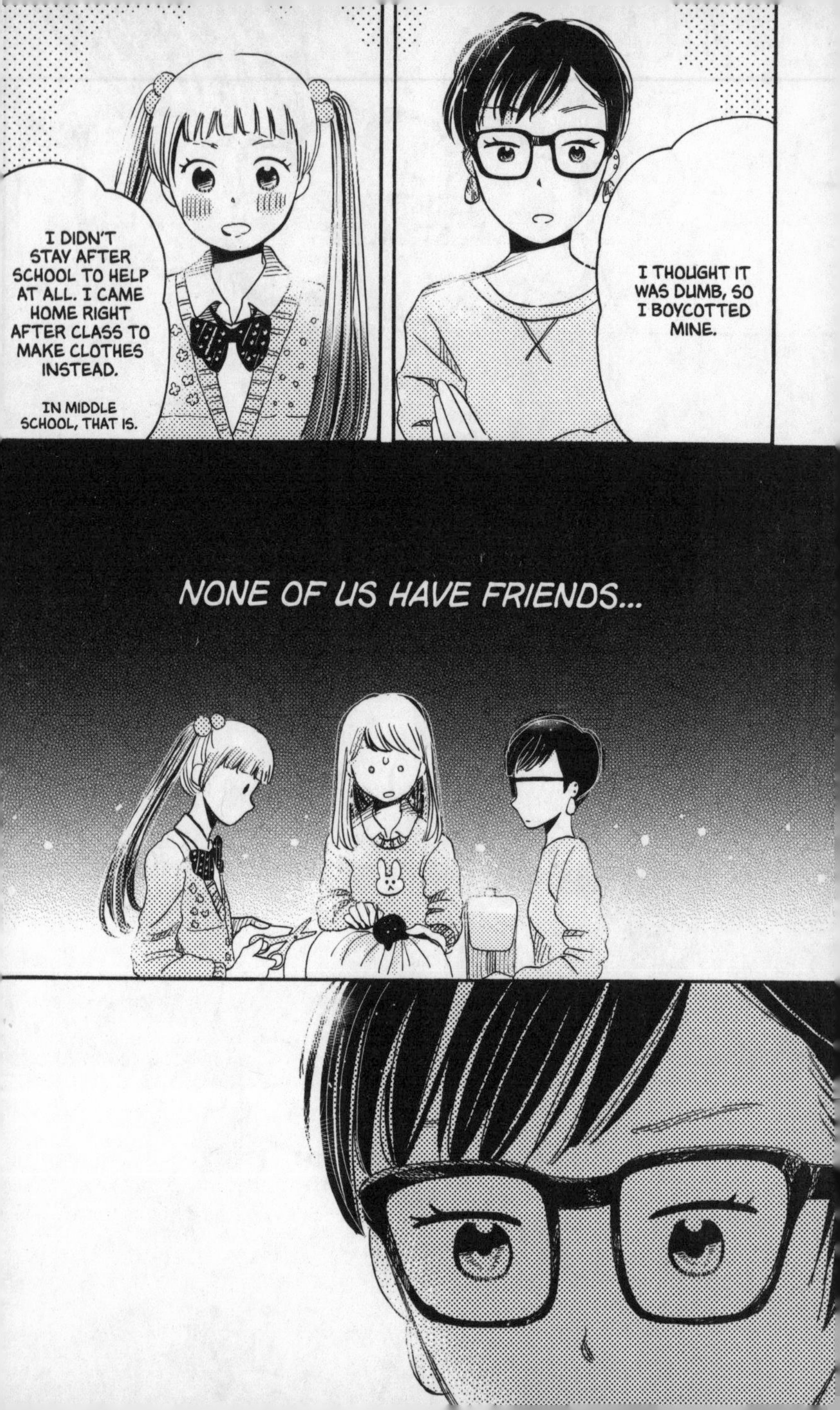
I THOUGHT IT WAS DUMB, SO I BOYCOTTED MINE.
I DIDN'T STAY AFTER SCHOOL TO HELP AT ALL. I CAME HOME RIGHT AFTER CLASS TO MAKE CLOTHES INSTEAD.
IN MIDDLE SCHOOL, THAT IS.
NONE OF US HAVE FRIENDS...

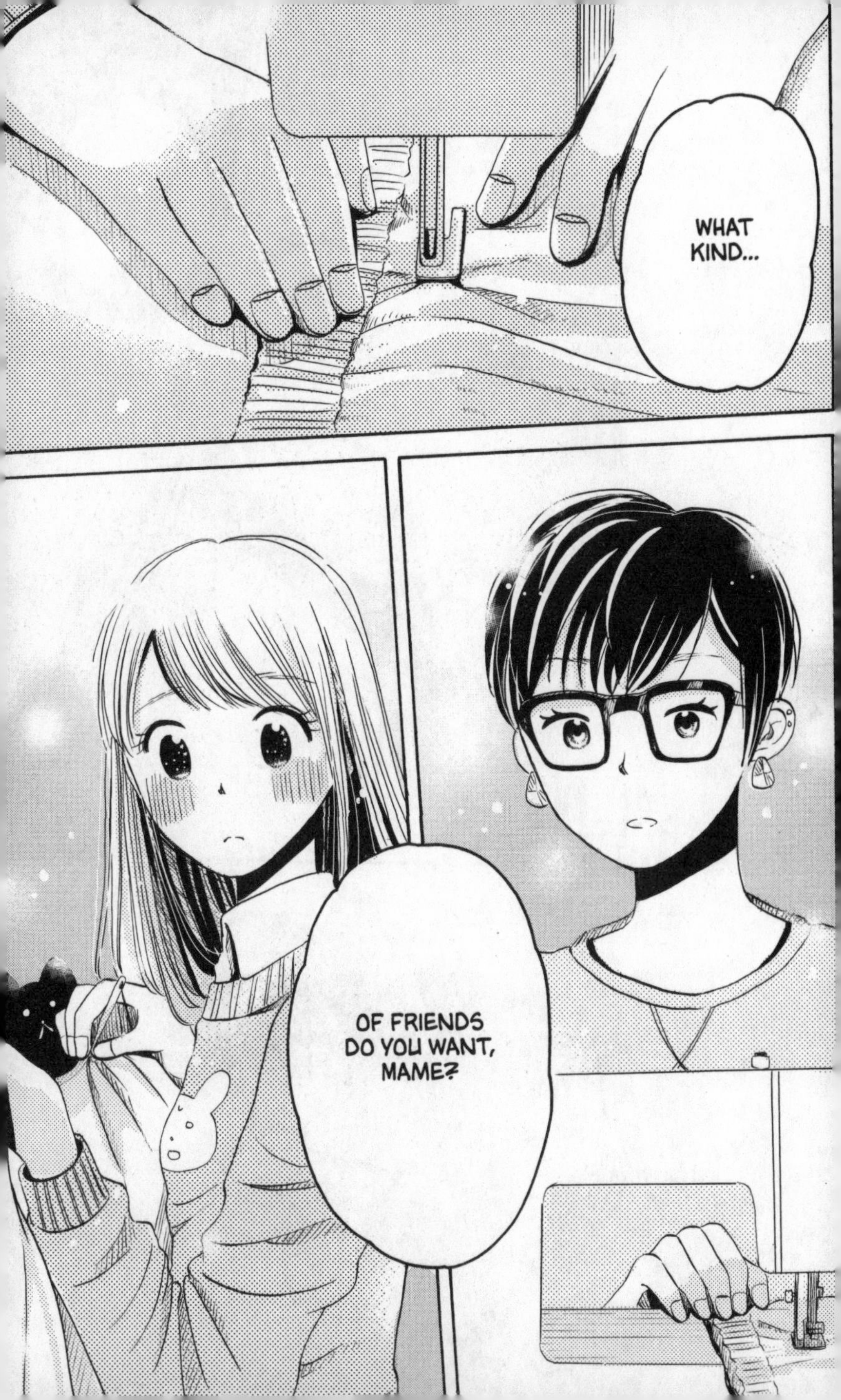
WHAT KIND...
OF FRIENDS DO YOU WANT, MAME?

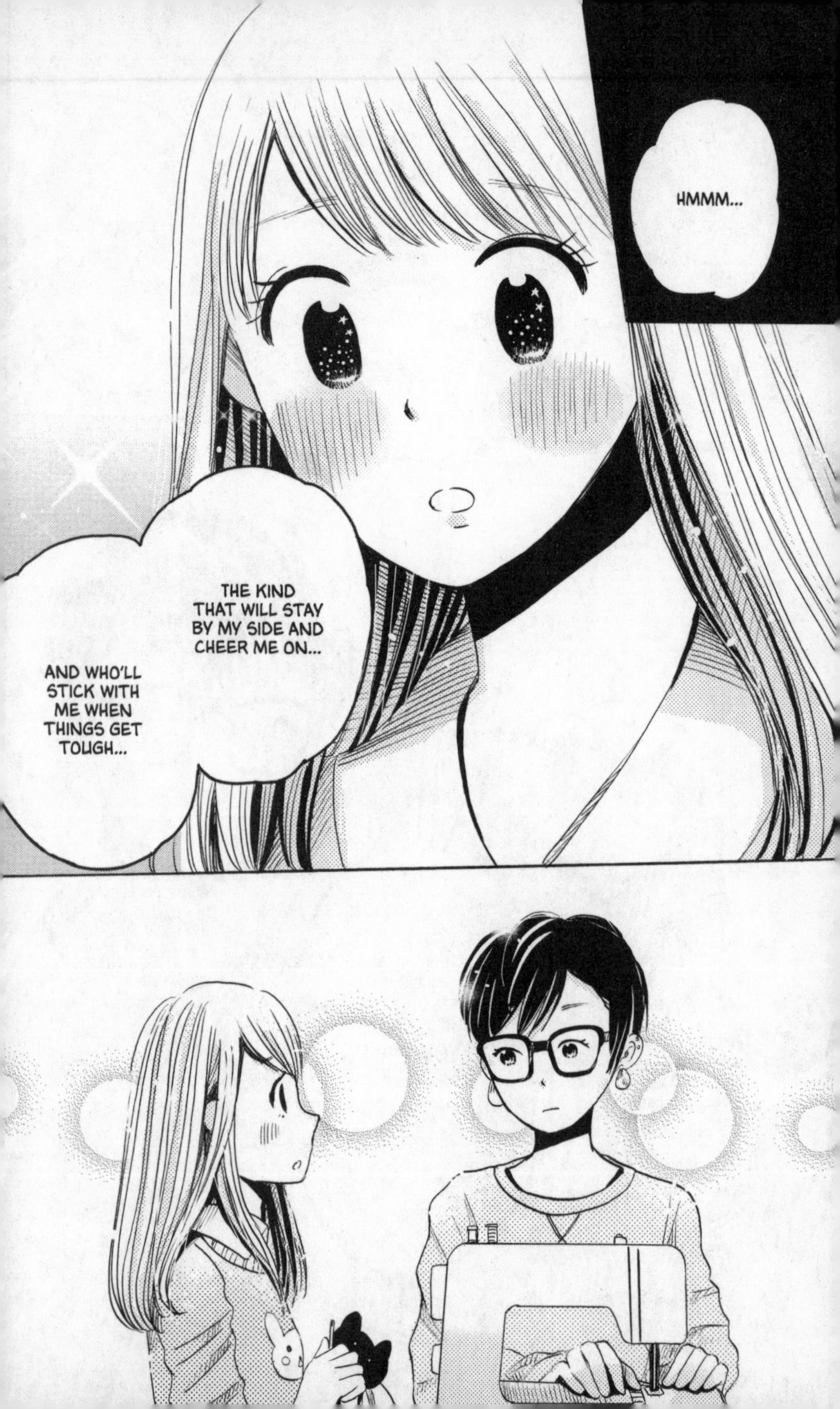
HMMM...
THE KIND THAT WILL STAY BY MY SIDE AND CHEER ME ON...
AND WHO'LL STICK WITH ME WHEN THINGS GET TOUGH...

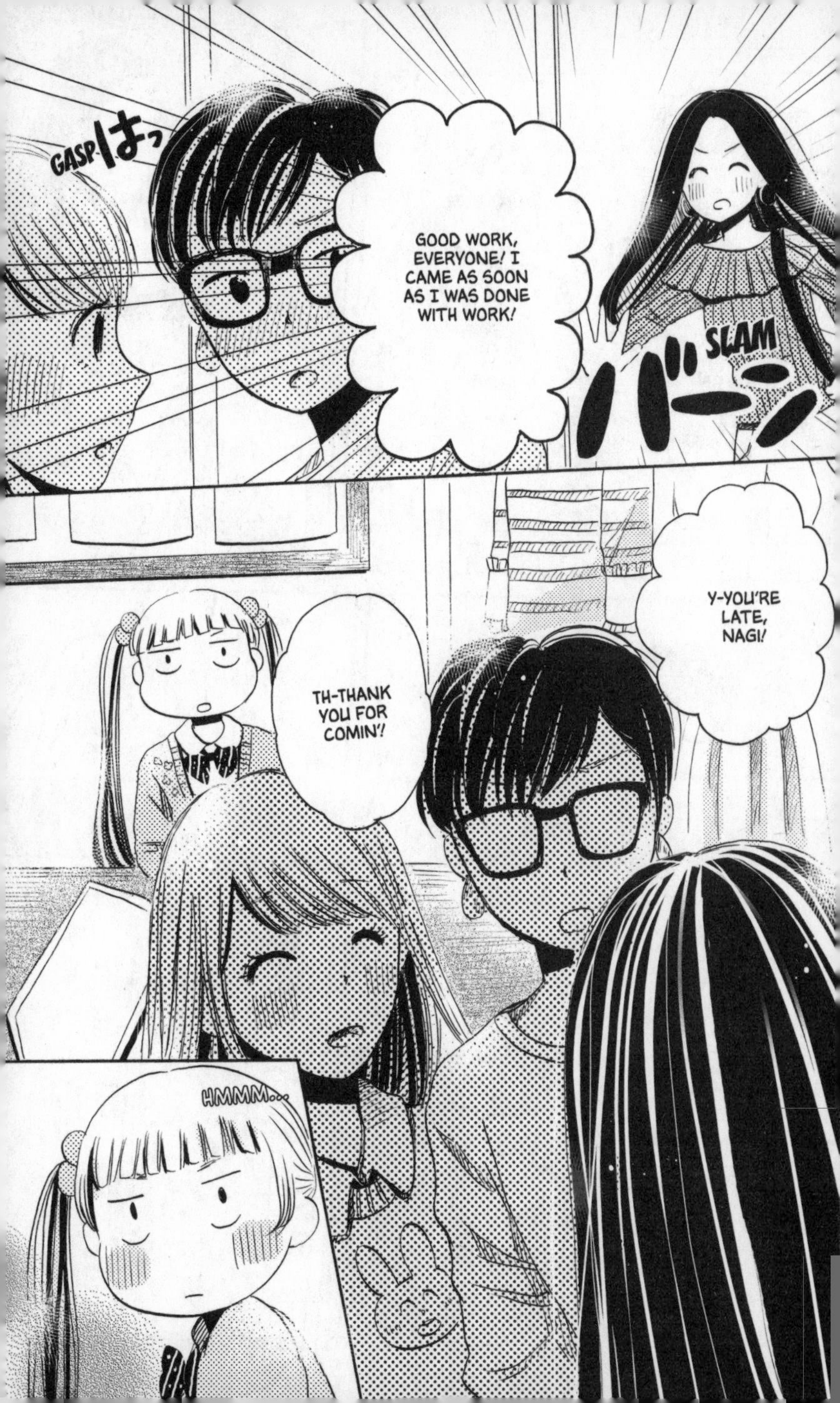

SLAM
GOOD WORK, EVERYONE! I CAME AS SOON AS I WAS DONE WITH WORK!
GASP はっ
Y-YOU'RE LATE, NAGI!
TH-THANK YOU FOR COMIN'!
HMMM...

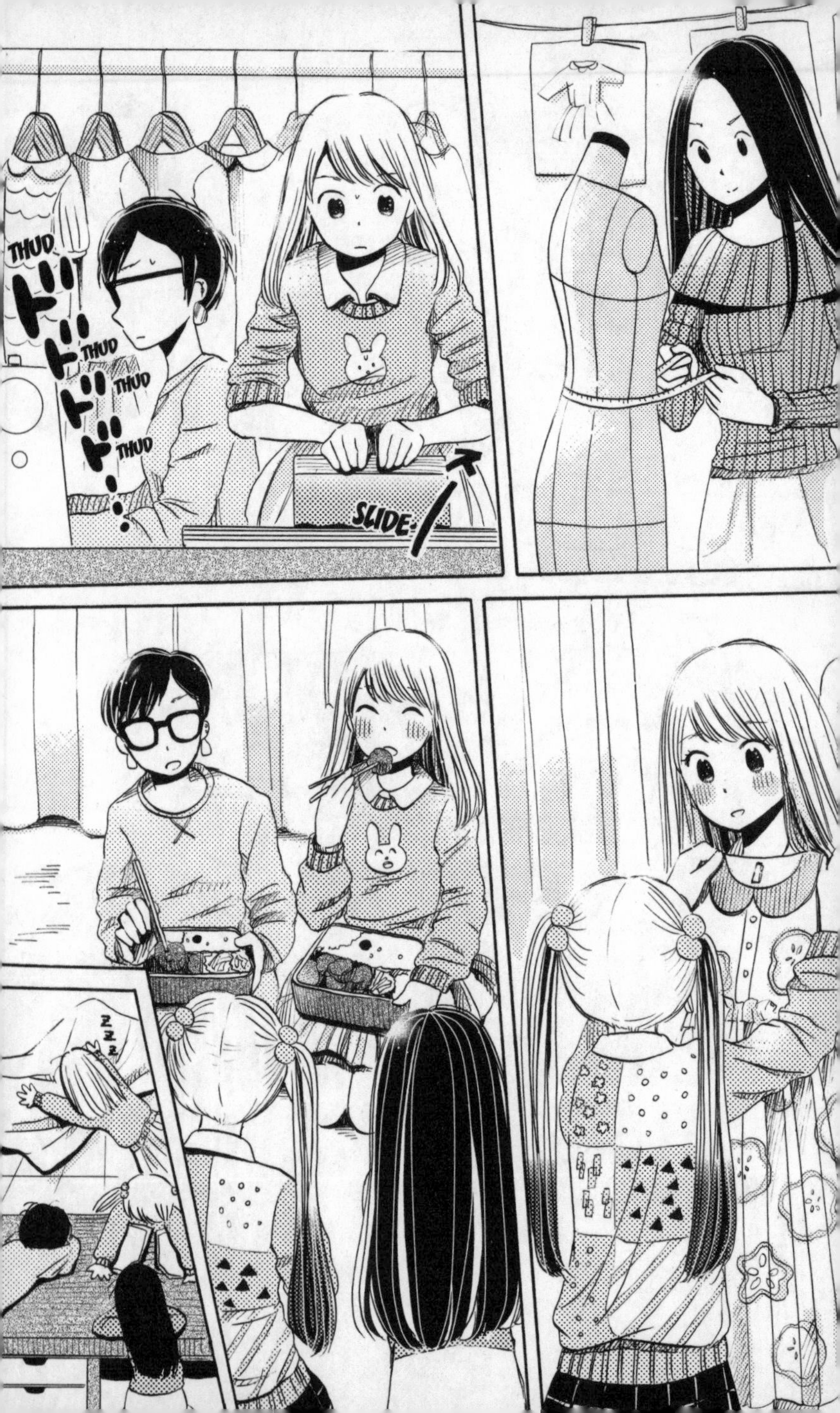
THUD
ドッ
THUD
ドッ
THUD
ドッ
THUD
ドッ…
SLIDE
ZZZ

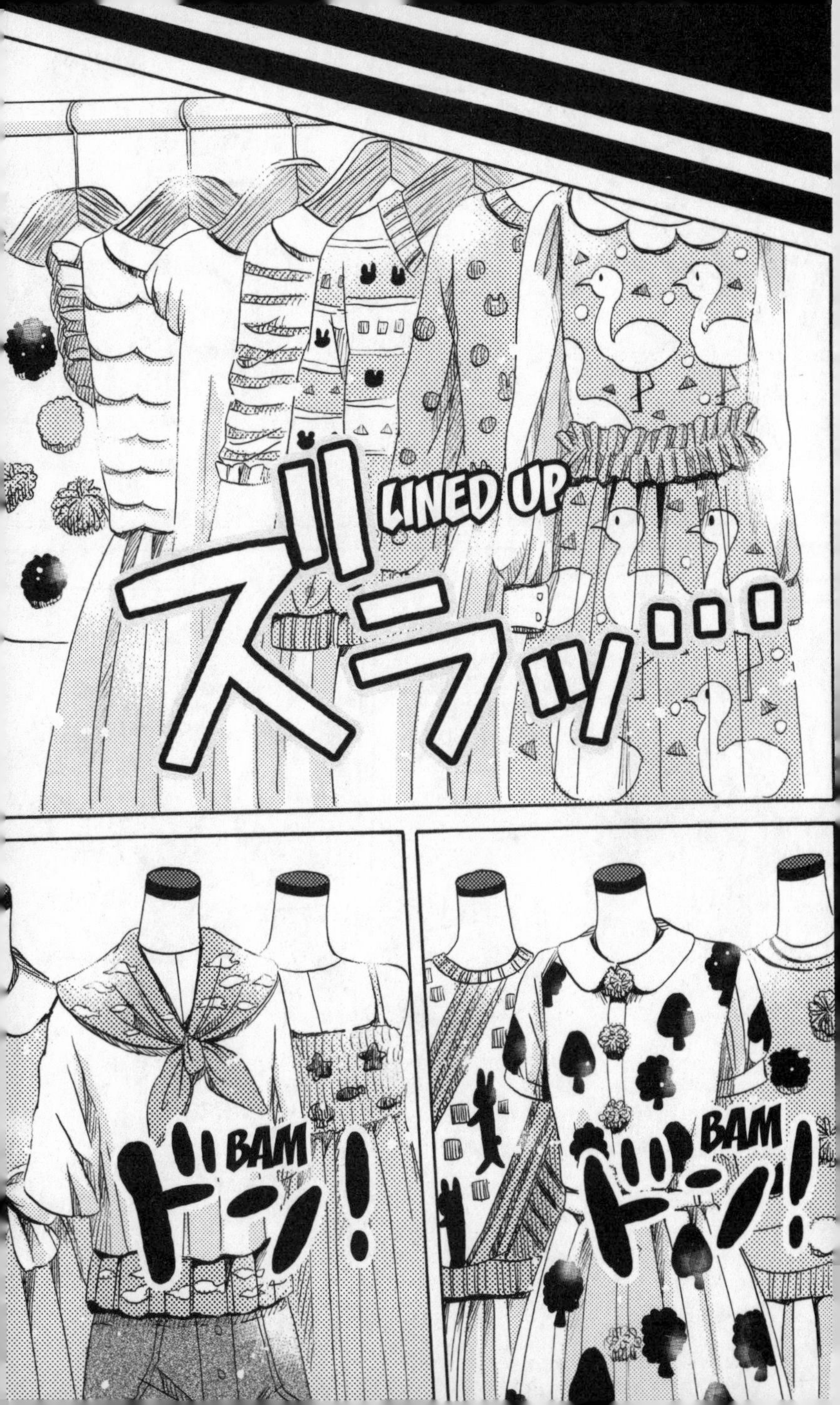
ズラッ…
LINED UP
ドーン!
BAM
ドーン!
BAM

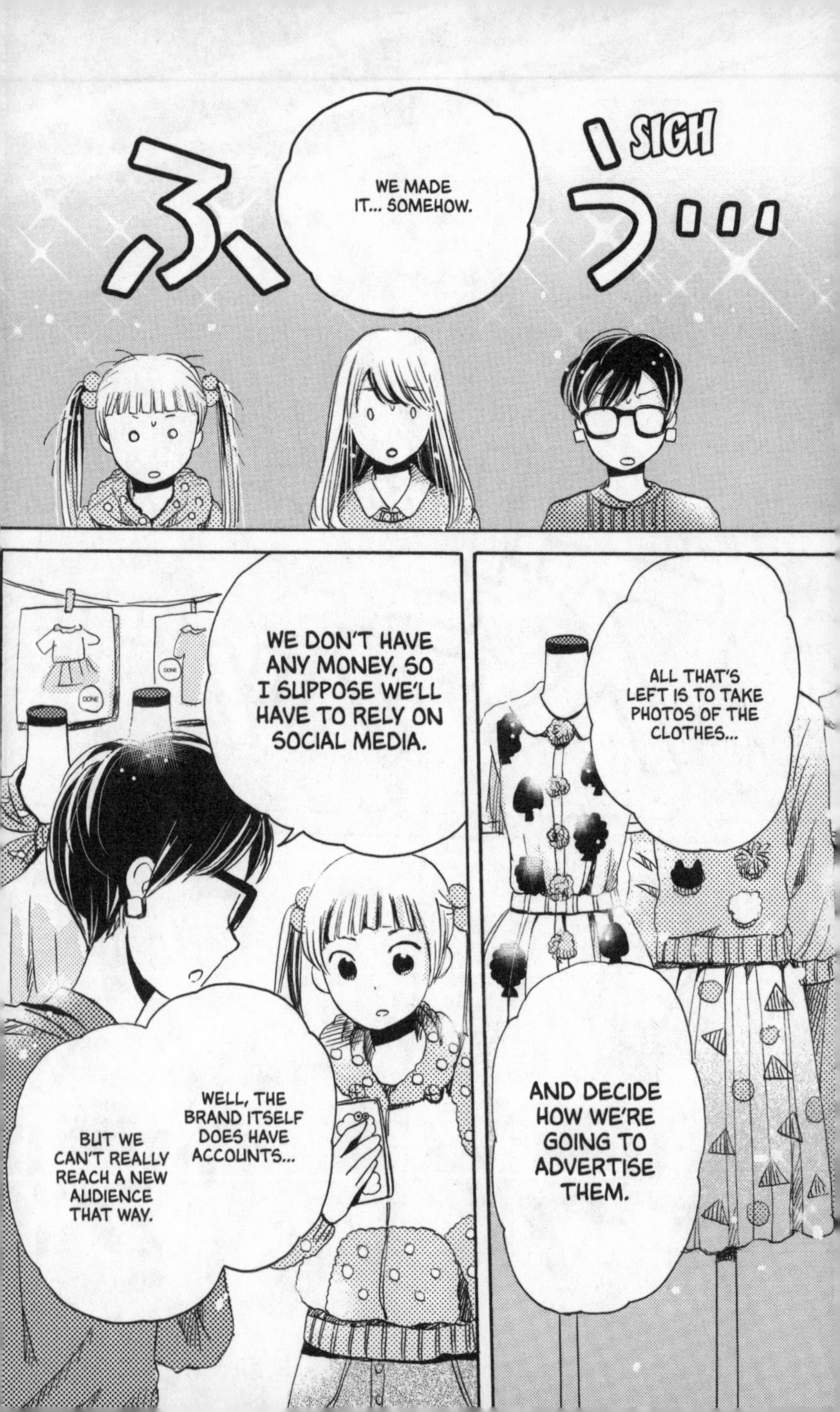
SIGH
WE MADE IT... SOMEHOW.
ふっ…
ALL THAT'S LEFT IS TO TAKE PHOTOS OF THE CLOTHES...
AND DECIDE HOW WE'RE GOING TO ADVERTISE THEM.
WE DON'T HAVE ANY MONEY, SO I SUPPOSE WE'LL HAVE TO RELY ON SOCIAL MEDIA.
WELL, THE BRAND ITSELF DOES HAVE ACCOUNTS...
BUT WE CAN'T REALLY REACH A NEW AUDIENCE THAT WAY.

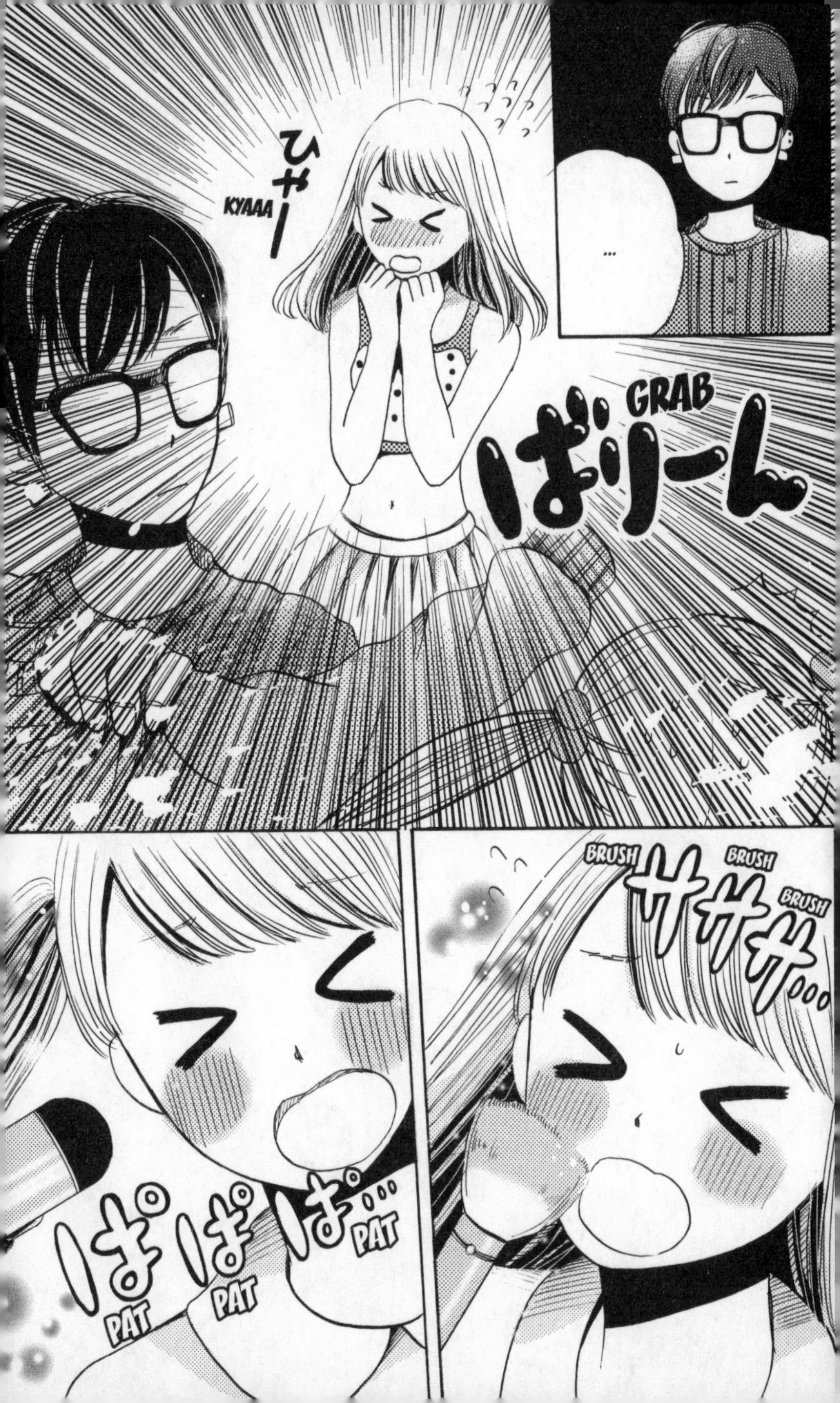
...
ひゃー
KYAAA
ぱりーん
GRAB
ささ さ...
BRUSH
BRUSH
BRUSH
ぱ ぱ ぱ...
PAT
PAT
PAT

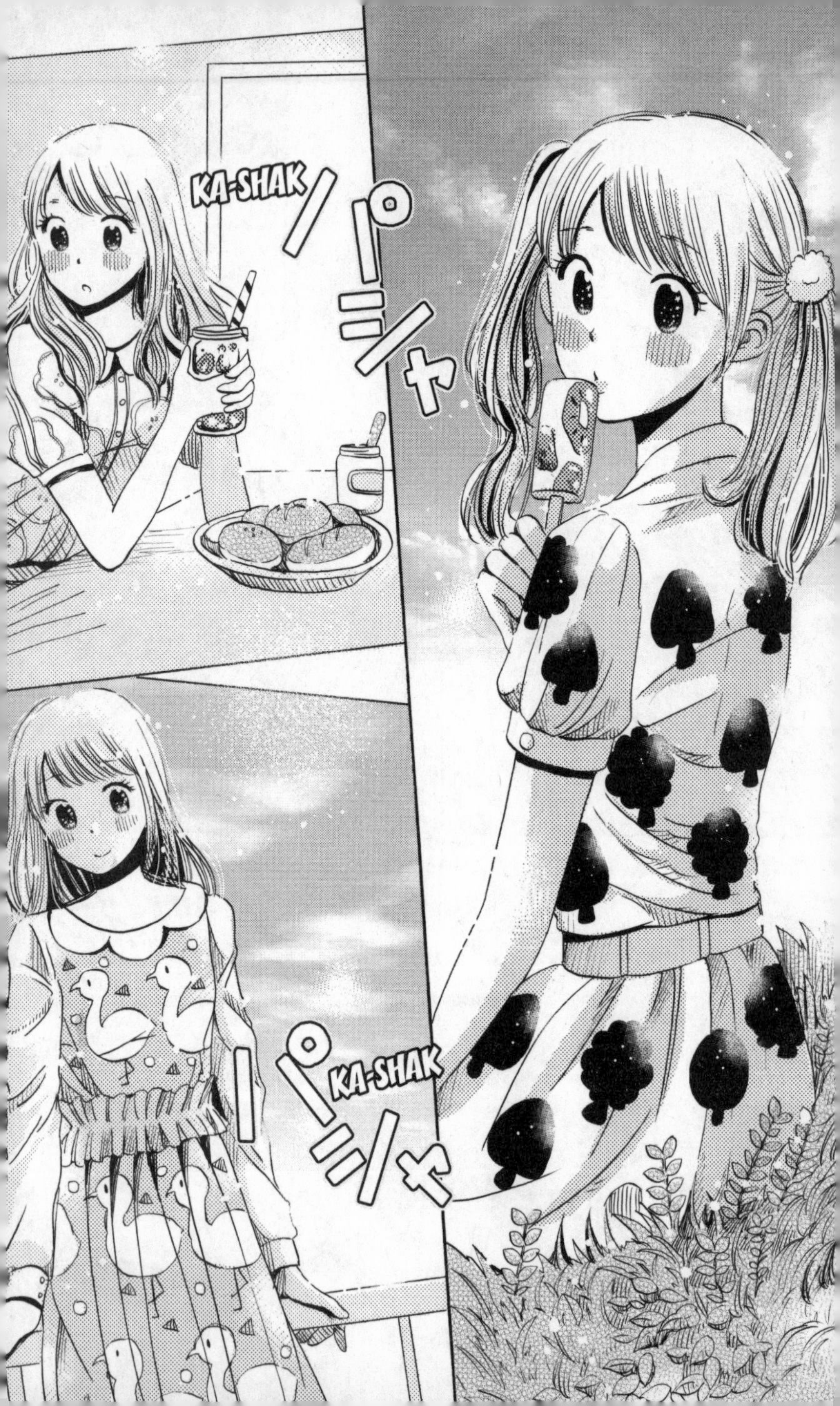
KA-SHAK
KA-SHAK

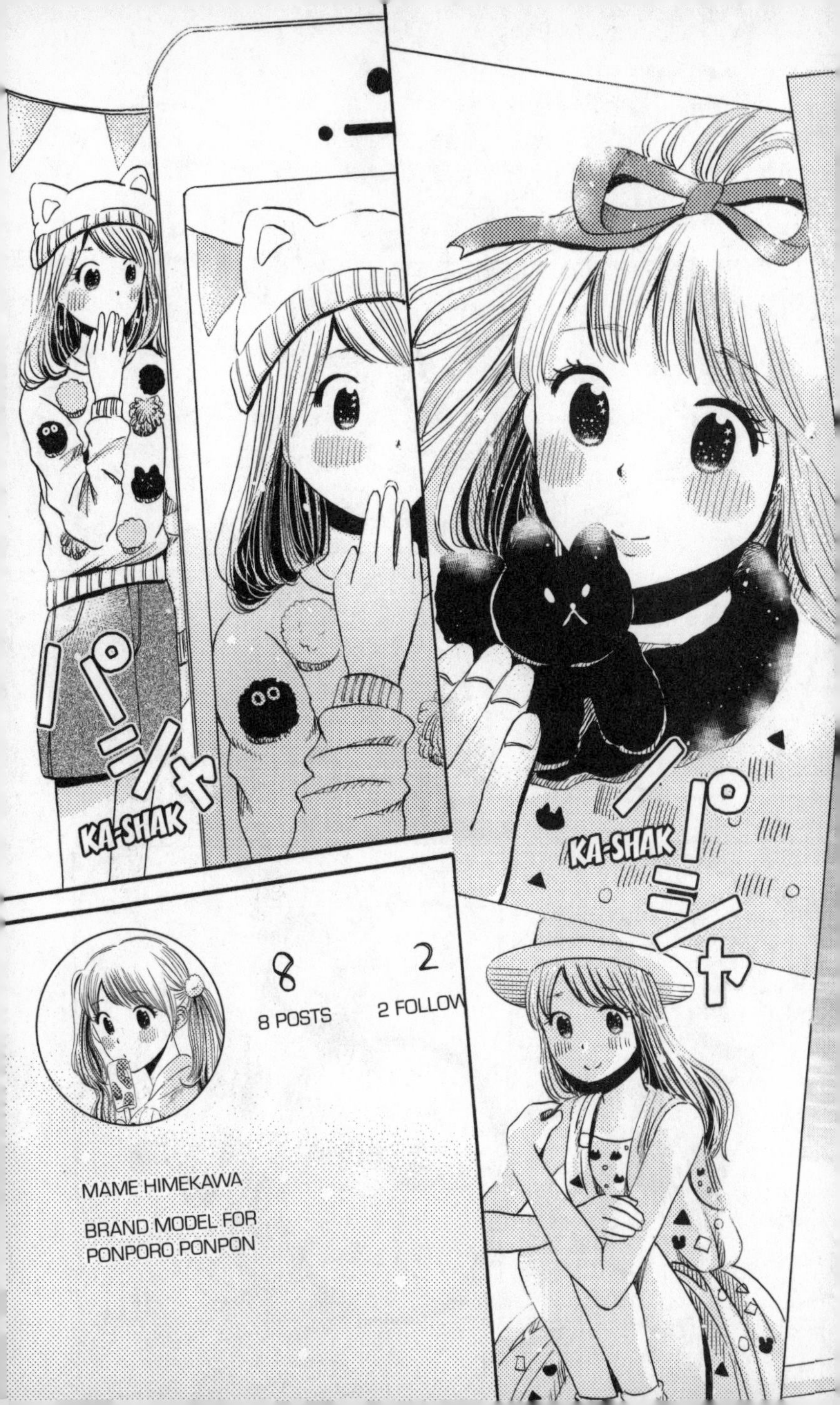
パシャ
KA-SHAK
パシャ
KA-SHAK
8
8 POSTS
2
2 FOLLOW
MAME HIMEKAWA
BRAND MODEL FOR PONPORO PONPON

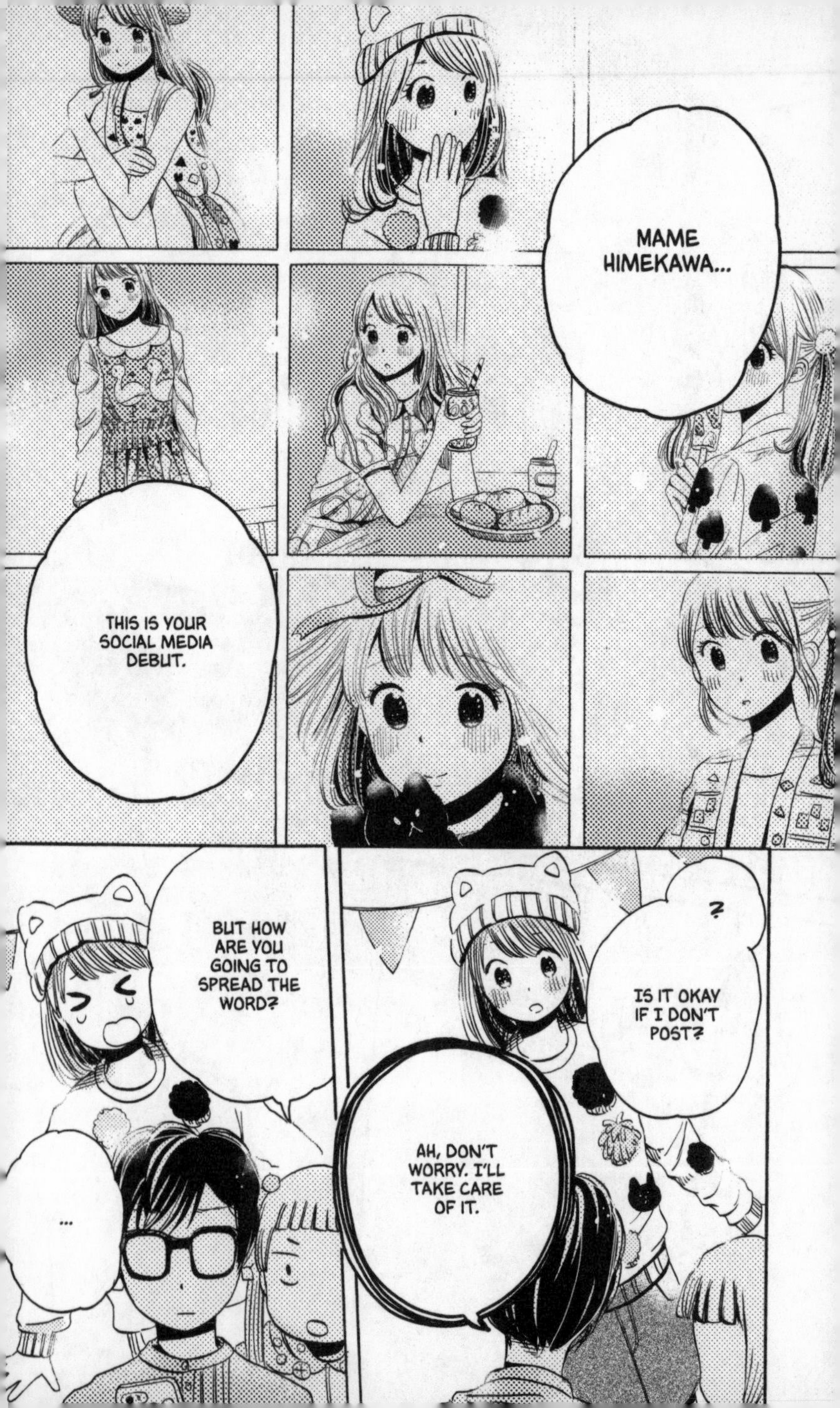
MAME HIMEKAWA...
THIS IS YOUR SOCIAL MEDIA DEBUT.
?
IS IT OKAY IF I DON'T POST?
AH, DON'T WORRY. I'LL TAKE CARE OF IT.
BUT HOW ARE YOU GOING TO SPREAD THE WORD?
...

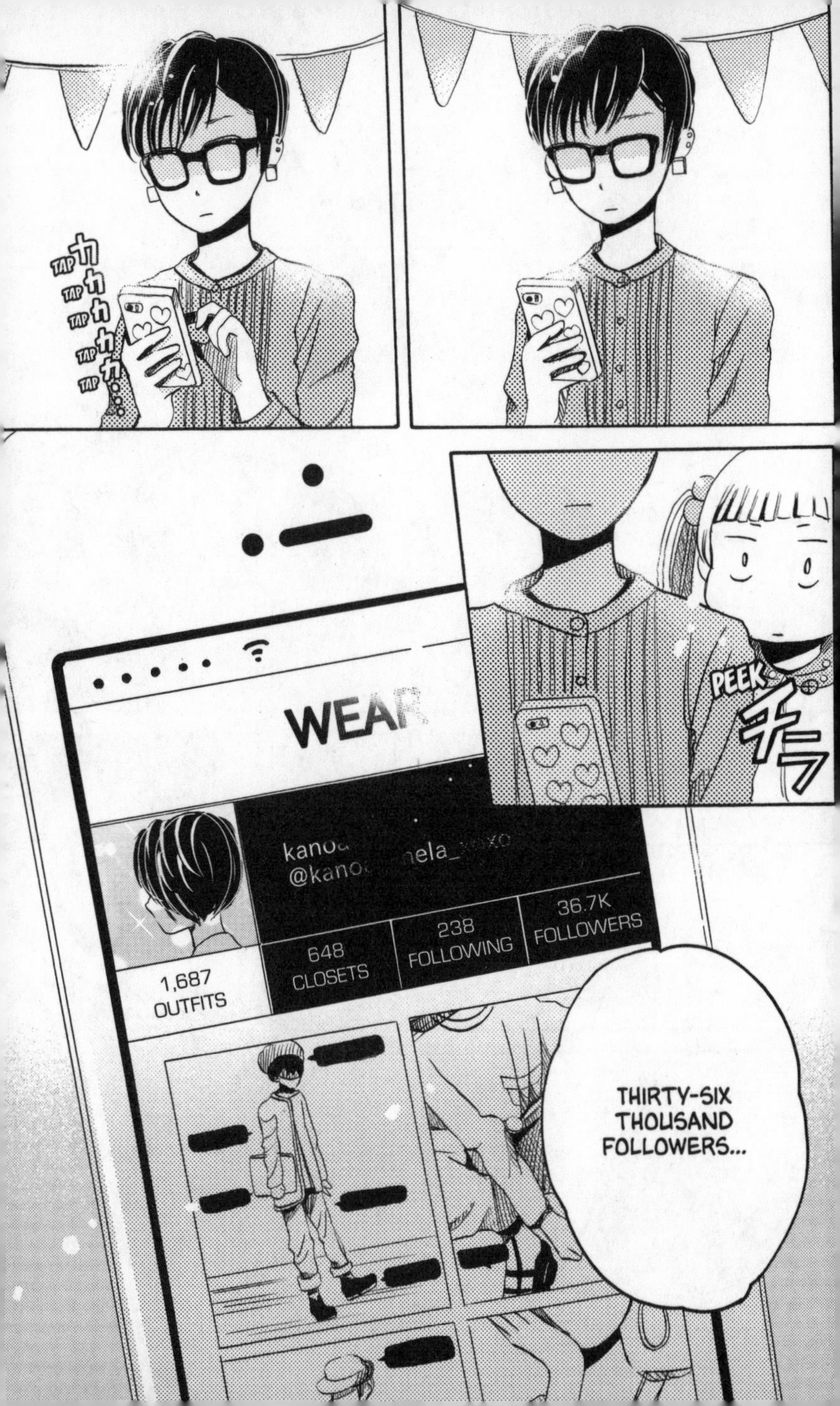
TAP TAP TAP TAP TAP
カカカカカ…
PEEK
チラ
WEAR
1,687 OUTFITS
648 CLOSETS
238 FOLLOWING
36.7K FOLLOWERS
THIRTY-SIX THOUSAND FOLLOWERS...

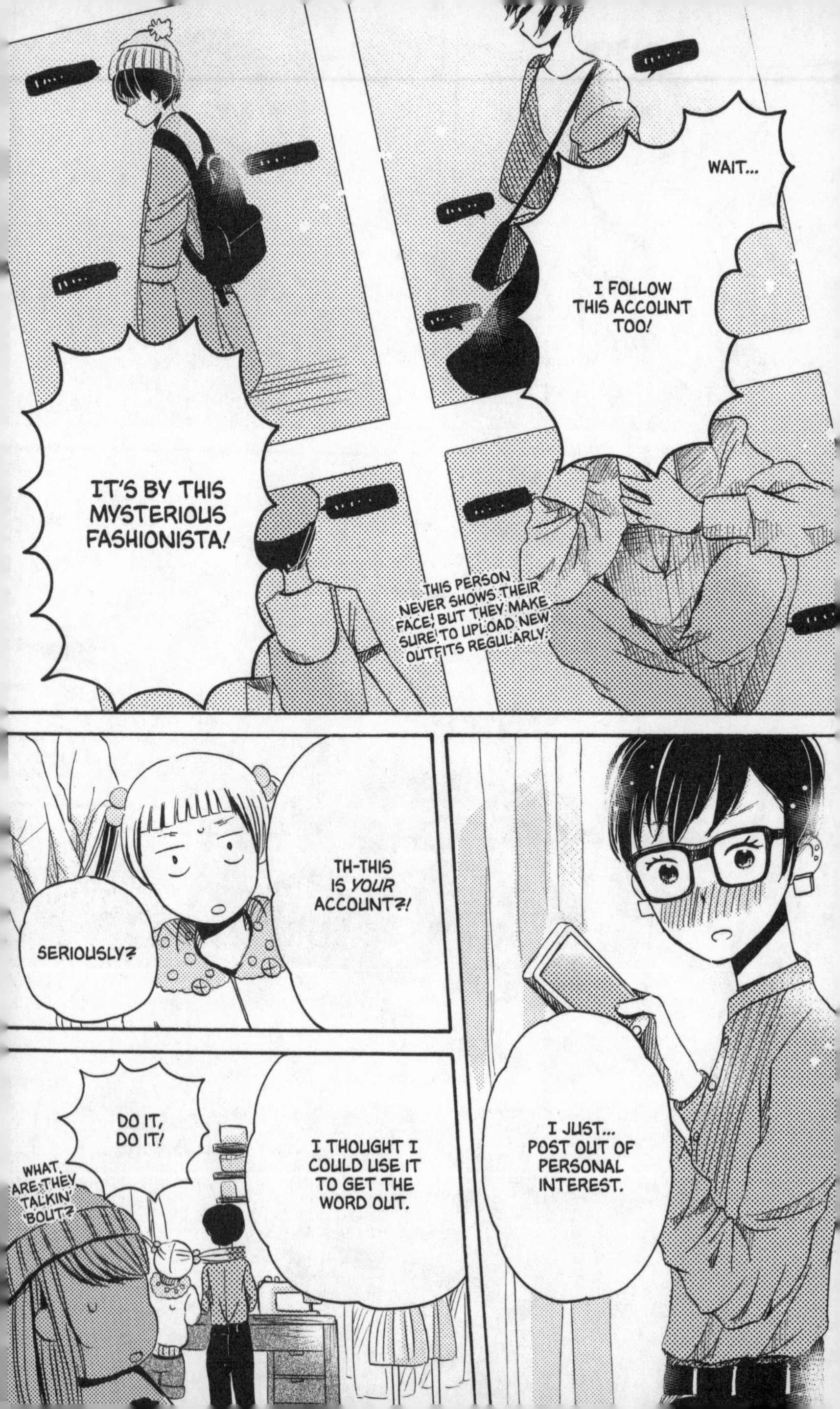
WAIT...
I FOLLOW THIS ACCOUNT TOO!
THIS PERSON NEVER SHOWS THEIR FACE, BUT THEY MAKE SURE TO UPLOAD NEW OUTFITS REGULARLY.
IT'S BY THIS MYSTERIOUS FASHIONISTA!
I JUST... POST OUT OF PERSONAL INTEREST.
TH-THIS IS *YOUR* ACCOUNT?!
SERIOUSLY?
I THOUGHT I COULD USE IT TO GET THE WORD OUT.
DO IT, DO IT!
WHAT ARE THEY TALKIN' 'BOUT?

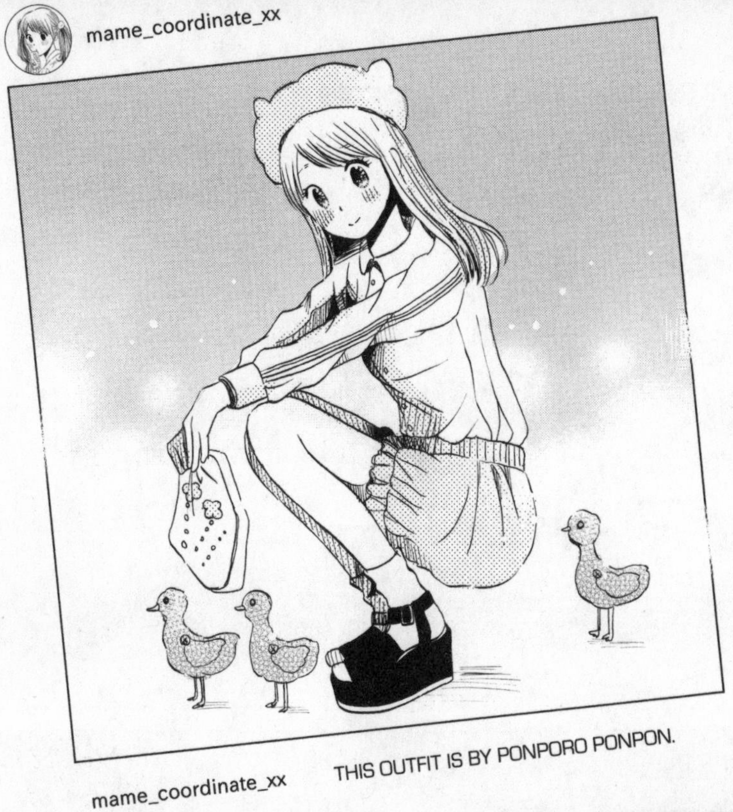
mame_coordinate_xx
mame_coordinate_xx
THIS OUTFIT IS BY PONPORO PONPON.

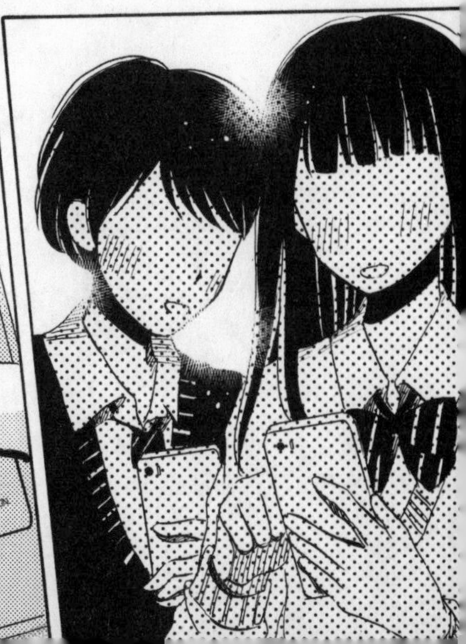

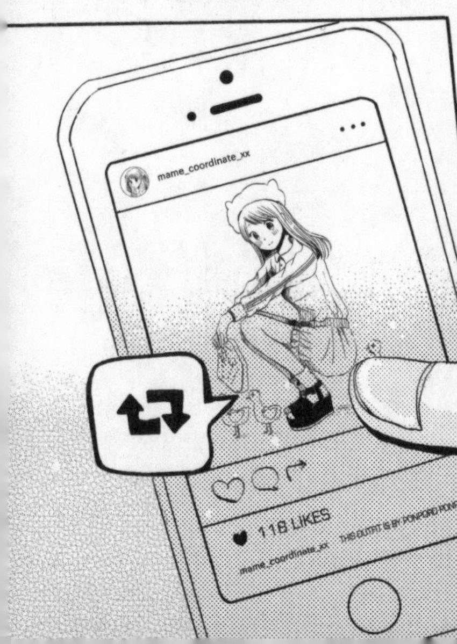
mame_coordinate_xx
118 LIKES
mame_coordinate_xx
THIS OUTFIT IS BY PONPORO PONPON.

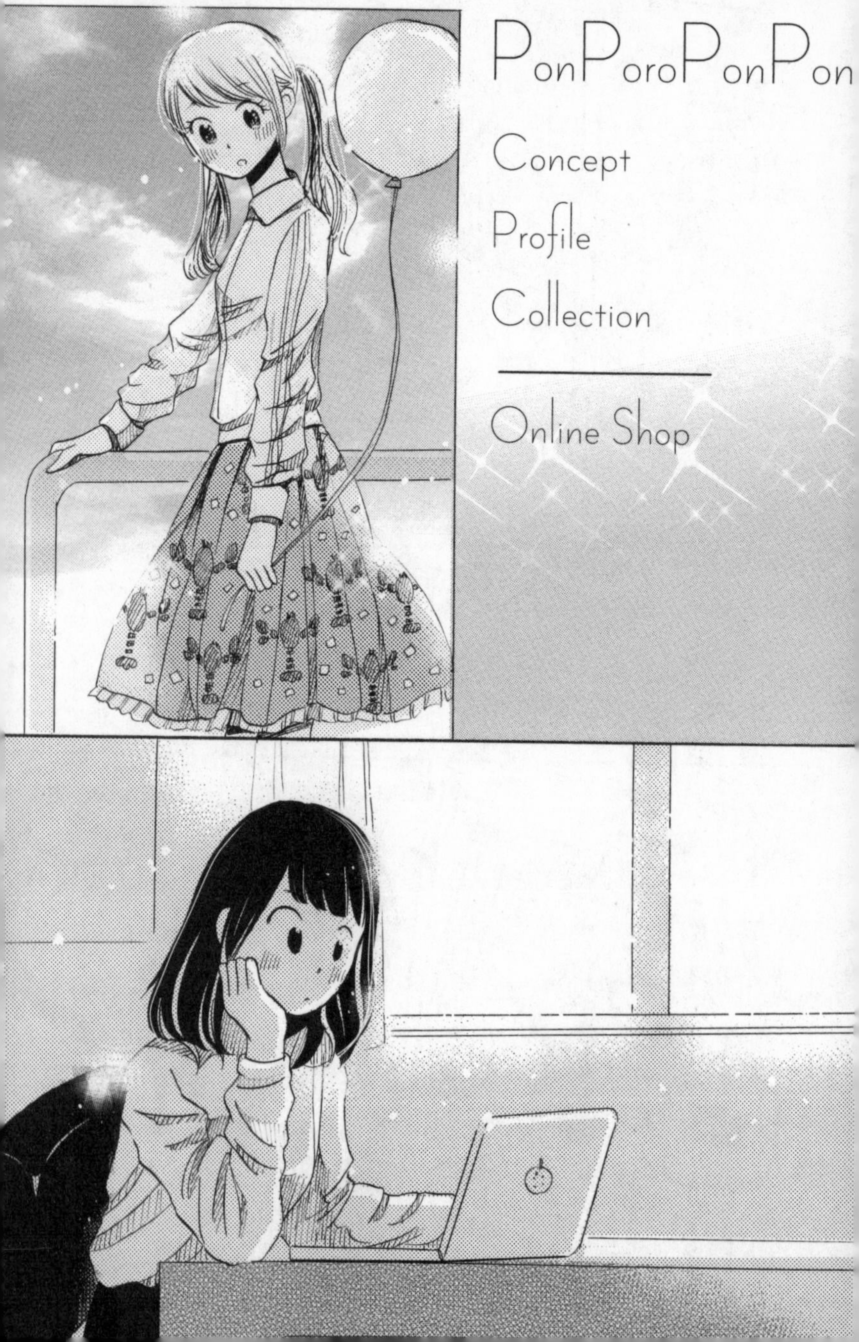
PonPoroPonPon
Concept
Profile
Collection
Online Shop

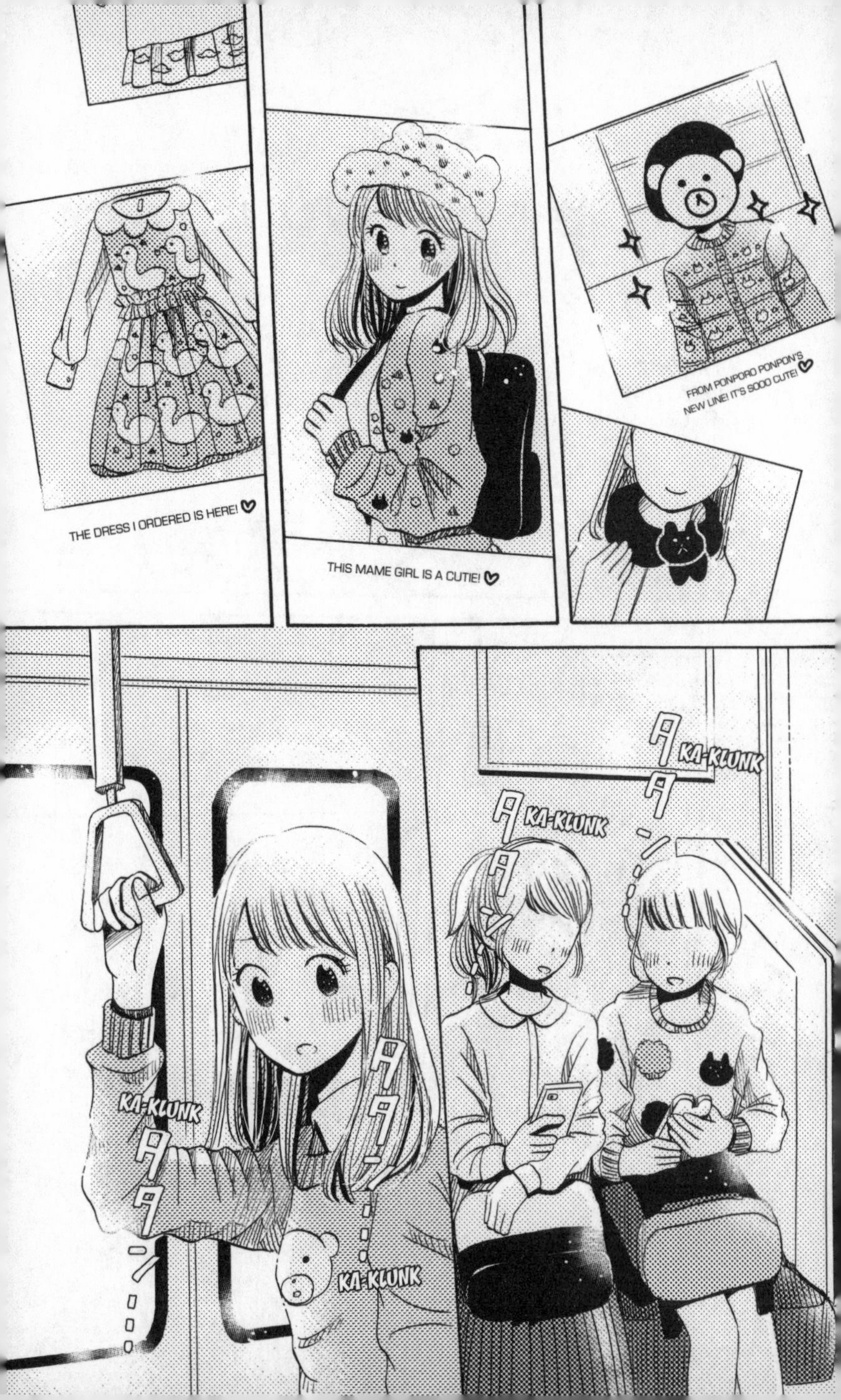

FROM PONPORO PONPON'S NEW LINE! IT'S SOOO CUTE! ♥
THIS MAME GIRL IS A CUTIE! ♥
THE DRESS I ORDERED IS HERE! ♥
KA-KLUNK
KA-KLUNK
KA-KLUNK
KA-KLUNK

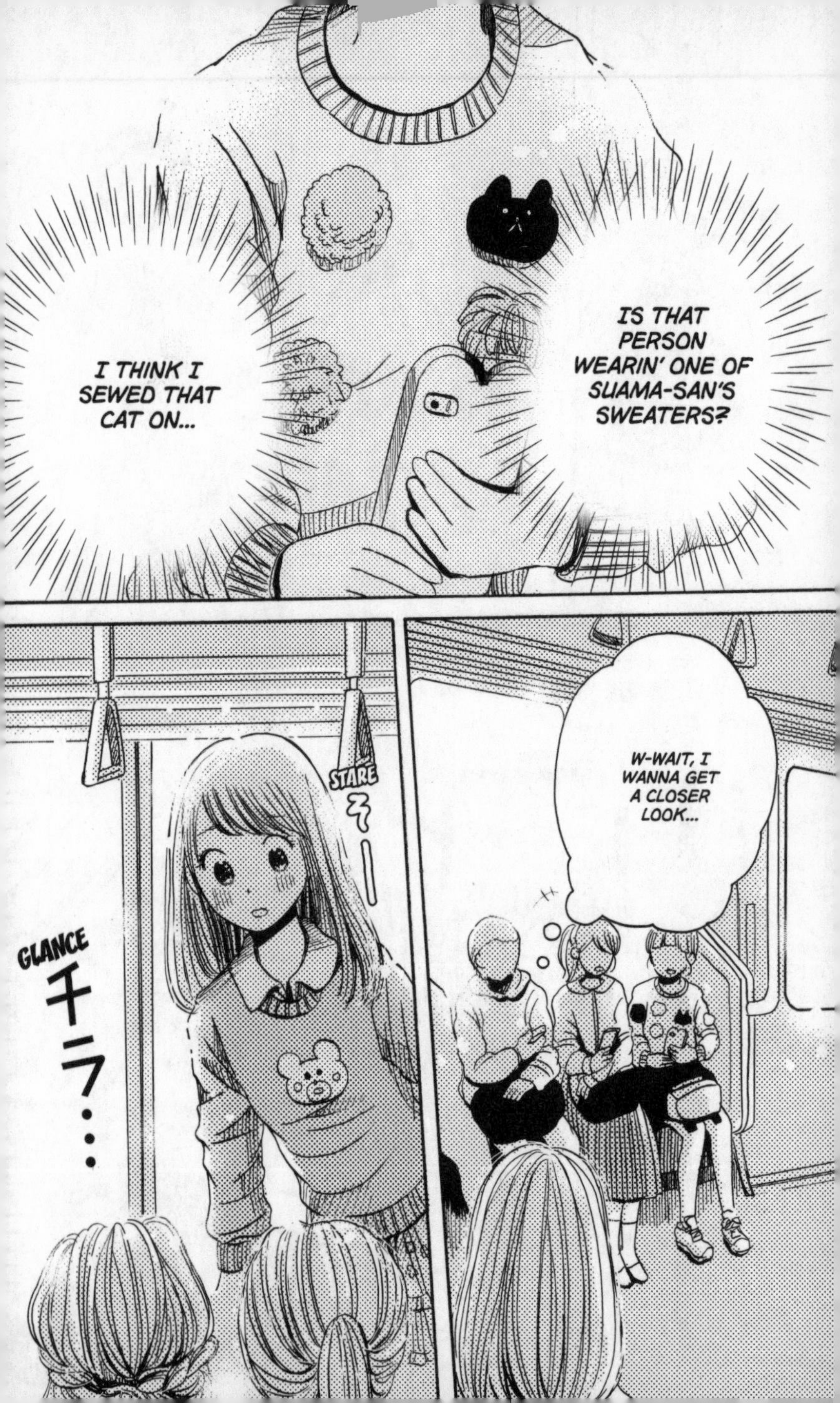
IS THAT PERSON WEARIN' ONE OF SUAMA-SAN'S SWEATERS?
I THINK I SEWED THAT CAT ON...
W-WAIT, I WANNA GET A CLOSER LOOK...
STARE
GLANCE
チラ…

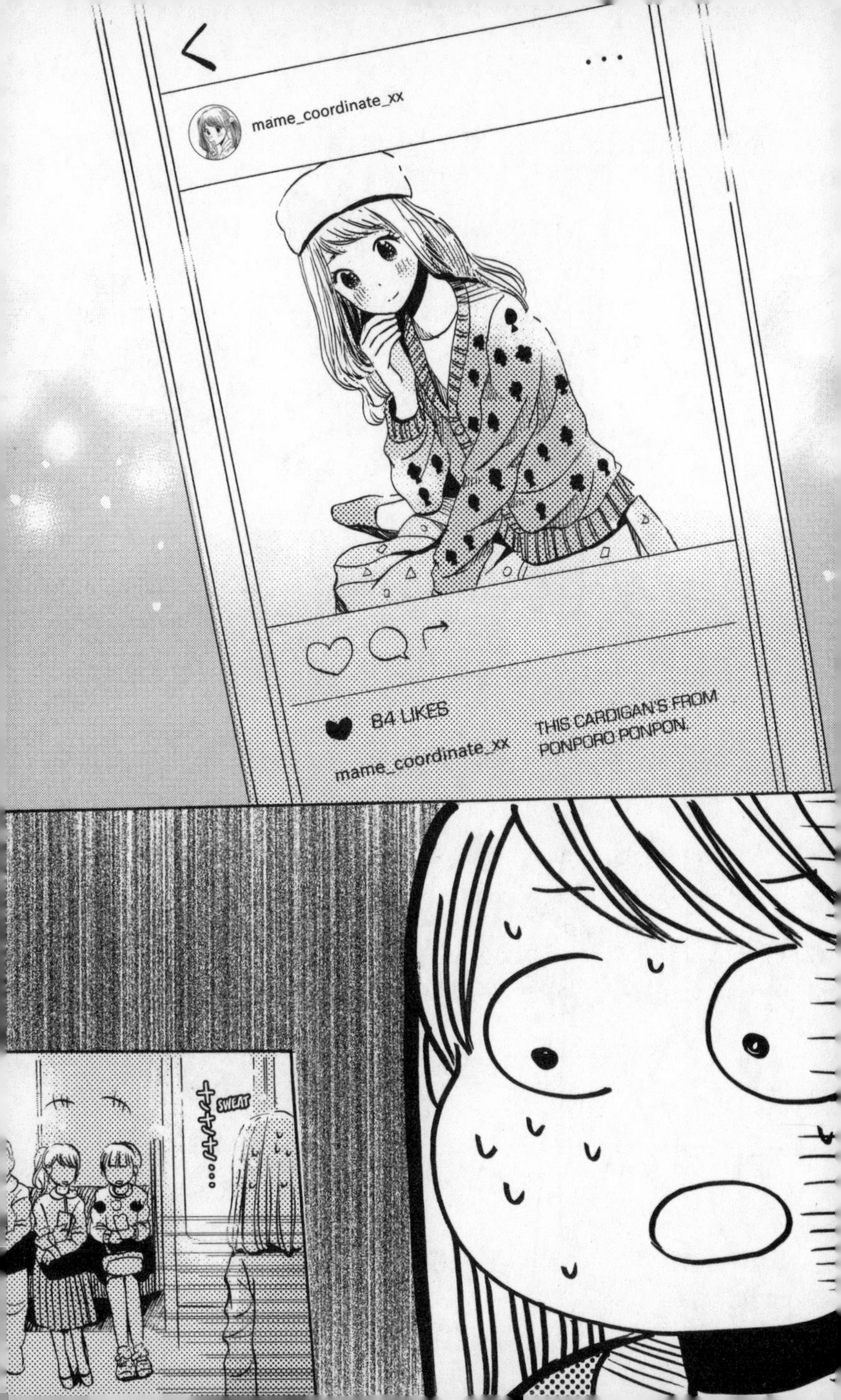
mame_coordinate_xx
84 LIKES
mame_coordinate_xx
THIS CARDIGAN'S FROM PONPORO PONPON.
SWEAT

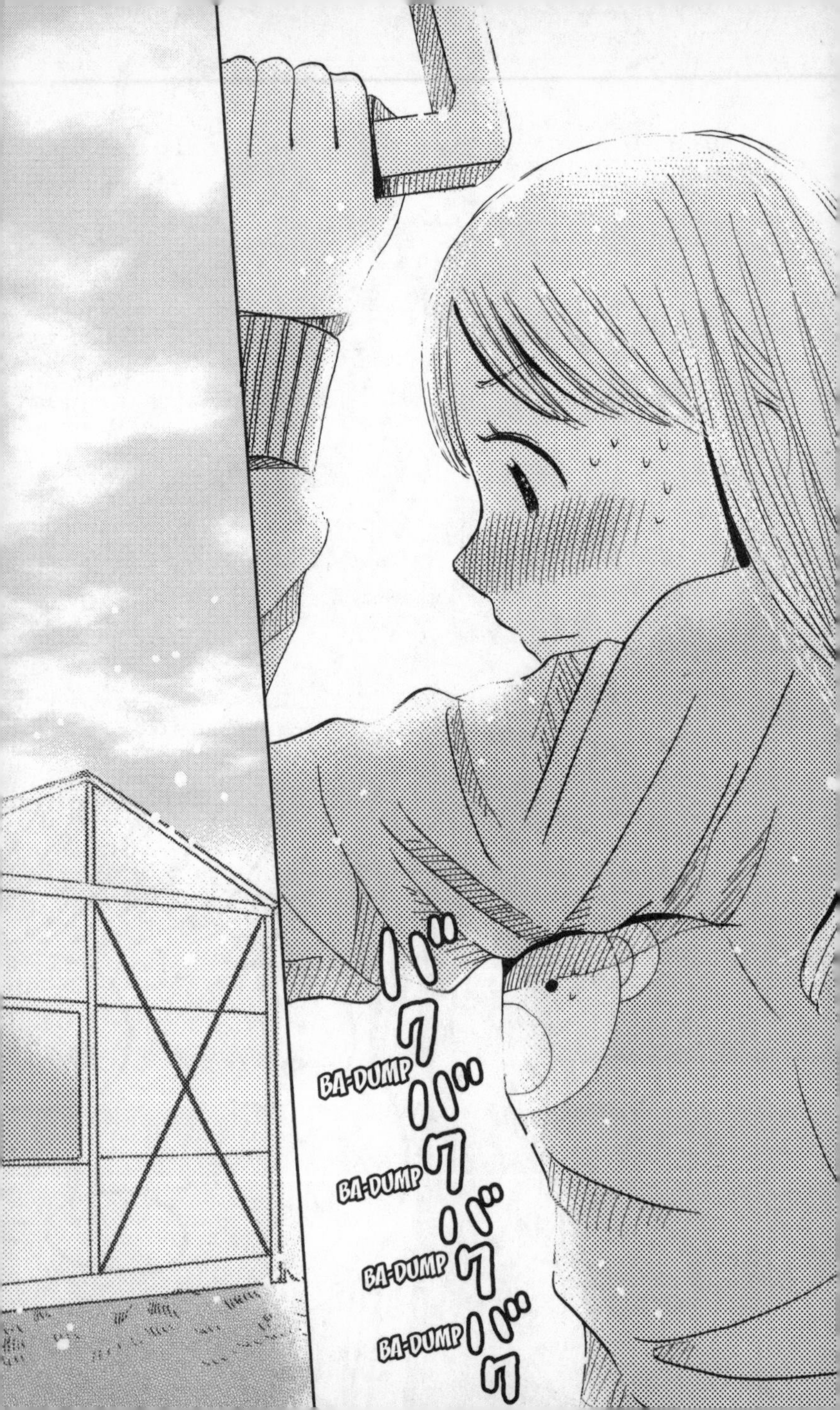
BA-DUMP
BA-DUMP
BA-DUMP
BA-DUMP

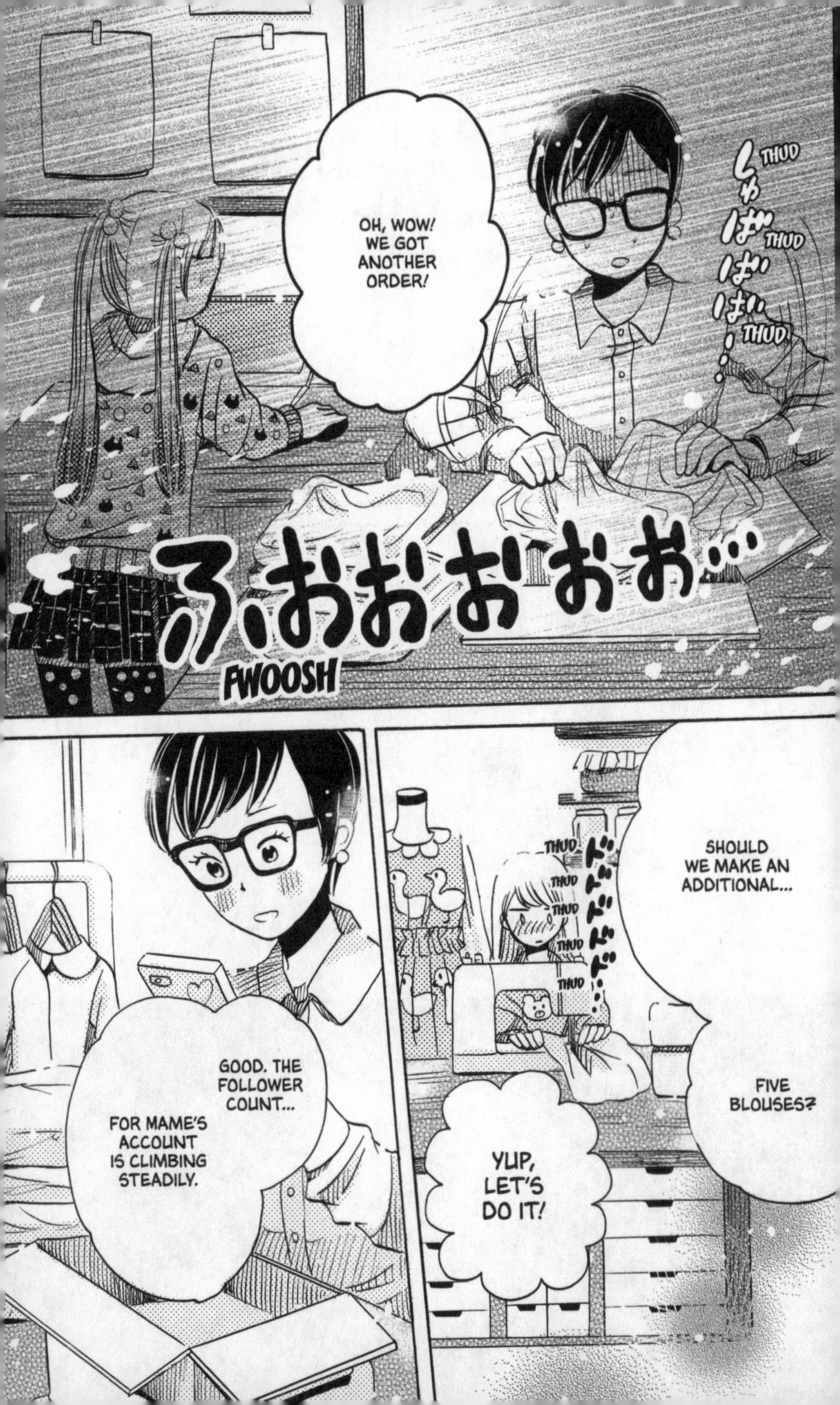
THUD
THUD
THUD
OH, WOW! WE GOT ANOTHER ORDER!
FWOOSH
SHOULD WE MAKE AN ADDITIONAL...
FIVE BLOUSES?
THUD
THUD
THUD
THUD
THUD
YUP, LET'S DO IT!
GOOD. THE FOLLOWER COUNT...
FOR MAME'S ACCOUNT IS CLIMBING STEADILY.

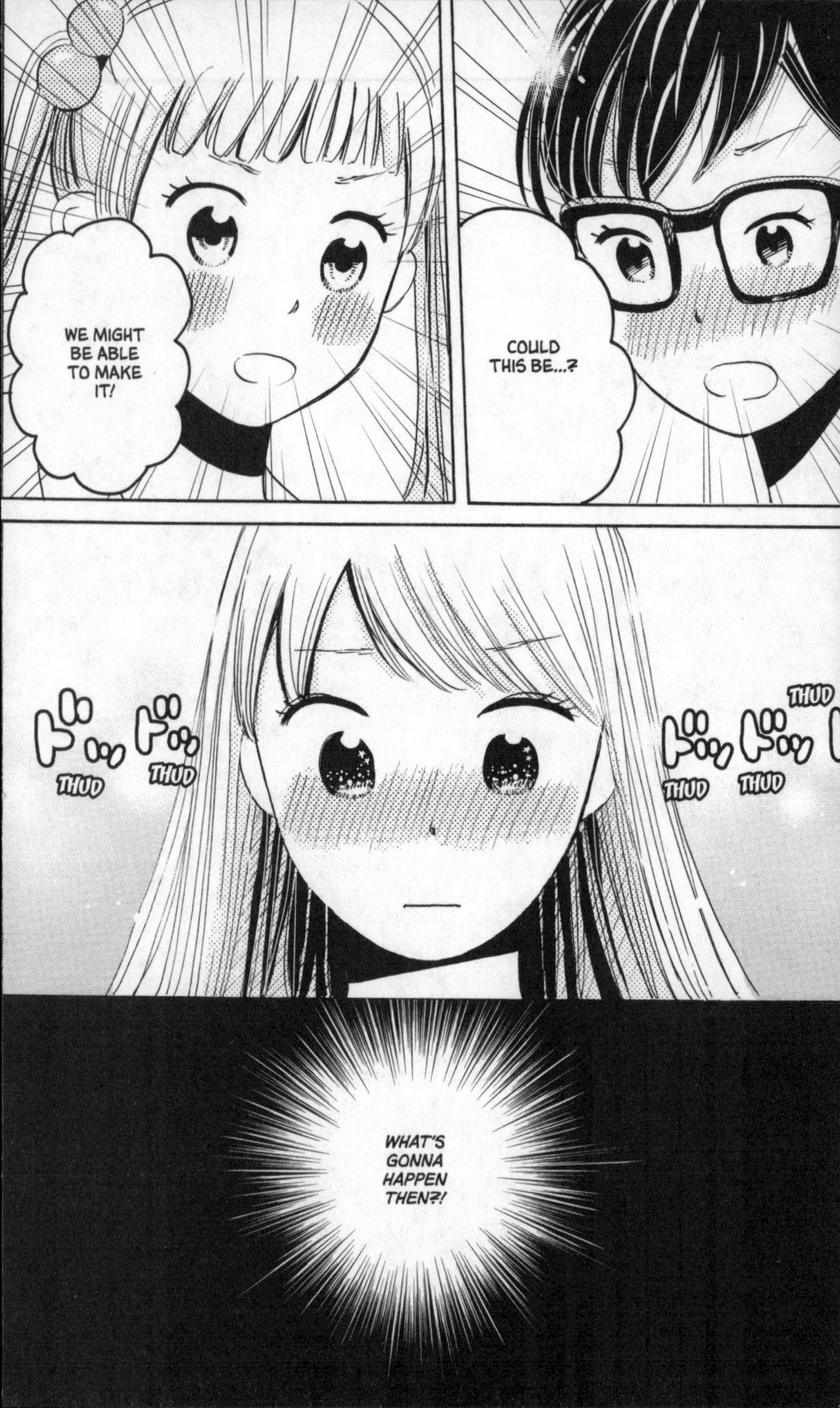
COULD THIS BE...?
WE MIGHT BE ABLE TO MAKE IT!
THUD
ドッ ドッ
THUD THUD
ドッ ドッ
THUD THUD
WHAT'S GONNA HAPPEN THEN?!

M A M E
coordinate

OOTD
CORNER
THE SAME AS ALWAYS
HER 15-YEAR-OLD DARK PAST VERSION
CASUAL AND REBELLIOUS PATTERN-ON-PATTERN!
HEADPHONES (JUST FOR SHOW)
POLKA-DOTTED BASEBALL JACKET
HEART-SHAPED BAG
POM-POM BRACELET
DRESS WITH THE UNION JACK ON IT
TIGER PRINT LEGGINGS
SNEAKERS WITH AN IMPACTFUL PATTERN

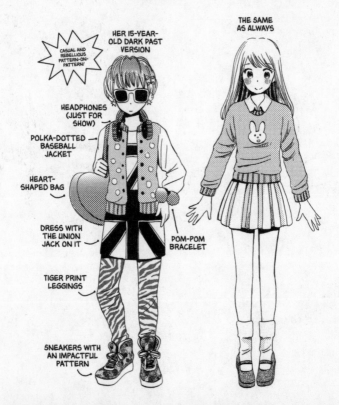

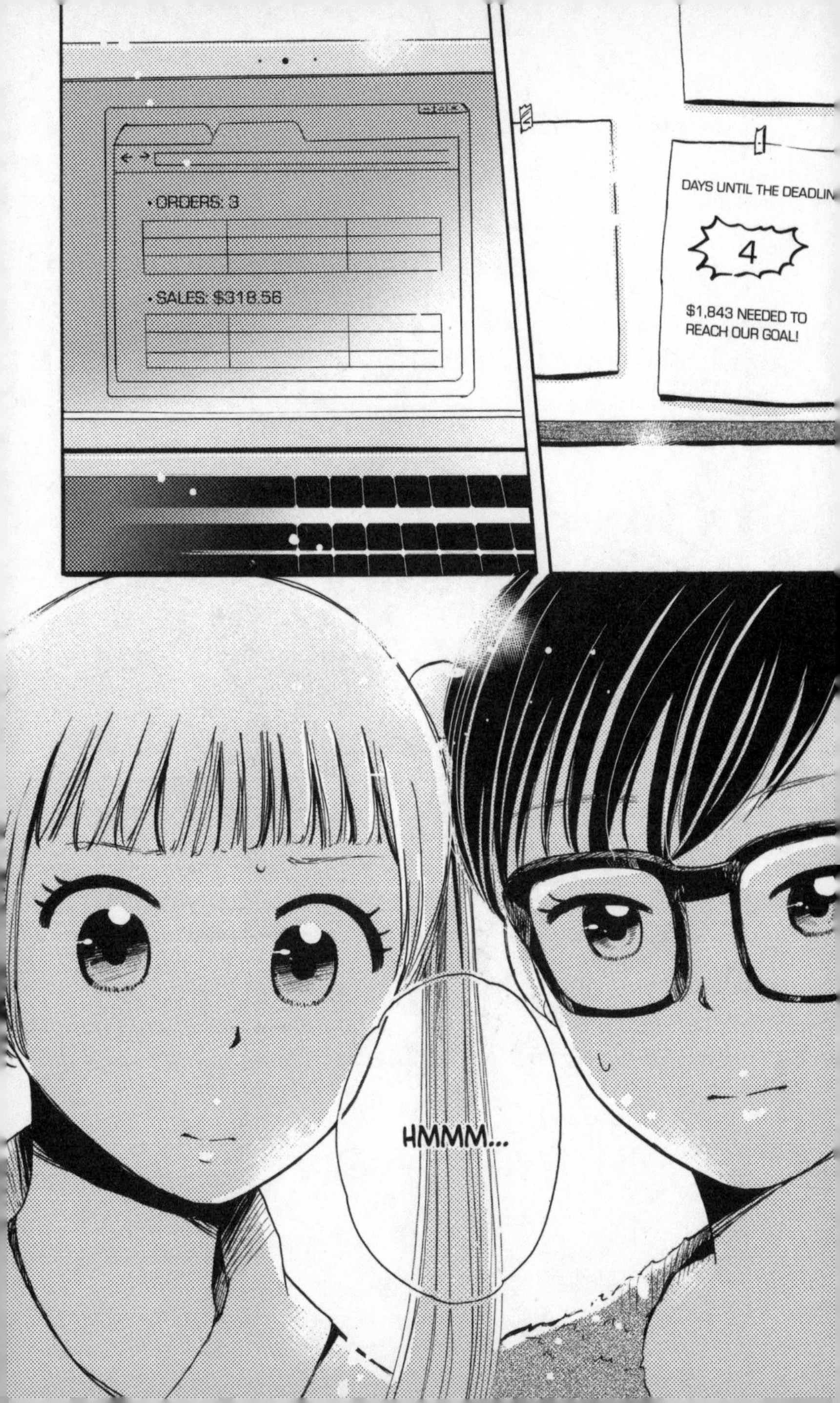
DAYS UNTIL THE DEADLIN
4
$1,843 NEEDED TO REACH OUR GOAL!
•ORDERS: 3
•SALES: $318.56
HMMM...

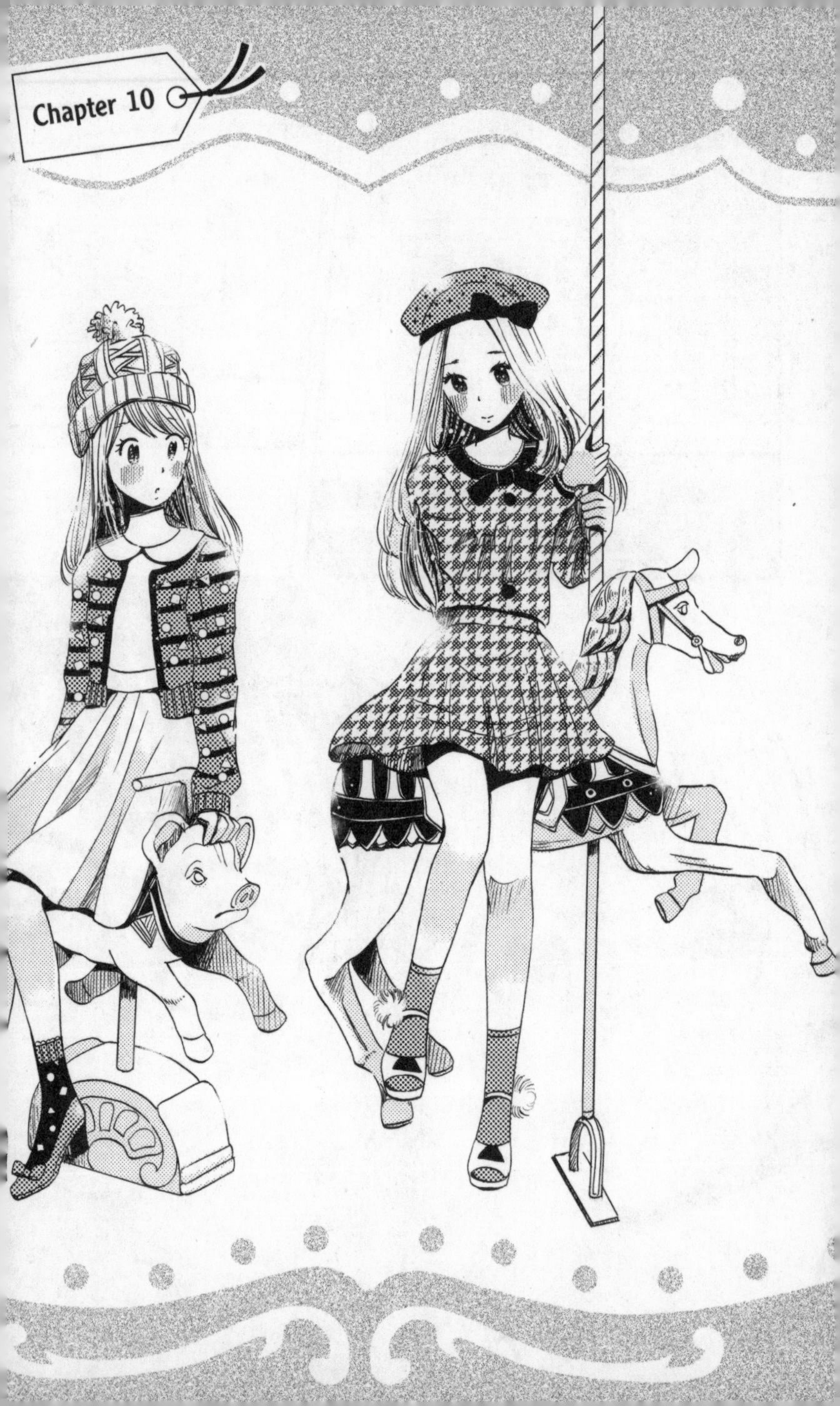
Chapter 10

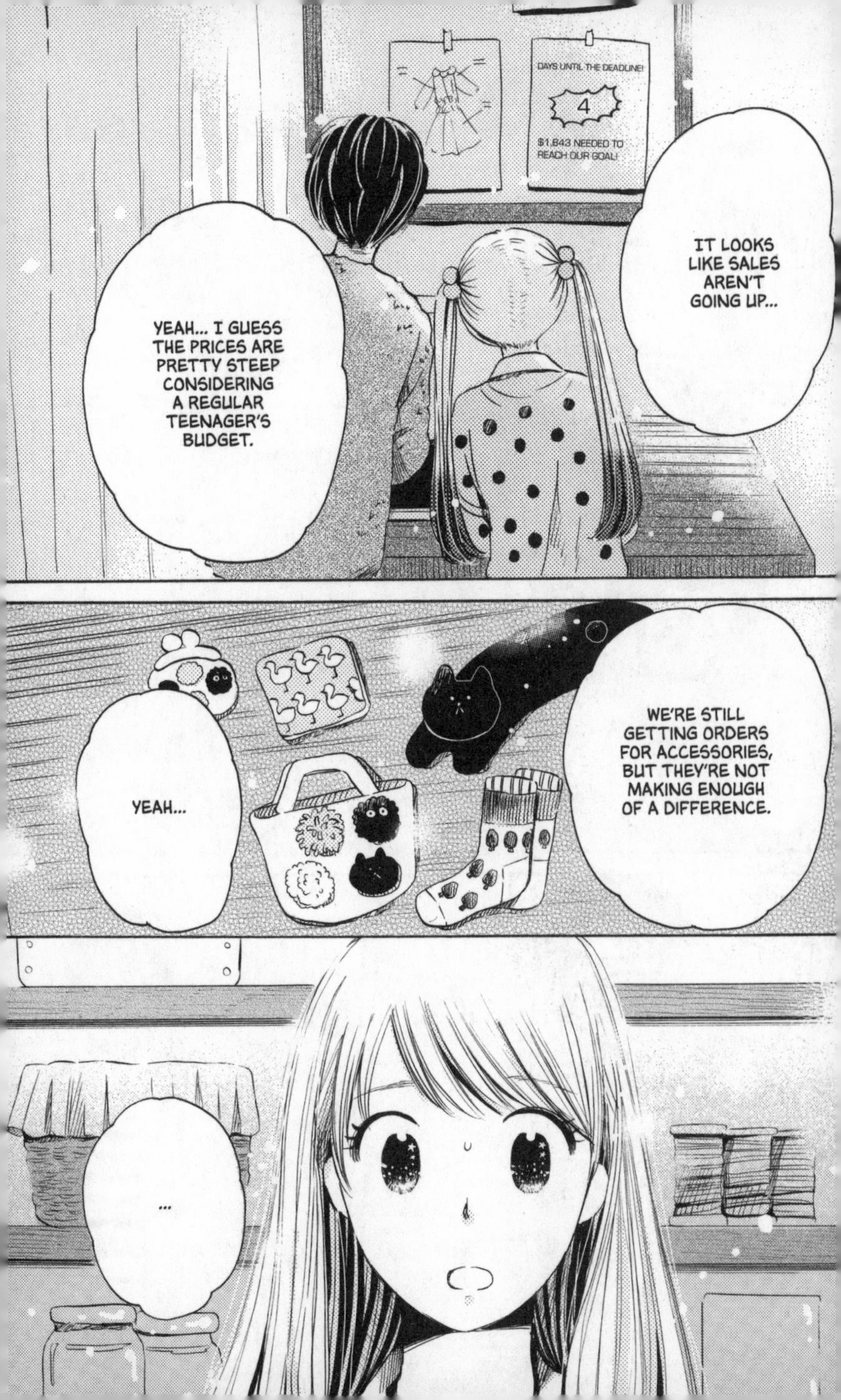
DAYS UNTIL THE DEADLINE!
4
$1,843 NEEDED TO REACH OUR GOAL!
IT LOOKS LIKE SALES AREN'T GOING UP...
YEAH... I GUESS THE PRICES ARE PRETTY STEEP CONSIDERING A REGULAR TEENAGER'S BUDGET.
WE'RE STILL GETTING ORDERS FOR ACCESSORIES, BUT THEY'RE NOT MAKING ENOUGH OF A DIFFERENCE.
YEAH...
...

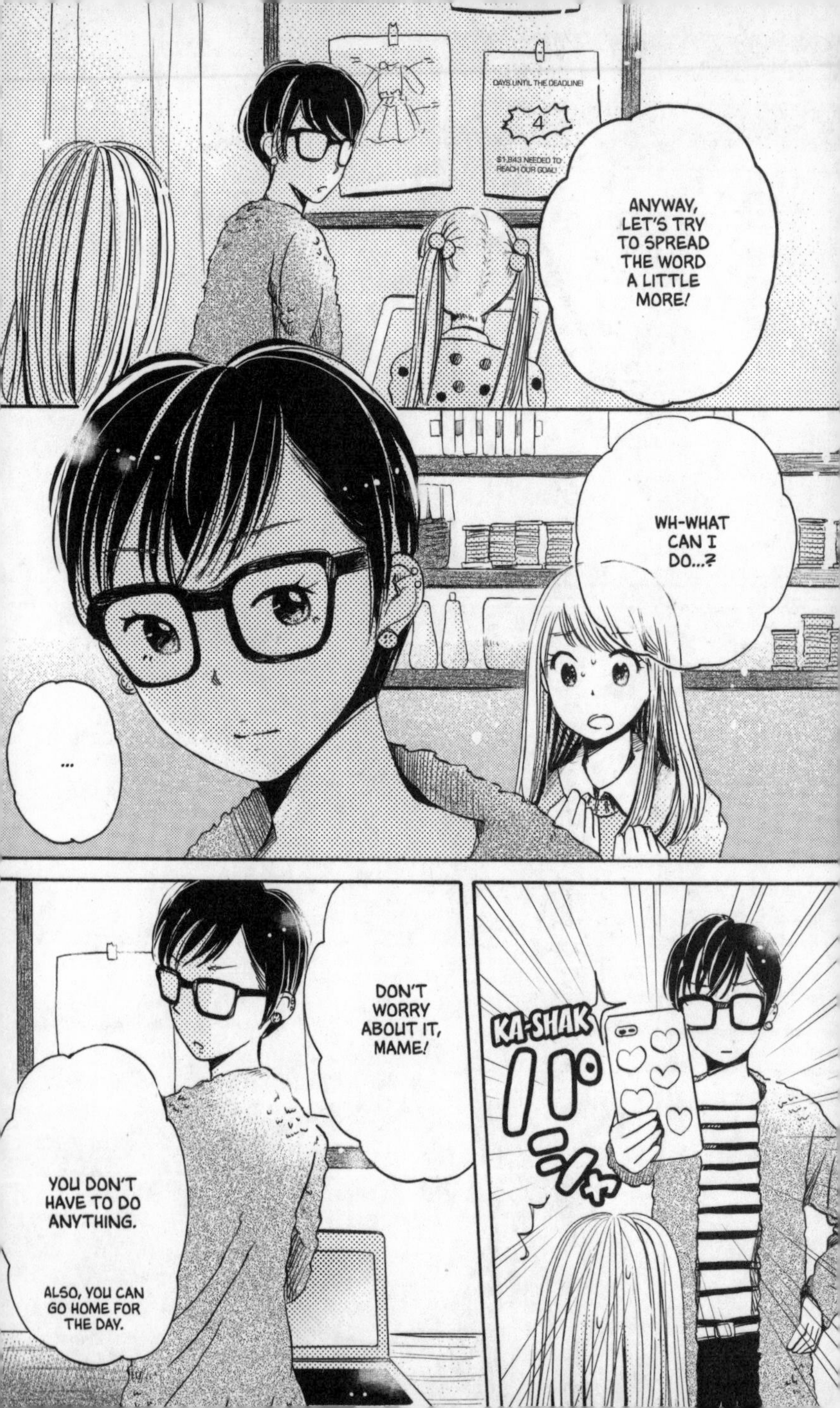
ANYWAY, LET'S TRY TO SPREAD THE WORD A LITTLE MORE!
DAYS UNTIL THE DEADLINE!
4
$1,843 NEEDED TO REACH OUR GOAL!
WH-WHAT CAN I DO...?
...
KA-SHAK
パシャ
DON'T WORRY ABOUT IT, MAME!
YOU DON'T HAVE TO DO ANYTHING.
ALSO, YOU CAN GO HOME FOR THE DAY.

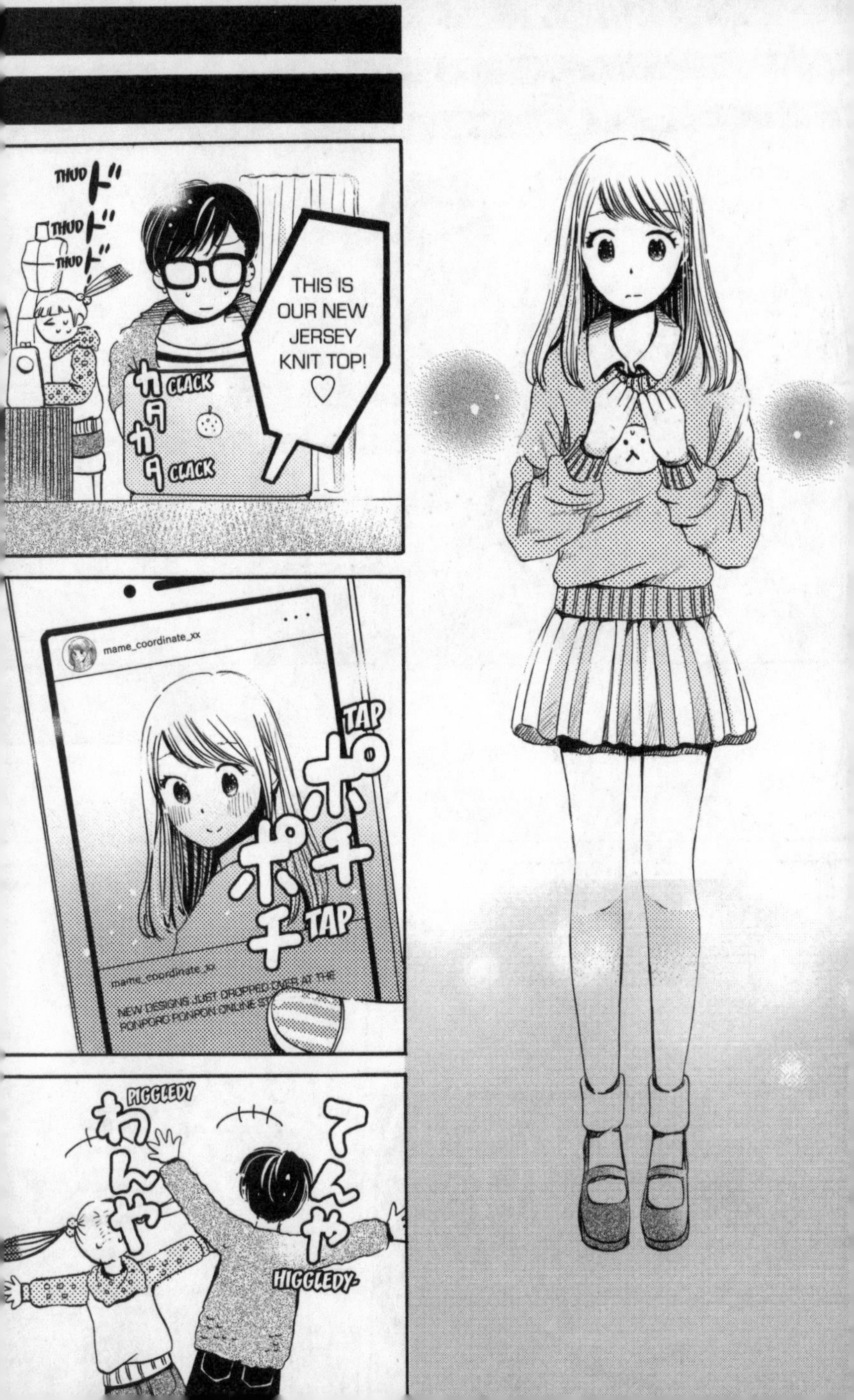
THUD ド
THUD ド
THUD ド
THIS IS OUR NEW JERSEY KNIT TOP! ♡
カタ CLACK
カタ CLACK
mame_coordinate_xx
TAP ポチ
TAP ポチ
mame_coordinate_xx
NEW DESIGNS JUST DROPPED OVER AT THE PONPORO PONPON ONLINE ST
てんや
HIGGLEDY-
わんや
PIGGLEDY

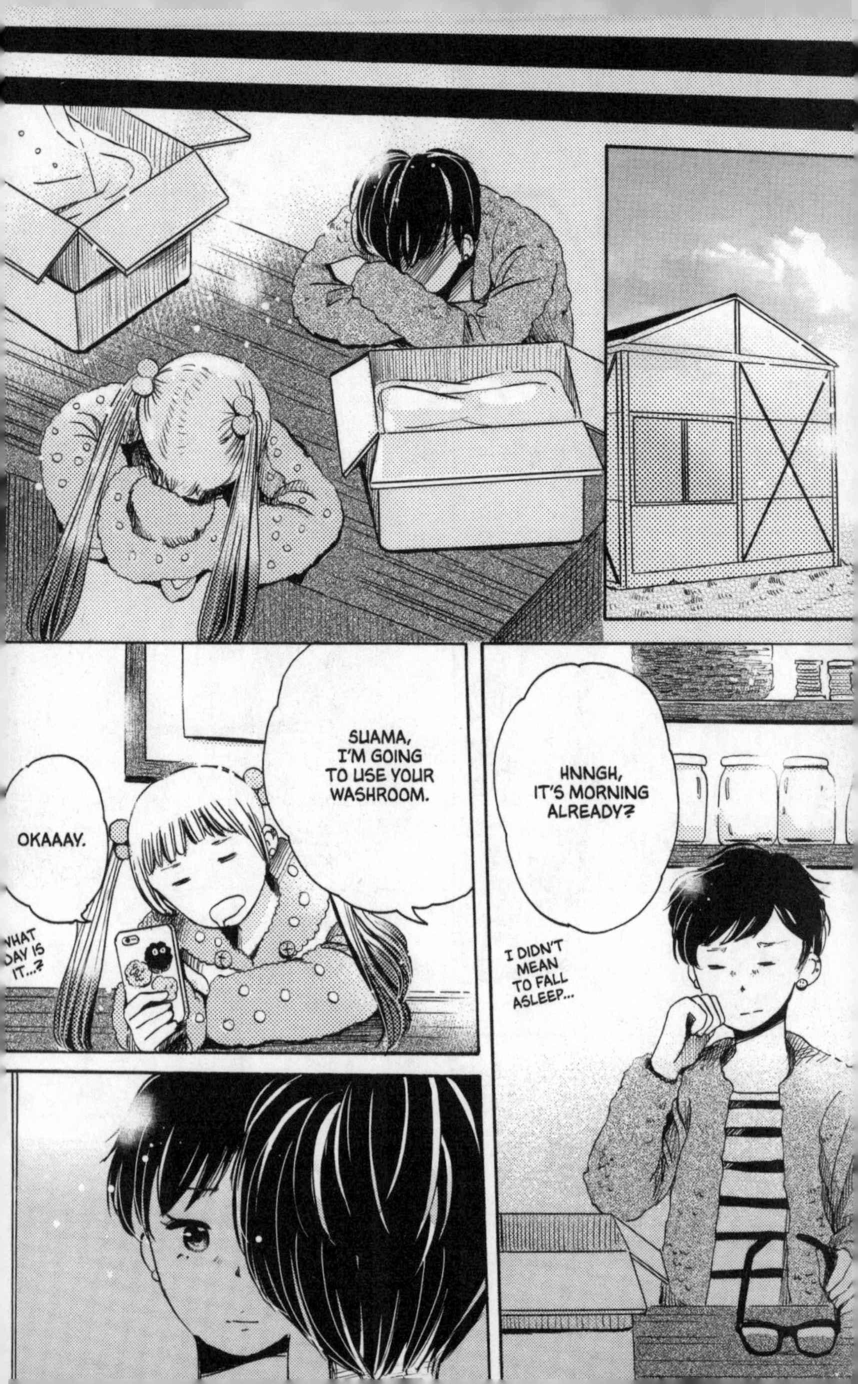
HNNGH, IT'S MORNING ALREADY?
I DIDN'T MEAN TO FALL ASLEEP...
SUAMA, I'M GOING TO USE YOUR WASHROOM.
OKAAAY.
WHAT DAY IS IT...?

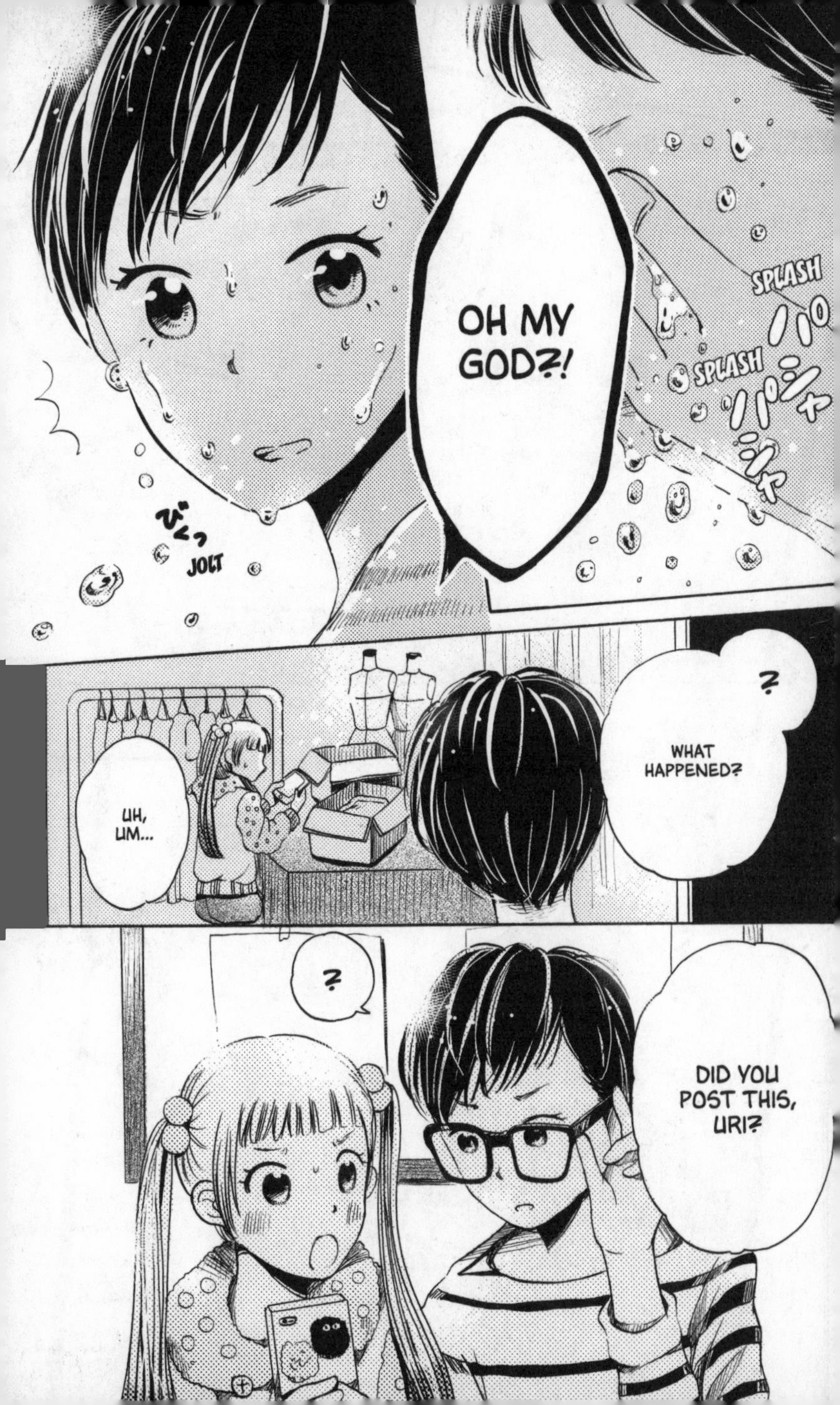
SPLASH
SPLASH
OH MY GOD?!
びくっ
JOLT
?
WHAT HAPPENED?
UH, UM...
DID YOU POST THIS, URI?
?

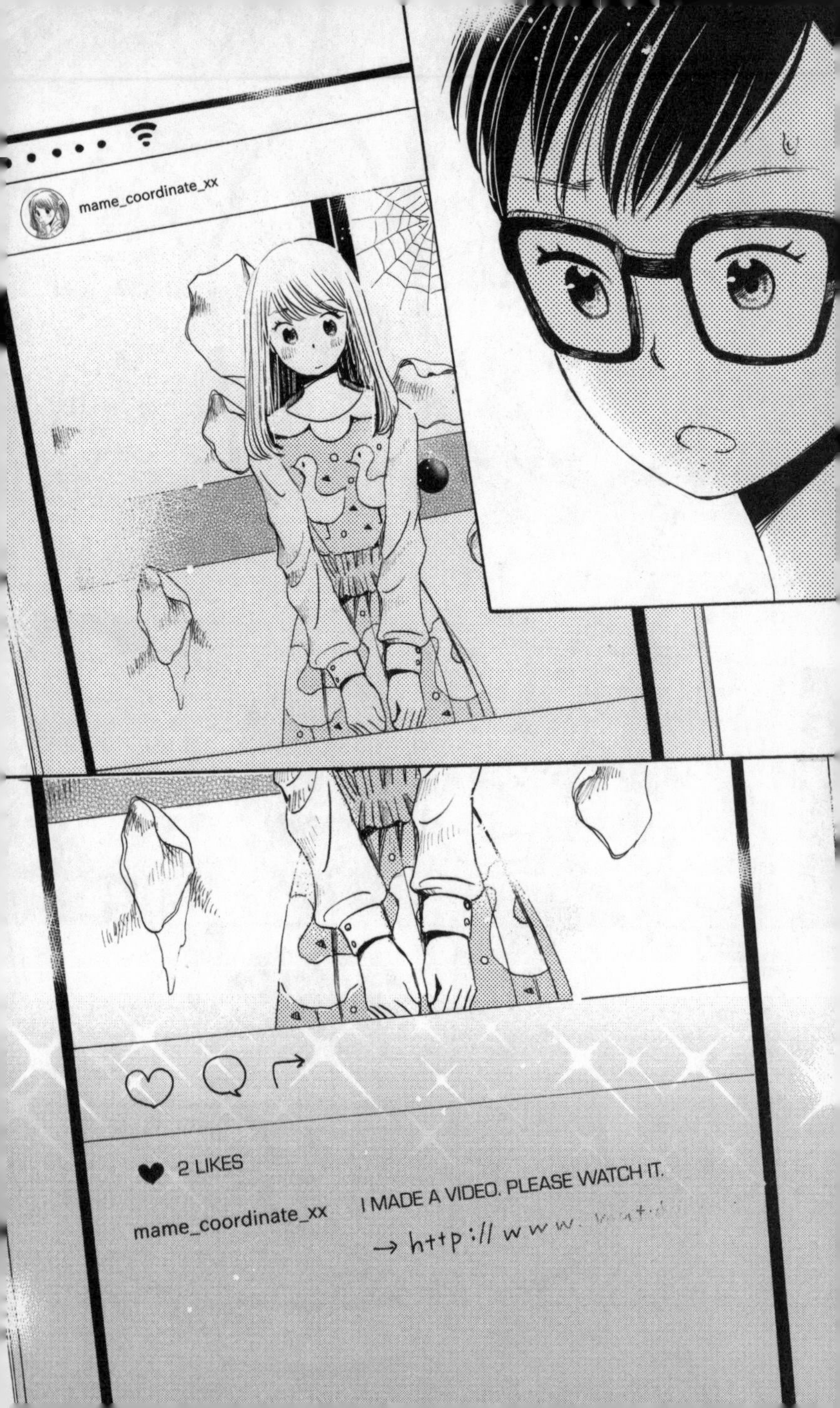
mame_coordinate_xx
2 LIKES
mame_coordinate_xx
I MADE A VIDEO. PLEASE WATCH IT.
→ http://www.

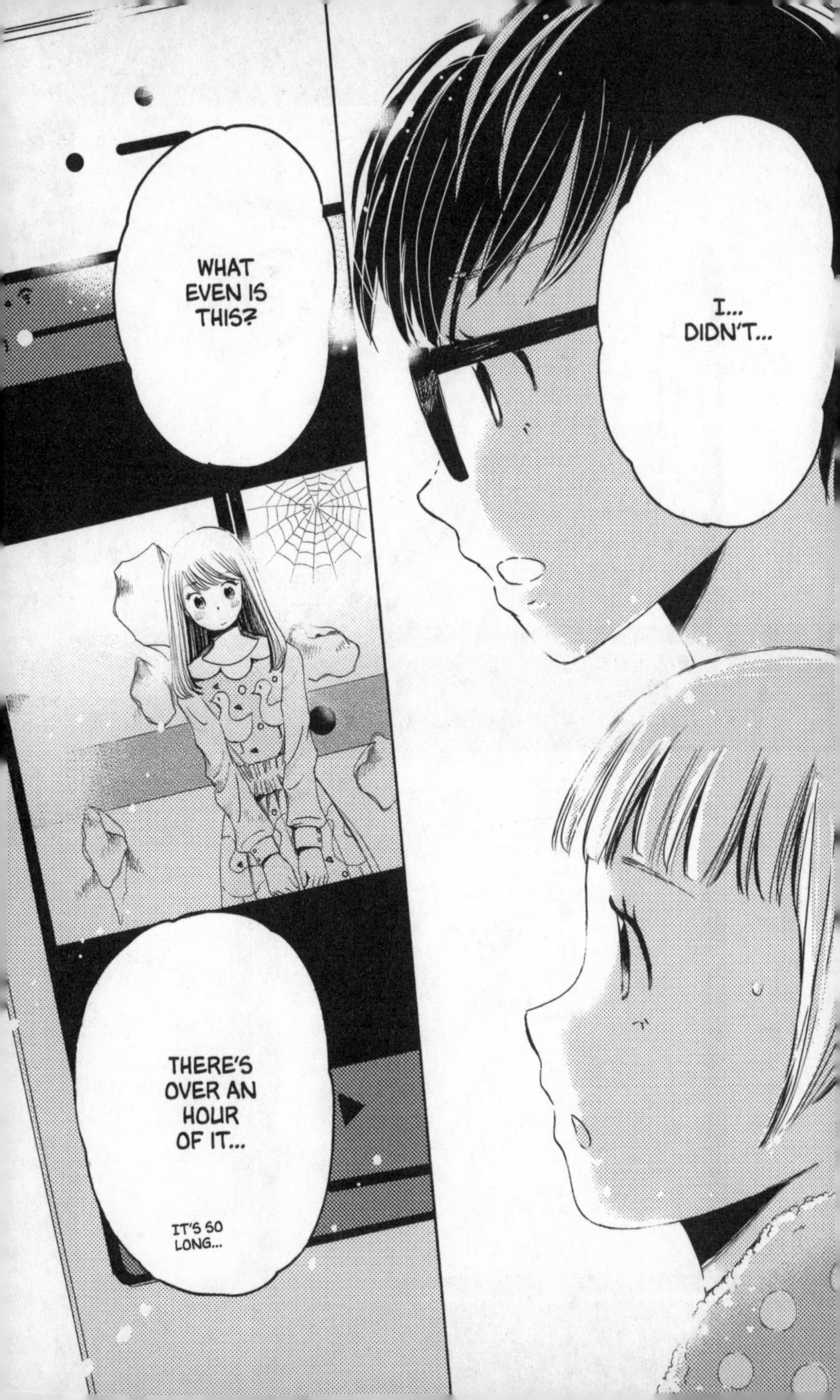
I... DIDN'T...
WHAT EVEN IS THIS?
THERE'S OVER AN HOUR OF IT...
IT'S SO LONG...

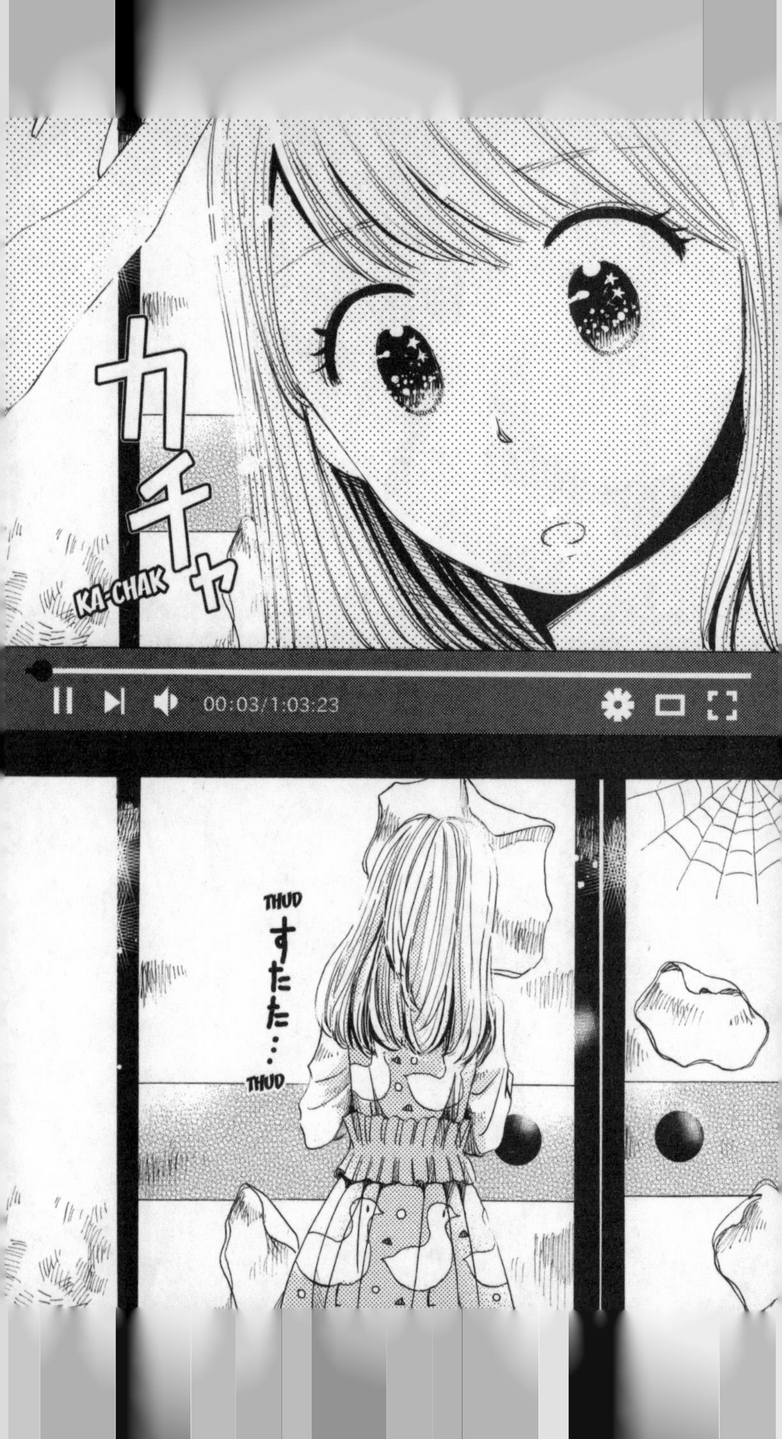
カチャ
KA-CHAK
00:03/1:03:23
THUD
すたた…
THUD

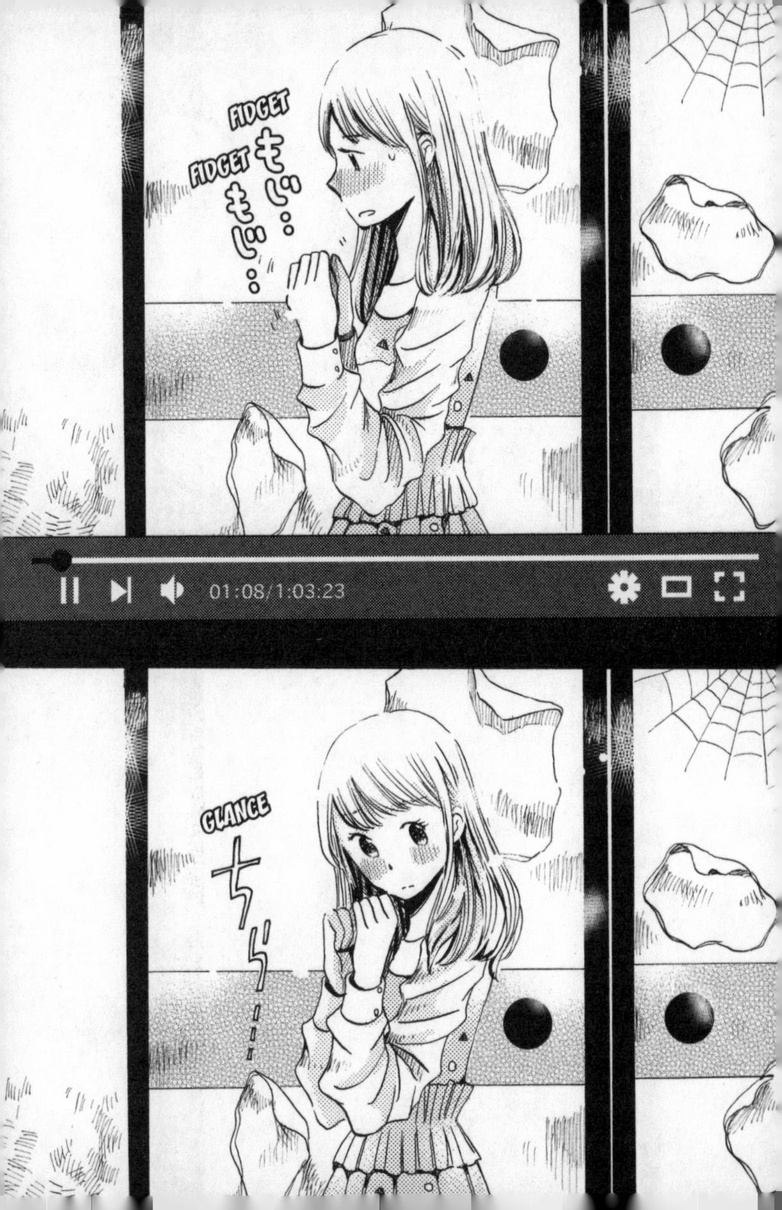
FIDGET もじ‥
FIDGET もじ‥
01:08/1:03:23
GLANCE ちら…

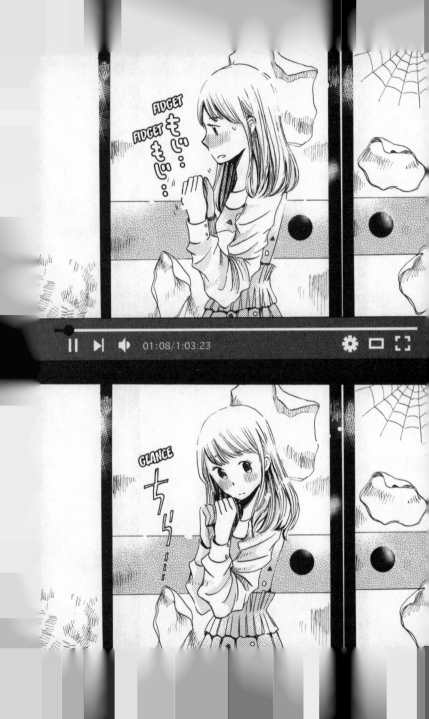

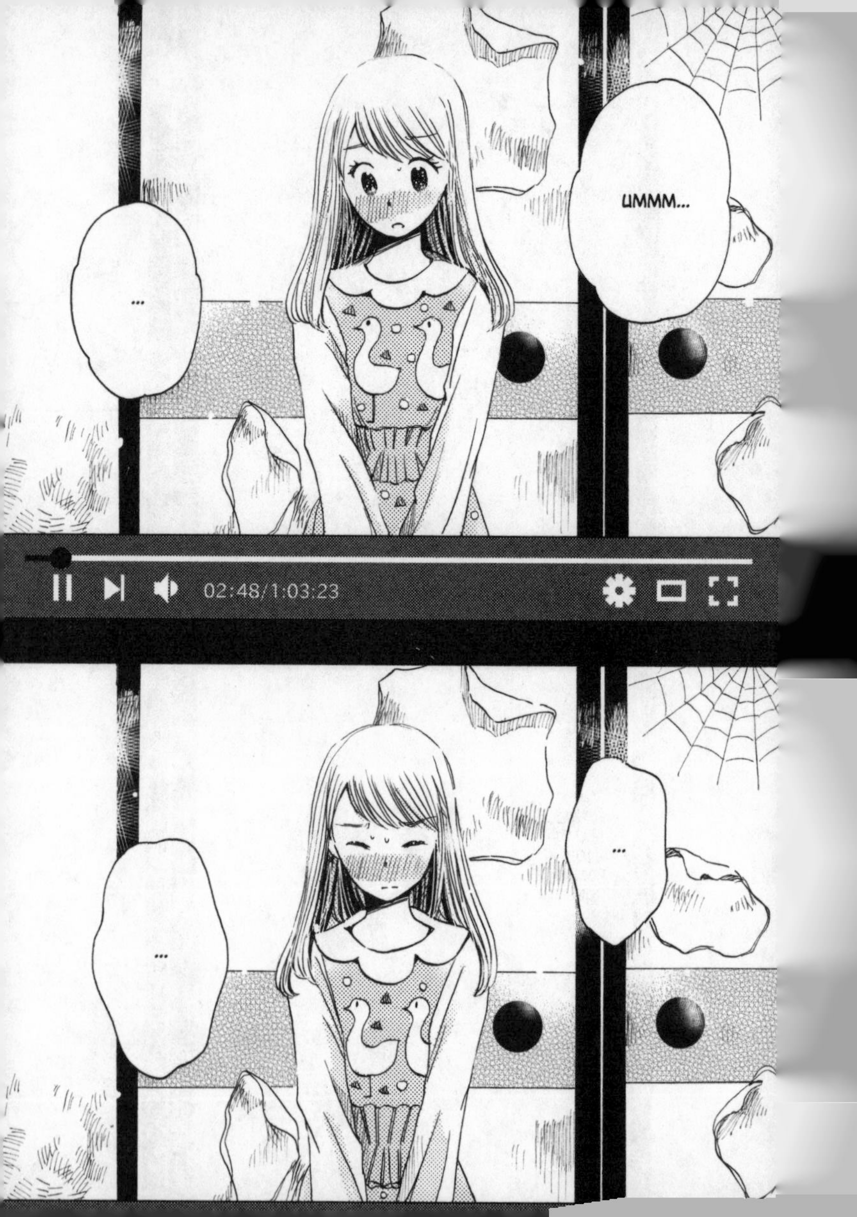
UMMM...
...
02:48/1:03:23
...
...

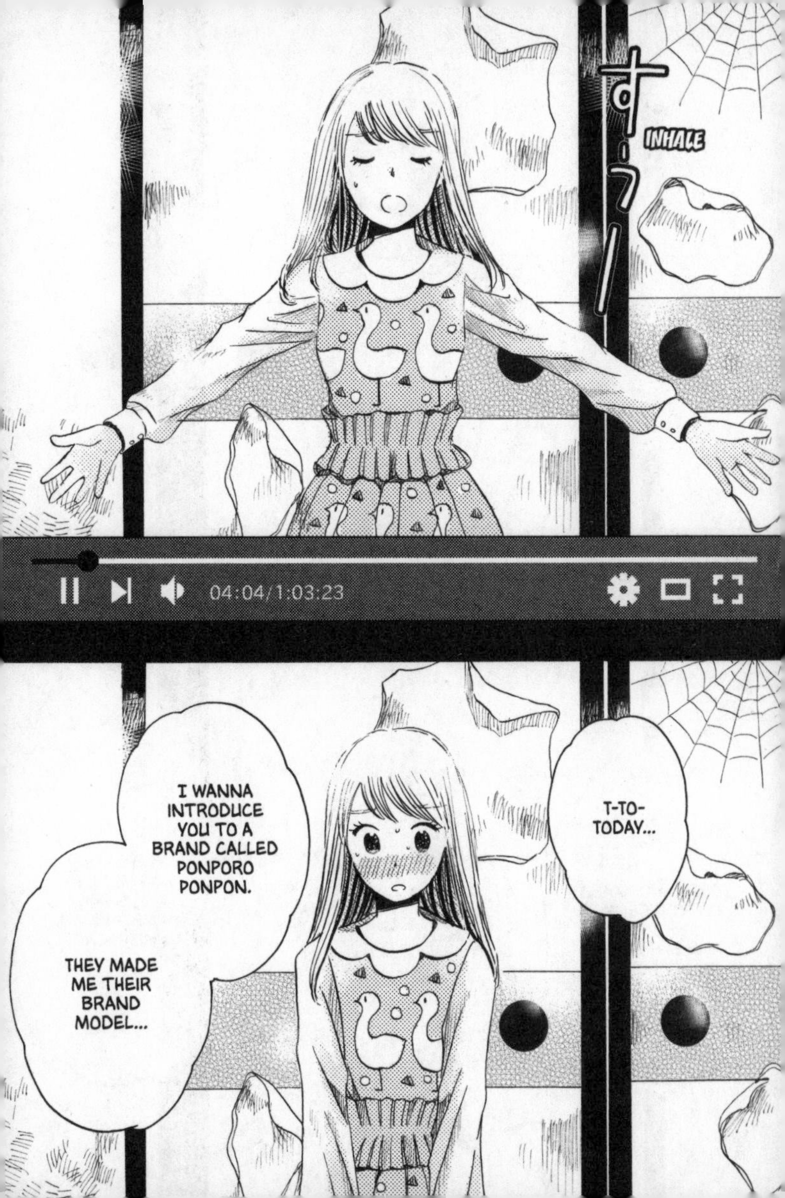
すーっ
INHALE
04:04/1:03:23
T-TO-TODAY...
I WANNA INTRODUCE YOU TO A BRAND CALLED PONPORO PONPON.
THEY MADE ME THEIR BRAND MODEL...

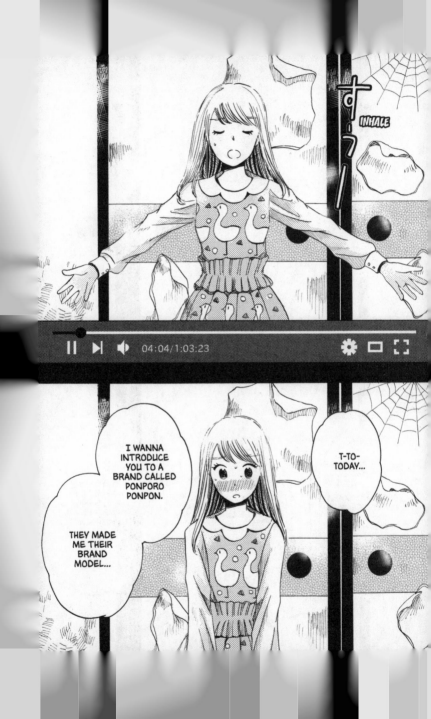

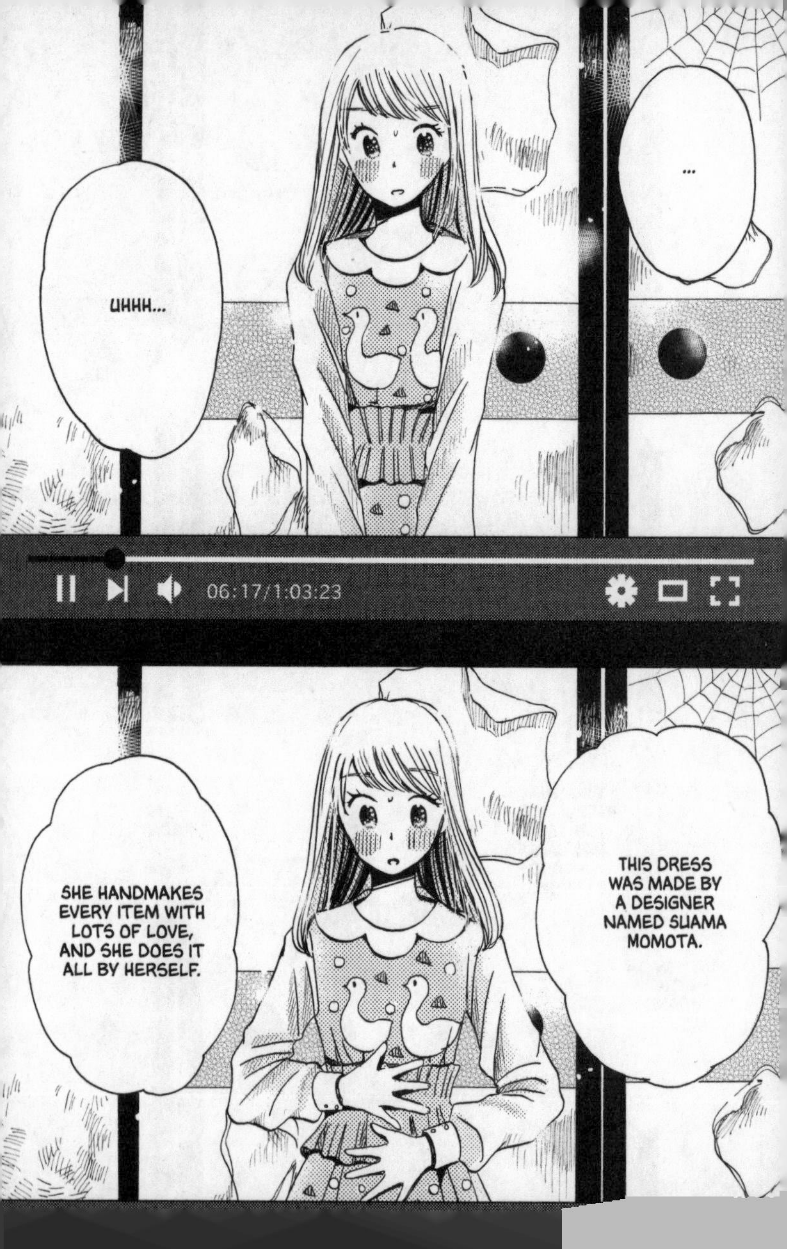
...
UHHH...
06:17/1:03:23
THIS DRESS WAS MADE BY A DESIGNER NAMED SUAMA MOMOTA.
SHE HANDMAKES EVERY ITEM WITH LOTS OF LOVE, AND SHE DOES IT ALL BY HERSELF.

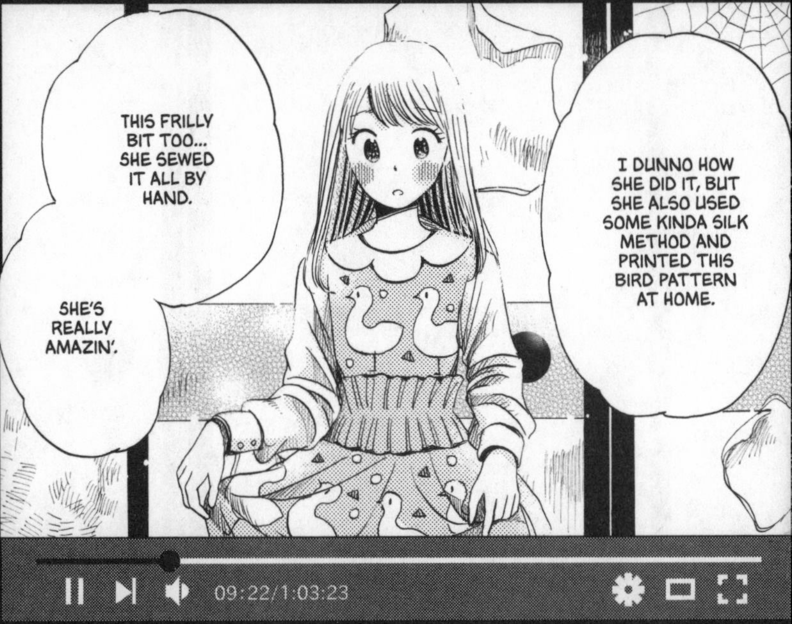
I DUNNO HOW SHE DID IT, BUT SHE ALSO USED SOME KINDA SILK METHOD AND PRINTED THIS BIRD PATTERN AT HOME.
THIS FRILLY BIT TOO... SHE SEWED IT ALL BY HAND.
SHE'S REALLY AMAZIN'.
09:22/1:03:23

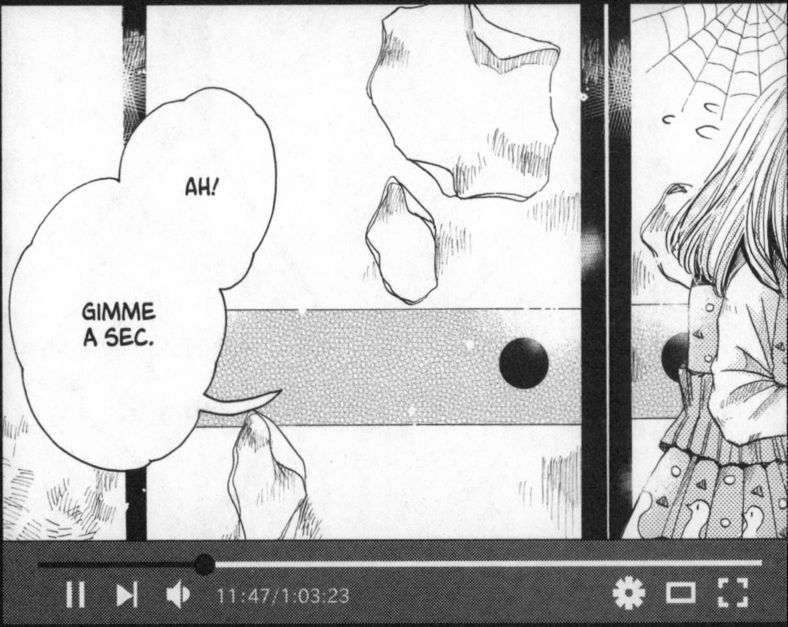
AH!
GIMME A SEC.
11:47/1:03:23

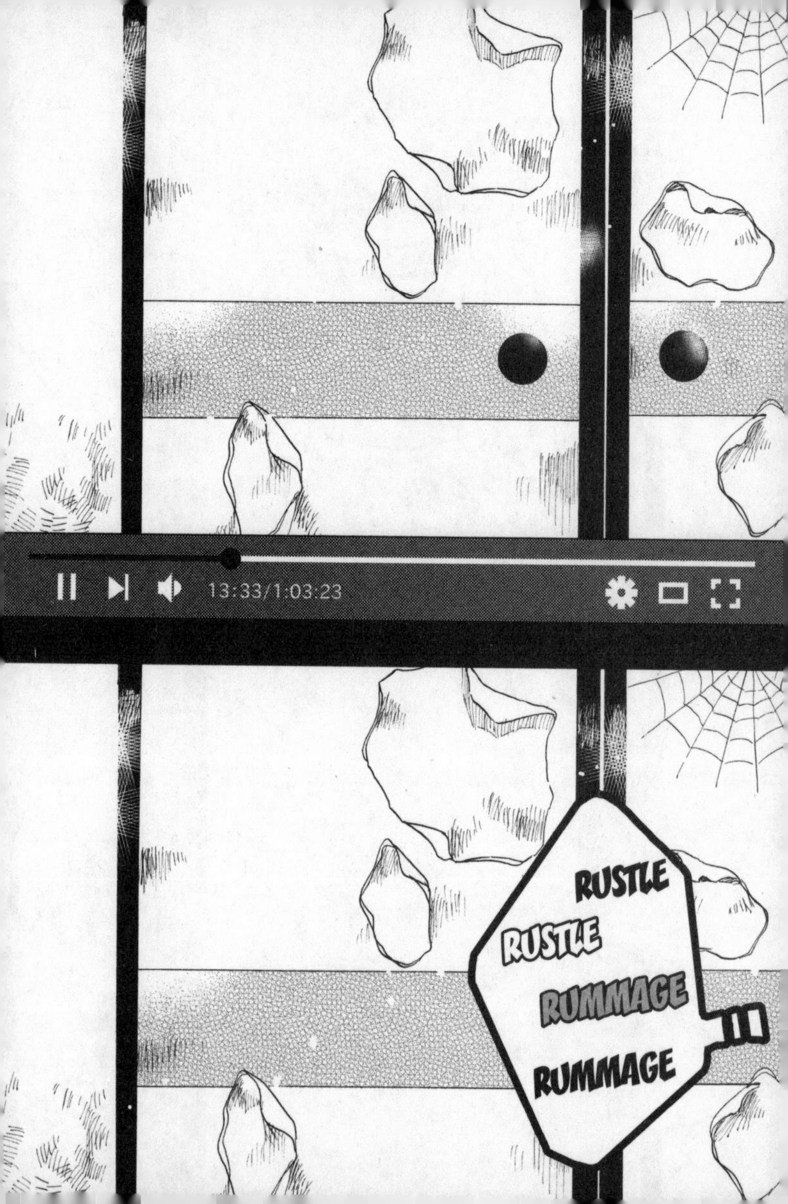
13:33/1:03:23
RUSTLE
RUSTLE
RUMMAGE
RUMMAGE

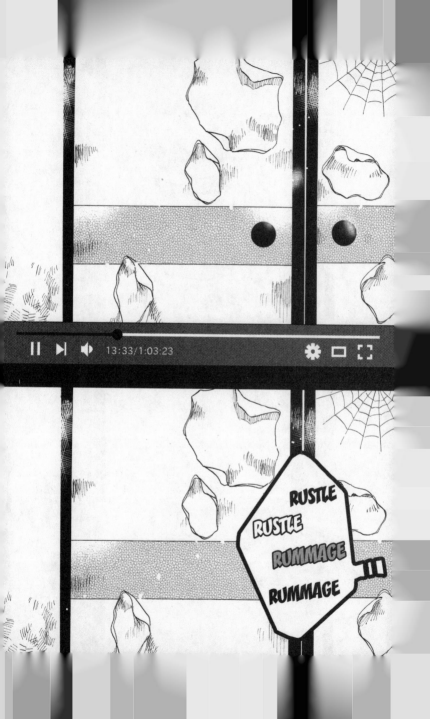

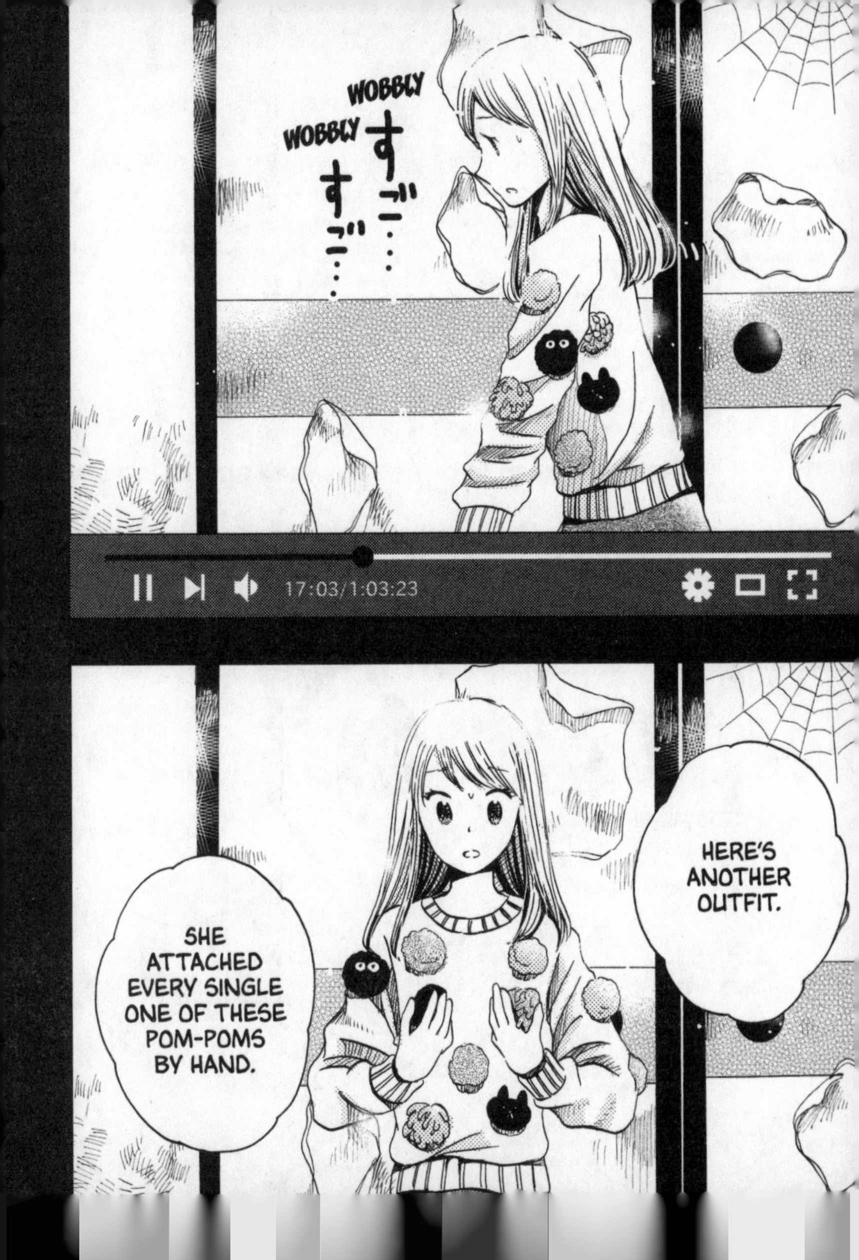
WOBBLY
WOBBLY
すごー…
すごー…
17:03/1:03:23
HERE'S ANOTHER OUTFIT.
SHE ATTACHED EVERY SINGLE ONE OF THESE POM-POMS BY HAND.

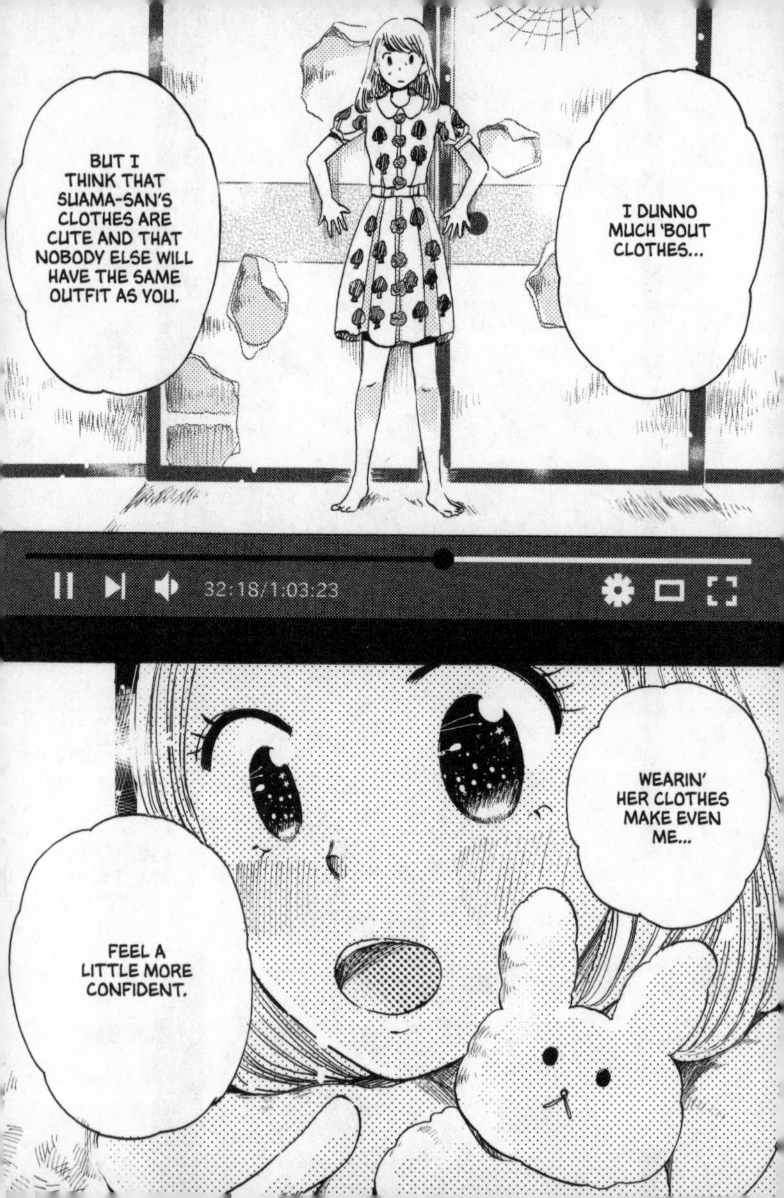
I DUNNO MUCH 'BOUT CLOTHES...
BUT I THINK THAT SUAMA-SAN'S CLOTHES ARE CUTE AND THAT NOBODY ELSE WILL HAVE THE SAME OUTFIT AS YOU.
32:18/1:03:23
WEARIN' HER CLOTHES MAKE EVEN ME...
FEEL A LITTLE MORE CONFIDENT.

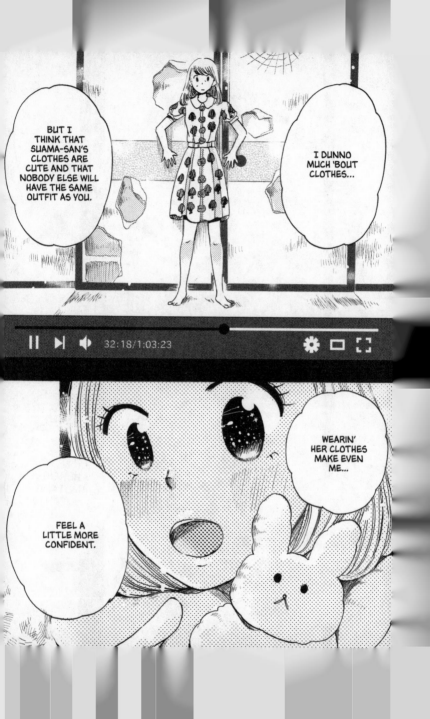

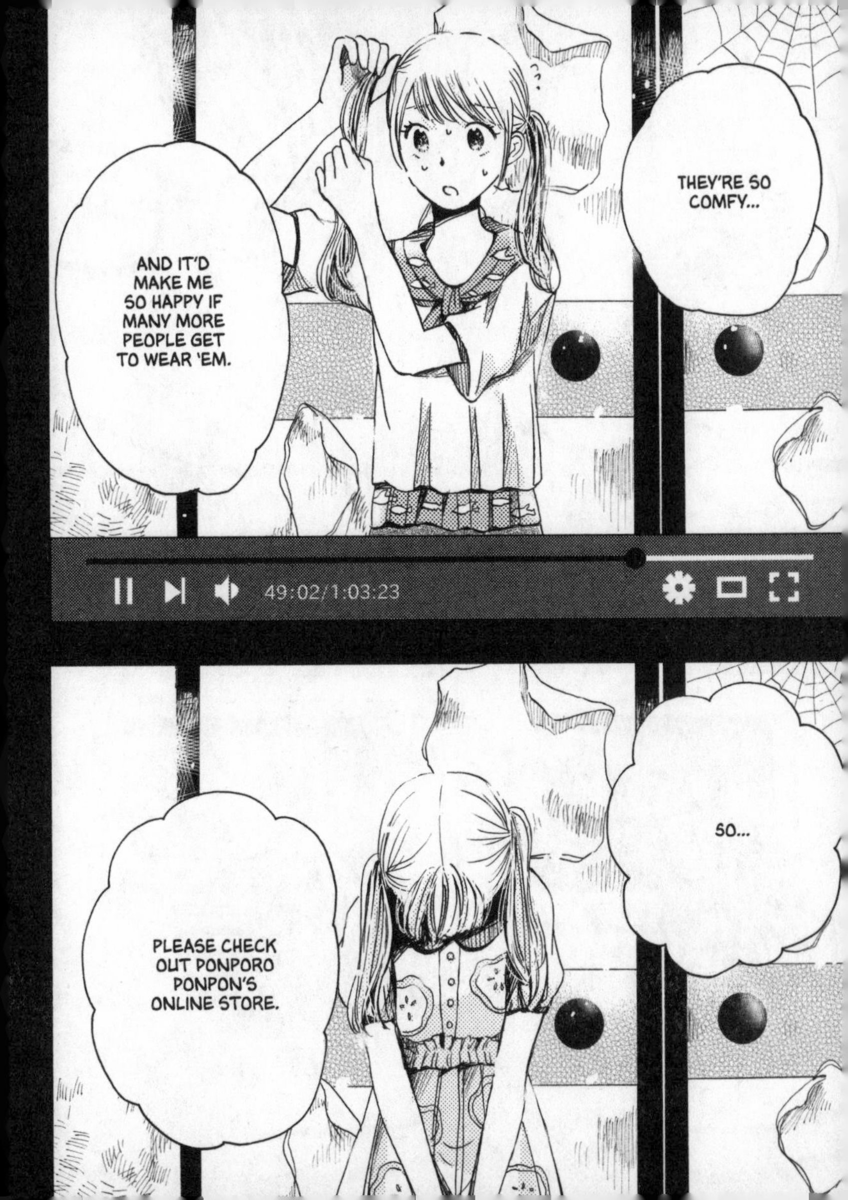
THEY'RE SO COMFY...
AND IT'D MAKE ME SO HAPPY IF MANY MORE PEOPLE GET TO WEAR 'EM.
49:02/1:03:23
SO...
PLEASE CHECK OUT PONPORO PONPON'S ONLINE STORE.

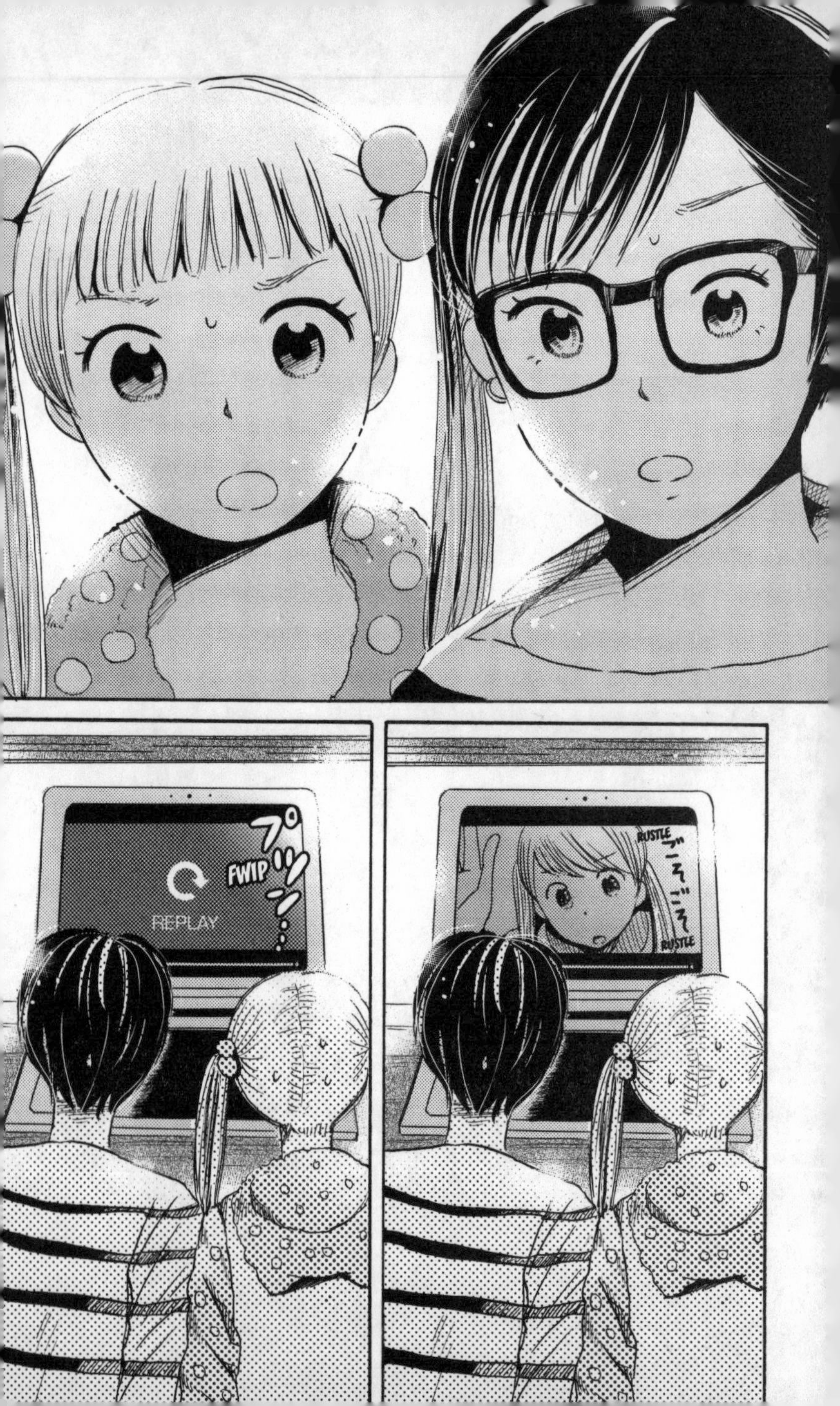
RUSTLE
RUSTLE
REPLAY
FWIP

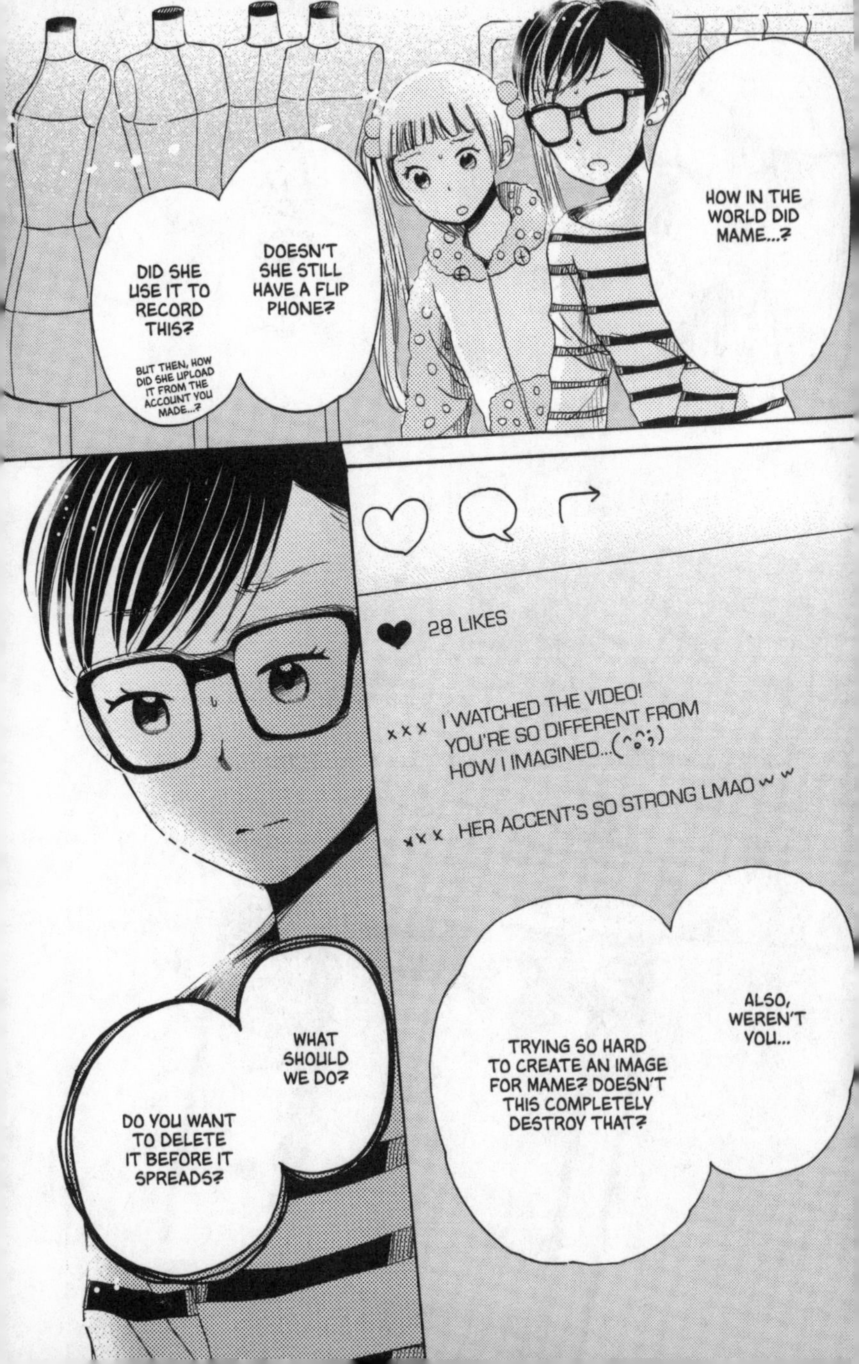

HOW IN THE WORLD DID MAME...?
DOESN'T SHE STILL HAVE A FLIP PHONE?
DID SHE USE IT TO RECORD THIS?
BUT THEN, HOW DID SHE UPLOAD IT FROM THE ACCOUNT YOU MADE...?
28 LIKES
××× I WATCHED THE VIDEO! YOU'RE SO DIFFERENT FROM HOW I IMAGINED...(^o^;)
××× HER ACCENT'S SO STRONG LMAO w w
ALSO, WEREN'T YOU...
TRYING SO HARD TO CREATE AN IMAGE FOR MAME? DOESN'T THIS COMPLETELY DESTROY THAT?
WHAT SHOULD WE DO?
DO YOU WANT TO DELETE IT BEFORE IT SPREADS?

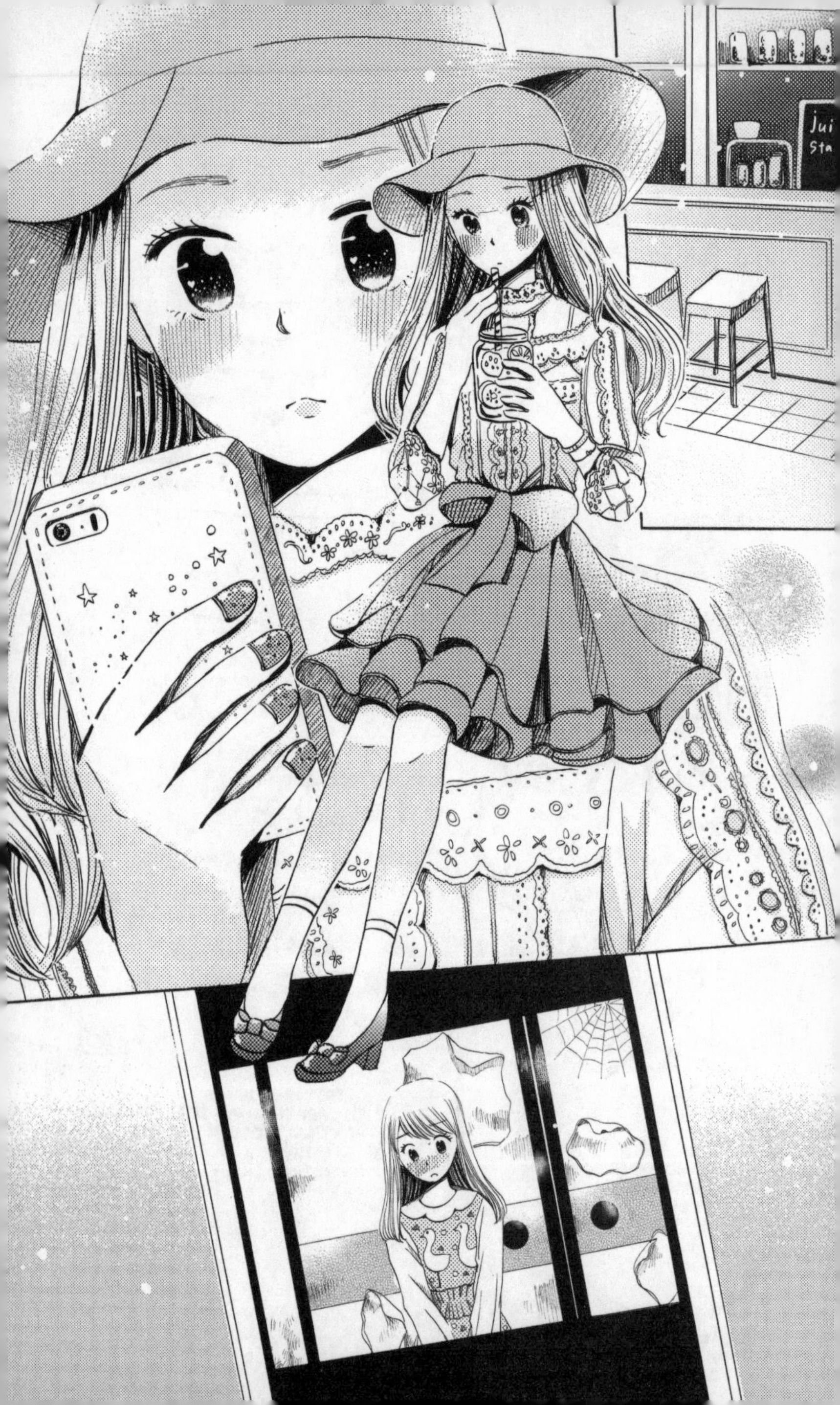

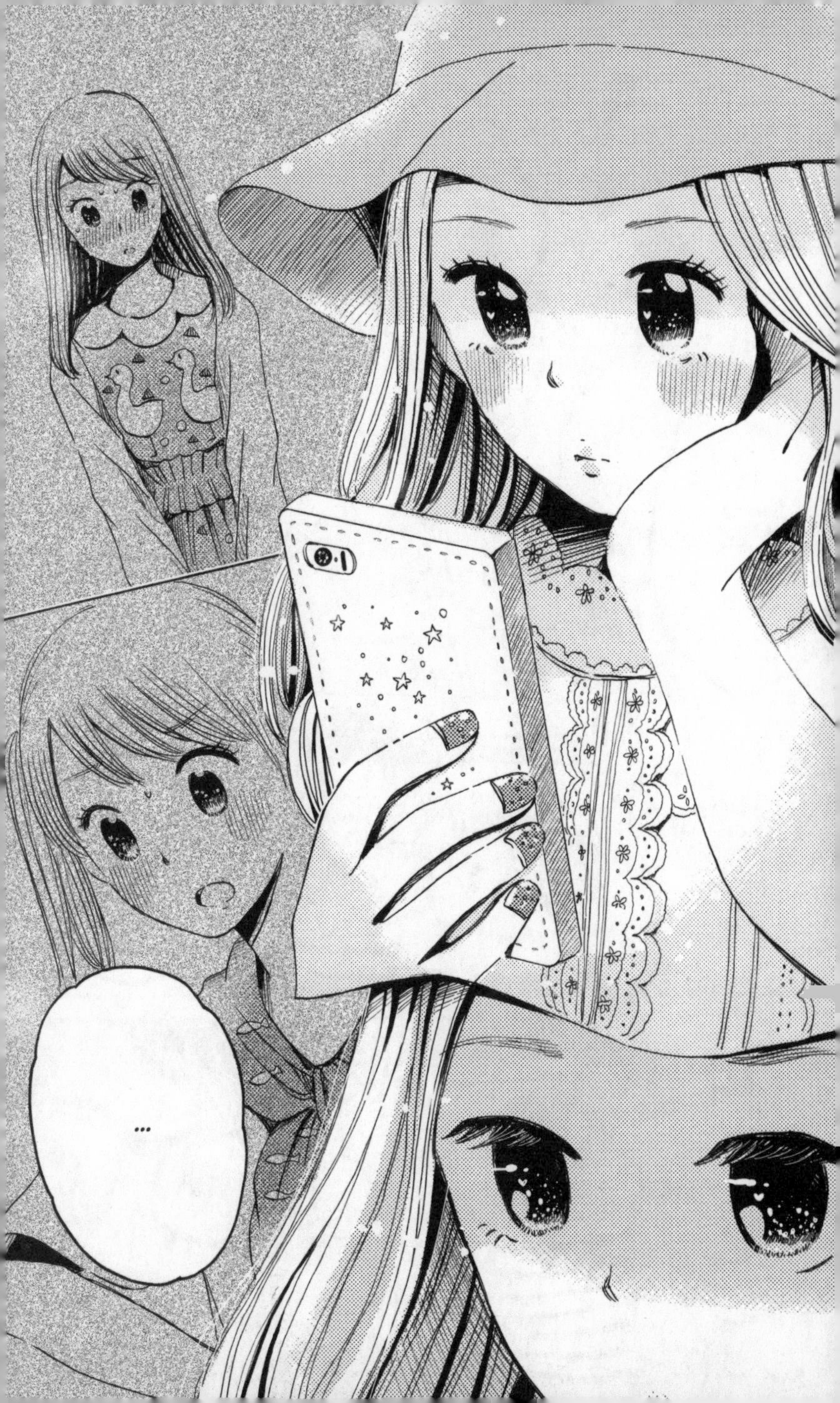
...

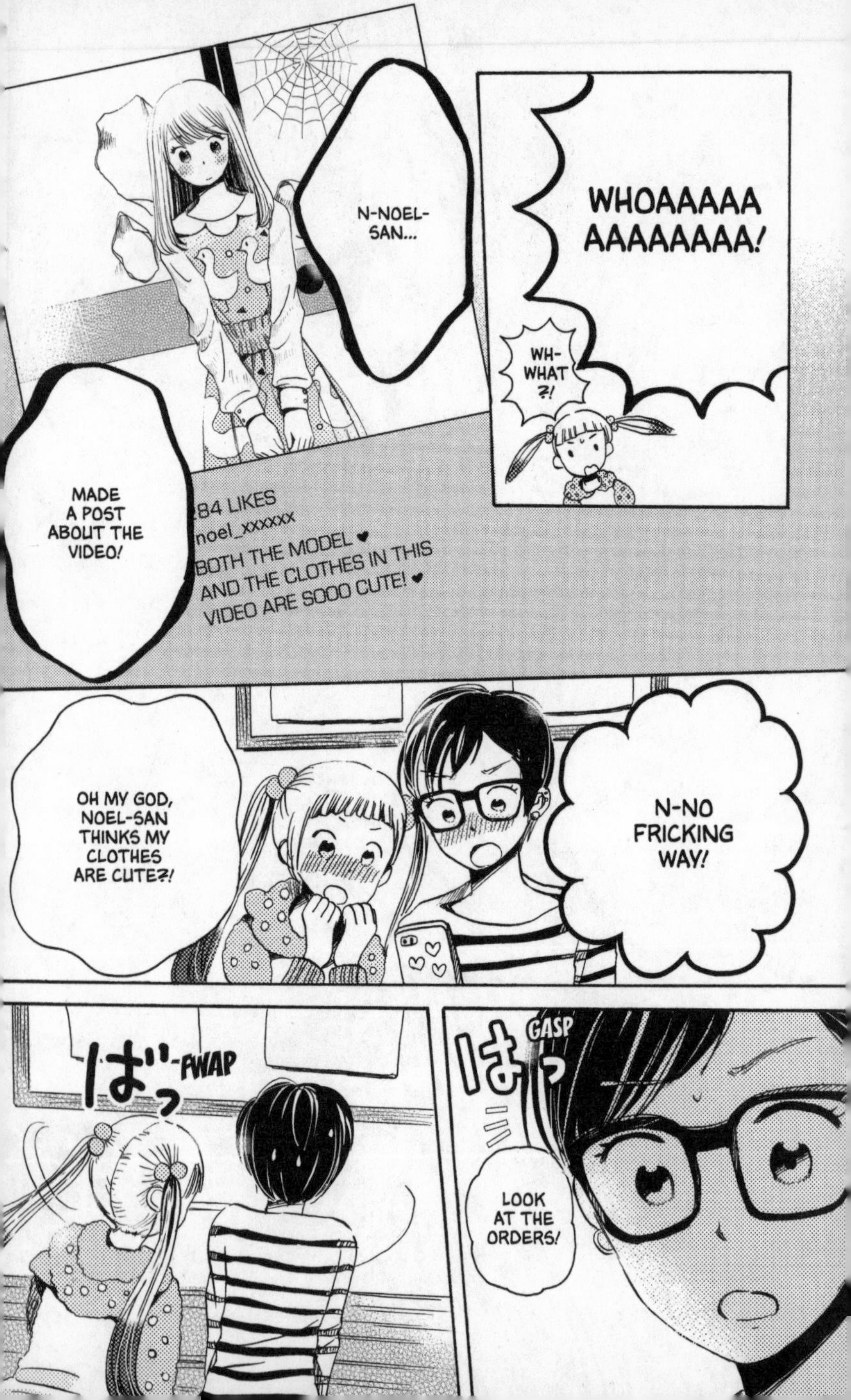
WHOAAAAA AAAAAAAA!
WH-WHAT?!
N-NOEL-SAN...
MADE A POST ABOUT THE VIDEO!
284 LIKES
noel_xxxxxx
BOTH THE MODEL ♥
AND THE CLOTHES IN THIS VIDEO ARE SOOO CUTE! ♥
N-NO FRICKING WAY!
OH MY GOD, NOEL-SAN THINKS MY CLOTHES ARE CUTE?!
はっ
GASP
LOOK AT THE ORDERS!
ばっ
FWAP

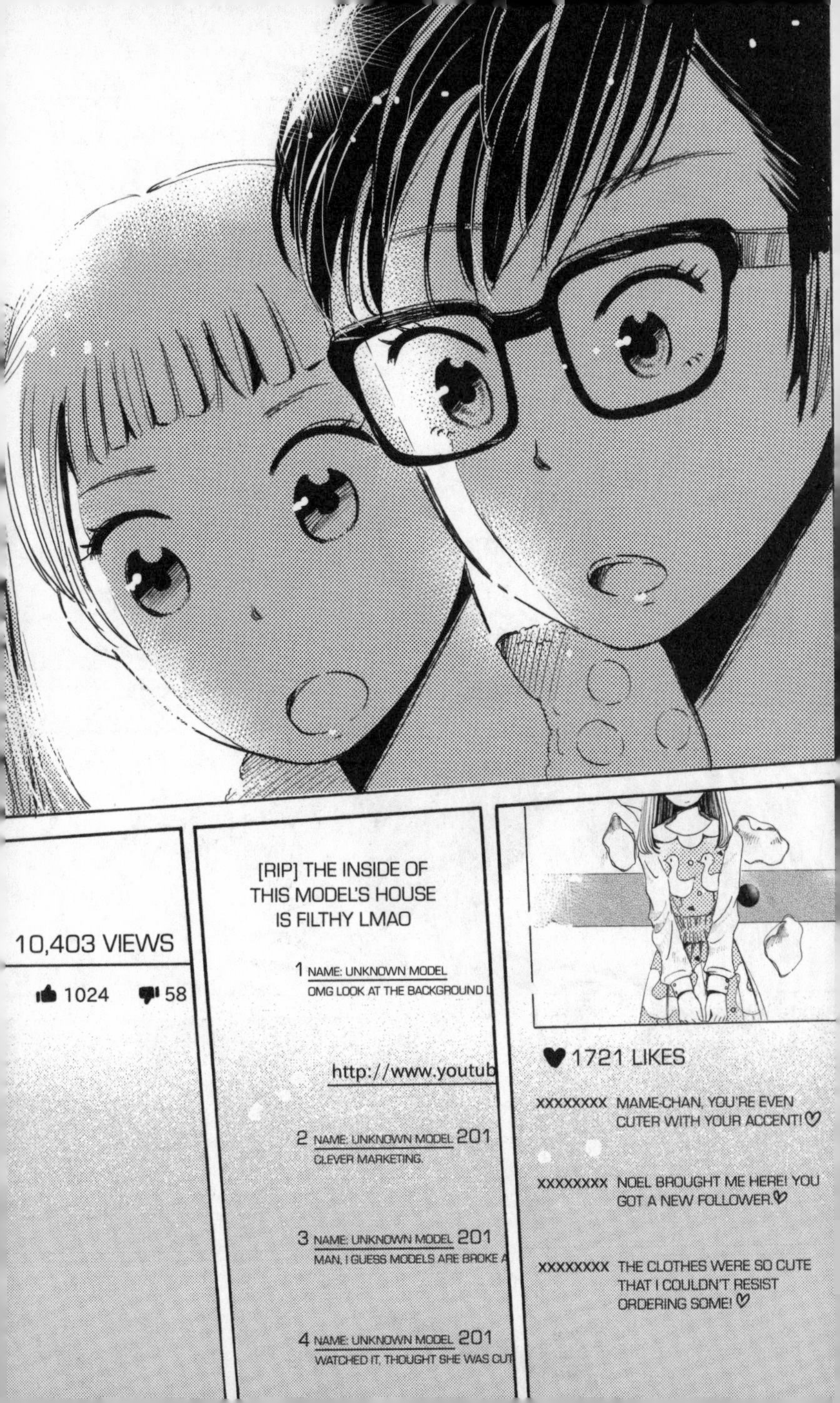
1721 LIKES
XXXXXXXX MAME-CHAN, YOU'RE EVEN CUTER WITH YOUR ACCENT!
XXXXXXXX NOEL BROUGHT ME HERE! YOU GOT A NEW FOLLOWER.
XXXXXXXX THE CLOTHES WERE SO CUTE THAT I COULDN'T RESIST ORDERING SOME!
[RIP] THE INSIDE OF THIS MODEL'S HOUSE IS FILTHY LMAO
1 NAME: UNKNOWN MODEL
OMG LOOK AT THE BACKGROUND L
http://www.youtub
2 NAME: UNKNOWN MODEL 201
CLEVER MARKETING.
3 NAME: UNKNOWN MODEL 201
MAN, I GUESS MODELS ARE BROKE A
4 NAME: UNKNOWN MODEL 201
WATCHED IT, THOUGHT SHE WAS CUT
10,403 VIEWS
1024
58

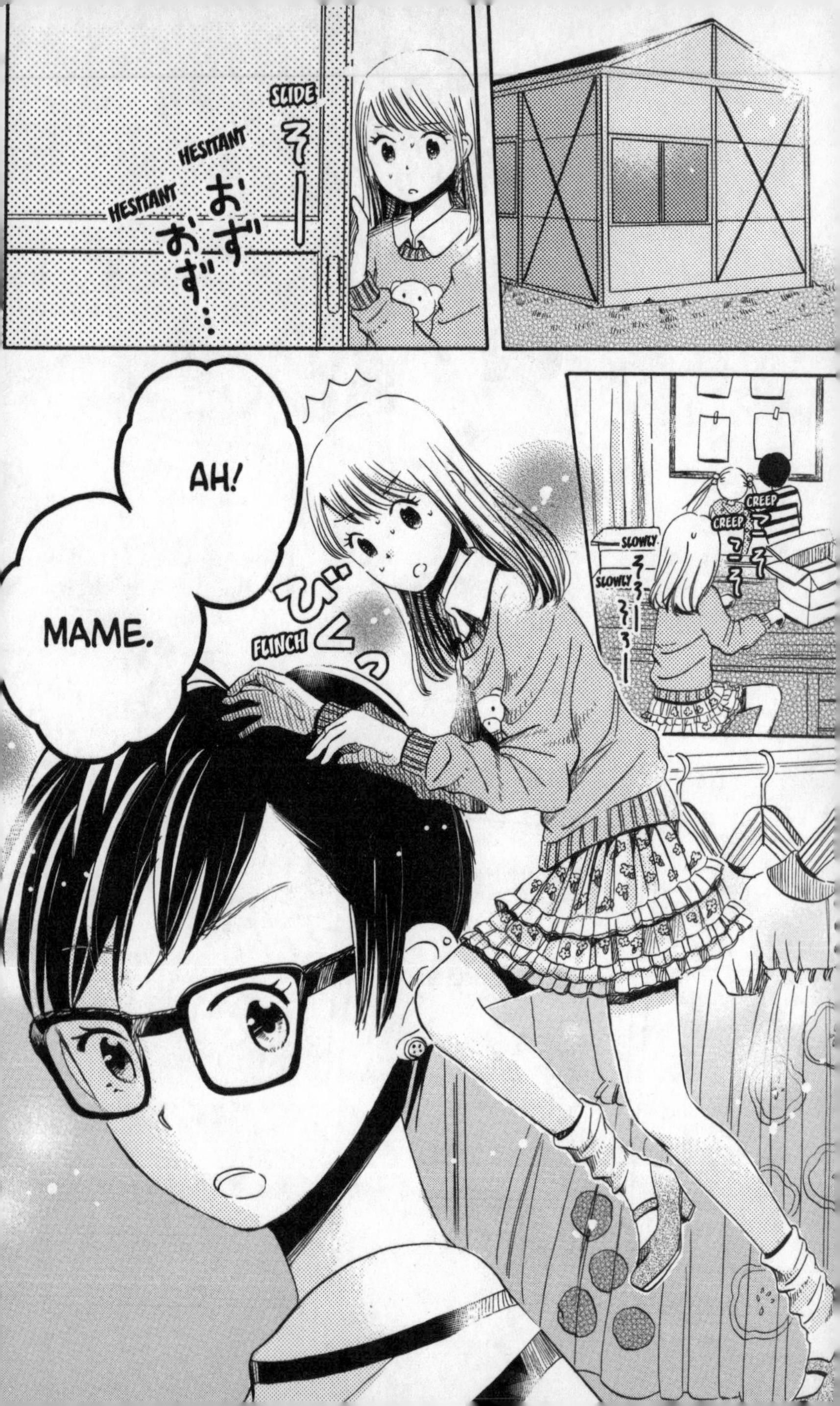
SLIDE
そー
HESITANT
HESITANT
おずおず…
CREEP
CREEP
SLOWLY
SLOWLY
びくっ
FLINCH
AH!
MAME.

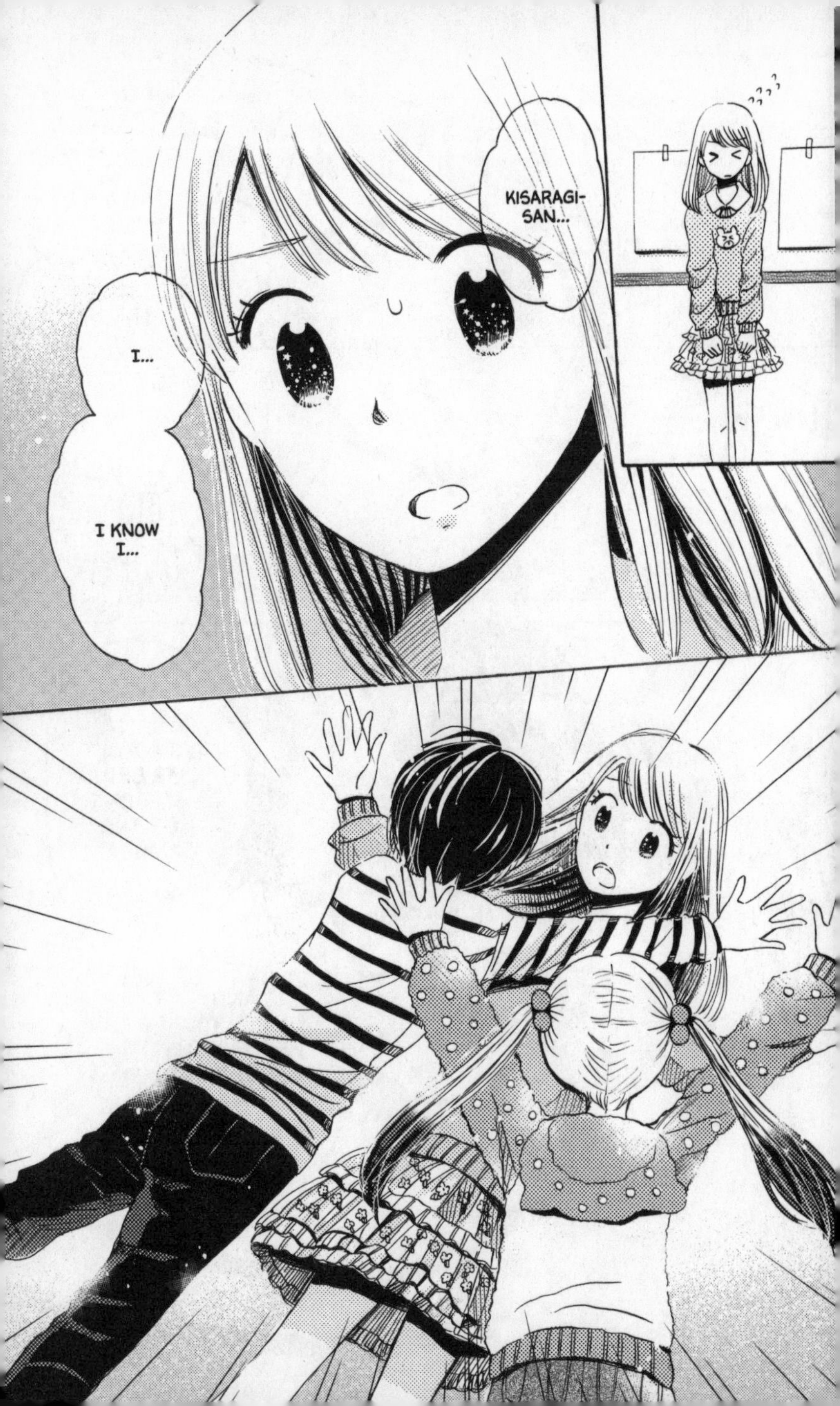
KISARAGI-SAN...
I...
I KNOW I...

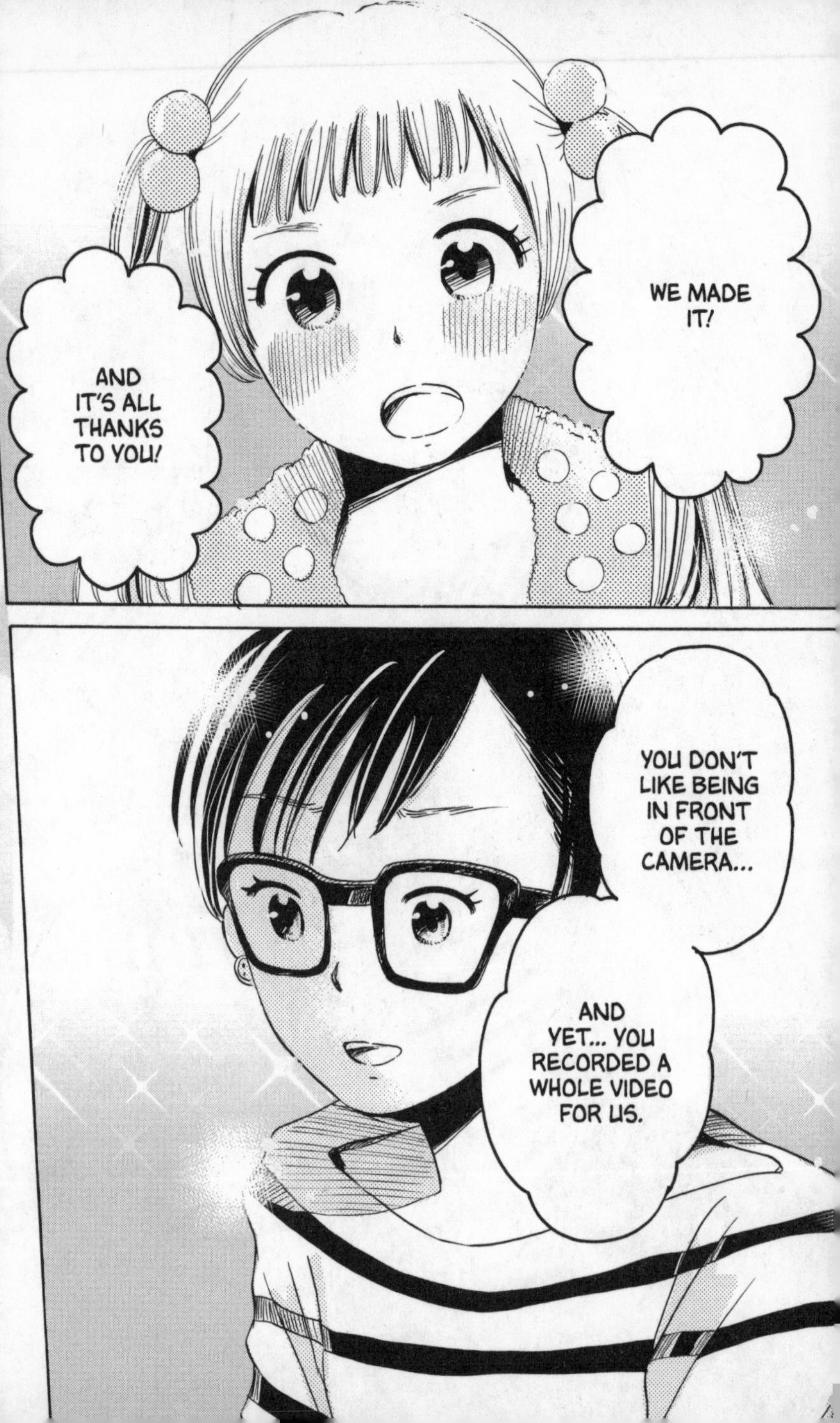
WE MADE IT!
AND IT'S ALL THANKS TO YOU!
YOU DON'T LIKE BEING IN FRONT OF THE CAMERA...
AND YET... YOU RECORDED A WHOLE VIDEO FOR US.

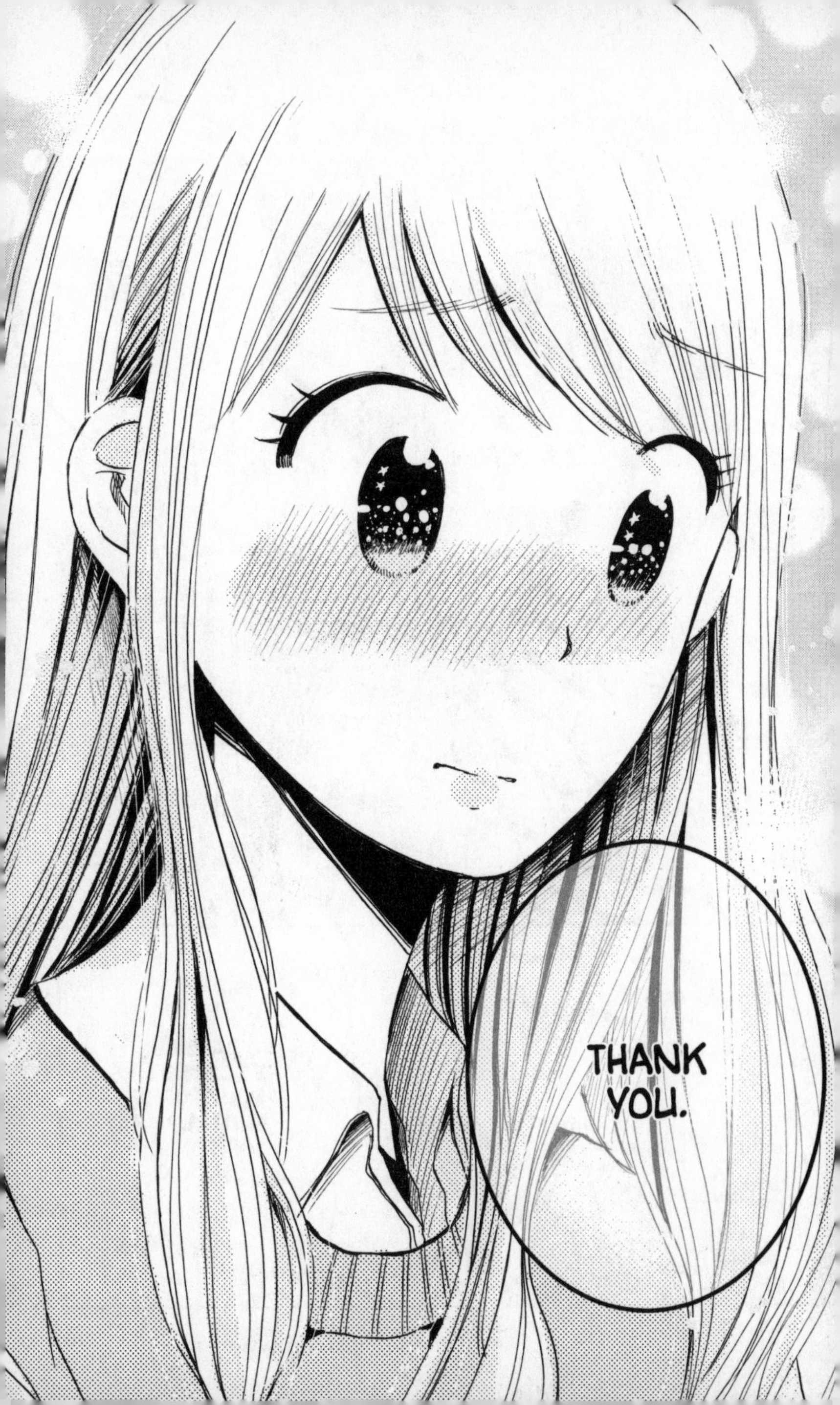
THANK YOU.

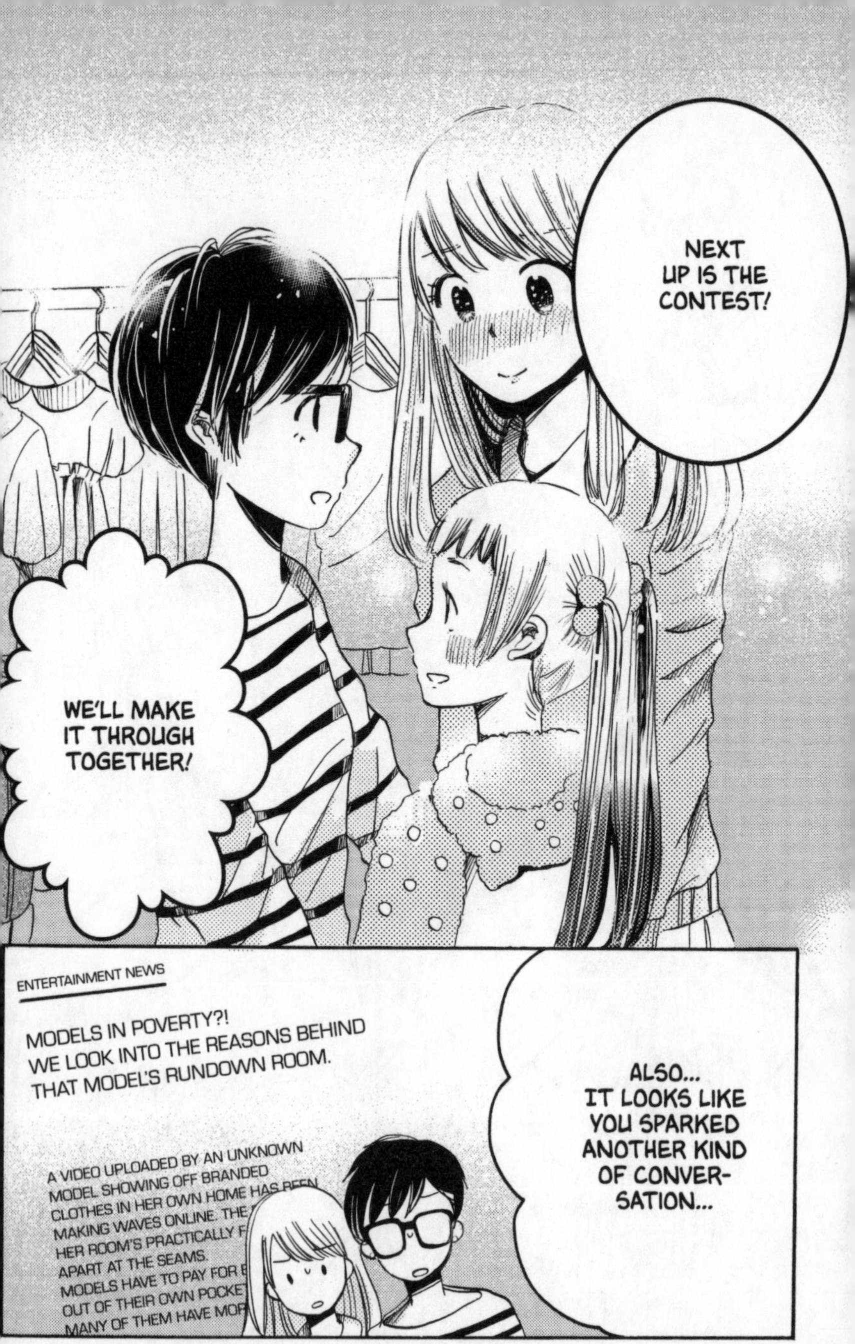
NEXT UP IS THE CONTEST!
WE'LL MAKE IT THROUGH TOGETHER!
ALSO... IT LOOKS LIKE YOU SPARKED ANOTHER KIND OF CONVER-SATION...
ENTERTAINMENT NEWS
MODELS IN POVERTY?! WE LOOK INTO THE REASONS BEHIND THAT MODEL'S RUNDOWN ROOM.
A VIDEO UPLOADED BY AN UNKNOWN MODEL SHOWING OFF BRANDED CLOTHES IN HER OWN HOME HAS BEEN MAKING WAVES ONLINE. THE HER ROOM'S PRACTICALLY APART AT THE SEAMS. MODELS HAVE TO PAY FOR OUT OF THEIR OWN POCKE MANY OF THEM HAVE MOR

# M A M E
## coordinate

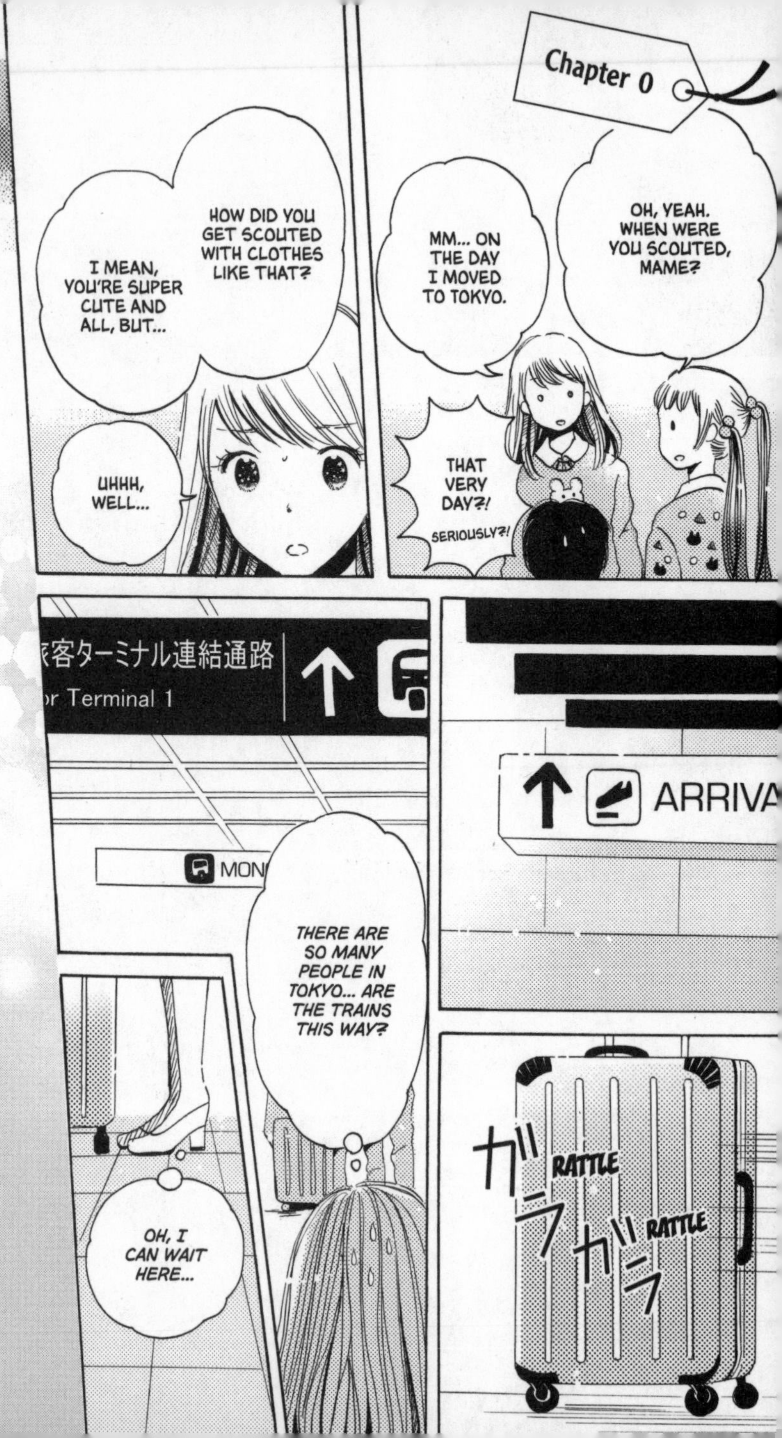

Chapter 0
OH, YEAH. WHEN WERE YOU SCOUTED, MAME?
MM... ON THE DAY I MOVED TO TOKYO.
THAT VERY DAY?!
SERIOUSLY?!
HOW DID YOU GET SCOUTED WITH CLOTHES LIKE THAT?
I MEAN, YOU'RE SUPER CUTE AND ALL, BUT...
UHHH, WELL...
ARRIVA
客ターミナル連結通路
Terminal 1
MON
THERE ARE SO MANY PEOPLE IN TOKYO... ARE THE TRAINS THIS WAY?
ガラ RATTLE
ガラ RATTLE
OH, I CAN WAIT HERE...

...

印旛日本医大 Inba
新遥子 Shi
成田 Nar
2 THE TRAIN ON

PLEASE STAND BEHIND THE WHITE LINE.

EXCUSE ME.

CAN I SPEAK TO YOU FOR A MOMENT?

A FEW DAYS LATER...

I WAS MAKING A BIG TRIP, SO I WAS WEARING A DRESS THAT I'D BORROWED FROM MY MOM.

FROM WHEN SHE WAS YOUNG...

YOU'RE *THAT* PERSON ?!

WHAT HAPPENED TO THE DRESS?

I SENT IT BACK HOME...

TO BE CONTINUED IN VOL. 3!

**TOKYOPOP** believes all types of romances deserve to be celebrated. *LOVE x LOVE* was born from that idea and our commitment to representing a variety of stories and voices as diverse as our fans.

TOKYOPOP

*Mai Naoi*

# YURI ESPOIR, VOLUME 1

## ♀LOVE-x-LOVE♀

After finding out she's to be forced into a marriage of convenience as soon as she graduates high school, Kokoro sees her life ending before her eyes at her father's wishes. And so, in her final year of high school, she decides to indulge in her love of other women — and create an incredible sketchbook of lesbian romance to leave behind as her legacy. As she observes the young women of her town, she learns more about their desires, their struggles, and the unpredictable whims of love.

# BREATH OF FLOWERS, VOLUME 1

*Caly*

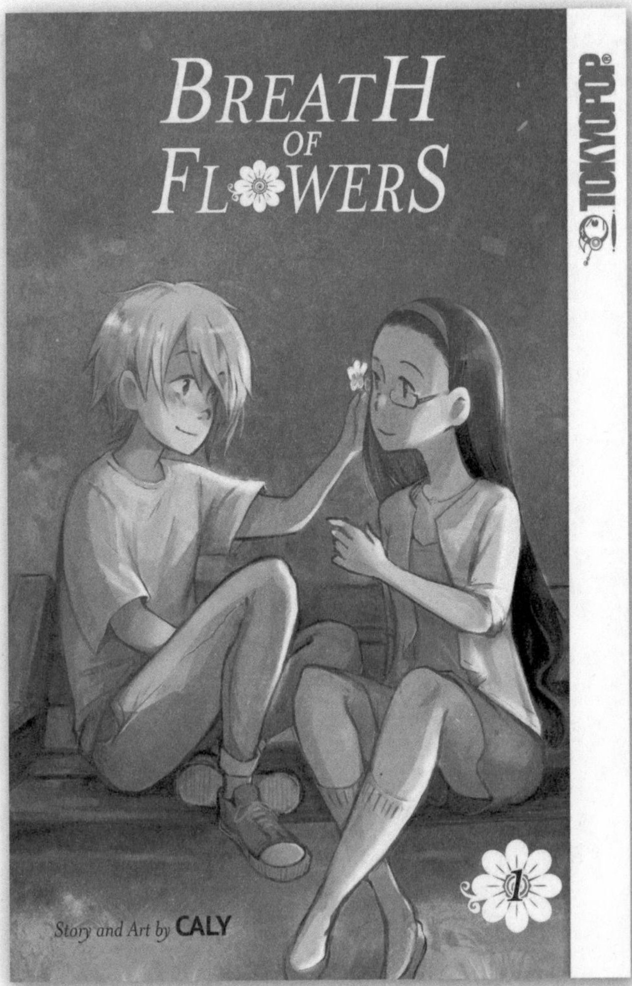
BREATH OF FLOWERS
TOKYOPOP
Story and Art by CALY
1

LOVE-x-LOVE

Azami has always been attracted only to boys, especially the handsome Gwyn. Intelligent, sporty, attractive and just a little older than Azami, she's sure he would be an ideal boyfriend. Then, on the day Azami finally gets the courage to confess her feelings, everything she believes is suddenly called into question when she finds out that Gwyn is actually a girl!

TOKYOPOP

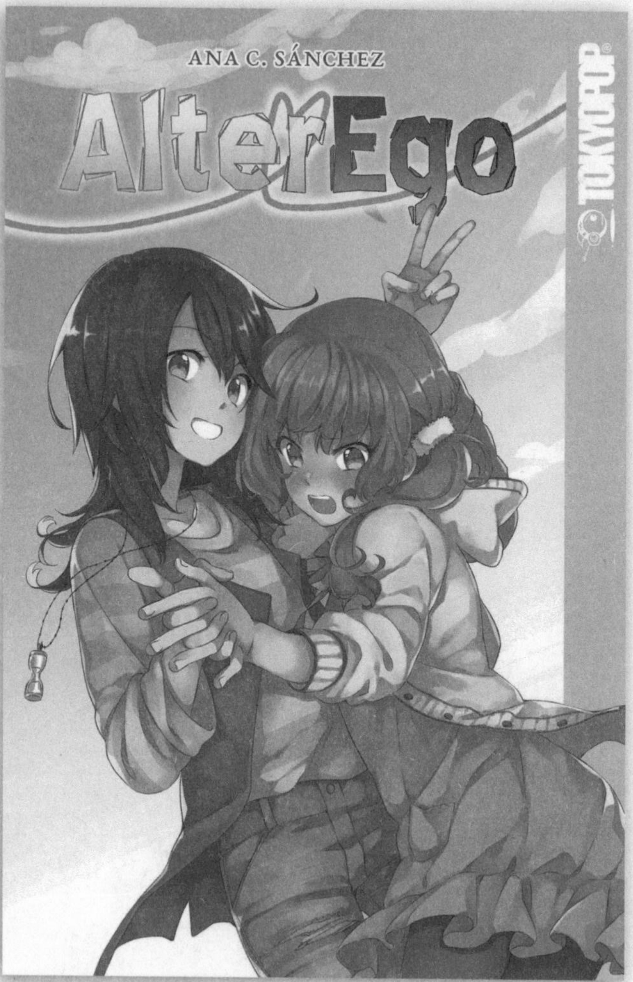
ANA C. SÁNCHEZ
AlterEgo
TOKYOPOP

# ALTER EGO

Ana C. Sánchez

LOVE-x-LOVE

Noel has always been in love with her best friend Elena, but she's never been able to find the courage to confess her feelings. Then, when her friend starts dating a boy, Noel's world collapses as she sees her chance at love slipping away.One night, in a moment of desperation, Noel ends up confessing her feelings for Elena to a complete stranger — but as fate would have it, this stranger turns out to be a girl named June, Elena's other best friend... and Noel's rival in love! Worst of all, now June knows Noel's secret. With everything suddenly going wrong, how can Noel ever win the girl of her dreams?

TOKYOPOP

# FUTARIBEYA: A ROOM FOR TWO, VOL 2
*Yukiko*

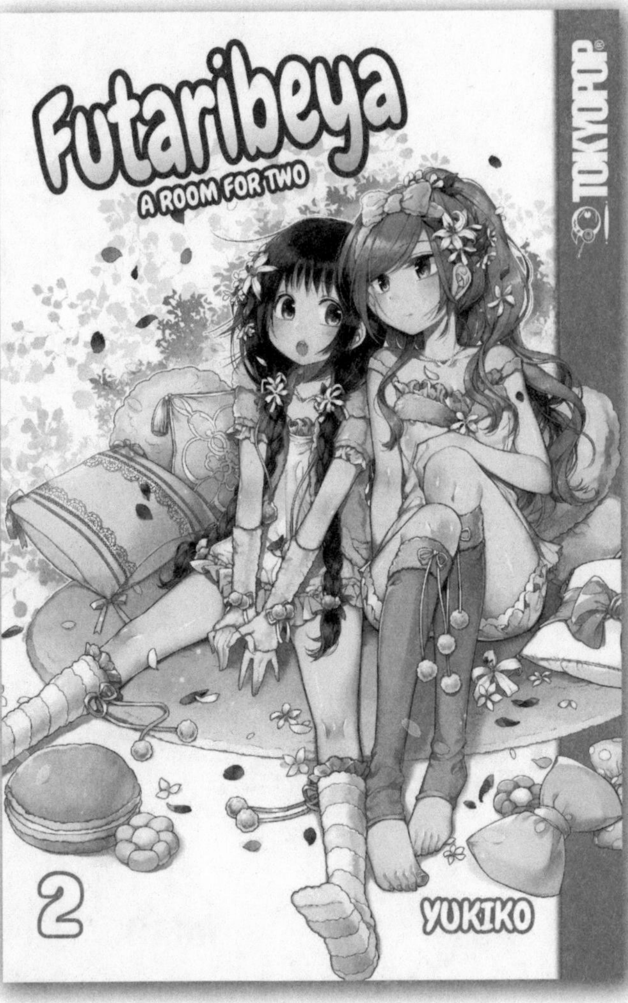
Futaribeya
A ROOM FOR TWO
TOKYOPOP
2
YUKIKO

**LOVE-x-LOVE**

***In terms of personality, Sakurako Kawawa couldn't be more at odds with her lackadaisical new roommate, Kasumi Yamabuki.*** But even though hardworking, friendly Sakurako might get top scores in class and do most of the cooking at home while Kasumi is constantly nodding off or snacking, these two roommates actually get along so well, you'll rarely see one without the other at her side. Whether they're just walking arm-in-arm to class, watching the cherry trees blossom, or sharing cotton candy at the summer festival, Sakurako and Kasumi are always having fun together!

TOKYOPOP

**STILL SICK, VOLUME 1**

*Akashi*

Makoto Shimizu is just an ordinary office worker, blending in seamlessly with her colleagues on the job... That is, until her coworker Akane Maekawa discovers her well-hidden secret: in her spare time, she draws and sells girls' love comics!

Akane is the last person Makoto would think of as a nerd, but as the two grow closer, it starts to seem like Akane may have a secret of her own...

# STILL SICK, VOLUME 2

*Akashi*

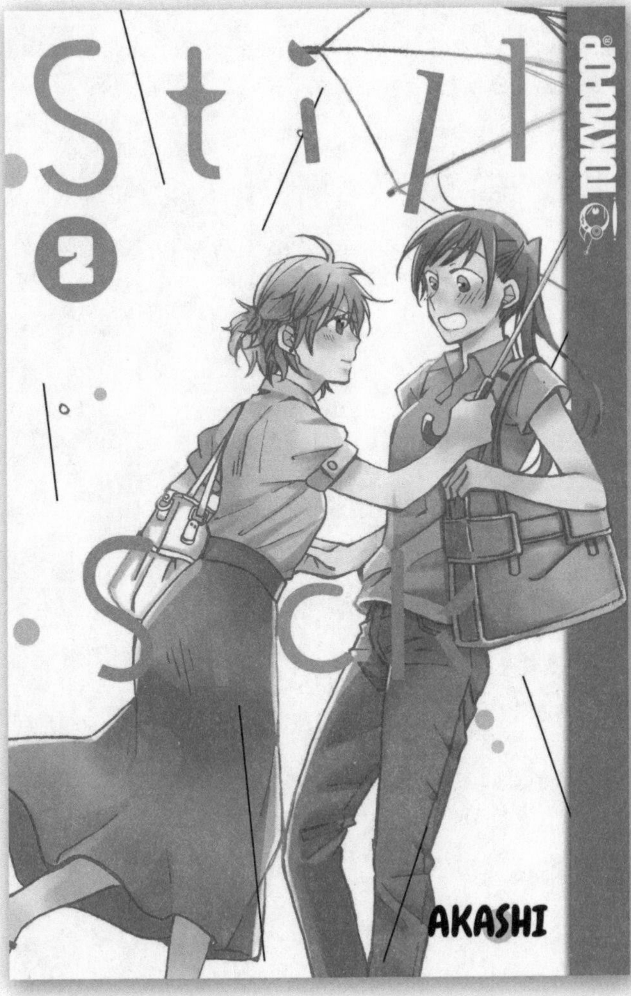

2
TOKYOPOP
AKASHI


LOVE-x-LOVE

After finding out that her coworker Akane used to be a manga creator, Makoto encourages her new friend to recapture that dream. As an amateur comic artist herself, Makoto looks up to Akane and tries to help her overcome the difficulties that made her give up that profession in the past. Although Akane is often her own worst critic, Makoto inspires her to try reshaping her attitude toward her art.

But matters become more complicated when Makoto realizes that, somewhere along the way, what started out as a professional friendship over a common interest has developed into... a serious crush!

TOKYOPOP

## THE TREASURE OF THE KING AND THE CAT

*You Kajika*

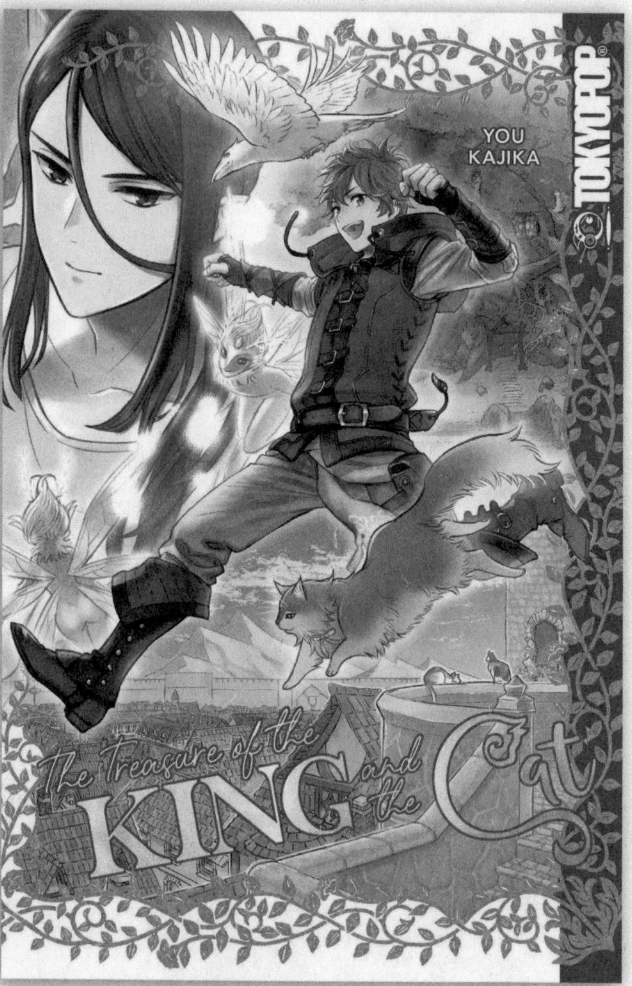
TOKYOPOP
YOU
KAJIKA
The Treasure of the KING and the Cat

**LOVE x LOVE**

***One day, a large number of people suddenly disappeared in the royal capital.*** When young King Castio goes out to investigate this occurrence, he comes across the culprit... but the criminal puts a spell on him! To help him out, the king calls the wizard O'Feuille to his castle, along with Prince Volks and his loyal retainer Nios. Together, they're determined to solve this strange, fluffy mystery full of cats, swords and magic!

TOKYOPOP

# KATAKOI LAMP
*Kyohei Azumi*

δLOVE-x-LOVEδ

***Kazuto Muronoi runs a cute little coffee shop, where many people enjoy doing some work or writing papers for school.*** Among his coffee shop's regulars is a college student named Jun, who often studies there. It was love at first sight for Kazuto! Will Kazuto be able to find the courage to confess his crush before Jun graduates college and stops frequenting the shop? And to make matters even more complicated... it seems Jun has his sights set on another worker at the café!

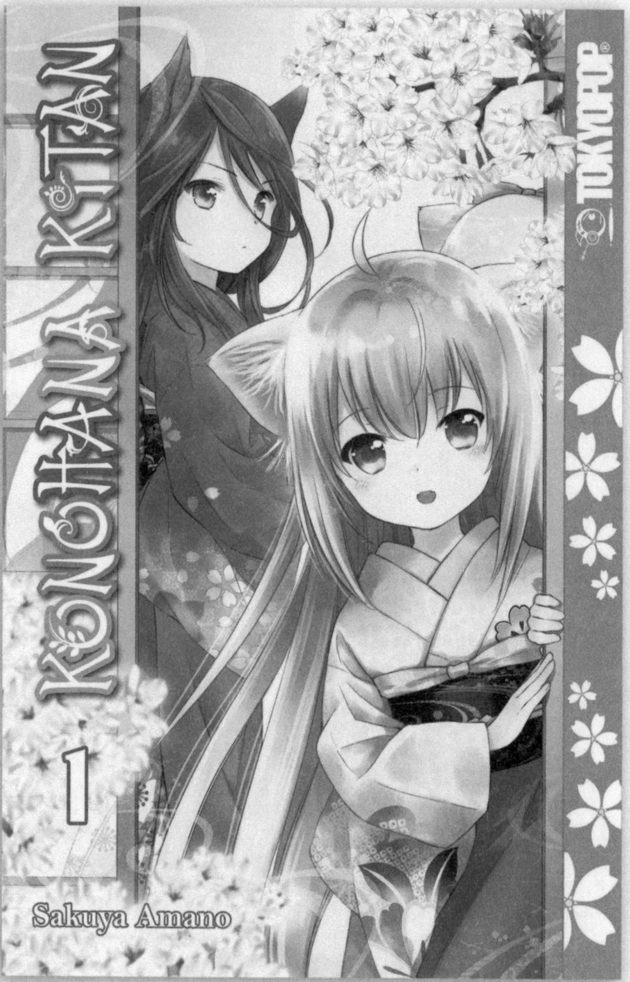
KONOHANA KITAN
1
Sakuya Amano
TOKYOPOP

# KONOHANA KITAN, VOL 1

Sakuya Amano

## FANTASY

***Yuzu is a brand new employee at Konohanatei, the hot-springs inn that sits on the crossroads between worlds.***

A simple, clumsy but charmingly earnest girl, Yuzu must now figure out her new life working alongside all the other fox-spirits who run the inn under one cardinal rule - at Konohanatei, every guest is a god!

# KONOHANA KITAN, VOL 2
*Sakuya Amano*

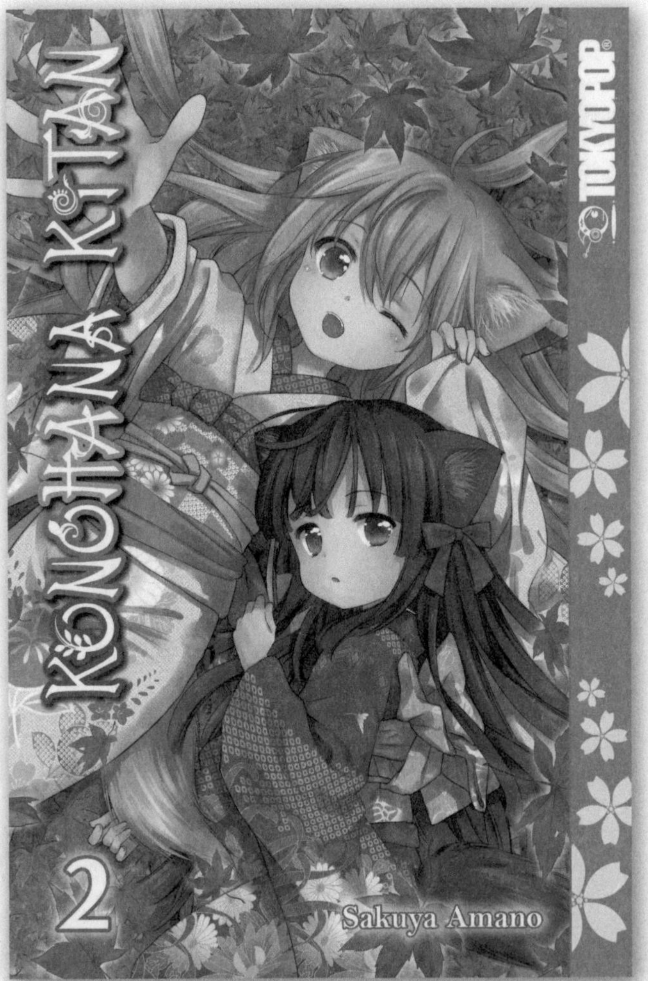
KONOHANA KITAN
2
Sakuya Amano
TOKYOPOP

**FANTASY**

***At Konohanatei, every guest is considered a god — but when an actual deity, the Great Spirit of Bubbles, comes to the inn for a bath, Yuzu and her fox friends get (many) more of her than they bargained for!***

Other guests stopping by the inn this time include a beautiful girl who weaves with the rain, a cursed Japanese doll, and... a mermaid?! Even Hiiragi, Satsuki's gorgeous older sister, drops in for a visit despite their rocky relationship. Perhaps the peaceful, otherworldly Konohanatei is just the right place to mend strained sibling bonds.

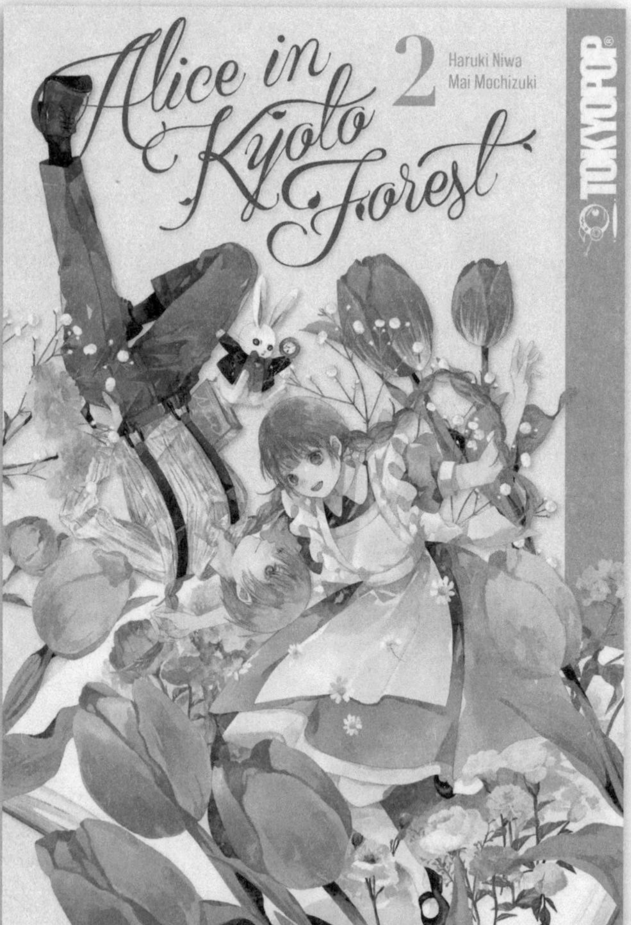
Alice in Kyoto Forest
2
Haruki Niwa
Mai Mochizuki
TOKYOPOP

# ALICE IN KYOTO FOREST, VOLUME 2

Mai Mochizuki & Haruki Niwa

**FANTASY**

Alice is certainly not in her world anymore! This version of Kyoto is magical and confusing — and Alice can't seem to find her childhood first love, Ren, the person she believes summoned her to this Kyoto in the first place. Strangely enough, the Imperial Crown Prince looks startlingly like Ren... but if he summoned her here, why doesn't he recognize her?

TOKYOPOP

# ALICE IN BISHOUNEN-LAND, VOLUME 2

*Yushi Kawata & Yukito*

**COMEDY**

After getting unexpectedly drawn into an idol dating sim, total newbie Alice Kagami doesn't have a clue how she's supposed to act like a proper producer, let alone save herself and her idol-obsessed friend Tamami. But after her group's crushing first loss, the only way to go is up! Together with her mismatched group of handsome boys, Alice learns to brave the gacha again, level up her idols, and join in summer festival fun. But will their group's newfound success transform digital dreams into reality?Includes excerpts from artist Yukito on the design and production process of the elegant FIORE Rose plastic model by popular kit-and-doll-making company VOLKS!

## *Mame Coordinate, Volume 2*
## Manga by Sachi Miyabe

Editor - Lena Atanassova
Translator - Caroline Wong
Quality Check - Nina Sawada
Proofreader - Katie Kimura
Copy Editor - M. Cara Carper
Graphic Designer - Sol DeLeo
Licensing Specialist - Arika Yanaka
Retouching and Lettering - Vibrraant Publishing Studio
Editorial Associate - Janae Young

A  Manga

TOKYOPOP and ⚙ are trademarks or registered trademarks of TOKYOPOP Inc.

TOKYOPOP Inc.
4136 Del Rey Ave., Suite 502
Marina del Rey, CA 90292-5604

E-mail: info@TOKYOPOP.com
Come visit us online at www.TOKYOPOP.com

f www.facebook.com/TOKYOPOP
🐦 www.twitter.com/TOKYOPOP
📷 www.instagram.com/TOKYOPOP

ISBN: 978-1-4278-6820-6
First TOKYOPOP Printing: May 2022
Printed in CANADA

# STOP

## THIS IS THE BACK OF THE BOOK!

**How do you read manga-style? It's simple! Let's practice -- just start in the top right panel and follow the numbers below!**

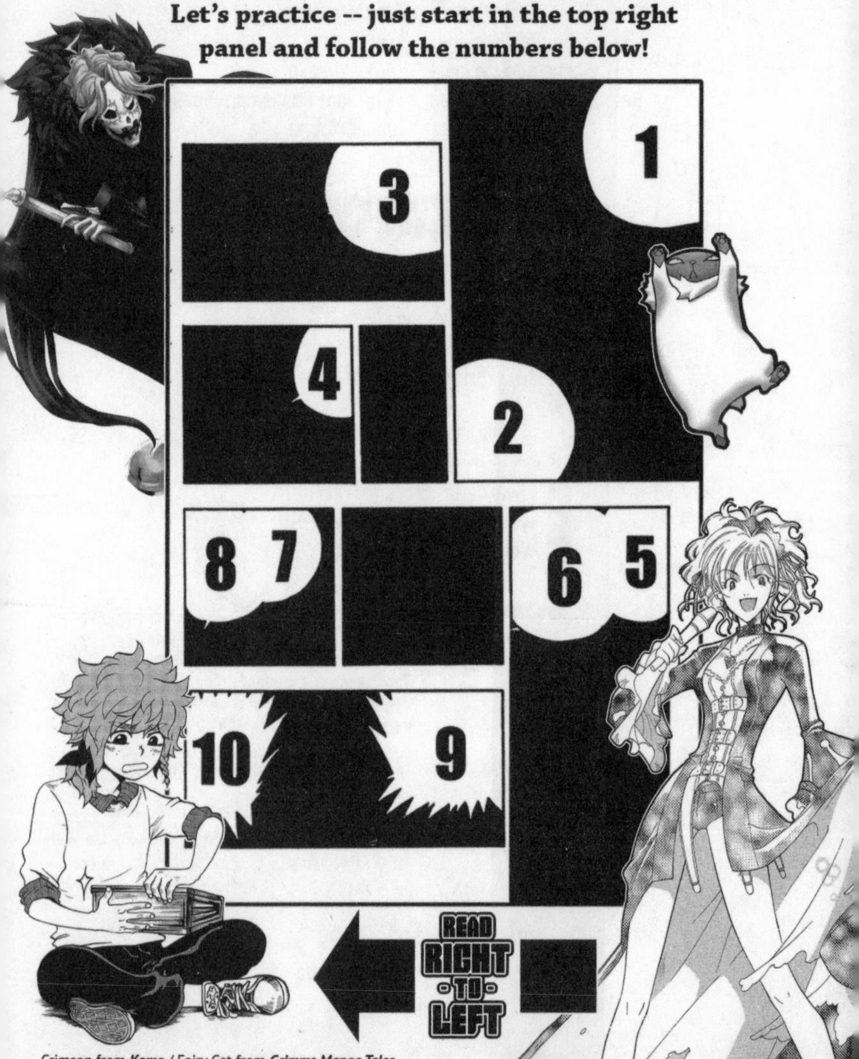
1
2
3
4
5
6
7
8
9
10
READ
RIGHT
-TO-
LEFT

Crimson from ***Kamo*** / Fairy Cat from ***Grimms Manga Tales***
Morrey from ***Goldfisch*** / Princess Ai from ***Princess Ai***